A-Z KINGSTON UPON THAMES and RICHMOND

Key to Map Pages	2-3
Map Pages	4-35

Large Scale Town Centre	36
Index	37-72

REFERENCE

Motorway	M4
A Road	A3
B Road	B358
Dual Carriageway	
One-way Street Traffic flow on A roads is also indicated by a heavy line on the drivers' left.	
Road Under Construction Opening dates are correct at the time of publication.	
Proposed Road	
Junction Name	KEW GREEN
Restricted Access	
Pedestrianized Road	
Residential Walkway	
Track / Footpath	
Low Emission Zone For information contact Transport for London www.tfl.gov.uk/modes/driving/	
Railway Stations: National Rail Network Overground Underground	Level Crossing / Tunnel
London Tramlink The boarding of Tramlink trams at stops may be limited to a single direction, indicated by the arrow.	Tunnel / Stop
Built-up Area	BOND ST.
Local Authority Boundary	
Posttown & London Postal District Boundary	
Postcode Boundary (within Posttown)	

Map Continuation	14 / Large Scale Town Centre 36
Car Park (selected)	P
Church or Chapel	†
Cycleway (selected)	
Fire Station	■
Hospital	H
House Numbers (A & B Roads only)	2 33
Information Centre	i
National Grid Reference	525
Park & Ride	Kingston upon Thames P+R
Police Station	▲
Post Office	★
River Bus Stop	R
Safety Camera with Speed Limit Fixed cameras and long term road works cameras. Symbols do not indicate camera direction.	30
Toilet: without facilities for the Disabled with facilities for the Disabled Disabled use only	▽ ▽ ▽
Educational Establishment	
Hospital or Healthcare Building	
Industrial Building	
Leisure or Recreational Facility	
Place of Interest	
Public Building	
Shopping Centre or Market	
Other Selected Buildings	

SCALE

Map Pages 4-35 1:19,000

0 — ¼ — ½ Mile

0 — 250 — 500 — 750 Metres

3.33 inches (8.47cm) to 1 mile   5.26cm to 1 km

Map Page 36 1:9,500

EDITION 7 2016

Copyright © Geograp...

Telephone: 01732 781000 (En...
01732 783422 (Ref...

© Crown copyright and database...

Safety camera information supplied by www.PocketGPSWorld.com.
Speed Camera Location Database Copyright 2015 © PocketGPSWorld.com

A-Z A-Z A to Z
registered trade marks of
Geographers' A-Z Map Company Ltd

www./az.co.uk

G000240795

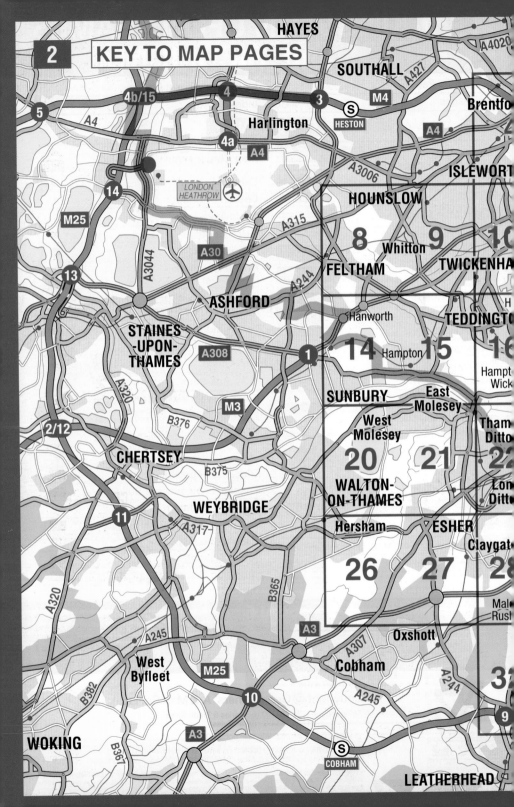

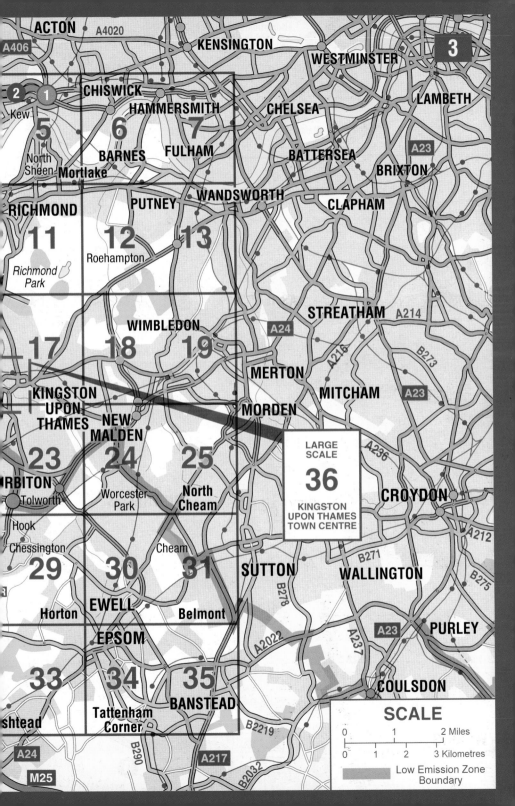

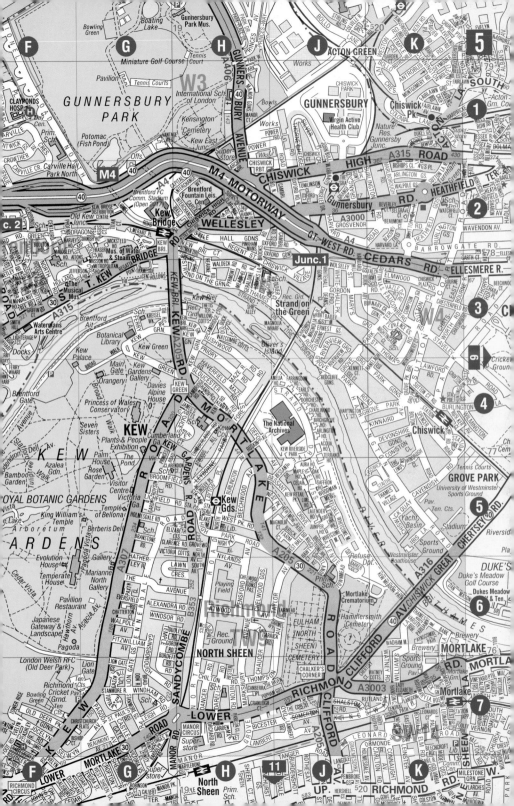

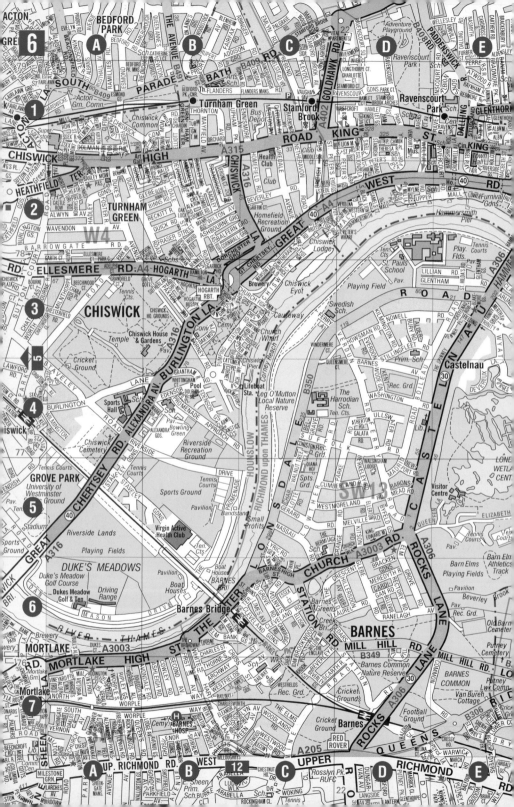

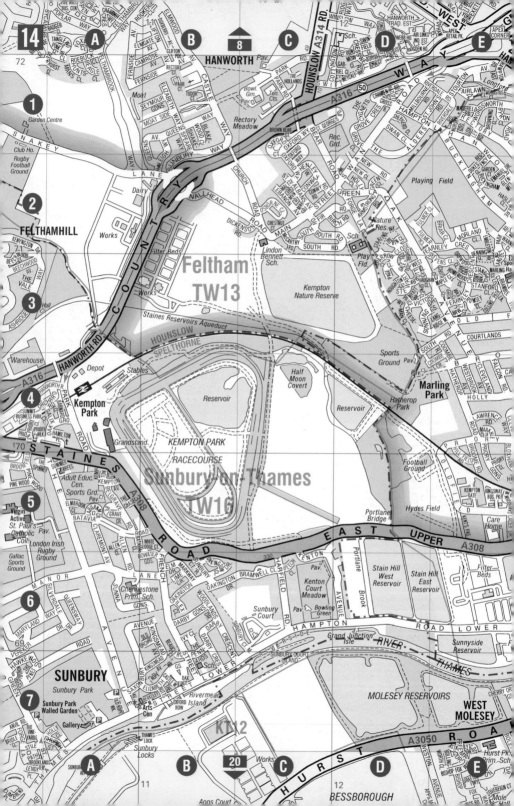

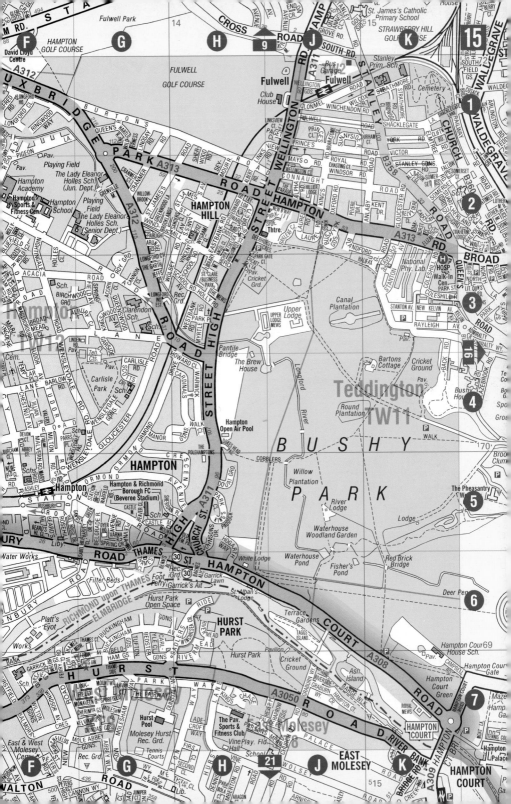

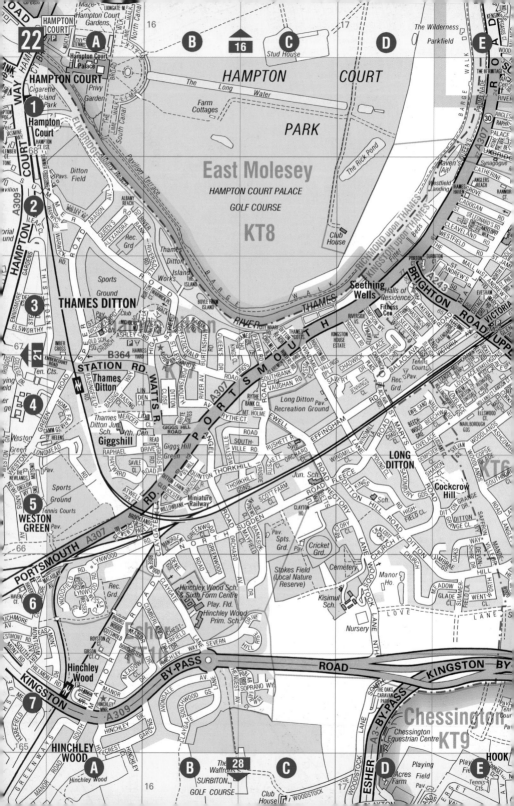

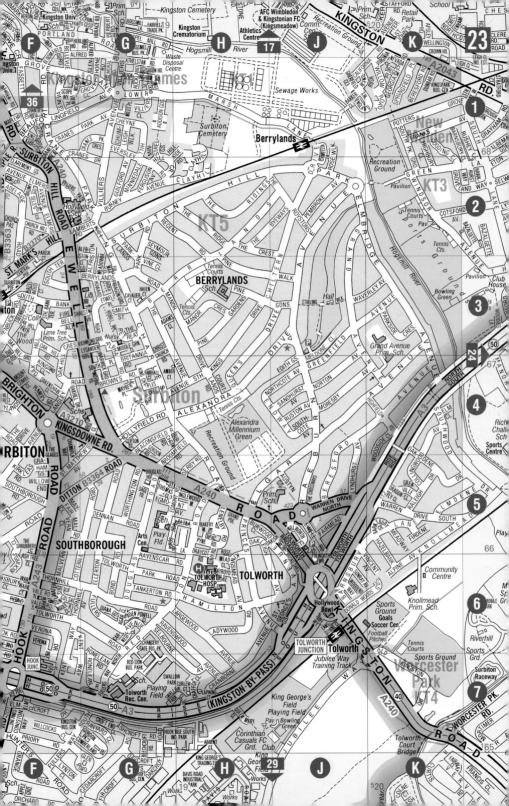

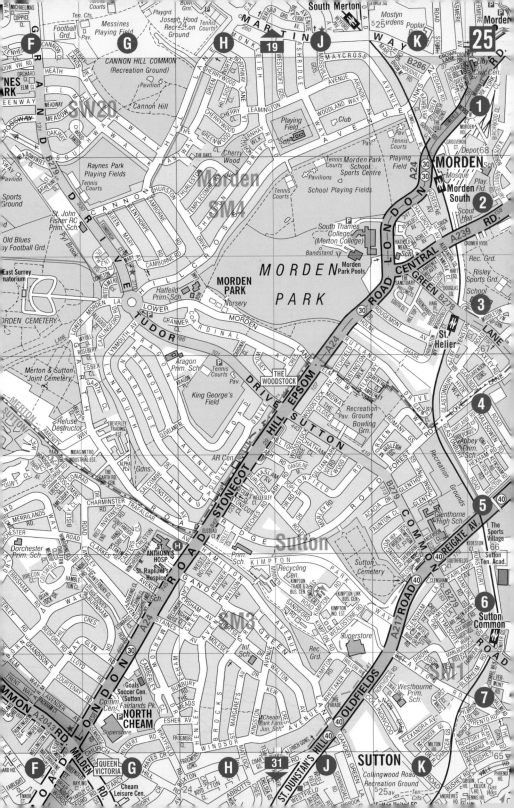

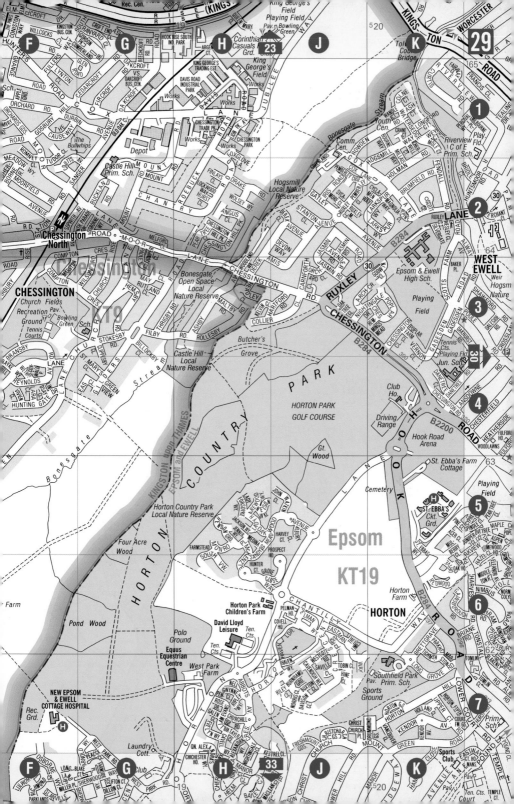

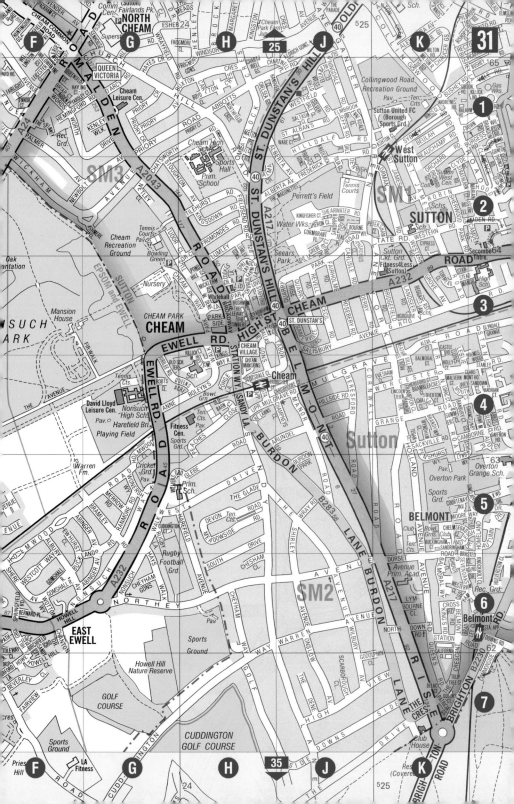

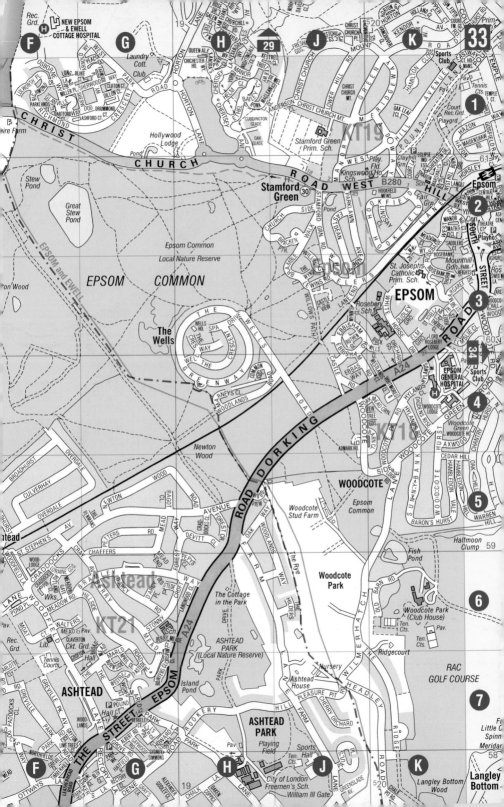

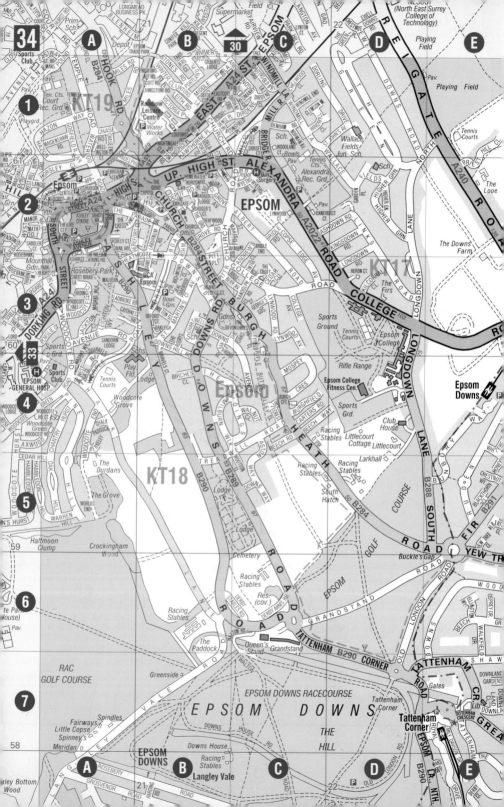

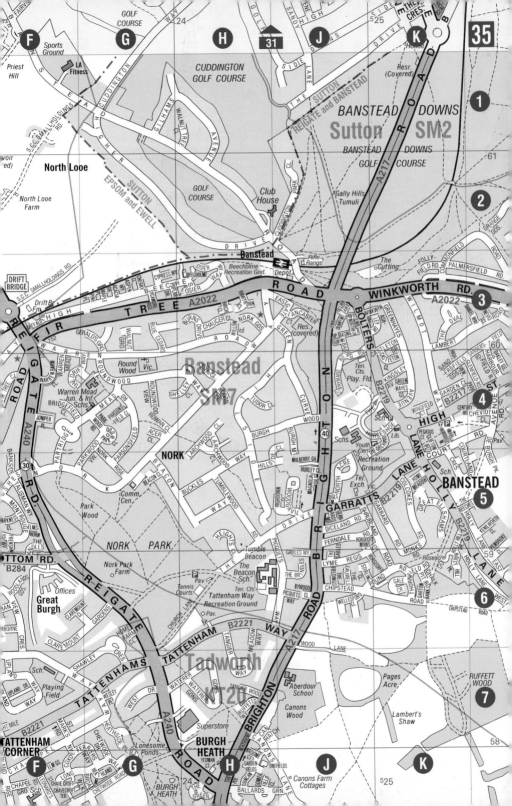

INDEX

Including Streets, Places & Areas, Hospitals etc., Industrial Estates,
Selected Flats & Walkways, Junction Names, Stations and Selected Places of Interest.

HOW TO USE THIS INDEX

1. Each street name is followed by its Postcode District, (or if outside the London Postcodes, by its Locality Abbreviation(s)) and then by its map reference;
e.g. **Abbotts Rd.** SM3: Cheam . . . .1H **31** is in the SM3 Postcode District and the Cheam Locality and is to be found in square 1H on page **31**.
The page number is shown in bold type.

2. A strict alphabetical order is followed in which Av., Rd., St., etc. (though abbreviated) are read in full and as part of the street name;
e.g. **Ash M.** appears after **Ashmere Cl.** but before **Ashmore Ho.**

3. Streets and a selection of flats and walkways that cannot be shown on the mapping, appear in the index with the thoroughfare to which they are
connected shown in brackets; e.g. **Abbot's Ho.** W14 . . . .1J **7** (off St Mary Abbot's Ter.)

4. Addresses that are in more than one part are referred to as not continuous.

5. Places and areas are shown in the index in BLUE TYPE and the map reference is to the actual map square in which the town centre or area is located and
not to the place name shown on the map; e.g. BANSTEAD 4K **35**

6. An example of a selected place of interest is Bourne Hall Mus. 5C **30**

7. Example of stations are: Ashtead Station (Rail) . . . .6F **33**; Cromwell Road Bus Station 2D **36** (5F **17**);
Kingston upon Thames (Park & Ride) . . . .5D **28**; Gunnersbury Station (Underground & Overground) 2J **5**;
Dundonald Road Stop (London Tramlink) . . . .4J **19**; Wandsworth Riverside Quarter Pier (River Bus) 1K **13**

8. Junction names are shown in the index in BOLD CAPITAL TYPE; e.g. APEX CORNER 7E **8**

9. An example of a Hospital, Hospice or selected Healthcare facility is BARNES HOSPITAL 7B **6**

10. Map references for entries that appear on large scale page **36** are shown first, with small scale map references shown in brackets;
e.g. **Acre Rd.** KT2: King T 1D **36** (5F **17**)

GENERAL ABBREVIATIONS

All. : Alley	**Dr.** : Drive	**La.** : Lane	**Rdbt.** : Roundabout
App. : Approach	**E.** : East	**Lit.** : Little	**Shop.** : Shopping
Arc. : Arcade	**Emb.** : Embankment	**Lwr.** : Lower	**Sth.** : South
Av. : Avenue	**Ent.** : Enterprise	**Mnr.** : Manor	**Sq.** : Square
Bri. : Bridge	**Est.** : Estate	**Mans.** : Mansions	**Sta.** : Station
B'way. : Broadway	**Fld.** : Field	**Mkt.** : Market	**St.** : Street
Bldg. : Building	**Flds.** : Fields	**Mdw.** : Meadow	**Ter.** : Terrace
Bldgs. : Buildings	**Gdns.** : Gardens	**Mdws.** : Meadows	**Twr.** : Tower
Bus. : Business	**Gth.** : Garth	**M.** : Mews	**Trad.** : Trading
Cvn. : Caravan	**Ga.** : Gate	**Mt.** : Mount	**Up.** : Upper
Cen. : Centre	**Gt.** : Great	**Mus.** : Museum	**Va.** : Vale
Chu. : Church	**Grn.** : Green	**Nth.** : North	**Vw.** : View
Cl. : Close	**Gro.** : Grove	**Pal.** : Palace	**Vs.** : Villas
Comn. : Common	**Hgts.** : Heights	**Pde.** : Parade	**Vis.** : Visitors
Cnr. : Corner	**Ho.** : House	**Pk.** : Park	**Wlk.** : Walk
Cotts. : Cottages	**Ho's.** : Houses	**Pas.** : Passage	**W.** : West
Ct. : Court	**Ind.** : Industrial	**Pl.** : Place	**Yd.** : Yard
Cres. : Crescent	**Info.** : Information	**Prom.** : Promenade	
Cft. : Croft	**Intl.** : International	**Ri.** : Rise	
Dpt. : Depot	**Junc.** : Junction	**Rd.** : Road	

LOCALITY ABBREVIATIONS

Ashtead: KT21 . . . . Asht	Esher: KT10 . . . . Esh	Isleworth: TW1,TW3,TW7 . . . . . . Isle	Sutton: SM1-3 . . . . Sutt
Banstead: KT17,SM2,SM7 . . . . . . Bans	Ewell: KT17,KT19,SM2 . . . . Ewe	Kew: TW9 . . . . Kew	Tadworth: KT18,KT20 . . . . Tad
Bedfont: TW14 . . . . Bedf	Feltham: TW13-14 . . . . Felt	Kingston upon Thames:	Tattenham Corner: KT18 . . . . . Tatt C
Brentford: TW7-8 . . . . Bford	Ham: TW10 . . . . Ham	KT1-2 . . . . King T	Teddington: TW1,TW11 . . . . Tedd
Cheam: KT17,SM2-3 . . . . Cheam	Hampton: TW12 . . . . Hamp	Leatherhead: KT9,KT22 . . . . Lea	Thames Ditton: KT7,KT10. . . . T Ditt
Chessington: KT9 . . . . Chess	Hampton Hill: TW12 . . . . Hamp H	Morden: SM4 . . . . Mord	Twickenham:
Claygate: KT10 . . . . Clay	Hampton Wick: KT1,TW11. . . . Hamp W	New Malden: KT3. . . . . N Mald	TW1-2,TW7,TW13 . . . . . . Twick
Cobham: KT11-12 . . . . Cobh	Hanworth: TW13. . . . . Hanw	Oxshott: KT10,KT22. . . . . Oxs	Walton-on-Thames: KT12 . . . . Walt T
East Molesey: KT8,TW12 . . . . E Mos	Hersham: KT10,KT12. . . . . Hers	Richmond: TW9-10 . . . . Rich	West Molesey: KT8 . . . . W Mole
Epsom: KT17-19 . . . . Eps	Hinchley Wood: KT10 . . . . . . Hin W	Sunbury: TW16 . . . . Sun	Whitton: TW2 . . . . Whitt
Epsom Downs: KT17-18. . . . . . Eps D	Hounslow: TW3-4,TW14 . . . . . . Houn	Surbiton: KT1,KT5-6,KT10 . . . . . Surb	Worcester Park: KT4,SM3 . . . Wor Pk

A

	Abingdon Lodge W8 . . . . . . .1K **7**	Acre Rd.	Adelaide Rd. KT6: Surb 2F **23**
	Abingdon Rd. W8 . . . . .1K **7**	KT2: King T 1D **36** (5F **17**)	KT12: Walt T 7A **20**
	Abingdon Vs. W8 . . . . .1K **7**	Acropolis Ho. KT1: King T 5E **36**	SW18 . . . . .2K **13**
Abbey Ct. TW12: Hamp 4F **15**	Abinger Av. SM2: Cheam 5F **31**	**ACTON GREEN** 1K **5**	TW9: Rich 1G **11**
Abbey Gdns. W6 . . . . .3H **7**	Abinger Gdns. TW7: Isle 1K **9**	Acton La. W4 . . . . .1K **5**	TW11: Tedd 3A **16**
Abbey M. TW7: Isle 5C **4**	Abinger Rd. W4 . . . . .1B **6**	(not continuous)	**Adelaide Ter.** TW8: Bford 2E **4**
Abbey Wlk. KT8: W Mole 7G **15**	Aboyne Dr. SW20 . . . . .6D **18**	Acuba Rd. SW18 . . . . .6K **13**	**Adelphi Cl.** W4 . . . . .3A **6**
Abbots Av. KT19: Eps 7H **29**	Acacia Av. TW8: Bford 4C **4**	Adams Cl. KT5: Surb 3G **23**	**Adelphi Rd.** KT17: Eps 2A **34**
Abbotsbury Rd. SM4: Mord 2K **25**	Acacia Dr. SM3: Sutt 5J **25**	Adams Dr. TW8: Bford 4D **4**	**Adeney Cl.** W6 . . . . .3G **7**
Abbot's Ho. W14 . . . . .1J **7**	SM7: Bans 3G **35**	Adams Wlk.	**Adie Ho.** W6 . . . . .1F **7**
(off St Mary Abbot's Ter.)	Acacia Gro. KT3: N Mald 7A **18**	KT1: King T 3C **36** (6F **17**)	**Admark Ho.** KT18: Eps 4J **33**
Abbotsleigh Cl. SM2: Sutt 4K **31**	Acacia Rd. TW12: Hamp 3F **15**	Adam Wlk. SW6 . . . . .4F **7**	**Admiral Ho.** TW11: Tedd 1B **16**
Abbotstone Rd. SW15 . . . . .7F **7**	Academy Pl. TW7: Isle 5A **4**	Addington Ct. SW14 . . . . .7A **6**	**Admiralty Bldg.** KT2: King T 2B **36**
Abbott Av. SW20 . . . . .5G **19**	Accommodation Rd.	Addington Bri. Pl. W14 . . . . .1J **7**	**Admiralty Rd.** TW11: Tedd 3A **16**
Abbott Cl. TW12: Hamp 3D **14**	KT17: Ewe 2D **30**	Addison Gdns. KT5: Surb 1G **23**	**Admiralty Way** TW11: Tedd 3A **16**
Abbotts Mead TW10: Ham 1E **16**	AC Court KT7: T Ditt 3B **22**	Addison Gro. W4 . . . . .1B **6**	**AFC Wimbledon** 7H **17**
Abbotts Rd. SM3: Cheam 1H **31**	Ace Pde. KT9: Chess 7F **23**	Addison Rd. TW11: Tedd 3C **16**	**Agar Cl.** KT6: Surb 6G **23**
Abbott's Tilt KT12: Hers 7D **20**	Acer Cl. KT17: Eps 5K **29**	W14 . . . . .1J **7**	**Agar Ho.** KT1: King T 6C **36**
Abercorn M. TW10: Rich 1G **11**	SM7: Bans 4G **35**	Addison Ter. W4 . . . . .1K **5**	**Agates La.** KT21: Asht 7E **32**
Abingdon W14 . . . . .1J **7**	Ackmar Rd. SW6 . . . . .5K **7**	(off Chiswick Rd.)	**Ailsa Av.** TW1: Twick 2B **10**
(off Kensington Village)	TW12: Hamp 3G **15**	Adecroft Way KT8: W Mole 7H **15**	**Ailsa Rd.** TW1: Twick 2C **10**
Abingdon Cl. KT4: Wor Pk 7E **24**	Acorns Way KT10: Esh 2H **27**	Adela Av. KT3: N Mald 2E **24**	**Aintree Est.** SW6 . . . . .4H **7**
	Acorn Cl. SM7: Bans 4H **35**	Adela Ho. W6 . . . . .2F **7**	**Aintree St.** SW6 . . . . .4H **7**
	Acqua Ho. TW9: Kew 4J **5**	(off Queen Caroline St.)	**Airedale Av.** W4 . . . . .1C **6**

Airedale Av. Sth.—Ashfield Cl.

Airedale Av. Sth. W4 2C **6**
Air Links Ind. Est. TW13: Hanw 7D **8**
Air Pk. Way TW13: Felt 6A **8**
Air Sea M. TW2: Twick 6J **9**
Aisgill Av. W14 2J **7**
(not continuous)
Aissele Pl. KT10: Esh 1G **27**
Aiten Pl. W6 1D **6**
Aitman Dr. TW8: Bford 2H **5**
Aitons Ho. TW8: Bford 2F **5**
Aits Vw. KT8: W Mole 7G **15**
Akehurst St. SW15 3D **12**
Akerman Rd. KT6: Surb 3D **22**
Alan Rd. SW19 2H **19**
Alba M. SW18 6K **13**
Albany Cl. KT10: Esh 5F **27**
SW14 1J **11**
Albany Cres. KT10: Clay 3K **27**
Albany M. KT2: King T 3E **16**
Albany Pde. TW8: Bford 3F **5**
Albany Pk. Rd. KT2: King T 3E **16**
Albany Pas. TW10: Rich 2F **11**
Albany Pl. TW8: Bford 3E **4**
Albany Reach KT7: T Ditt 2A **22**
Albany Rd. KT3: N Mald 1A **24**
KT12: Hers 1C **26**
SW19 2K **19**
TW8: Bford 3E **4**
TW10: Rich 2G **11**
Albany Ter. *TW10: Rich 2G* ***11***
(off Albany Pas.)
Albemarle SW19 6G **13**
Albemarle Av. TW2: Whitt 5E **8**
Albemarle Gdns. KT3: N Mald 1A **24**
Alberta Av. SM1: Sutt 1H **31**
Albert Dr. SW19 6H **13**
Albert Gro. SW20 5G **19**
Albertine Cl. KT17: Eps D 5E **34**
Albert Rd. KT1: King T 3E **36** (6G **17**)
KT3: N Mald 1C **24**
KT17: Eps 2C **34**
KT21: Asht 7G **33**
TW1: Twick 5A **10**
TW3: Houn 1F **9**
TW10: Rich 2F **11**
TW11: Tedd 3A **16**
TW12: Hamp H 2H **15**
Albert Ter. *W6 2D* ***6***
(off Beavor La.)
Albion Ct. *W6 1E* ***6***
(off Albion Pl.)
Albion Gdns. W6 1E **6**
Albion M. W6 1E **6**
Albion Pl. W6 1E **6**
Albion Rd. KT2: King T 5K **17**
TW2: Twick 5K **9**
TW3: Houn 1F **9**
Albon Ho. *SW18 3K* ***13***
(off Neville Gill Cl.)
Albury Av. SM2: Cheam 5F **31**
TW7: Isle 4A **4**
Albury Cl. KT19: Eps 5J **29**
TW12: Hamp 3G **15**
Albury Pl. KT10: Clay 3K **27**
Albury Rd. KT9: Chess 2F **29**
Alcorn Cl. SM3: Sutt 6K **25**
Aldensley Rd. W6 1E **6**
Alderbury Rd. SW13 3D **6**
Alder Lodge SW6 5F **7**
Alderman Judge Mall
KT1: King T 4C **36**
Alder Rd. SW14 7A **6**
Alders, The TW13: Hanw 1D **14**
Aldersbrook Dr. KT2: King T 3G **17**
Alders Gro. KT8: E Mos 2J **21**
Alderton Ct. *KT8: W Mole 1E* ***20***
(off Dunstable Rd.)
Alderville Rd. SW6 6J **7**
Aldrich Gdns. SM3: Cheam 7J **25**
Aldridge Ri. KT3: N Mald 4B **24**
Alexa Ct. SM2: Sutt 3K **31**
W8 1K **7**
Alexander Cl. TW2: Twick 6K **9**
Alexander Godley Cl.
KT21: Asht 7G **33**
Alexander Ho. KT2: King T 2C **36**
Alexandra Av. SM1: Sutt 7K **25**
W4 4A **6**
Alexandra Cl. KT12: Walt T 6A **20**
Alexandra Dr. KT5: Surb 4H **23**
Alexandra Gdns. W4 4B **6**
Alexandra Ho. *W6 2F* ***7***
(off Queen Caroline St.)
Alexandra Mans. *KT17: Eps 2C* ***34***
(off Alexandra Rd.)
Alexandra M. SW19 3J **19**
Alexandra Rd. KT2: King T 4H **17**
KT7: T Ditt 2A **22**
KT17: Eps 2C **34**
SW14 7A **6**
SW19 3J **19**
TW1: Twick 3D **10**
TW3: Houn 1G **9**
TW8: Bford 3E **4**
TW9: Kew 6G **5**
Alexandra Sq. SM4: Mord 2K **25**
Alexandra Way KT19: Eps 7H **29**
Alfred Cl. W4 1A **6**
Alfred Rd. KT1: King T 6D **36** (7F **17**)
TW13: Felt 6B **8**
Alfreton Cl. SW19 7G **13**
Alfriston KT5: Surb 3G **23**
Alfriston Cl. KT5: Surb 2G **23**
Algar Cl. TW7: Isle 7B **4**
Algar Rd. TW7: Isle 7B **4**
Alice Gilliatt Ct. *W14 3J* ***7***
(off Star Rd.)
Alice M. TW11: Tedd 2A **16**
Alice Way TW3: Houn 1G **9**
Alkerden Rd. W4 2B **6**
Allan Cl. KT3: N Mald 2A **24**
Allbrook Cl. TW11: Tedd 2K **15**
Allen Cl. TW16: Sun 5A **14**
Allenford Ho. *SW15 3C* ***12***
(off Tunworth Cres.)
Allen Rd. TW16: Sun 5A **14**
Allen St. W8 1K **7**
Allenswood SW19 5H **13**
Allestree Rd. SW6 4H **7**
Allgood Cl. SM4: Mord 3G **25**
Alliance Cl. TW4: Houn 2E **8**
Allington Cl. SW19 2G **19**
All Saints Pas. SW18 2K **13**
Alma Cres. SM1: Sutt 2H **31**
Alma Ho. TW8: Bford 3F **5**
Alma Rd. KT10: Esh 5K **21**
Alma Ter. W8 1K **7**
Almer Rd. SW20 4D **18**
Almond Gro. TW8: Bford 4C **4**
Almond Rd. KT19: Eps 7A **30**
Almshouse La. KT9: Chess 5D **28**
Alpha Pl. SM4: Mord 5G **25**
Alpha Rd. KT5: Surb 3G **23**
TW11: Tedd 2J **15**
Alpine Av. KT5: Surb 6K **23**
Alpine Cl. KT19: Ewe 2K **29**
Alpine Rd. KT12: Walt T 4A **20**
Alric Av. KT3: N Mald 7B **18**
Alsager *KT22: Lea 7B* ***32***
(off Clements Mead)
Alsom Av. KT4: Wor Pk 1D **30**
Alston Cl. KT6: Surb 4C **22**
Alstonfield KT10: Esh 2H **27**
Alt Gro. SW19 4J **19**
Alton Cl. TW7: Isle 6A **4**
Alton Gdns. TW2: Whitt 4J **9**
Alton Rd. SW15 5D **12**
TW9: Rich 1F **11**
Alverstone Av. SW19 6K **13**
Alverstone Rd. KT3: N Mald 1C **24**
Alway Av. KT19: Ewe 2A **30**
Alwyn Av. W4 2A **6**
Alwyne Rd. SW19 3J **19**
Amalgamated Dr. TW8: Bford 3C **4**
Amber Cl. KT17: Eps D 4E **34**
Amber Ct. KT5: Surb 4G **23**
Amberley Gdns. KT19: Ewe 1C **30**
Amberley Way SM4: Mord 4J **25**
TW4: Houn 2B **8**
Amberside Cl. TW7: Isle 3J **9**
Amberwood Ri. KT3: N Mald 3B **24**
Amblecote KT11: Cobh 7D **26**
Ambleside SW19 5H **13**
Ambleside Av. KT12: Walt T 5B **20**
Amelia Ho. TW9: Kew 4J **5**
W6 2F ***7***
(off Queen Caroline St.)
Amenity Way SM4: Mord 4F **25**
American International
University in London,
The Richmond Hill Campus
3F **11**
Amerland Rd. SW18 2J **13**
Amesbury Cl. KT4: Wor Pk 5F **25**
Amesbury Rd. TW13: Felt 6C **8**
Amhurst Gdns. TW7: Isle 6B **4**
Amis Av. KT19: Ewe 3J **29**
Amity Gro. SW20 5E **18**
Amor Rd. W6 1F **7**
Amyand Cotts. TW1: Twick 3C **10**
Amyand La. TW1: Twick 4C **10**
Amyand Pk. Gdns. TW1: Twick 4C **10**
Amyand Pk. Rd. TW1: Twick 4B **10**
Ancaster Cres. KT3: N Mald 3D **24**
Anchorage Cl. SW19 2K **19**
Ancill Cl. W6 3H **7**
Anderson Cl. KT19: Eps 1J **33**
SM3: Sutt 5K **25**
Anderson Pl. TW3: Houn 1G **9**
Andover Cl. KT19: Eps 7A **30**
Andover Rd. TW2: Twick 5J **9**
Andover Ter. *W6 1E* ***6***
(off Raynham Rd.)
Andrewes Ho. SM1: Sutt 1K **31**
Andrew Reed Ho. *SW18 4H* ***13***
(off Linstead Way)
Andrew's Cl. KT17: Eps 3C **34**
Andrews Cl. KT4: Wor Pk 6F **25**
Angel Cl. TW12: Hamp H 2H **15**
Angelfield TW3: Houn 1G **9**
Angel M. SW15 4D **12**
Angel Rd. KT7: T Ditt 4B **22**
Angel Wlk. W6 1F **7**
Anglers, The KT1: King T 5B **36**
Anglers Cl. TW10: Ham 1D **16**
Anglers Reach KT6: Surb 2E **22**
Anglesea Ho. KT1: King T 7B **36**
Anglesea Rd.
KT1: King T 7B **36** (1E **22**)
Angus Cl. KT9: Chess 2H **29**
Anlaby Rd. TW11: Tedd 2K **15**
Annaleigh Pl. KT12: Hers 1C **26**
Annandale Rd. W4 2B **6**
Anne Boleyn's Wlk.
KT2: King T 2F **17**
SM3: Cheam 4G **31**
Anne Case M. KT3: N Mald 7A **18**
Anne Way KT8: W Mole 1G **21**
Anselm Rd. SW6 3K **7**
Anstice Cl. W4 4B **6**
Antelope Wlk. KT6: Surb 2E **22**
Anton Cres. SM1: Sutt 7K **25**
Antrobus Cl. SM1: Sutt 2J **31**
Antrobus Rd. W4 1K **5**
Anvil Rd. TW16: Sun 7A **14**
Aperdele Rd. KT22: Lea 7B **32**
APEX CORNER **7E 8**
Apex Retail Pk. TW13: Hanw 7E **8**
Appleby Cl. TW2: Twick 6J **9**
Appleby Ho. KT19: Eps 7A **30**
Apple Gth. TW8: Bford 1E **4**
Applegarth KT10: Clay 2A **28**
Apple Gro. KT9: Chess 1F **29**
TW1: Twick 3B **10**
Apple Mkt. KT1: King T 4B **36**
Appleton Gdns. KT3: N Mald 3D **24**
Approach Rd. KT8: W Mole 2F **21**
SW20 6F **19**
Apps Mdw. Cl. KT8: W Mole 1E **20**
April Cl. KT21: Asht 7G **33**
TW13: Felt 7A **8**
Apsley Ho. *SW15 3D* ***12***
(off Holford Way)
TW4: Houn 1E **8**
Apsley Rd. KT3: N Mald 7K **17**
Aquarius TW1: Twick 5C **10**
Arabella Dr. SW15 1B **12**
Aragon Av. KT7: T Ditt 2A **22**
KT17: Ewe 6E **30**
Aragon Ct. KT8: E Mos 1H **21**
Aragon Pl. SM4: Mord 4H **25**
Aragon Rd. KT2: King T 2F **17**
SM4: Mord 3G **25**
Arbor Ho. TW8: Bford 4D **4**
Arbrook Chase KT10: Esh 3H **27**
Arbrook Hall KT10: Clay 3A **28**
Arbrook La. KT10: Esh 3H **27**
Arcade Pde. KT9: Chess 2E **28**
Arcadia M. KT3: N Mald 7B **18**
Arcadian Pl. SW18 4J **13**
Archdale Pl. KT3: N Mald 7J **17**
Archel Rd. W14 3J **7**
Archer Cl. KT2: King T 4F **17**
Archer M. TW12: Hamp H 3H **15**
Arch Rd. KT12: Hers 7C **20**
Archway Cl. SW19 7K **13**
Archway M. *SW15 1H* ***13***
(off Putney Bri. Rd.)
Archway St. SW13 7B **6**
Arden Cl. TW2: Whitt 4E **8**
Ardingly Ct. KT18: Eps 3A **34**
Ardleigh Gdns. SM3: Sutt 4K **25**
Ardmay Gdns. KT6: Surb 2F **23**
Ardrossan Gdns. KT4: Wor Pk 7D **24**
Ardshiel Cl. SW15 7G **7**
Argent Ct. KT6: Surb 7H **23**
Argenton Twr. *SW18 3K* ***13***
(off Mapleton Cres.)
Argon M. SW6 4K **7**
Argyle Av. TW3: Houn 3F **9**
Argyle Pl. W6 1E **6**
Argyle Rd. TW3: Houn 2G **9**
Argyll Mans. *W14 1H* ***7***
(off Hammersmith Rd.)
Ark, The *W6 2G* ***7***
(off Talgarth Rd.)
Arklow M. KT6: Surb 6F **23**
Arlesey Cl. SW15 2H **13**
Arlington Cl. SM1: Sutt 6K **25**
TW1: Twick 3D **10**
Arlington Gdns. W4 2K **5**
Arlington Ho. TW9: Kew 4J **5**
Arlington Pk. Mans. *W4 2K* ***5***
(off Sutton La. Nth.)
Arlington Pas. TW11: Tedd 1A **16**
Arlington Rd. KT6: Surb 3E **22**
TW1: Twick 3D **10**
TW10: Ham 6E **10**
TW11: Tedd 1A **16**
Armadale Rd. SW6 4K **7**
TW14: Felt 2A **8**
Armfield Cl. KT8: W Mole 2E **20**
Armoury Way SW18 2K **13**
Armstrong Rd. TW13: Hanw 2D **14**
Arnal Cres. SW18 4H **13**
Arndale Wlk. SW18 2K **13**
Arnewood Cl. SW15 5D **12**
Arnison Rd. KT8: E Mos 1J **21**
Arnold Cres. TW7: Isle 2J **9**
Arnold Dr. KT9: Chess 3E **28**
Arnold Mans. *W14 3J* ***7***
(off Queen's Club Gdns.)
Arnold Way KT19: Eps 1G **33**
Arnott Cl. W4 1A **6**
Arosa Rd. TW1: Twick 3E **10**
Arragon Rd. SW18 5K **13**
TW1: Twick 4B **10**
Arran Way KT10: Esh 6G **21**
Arrow Ct. *SW5 1K* ***7***
(off W. Cromwell Rd.)
Artemis Pl. SW18 4J **13**
Arterberry Rd. SW20 4F **19**
Arthur Henderson Ho. *SW6 6J* ***7***
(off Fulham Rd.)
Arthur Rd. KT2: King T 4H **17**
KT3: N Mald 2E **24**
SW19 2J **19**
Artichoke Wlk. *TW9: Rich 2E* ***10***
(off Red Lion St.)
Arundale *KT1: King T 1E* ***22***
(off Anglesea Rd.)
Arundel Av. KT17: Ewe 6E **30**
SM4: Mord 1J **25**
Arundel Cl. TW12: Hamp H 2G **15**
Arundel Ct. *SW13 3E* ***6***
(off Arundel Ter.)
Arundel Mans. *SW6 5J* ***7***
(off Kelvedon Rd.)
Arundel Rd. KT1: King T 6J **17**
SM2: Cheam, Sutt 4J **31**
(not continuous)
TW4: Houn 1B **8**
Arundel Ter. SW13 3E **6**
Arun Ho. KT2: King T 1B **36** (5E **16**)
Asbridge Ct. *W6 1E* ***6***
(off Dalling Rd.)
Ashbourne Gro. W4 2B **6**
Ashbourne Ter. SW19 4J **19**
Ashburnham Pk. KT10: Esh 1H **27**
Ashburnham Rd. TW10: Ham 7C **10**
Ashburton Ent. Cen. SW15 3F **13**
Ashby Av. KT9: Chess 3H **29**
Ash Cl. KT3: N Mald 6A **18**
SM7: Bans 4H **35**
TW7: Isle 5A **4**
Ashcombe Av. KT6: Surb 4E **22**
Ashcombe Rd. SW19 2K **19**
Ashcombe Sq. KT3: N Mald 7K **17**
Ashcombe St. SW6 6K **7**
Ash Ct. KT19: Ewe 1K **29**
SW19 4H **19**
Ashcroft Rd. KT9: Chess 7G **23**
Ashcroft Sq. W6 1F **7**
Ashdale Cl. TW2: Whitt 4H **9**
Ashdale Way TW2: Whitt 4G **9**
Ashdown Pl. KT7: T Ditt 4B **22**
KT17: Ewe 4C **30**
Ashdown Rd.
KT1: King T 4C **36** (6F **17**)
KT17: Eps 2C **34**
Ashe Ho. TW1: Twick 3E **10**
Ashen Gro. SW19 7K **13**
Ashfield Av. TW13: Felt 5A **8**
Ashfield Cl. TW10: Ham 5F **11**

Ashfield Ho.—Beadon Rd.

Ashfield Ho. *W14* *2J 7*
(off W. Cromwell Rd.)
Ashford Ct. KT19: Eps 1G **33**
Ashington Rd. SW6 . . . . 6J **7**
Ash Island KT8: E Mos 7J **15**
Ashleigh Ct. *W5* *1E 4*
(off Murray Rd.)
Ashleigh Rd. SW14 . . . . 7B **6**
Ashley Av. KT18: Eps 2A **34**
SM4: Mord 2K **25**
Ashley Cen. KT18: Eps 2A **34**
Ashley Ct. KT18: Eps 2A **34**
Ashley Dr. KT12: Walt T 7A **20**
SM7: Bans 3K **35**
TW2: Whitt 4G **9**
Ashley Gdns. TW10: Ham 6E **10**
ASHLEY PARK **7A 20**
Ashley Pk. Rd.
KT12: Walt T 7A **20**
Ashley Rd. KT7: T Ditt 3A **22**
KT18: Eps, Eps D 2A **34**
TW9: Rich 7F **5**
TW12: Hamp 5F **15**
Ashley Sq. *KT18: Eps* *2A 34*
(off South St.)
Ashlone Rd. SW15 . . . . 7F **7**
Ashlyns Way KT9: Chess 3E **28**
Ashmere Cl. SM3: Cheam 2G **31**
Ash M. KT18: Eps 2B **34**
Ashmore Ho. *W14* *1H 7*
(off Russell Rd.)
Ashmount Ter. W5 . . . . 1E **4**
Ashridge Way SM4: Mord 7J **19**
TW16: Sun 3A **14**
Ash Rd. SM3: Sutt 4H **25**
ASHTEAD **7G 33**
Ashtead Common
(National Nature Reserve)
. . . . 4D **32**
Ashtead Gap KT22: Lea 5C **32**
ASHTEAD PARK **7H 33**
Ashtead Pk. (Local Nature Reserve)
. . . . 6H **33**
Ashtead Station (Rail) 6F **33**
Ashtead Woods Rd.
KT21: Asht 6D **32**
Ashton Cl. KT12: Hers 3A **26**
SM1: Sutt 1K **31**
Ashton Gdns. TW4: Houn 1E **8**
Ashton Pl. KT10: Clay 4A **28**
Ash Tree Cl. KT6: Surb 6F **23**
Ashurst KT18: Eps 3A **34**
Ashway Cen., The
KT2: King T 2D **36** (5F **17**)
Askill Dr. SW15 . . . . 2H **13**
Aspen Cl. KT1: Hamp W 5D **16**
KT19: Eps 5A **30**
Aspen Gdns. W6 . . . . 2E **6**
Aspenlea Rd. W6 . . . . 3G **7**
Aspen Way SM7: Bans 3G **35**
TW13: Felt 7A **8**
Asquith Ho. *SM7: Bans* *4J 35*
(off Dunnymans Rd.)
Assher Rd. KT12: Hers 7D **20**
Astede Pl. KT21: Asht 7G **33**
Astley Ho. *SW13* *3E 6*
(off Wyatt Dr.)
Aston Cl. KT21: Asht 7D **32**
Aston Rd. KT10: Clay 2K **27**
SW20 . . . . 6F **19**
Astonville St. SW18 . . . . 5K **13**
Aston Way KT18: Eps 4C **34**
Astor Cl. KT2: King T 3J **17**
Astrid Ho. TW13: Felt 6B **8**
Atalanta St. SW6 . . . . 4G **7**
Atbara Rd. TW11: Tedd 3C **16**
Atcham Rd. TW3: Houn 1H **9**
Athelstan Ho. *KT1: King T* *1G 23*
(off Athelstan Rd.)
Athelstan Rd. KT1: King T 1G **23**
Athena Cl.
KT1: King T 5E **36** (7G **17**)
Atherley Way TW4: Houn 4E **8**
Atherton Dr. SW19 . . . . 1G **19**
Atherton Rd. SW13 . . . . 4D **6**
Athlone KT10: Clay 3K **27**
Atkinson Cl. SW20 . . . . 4D **18**
Atney Rd. SW15 . . . . 1H **13**
Attfield Ct. KT1: King T 4E **36**
Atwell Pl. KT7: T Ditt 5A **22**
Atwood Av. TW9: Kew 6H **5**
Atwood Ho. *W14* *1J 7*
(off Beckford Cl.)
Atwood Rd. W6 . . . . 1E **6**
Atwoods All. TW9: Kew 5H **5**
Aubyn Sq. SW15 . . . . 2D **12**
Auckland Rd.
KT1: King T 1G **23**
Auden Pl. SM3: Cheam 1F **31**
Audley Ct. TW2: Twick 7J **9**
Audley Firs KT12: Hers 1B **26**
Audley Pl. SM2: Sutt 4K **31**
Audley Rd. TW10: Rich 2G **11**
Audric Cl. KT2: King T 5H **17**
Augusta Cl. KT8: W Mole 7E **14**
Augusta Rd. TW2: Twick 6H **9**
Augustine Rd. W14 . . . . 1G **7**
Augustus Cl. TW8: Bford 4D **4**
Augustus Ct. TW13: Hanw 1E **14**
Augustus Rd. SW19 . . . . 5G **13**
Aura Ho. TW9: Kew 5J **5**
Auriol Cl. KT4: Wor Pk 7B **24**
Auriol Mans. *W14* *1H 7*
(off Edith Rd.)
Auriol Pk. Rd.
KT4: Wor Pk 7B **24**
Auriol Rd. W14 . . . . 1H **7**
Aurora Apartments *SW18* *2K 13*
(off Buckhold Rd.)
Austin Cl. TW1: Twick 2D **10**
Austyn Gdns. KT5: Surb 5J **23**
Austyns Pl. KT17: Ewe 5D **30**
Autumn Dr. SM2: Sutt 5K **31**
Avalon Cl. SW20 . . . . 6H **19**
Avante KT1: King T 5B **36** (7E **16**)
Avebury Pk. KT6: Surb 4E **22**
Avebury Rd. SW19 . . . . 5J **19**
Avening Rd. SW18 . . . . 4K **13**
Avening Ter. SW18 . . . . 4K **13**
Avenue, The
KT4: Wor Pk 6C **24**
KT5: Surb 3G **23**
KT10: Clay 3K **27**
KT17: Ewe 4E **30**
KT22: Oxs 7A **28**
SM2: Cheam 5J **31**
SM3: Cheam 4F **31**
TW1: Twick 2C **10**
TW3: Houn 2G **9**
TW9: Kew 6G **5**
TW12: Hamp 3E **14**
TW16: Sun 5A **14**
W4 . . . . 1B **6**
Avenue Elmers KT6: Surb 2F **23**
Avenue Gdns. SW14 . . . . 7B **6**
TW11: Tedd 4A **16**
Avenue Pde. TW16: Sun 7A **14**
Avenue Rd.
KT1: King T 5D **36** (7F **17**)
KT3: N Mald 1B **24**
KT18: Eps 3A **34**
SM2: Sutt 6K **31**
SM7: Bans 4K **35**
SW20 . . . . 6E **18**
TW7: Isle 5A **4**
TW8: Bford 2D **4**
TW11: Tedd 4B **16**
TW12: Hamp 5G **15**
Avenue Sth. KT5: Surb 4H **23**
Avenue Ter. KT3: N Mald 7K **17**
Averill St. W6 . . . . 3G **7**
Avern Gdns. KT8: W Mole 1G **21**
Avern Rd. KT8: W Mole 1G **21**
Avershaw Ho. SW15 . . . . 2G **13**
Avon Cl. KT4: Wor Pk 6D **24**
Avon Ct. SW15 . . . . 2H **13**
Avondale Av.
KT4: Wor Pk 5C **24**
KT10: Hin W 7B **22**
Avondale Cl. KT12: Hers 2B **26**
Avondale Gdns. TW4: Houn 2E **8**
Avondale Mans. *SW6* *5J 7*
(off Rostrevor Rd.)
Avondale Rd. SW14 . . . . 7B **6**
SW19 . . . . 2K **19**
Avon Ho.
KT2: King T 1B **36** (5E **16**)
W14 . . . . *1J 7*
(off Kensington Village)
Avonmore Gdns. W14 . . . . 1J **7**
Avonmore Mans. *W14* *1H 7*
(off Avonmore Rd.)
Avonmore Pl. W14 . . . . 1H **7**
Avonmore Rd. W14 . . . . 1H **7**
Axwood KT18: Eps 4K **33**
Aylett Rd. TW7: Isle 6A **4**
Ayliffe Cl. KT1: King T 6H **17**
Aylward Rd. SW20 . . . . 6J **19**
Aynhoe Mans. *W14* *1G 7*
(off Aynhoe Rd.)
Aynhoe Rd. W14 . . . . 1G **7**
Aynscombe Path SW14 . . . . 6K **5**
Azalea Ho. TW13: Felt 5A **8**
Azure Pl. TW3: Houn 1G **9**

B

Babbacombe Cl. KT9: Chess 2E **28**
Baber Bri. Cvn. Site TW14: Felt . . 2B **8**
Baber Bri. Pde. TW14: Felt 3B **8**
Baber Dr. TW14: Felt 3B **8**
Back Grn. KT12: Hers 3B **26**
Back La. TW8: Bford 3E **4**
TW10: Ham 7D **10**
Back Rd. TW11: Tedd 4K **15**
Baddeley Ho. *KT8: W Mole* *2F 21*
(off Down St.)
Baden Powell Cl. KT6: Surb 6G **23**
Bader Way SW15 . . . . 3D **12**
Badger Cl. TW13: Felt 7A **8**
Badgers Copse KT4: Wor Pk 6C **24**
Badger's Ct. KT17: Eps 2B **34**
Badger's Lodge KT17: Eps 2B **34**
Badgers Wlk. KT3: N Mald 6B **18**
Bagley's La. SW6 . . . . 5K **7**
Bagot Cl. KT21: Asht 5G **33**
Bahram Rd. KT19: Eps 6A **30**
Bailey Cres. KT9: Chess 4E **28**
Bailey M. W4 . . . . 3J **5**
Bainbridge Cl. TW10: Ham 2F **17**
Bakehouse M. TW12: Hamp 4F **15**
Baker Pl. KT19: Ewe 3K **29**
Bakers End SW20 . . . . 6H **19**
Bakery M. KT6: Surb 5H **23**
Bakewell Way KT3: N Mald 6B **18**
Balaam Ho. SM1: Sutt 1K **31**
Balaclava Rd. KT6: Surb 4D **22**
Balfern Gro. W4 . . . . 2B **6**
Balfour Pl. SW15 . . . . 1E **12**
Balgowan Cl. KT3: N Mald 2B **24**
Ballard Cl. KT2: King T 4A **18**
Ballards Grn. KT20: Tad 7H **35**
Balmain Lodge *KT5: Surb* *1F 23*
(off Cranes Pk. Av.)
Balmoral Cl. SW15 . . . . 3G **13**
Balmoral Ct. KT4: Wor Pk 6E **24**
SM2: Sutt 4K **31**
Balmoral Cres. KT8: W Mole 7F **15**
Balmoral Ho. *W14* *1H 7*
(off Windsor Way)
Balmoral Rd.
KT1: King T 7E **36** (1G **23**)
KT4: Wor Pk 7E **24**
Balmoral Way SM2: Sutt 6K **31**
Balmuir Gdns. SW15 . . . . 1F **13**
Balquhain Cl. KT21: Asht 6E **32**
Baltic Av. TW8: Bford 2E **4**
Balvernie Gro. SW18 . . . . 4J **13**
Balvernie M. SW18 . . . . 4K **13**
Banbury Ct. SM2: Sutt 4K **31**
Bangalore St. SW15 . . . . 7F **7**
Banim St. W6 . . . . 1E **6**
Bank La. KT2: King T 4F **17**
SW15 . . . . 2B **12**
Bank of England Sports Cen. **2B 12**
Banksian Wlk. TW7: Isle 5A **4**
Bankside KT17: Eps D 5F **35**
Bankside Cl. TW7: Isle 1A **10**
Bankside Dr. KT7: T Ditt 5C **22**
Bannow Cl. KT19: Ewe 1B **30**
BANSTEAD **4K 35**
Banstead Downs Golf Course . . . **7K 31**
Banstead Rd. KT17: Ewe 6E **30**
SM7: Bans 6E **30**
Banstead Station (Rail) **3J 35**
Barbara Castle Cl. SW6 . . . . 3J **7**
Barb M. W6 . . . . 1F **7**
Barclay Cl. SW6 . . . . 4K **7**
Barclay Rd. SW6 . . . . 4K **7**
Bardolph Rd. TW9: Rich 7G **5**
Bargate Cl. KT3: N Mald 4D **24**
Barge Wlk.
KT1: Hamp W 5A **36** (7E **16**)
KT1: King T 2B **36** (5E **16**)
KT8: E Mos 3B **22**
(Boyle Farm Island)
KT8: E Mos 7J **15**
(Hampton Ct. Cres.)
Barham Rd. SW20 . . . . 4D **18**
Barker Cl. KT3: N Mald 1J **23**
TW9: Kew 6J **5**
Barkston Gdns. SW5 . . . . 1K **7**
Barley Mow Pas. W4 . . . . 2A **6**
Barlow Rd. TW12: Hamp 4F **15**
Barnard Cl. TW16: Sun 4A **14**
Barnard Gdns. KT3: N Mald 1D **24**
Barnby Cl. KT21: Asht 6D **32**
Barn Cl. KT18: Eps 4K **33**
Barneby Cl. TW2: Twick 5K **9**
Barn Elms Athletics Track **6E 6**
Barn Elms Cl. KT4: Wor Pk 7C **24**
Barn Elms Pk. SW15 . . . . 7F **7**
BARNES **6C 6**
Barnes All. TW12: Hamp 6H **15**
Barnes Av. SW13 . . . . 4D **6**
Barnes Bri. W4 . . . . 6B **6**
Barnes Bridge Station (Rail) **6C 6**
Barnes Common Nature Reserve
. . . . **7D 6**
Barnes End KT3: N Mald 2D **24**
Barnes High St. SW13 . . . . 6C **6**
BARNES HOSPITAL **7B 6**
Barnes Station (Rail) **7D 6**
Barnett Wood La. KT21: Asht 7D **32**
Barnfield KT3: N Mald 3B **24**
Barnfield Av. KT2: King T 1E **16**
Barnfield Gdns. KT2: King T 1F **17**
Barnlea Cl. TW13: Hanw 6D **8**
Barnsbury Cl. KT3: N Mald 1K **23**
Barnsbury Cres. KT5: Surb 5K **23**
Barnsbury La. KT5: Surb 6J **23**
Barnscroft SW20 . . . . 7E **18**
Barn Theatre, The
West Molesey **1F 21**
Barons, The TW1: Twick 3C **10**
BARONS COURT **2H 7**
Baron's Ct. Rd. W14 . . . . 2H **7**
Barons Court Station
(Underground) **2H 7**
Barons Court Theatre ***2H 7***
(off Comeragh Rd.)
Baronsfield Rd. TW1: Twick 3C **10**
Barons Ga. W4 . . . . 1K **5**
Baron's Hurst KT18: Eps 5K **33**
Barons Keep W14 . . . . 2H **7**
Baronsmead Rd. SW13 . . . . 5D **6**
Barrack Rd. TW4: Houn 1C **8**
Barrington Rd. SM3: Sutt 6K **25**
Barrowgate Rd. W4 . . . . 2K **5**
Barrow Hill KT4: Wor Pk 6B **24**
Barrow Hill Cl. KT4: Wor Pk 6B **24**
Barrow Wlk. TW8: Bford 3D **4**
Bartlett Ho. *KT4: Wor Pk* *6C 24*
(off The Avenue)
Barton Ct. *W14* *2H 7*
(off Baron's Ct. Rd.)
Barton Grn. KT3: N Mald 6A **18**
Barton Rd. W14 . . . . 2H **7**
Barwell Bus. Pk. KT9: Chess 4E **28**
Barwell Ct. KT9: Chess 4C **28**
Barwell La. KT9: Chess 4D **28**
Basden Gro. TW13: Hanw 6F **9**
Basden Ho. TW13: Hanw 6F **9**
Basildene Rd. TW4: Houn 1C **8**
Basing Cl. KT7: T Ditt 4A **22**
Basingfield Rd. KT7: T Ditt 4A **22**
Basing Rd. SM7: Bans 3J **35**
Basing Way KT7: T Ditt 4A **22**
Basuto Rd. SW6 . . . . 5K **7**
Batavia Cl. TW16: Sun 5A **14**
Batavia Rd. TW16: Sun 5A **14**
Bat Gdns. KT2: King T 3G **17**
Bathgate Rd. SW19 . . . . 7G **13**
Bath Pas. KT1: King T . . 4B **36** (6E **16**)
Bath Pl. *W6* *2F 7*
(off Peabody Est.)
Bath Rd. TW3: Houn 1F **9**
W4 . . . . 1B **6**
Bathurst Av. SW19 . . . . 5K **19**
Baulk, The SW18 . . . . 4K **13**
Baygrove M.
KT1: Hamp W 1A **36** (5D **16**)
Bayleaf Cl. TW12: Hamp H 2J **15**
Baylis M. TW1: Twick 4B **10**
Bayonne Rd. W6 . . . . 3H **7**
Bazalgette Cl. KT3: N Mald 2A **24**
Bazalgette Gdns. KT3: N Mald . . . 2A **24**
Beach Gro. TW13: Hanw 6F **9**
Beach Ho. *SW5* *2K 7*
(off Philbeach Gdns.)
TW13: Hanw 6F **9**
Beacon Cl. SM7: Bans 5G **35**
Beaconsfield Cl. W4 . . . . 2K **5**
Beaconsfield Gdns. KT10: Clay . . . 4K **27**
Beaconsfield Pl. KT17: Eps 1B **34**
Beaconsfield Rd. KT3: N Mald . . . 6A **18**
KT5: Surb 4G **23**
KT10: Clay 4K **27**
TW1: Twick 3C **10**
W4 . . . . 1A **6**
Beaconsfield Wlk. SW6 . . . . 5J **7**
Beacon Way SM7: Bans 5G **35**
Beadon Rd. W6 . . . . 1F **7**

Beaford Gro. SW20 .....7H 19
Beagle Cl. TW13: Felt 1A 14
Beard Rd. KT2: King T 2G 17
Beard's Hill TW12: Hamp 5F 15
Beard's Hill Cl. TW12: Hamp 5F 15
Bear Rd. TW13: Hanw 1C 14
Beatrice Ho. W6 .....2F 7
 (off Queen Caroline St.)
Beatrice Rd. TW10: Rich 2G 11
Beauchamp Rd.
 KT8: W Mole, E Mos 2G 21
 SM1: Sutt 1K 31
 TW1: Twick 4B 10
Beauchamp Ter. SW15 .....7E 6
Beauclerc Ct. TW16: Sun 6B 14
Beauclerk Cl. TW13: Felt 5A 8
Beaufort Cl. SW15 .....4E 12
Beaufort Ct. SW6 .....3K 7
 TW10: Ham 1D 16
Beaufort M. SW6 .....3J 7
Beaufort Rd.
 KT1: King T 7D 36 (1F 23)
 TW1: Twick 4D 10
 TW10: Ham 1D 16
Beaufort Way KT17: Ewe 4D 30
Beaulieu Cl. TW1: Twick 3E 10
 TW4: Houn 2E 8
Beaulieu Pl. W4 .....1K 5
Beaumont W14 .....1J 7
 (off Kensington Village)
Beaumont Av. TW9: Rich 7G 5
 W14 .....2J 7
Beaumont Cl. KT2: King T 4H 17
Beaumont Cres. W4 .....2K 5
Beaumont Cres. W14 .....2J 7
Beaumont Dr.
 KT4: Wor Pk 4E 24
Beaumont Pl. TW7: Isle 2A 10
Beaumont Rd. SW19 .....4H 13
 W4 .....1K 5
Beaver Cl. SM4: Mord 4F 25
 TW12: Hamp 5G 15
Beavers Cres. TW4: Houn 1B 8
Beavers La. TW4: Houn 1B 8
Beavers La. Campsite
 TW4: Houn 1C 8
Beavor Gro. W6 .....2D 6
 (off Beavor La.)
Beavor La. W6 .....2D 6
Bechtel Ho. W6 .....1G 7
 (off Hammersmith Rd.)
Becketts Cl. TW14: Felt 3A 8
Becketts Pl.
 KT1: Hamp W 2A 36 (5E 16)
Becketts Wharf KT1: Hamp W 2A 36
Beckford Cl. W14 .....1J 7
Bective Pl. SW15 .....1J 13
Bective Rd. SW15 .....1J 13
Bedfont La. TW13: Felt 5A 8
 TW14: Felt 5A 8
Bedford Cl. W4 .....3B 6
Bedford Cnr. W4 .....1B 6
 (off South Pde.)
BEDFORD PARK 1A 6
Bedford Pk. Cnr. W4 .....1B 6
Bedford Pk. Mans. W4 .....1A 6
Bedford Pas. SW6 .....4H 7
 (off Dawes Rd.)
Bedford Rd. KT4: Wor Pk 6F 25
 TW2: Twick 7J 9
 W4 .....1A 6
Bedgebury Gdns. SW19 .....6H 13
Bedster Gdns. KT8: W Mole 6G 15
Beech Av. TW8: Bford 4C 4
Beech Cl. KT11: Cobh 7F 27
 KT12: Hers 1B 26
 SW15 .....4D 12
 SW19 .....3F 19
 TW16: Sun 6C 14
Beech Cl. Ct. KT11: Cobh 7E 26
Beech Cl. KT6: Surb 4E 22
Beechcroft Av. KT3: N Mald 5K 17
Beechcroft Rd. KT9: Chess 7G 23
 SW14 .....7K 5
Beechen Cliff Way TW7: Isle 6A 4
Beeches SM7: Bans 5K 35
Beeches Rd. SM3: Sutt 5H 25
Beech Gro. KT3: N Mald 7A 18
 KT18: Tatt C 6E 34
Beechmore Gdns.
 SM3: Cheam 6G 25
Beecholme SM7: Bans 3H 35
Beech Rd. KT17: Eps 4C 34
Beechrow TW10: Ham 1F 17
Beech Wlk. KT17: Ewe 7D 30

Beech Way KT17: Eps 4C 34
 TW2: Twick 7F 9
Beechwood Av. TW9: Kew 5H 5
 TW16: Sun 3A 14
Beechwood Cl. KT6: Surb 4D 22
Beechwood Ct. KT12: Walt T 7A 20
 (off Station Rd.)
 TW16: Sun 3A 14
 W4 .....3A 6
Beechwood Dr. KT11: Cobh 7F 27
Beechwood Gro. KT6: Surb 4D 22
Beecot La. KT12: Walt T 6B 20
Beeston Way TW14: Felt 3B 8
BEGGAR'S HILL 3C 30
Beggar's Hill KT17: Ewe 4C 30
Beggars Roost La. SM1: Sutt 3K 31
Begonia Pl. TW12: Hamp 3F 15
Beldam Way TW3: Houn 1E 8
Beldham Gdns. KT8: W Mole 6G 15
Belfield Rd. KT19: Ewe 5A 30
Belgrade Rd. TW12: Hamp 5G 15
Belgrave Cl. KT12: Hers 1A 26
Belgrave Ct. W4 .....2K 5
Belgrave Cres. TW16: Sun 5A 14
Belgrave Rd. SW13 .....4C 6
 TW4: Houn 1E 8
 TW16: Sun 5A 14
Belgravia M. KT1: King T 1E 22
Bellamy Cl. W14 .....2J 7
Bel La. TW13: Hanw 7D 8
Bell Dr. SW18 .....4H 13
Bellevue Cl. TW3: Houn 1F 9
Bellevue Rd.
 KT1: King T 6D 36 (7F 17)
 (not continuous)
 SW13 .....6D 6
Bell Ind. Est. W4 .....1K 5
Bell La. TW1: Twick 5B 10
Bell Rd. KT8: E Mos 2J 21
 TW3: Houn 1G 9
Bells All. SW6 .....6K 7
BELMONT 6K 31
Belmont Av. KT3: N Mald 2D 24
Belmont Gro. W4 .....1A 6
Belmont M. SW19 .....6G 13
Belmont Ri. SM2: Sutt 4J 31
Belmont Rd. SM2: Sutt 6K 31
 TW2: Twick 6J 9
 W4 .....1A 6
Belmont Station (Rail) 6K 31
Belmont Ter. W4 .....1A 6
Beloe Cl. SW15 .....1D 12
Belsize Av. SW13 .....1C 4
Beltane Dr. SW19 .....7G 13
Beltran Rd. SW6 .....2H 7
Belvedere Av. SW19 .....2H 19
Belvedere Cl. KT10: Esh 2G 27
Belvedere Ct. SW15 .....1F 13
 TW11: Tedd 2K 15
Belvedere Dr. SW19 .....2H 19
Belvedere Gdns. KT8: W Mole 2E 20
Belvedere Gro. SW19 .....2H 19
Belvedere Sq. SW19 .....2H 19
Bembridge Ho. KT2: King T 6H 17
 (off Coombe Rd.)
Bemish Rd. SW15 .....7G 7
Bench, The TW10: Ham 7D 10
Bendemeer Rd. SW15 .....7G 7
Benfleet Cl. KT11: Cobh 7D 26
Biggs Row SW15 .....7G 7
Benham Cl. KT9: Chess 3D 28
Benham Gdns. TW4: Houn 2E 8
Benkart M. SW15 .....3D 12
Bennet Cl. KT1: Hamp W 5D 16
Bennett Cl. TW4: Houn 2D 8
Bennett St. W4 .....3B 6
Benn's All. TW12: Hamp 6G 15
Benns Wlk. TW9: Rich 1F 11
 (off Michelsdale Dr.)
Bensbury Cl. SW15 .....4E 12
Benson Cl. TW3: Houn 1F 9
Bentall Cen., The
 KT1: King T 3B 36 (6E 16)
Bentley Cl. SW19 .....7K 13
Berberis Ho. TW13: Felt 6A 8
Beresford Av. KT5: Surb 5J 23
 TW1: Twick 3D 10
Beresford Gdns. TW4: Houn 2E 8
Beresford Rd.
 KT2: King T 1E 36 (5G 17)
 KT3: N Mald 1K 23
 SM2: Sutt 4J 31
Berestede Rd. W6 .....2C 6
Bergenia Ho. TW13: Felt 5A 8
Berkeley Cl. KT2: King T 4F 17
Berkeley Ct. KT6: Surb 4E 22
 KT21: Asht 7G 33

Berkeley Dr. KT8: W Mole 7E 14
Berkeley Gdns. KT10: Clay 3B 28
Berkeley Ho. TW8: Bford 3E 4
 (off Albany Rd.)
Berkeley M. TW16: Sun 7B 14
Berkeley Pl. KT18: Eps 4A 34
 SW19 .....3G 19
Berkeley Rd. SW13 .....5D 6
Berkley Cl. TW2: Twick 7K 9
 (off Wellesley Rd.)
Bernard Gdns. SW19 .....2J 19
Bernard Pl. KT17: Ewe 6F 31
Berry Ct. TW4: Houn 2E 8
BERRYLANDS 3H 23
Berrylands KT5: Surb 3G 23
 SW20 .....7F 19
Berrylands Rd. KT5: Surb 3G 23
Berrylands Station (Rail) 1J 23
Berry La. KT12: Hers 2C 26
 (off New Berry La.)
Berry Meade KT21: Asht 6G 33
Berry Meade Cl. KT21: Asht 6G 33
Bertelli Pl. TW13: Felt 5A 8
Bertram Cotts. SW19 .....4K 19
Berwick Cl. TW2: Whitt 5F 9
Berwyn Rd. TW10: Rich 1J 11
Beryl Rd. W6 .....2G 7
Berystede KT2: King T 4J 17
Bessant Dr. TW9: Kew 5J 5
Bessborough Rd. SW15 .....5D 12
Betley Ct. KT12: Walt T 7A 20
Betbridge Rd. SW6 .....6J 7
Betts Way KT6: Surb 5C 22
Beulah Rd. SM1: Sutt 1K 31
 SW19 .....4J 19
Bevan Ho. TW1: Twick 3E 10
Bevan Pk. KT17: Ewe 6C 30
Beveree Stadium 5G 15
 TW4: Houn 1E 8
Beverley Cl. KT9: Chess 1D 28
 KT17: Ewe 7F 31
 SW13 .....6D 6
Beverley Cotts. SW15 .....7B 12
Beverley Ct. TW4: Houn 1E 8
 W4 .....2K 5
Beverley Gdns. KT4: Wor Pk 5D 24
 SW13 .....7C 6
Beverley La. KT2: King T 4B 18
 SW13 .....7C 6
Beverley Meads & Fishpond Woods
 Nature Reserve 3C 18
Beverley Path SW13 .....6C 6
Beverley Rd. KT1: Hamp W 5D 16
 KT3: N Mald 1D 24
 KT4: Wor Pk 6F 25
 SW13 .....7C 6
 W4 .....2C 6
Beverley Trad. Est.
 SM4: Mord 4G 25
Beverley Way KT3: N Mald 1D 24
 SW20 .....5C 18
Bexhill Cl. TW13: Felt 6D 8
Bexhill Rd. SW14 .....7K 5
Bicester Rd. TW9: Rich 7H 5
Bideford Cl. TW13: Hanw 7E 8
Biggin Hill Cl. KT2: King T 2D 16
Biggs Row SW15 .....7G 7
Billockby Cl. KT9: Chess 3G 29
Binley Ho. SW15 .....3D 12
Binns Rd. W4 .....2B 6
Binns Ter. W4 .....2B 6
Birch Cl. SM7: Bans 3H 35
 TW8: Bford 4C 4
 TW11: Tedd 2B 16
Birches, The TW4: Houn 4E 8
Birches Cl. KT18: Eps 4B 34
Birchfield Cl. KT12: Walt T 4A 20
 (off Grove Cres.)
Birchfield Gro. KT17: Ewe 6F 31
Birchgrove Ho. TW9: Kew 4J 5
Birchington Rd. KT5: Surb 4G 23
Birch Rd. TW13: Hanw 2C 14
Birchwood Cl. SM4: Mord 1K 25
Birchwood Gro. TW12: Hamp 3F 15
Birchwood La. KT10: Esh 5J 27
 KT22: Oxs 5J 27
Bird Wlk. TW2: Whitt 5E 8
Birdwood Cl. TW11: Tedd 1K 15
Birkbeck Rd. W5 .....1D 4
Birkenhead Av.
 KT2: King T 3E 36 (6G 17)
Biscay Rd. W6 .....2G 7
Bishop Ct. TW9: Rich 7F 5
Bishop Fox Way KT8: W Mole 1E 20

Bishop King's Rd. W14 .....1H 7
Bishop's Av. SW6 .....6G 7
Bishop's Cl. SM1: Sutt 7K 25
Bishops Cl. TW10: Ham 7E 10
 W4 .....2K 5
Bishop's Gro. TW12: Hamp 1E 14
Bishops Gro. Cvn. Site
 TW12: Hamp, Hamp H 1F 15
Bishop's Hall
 KT1: King T 3B 36 (6E 16)
Bishop's Mans. SW6 .....6G 7
Bishopsmead Cl. KT19: Ewe 6A 30
Bishopsmead Ct. KT19: Ewe 6B 30
Bishop's Pk. Rd. SW6 .....6G 7
Bishops Rd. SW6 .....5H 7
Bisley Cl. KT4: Wor Pk 5F 25
Bison Ct. TW14: Felt 4A 8
Bittoms, The
 KT1: King T 5B 36 (7E 16)
Bittoms Ct.
 KT1: King T 5B 36 (7E 16)
Bkackthorn Cl. KT17: Eps D 5E 34
Blackburn Way TW4: Houn 2D 8
Blackett St. SW15 .....7G 7
Blackford's Path SW15 .....4D 12
Blackhills KT10: Esh 5E 26
Black Lion La. W6 .....1D 6
Black Lion M. W6 .....1D 6
Blackmore's Gro.
 TW11: Tedd 3B 16
Blacksmith Cl. KT21: Asht 7G 33
Blacks Rd. W6 .....2F 7
Blade M. SW15 .....1J 13
Blades Cl. SW15 .....1J 13
 W6 .....2E 6
 (off Lower Mall)
Blagdon Rd. KT3: N Mald 1C 24
Blagdon Wlk. TW11: Tedd 3D 16
Blagrove Rd. TW11: Hamp W 4C 16
Blair Av. KT10: Esh 6H 21
Blake Ct. KT19: Eps 1G 33
Blakeden Dr. KT10: Clay 3A 28
Blake Gdns. SW6 .....5K 7
Blake M. TW9: Kew 5H 5
Blakemore Gdns. SW13 .....3E 6
Blakeney Cl. KT19: Eps 7A 30
Blakes Av. KT3: N Mald 2C 24
Blakes La. KT3: N Mald 2C 24
Blakesley Wlk. SW20 .....6J 19
Blakes Ter. KT3: N Mald 2D 24
Blakewood Cl. TW13: Hanw 1B 14
Blanchard Ho. TW1: Twick 3E 10
 (off Clevedon Rd.)
Blandford Av. TW2: Whitt 5G 9
Blandford Rd. TW11: Tedd 2J 15
Bleak Ho. La. W4 .....2A 6
 (off Chiswick High Rd.)
Blendworth Point SW15 .....5E 12
Blenheim Cl. SW20 .....7F 19
Blenheim Gdns. KT2: King T 4J 17
Blenheim Ho. TW3: Houn 1F 9
Blenheim Pl. TW11: Tedd 2A 16
Blenheim Rd. KT19: Eps 7A 30
 SM1: Sutt 7K 25
 SW20 .....7F 19
 W4 .....1B 6
Blenheim Way TW7: Isle 5B 4
Blincoe Cl. SW19 .....6G 13
Blondin Av. W5 .....1D 4
Blondin Pk. & Nature Area 1C 4
Bloomfield Rd.
 KT1: King T 7D 36 (1F 23)
Bloom Pk. Rd. SW6 .....4J 7
Bloomsbury Ct. KT19: Eps 6A 30
Bloxham Cres. TW12: Hamp 4E 14
Blue Anchor All. TW9: Rich 1F 11
Blue Cedars SM7: Bans 3G 35
Blue Cedars Pl. KT11: Cobh 7C 26
Bluefield Cl. TW12: Hamp 2F 15
Bluegates KT17: Ewe 4D 30
Blunden Ct. SW6 .....4K 7
 (off Farm La.)
Blyth Cl. TW1: Twick 3A 10
Blythe Rd. W14 .....1G 7
Boars Head Yd. TW8: Bford 4D 4
Bockhampton Rd.
 KT2: King T 4G 17
Boddicott Cl. SW19 .....6H 13
Boddington Ho. SW13 .....3E 6
 (off Wyatt Dr.)
Bodicea M. TW4: Houn 3E 8
Bodley Cl. KT3: N Mald 2B 24
Bodley Rd. KT3: N Mald 3A 24
Bodmin St. SW18 .....5K 13
Bodnant Gdns. SW20 .....7D 18
Boileau Rd. SW13 .....7C 6

lander Gro. Nth. SW6 ....3K 7
(off Seagrave Rd.)
lander Gro. Sth. SW6 ....3K 7
(off Seagrave Rd.)
pleyn Av. KT17: Ewe 6E 30
pleyn Ct. KT8: E Mos 1J 21
(off Bridge Rd.)
pleyn Dr. KT8: W Mole 7E 14
pllo La. W3 ....1J 5
W4 ....1K 5
plney Way TW13: Hanw 7D 8
plters La. SM7: Bans 3J 35
plton Cl. KT9: Chess 3E 28
plton Gdns. TW11: Tedd 3B 16
plton Rd. KT9: Chess 3E 28
W4 ....4K 5
ond Ho. TW8: Bford 2E 4
ond Rd. KT6: Surb 6G 23
ond St. W4 ....1A 6
onesgate Open Space
Local Nature Reserve 3H 9
onner Hill Rd. KT1: King T 6G 17
onor Rd. TW1: Twick 6A 10
ooth Ho. TW8: Bford 4D 4
(off High St.)
ordesley Rd. SM4: Mord 2K 25
ordeston Ct. TW8: Bford 4D 4
(off The Ham)
ordon Wlk. SW15 ....4D 12
orland Ter. TW11: Tedd 4C 16
orneo St. SW18 ....7F 7
orough Rd. KT2: King T 5H 17
TW7: Isle 5A 4
orough Sports Ground 1K 31
oscombe Rd. KT4: Wor Pk 5F 25
SW19 ....5K 19
oston Bus. Pk. W7 ....1A 4
oston Gdns. TW8: Bford 1B 4
W4 ....3B 6
W7 ....1B 4
oswell Ct. KT2: King T 5G 17
(off Clifton Rd.)
W14 ....1G 7
(off Blythe Rd.)
othwell St. W6 ....3G 7
otsford Rd. SW20 ....6H 19
oucher Cl. TW11: Tedd 2A 16
oulton Ho. TW8: Bford 2F 5
oundaries Rd. TW13: Felt 5B 8
oundary Cl. KT1: King T 7J 17
ourne Ct. T Ditt 6A 22
TW7: Isle 7A 4
ourne Ct. W4 ....3K 5
ourne Gro. KT21: Asht 7E 32
ourne Hall Mus. 5C 30
ournemouth Rd. SW19 ....5K 19
ourne Pl. W4 ....2A 6
ourne Way KT19: Ewe 1K 29
SM1: Sutt 2J 31
owater Gdns. TW16: Sun 6B 14
owerdean St. SW6 ....5K 7
owes Rd. KT12: Walt T 6A 20
owfell Rd. W6 ....3F 7
owie Ho. SM4: Mord 3H 25
owline Ct. TW8: Bford 3D 4
owling Grn. Cl. SW15 ....4E 12
owman M. SW18 ....5J 13
owness Cres. SW15 ....2B 18
owness Dr. TW4: Houn 1D 8
owyers Cl. KT21: Asht 7G 33
owyers Ct. TW1: Isle 1C 10
oyd Cl. KT2: King T 4H 17
oyle Farm Island
KT7: T Ditt 3B 22
oyle Farm Rd. KT7: T Ditt 3B 22
rackenbury Rd. W6 ....1E 6
racken Cl. TW2: Whitt 4F 9
racken End TW7: Isle 2J 9
racken Gdns. SW13 ....6D 6
rackenhill KT11: Cobh 7G 27
racken Path KT18: Eps 2J 33
rackley Rd. W4 ....2B 6
rackley Ter. W4 ....2B 6
racondale KT10: Esh 2H 27
radbourne St. SW6 ....6K 7
raddock Cl. TW7: Isle 6A 4
raddon Rd. TW9: Rich 7G 5

Bradford Dr. KT19: Ewe 3C 30
Bradley Cl. SM2: Sutt 6K 31
Bradmore Pk. Rd. W6 ....1E 6
Bradshaw Cl. SW19 ....3K 19
Bradstock Rd. KT17: Ewe 2D 30
Brae Ct. KT2: King T 5H 17
Braemar SW15 ....3G 13
Braemar Av. SW19 ....6K 13
Braemar Rd. KT4: Wor Pk 7E 24
TW8: Bford 3E 4
Braeside Av. SW19 ....5H 19
Braid Cl. TW13: Hanw 6E 8
Brainton Av. TW14: Felt 4A 8
Bramber Ct. TW8: Bford 1F 5
W14 ....3J 7
(off Bramber Rd.)
Bramber Ho. KT2: King T 2C 36
Bramber Rd. W14 ....3J 7
Brambleacres Cl. SM2: Sutt 4K 31
Bramble La. TW12: Hamp 3E 14
Brambles, The SW19 ....2J 19
(off Woodside)
Brambles Cl. TW7: Isle 4C 4
Bramble Wlk. KT18: Eps 3J 33
Bramcote Av. SW15 ....1E 12
Bramham Gdns. KT9: Chess 1E 28
Bramley Cl. TW2: Whitt 3H 9
Bramley Ho. SW15 ....3C 12
(off Tunworth Cres.)
TW4: Houn 1E 8
Bramley Rd. SM2: Cheam 5G 31
W5 ....1D 4
Bramley Way KT21: Asht 6G 33
TW4: Houn 2E 8
Brampton Gdns. KT12: Hers 2B 26
Bramshaw Ri. KT3: N Mald 3B 24
Bramwell Cl. TW16: Sun 6C 14
Brandlehow Rd. SW15 ....1J 13
Brandon Mans. W14 ....3H 7
(off Queen's Club Gdns.)
Brandon Rd. SM1: Sutt 1K 31
Brandy Way SM2: Sutt 4K 31
Brangwyn Ct. W14 ....1H 7
(off Blythe Rd.)
Branksea St. SW6 ....4H 7
Branksome Cl. KT12: Walt T 6C 20
TW11: Tedd 1J 15
Branksome Rd. SW19 ....5K 19
Branksome Way KT3: N Mald 5K 17
Bransby Rd. KT9: Chess 3F 29
Branstone Rd. TW9: Kew 5G 5
Brantwood Av. TW7: Isle 1B 10
Brasenose Dr. SW13 ....3F 7
Brasted Cl. SM2: Sutt 6K 31
Brathway Rd. SW18 ....4K 13
Braybourne Dr. TW7: Isle 4A 4
Braycourt Av. KT12: Walt T 4A 20
Breamore Cl. SW15 ....5D 12
Breamwater Gdns.
TW10: Ham 7C 10
Breasley Cl. SW15 ....1E 12
Brecon Cl. KT4: Wor Pk 6F 25
Brecon Rd. W6 ....3H 7
Brende Gdns. TW8: W Mole 1G 21
Brendon Cl. KT10: Esh 3H 27
Brendon Dr. KT10: Esh 3H 27
BRENTFORD 3E 4
Brentford Bus. Cen. TW8: Bford 4D 4
BRENTFORD END 4C 4
Brentford FC 3E 4
Brentford Fountain Leisure Cen.
....2H 5
Brentford Ho. TW1: Twick 4C 10
Brentford Station (Rail) 3D 4
Brent Lea TW8: Bford 4D 4
Brent Rd. TW8: Bford 3D 4
Brent Side TW8: Bford 3D 4
Brentside Executive Cen.
TW8: Bford 3C 4
Brent Way TW8: Bford 4E 4
Brentwick Gdns. TW8: Bford 1F 5
Brettgrave KT19: Eps 6K 29
Brett Ho. Cl. SW15 ....4G 13
Brewers La. TW9: Rich 2E 10
Brewery La. TW1: Twick 4A 10
Brewery M. Cen. TW7: Isle 7B 4
Brewhouse La. SW15 ....7H 7
Brewster Pl. KT1: King T 6K 17
Briane Rd. KT19: Eps 6K 29
Briar Cl. TW7: Isle 2A 10
TW12: Hamp 2E 14
Briar Ct. SM3: Cheam 1F 31
SW15 ....1E 12
Briar Rd. TW2: Twick 5K 9

Briar Wlk. SW15 ....1E 12
Briarwood Ct. KT4: Wor Pk 5D 24
(off The Avenue)
Briarwood Rd. KT17: Ewe 3D 30
Briavels Ct. KT18: Eps 4B 34
Brick Farm Cl. TW9: Kew 5J 5
Brickfield Cl. TW8: Bford 4D 4
Bridge Av. W6 ....1F 7
Bridge Av. Mans. W6 ....2F 7
(off Bridge Av.)
Bridge Cl. TW11: Tedd 1A 16
Bridge End Cl. KT2: King T 5H 17
Bridgefield Cl. SM7: Bans 4F 35
Bridgefield Rd. SM1: Sutt 3K 31
Bridge Gdns. KT8: E Mos 1J 21
Bridgeman Ho. W14 ....1J 7
(off Radnor Rd.)
Bridgeman Rd. TW11: Tedd 3B 16
Bridgepark SW18 ....2K 13
Bridge Rd. KT8: E Mos 1J 21
KT9: Chess 2F 29
KT17: Eps 1C 34
TW1: Twick 3C 10
TW7: Isle 1J 9
Bridges Pl. SW6 ....5J 7
Bridges Rd. SW19 ....3K 19
Bridge Rd. M. SW19 ....3K 19
Bridge St. TW9: Rich 2E 10
W4 ....1A 6
Bridge Vw. W6 ....2F 7
Bridge Way TW2: Whitt 4H 9
Bridge Wharf Rd. TW7: Isle 7C 4
Bridgewood Rd. KT4: Wor Pk 1D 30
Bridle Cl. KT1: King T 7B 36 (1E 22)
KT19: Ewe 2A 30
TW16: Sun 7A 14
Bridle End KT17: Eps 2C 34
Bridle La. TW1: Twick 3C 10
Bridle Path, The KT17: Ewe 6F 31
Bridle Rd. KT10: Clay 3C 28
KT17: Eps 2C 34
Bridleway Cl. KT17: Ewe 6F 31
Brighton Rd. KT6: Surb 3D 22
SM2: Bans, Sutt 7K 31
SM7: Bans 7H 35
Brindles, The SM7: Bans 6J 35
Brinkley KT1: King T 6H 17
Brinkley Rd. KT4: Wor Pk 6E 24
Brinsworth Cl. TW2: Twick 5J 9
Brinsworth Ho. TW2: Twick 6J 9
Brisbane Av. SW19 ....5K 19
Briscoe M. TW2: Twick 6J 9
Brisson Cl. KT10: Esh 3E 26
Bristol Cl. TW4: Houn 4F 9
Bristol Gdns. SW15 ....4F 13
Bristow Rd. TW3: Houn 1H 9
Britannia Cl. KT17: Epsom 1B 36
Britannia La. TW2: Whitt 4H 9
Britannia Rd. KT5: Surb 4G 23
SW6 ....4K 7
British Gro. W4 ....2C 6
British Gro. Pas. W4 ....2C 6
British Gro. Sth. W4 ....2C 6
Brittain Rd. KT12: Hers 2C 26
Broad Cl. KT12: Hers 7C 20
Broadfields KT8: E Mos 3K 21
Broadhurst TW10: Rich 2G 11
Broadlands TW13: Hanw 7F 9
Broadlands Ct. TW9: Kew 4H 5
(off Kew Gdns. Rd.)
Broadlands Way KT3: N Mald 3C 24
Broad La. TW12: Hamp 4E 14
Broadmead KT21: Asht 6G 33
W14 ....1H 7
Broadmead Av. KT4: Wor Pk 4D 24
Broadmead Cl. TW12: Hamp 3F 15
Broadoaks KT6: Surb 6J 23
Broad St. TW11: Tedd 3A 16
Broad Wlk. KT18: Tatt C 7G 35
TW9: Kew 4G 5
Broad Wlk., The KT8: E Mos 1A 22
Broadway, The KT7: T Ditt 5K 21
SM3: Cheam 3H 31
SW13 ....6B 6
SW19 ....3J 19
Broadway Arc. W6 ....1F 7
(off Hammersmith B'way)
Broadway Cen., The W6 ....1F 7
Broadway Chambers W6 ....1F 7
(off Hammersmith B'way)
Broadway Ct. SW19 ....3K 19
Broadway Mans. SW6 ....4K 7
(off Fulham Rd.)
Broadway Pl. SW19 ....3J 19

Broadwood Ter. W8 ....1J 7
Brockbridge Ho. SW15 ....3C 12
Brockenhurst KT8: W Mole 2E 20
Brockenhurst Av. KT4: Wor Pk 5B 24
Brockham Cl. SW19 ....2J 19
Brocks Dr. SM3: Cheam 7H 25
Brockshot Cl. TW8: Bford 2E 4
Brompton Cemetery 3K 7
Brompton Cl. TW4: Houn 2E 8
Brompton Pk. Cres. SW6 ....3K 7
Brompton Vs. SW6 ....3K 7
(off Lillie Rd.)
Bronsart Rd. SW6 ....4H 7
Bronson Rd. SW20 ....6G 19
Bronte Ct. W14 ....1G 7
(off Girdler's Rd.)
Brook Cl. KT19: Ewe 5B 30
SW20 ....7E 18
Brookers Cl. KT21: Asht 6D 32
Brookfield Cl. KT10: Clay 3A 28
Brook Gdns. KT2: King T 5K 17
SW13 ....7C 6
BROOK GREEN 1G 7
Brook Grn. W6 ....1G 7
Brook Grn. Flats W14 ....1G 7
(off Dunsany Rd.)
Brook Ho. W6 ....1F 7
(off Shepherd's Bush Rd.)
Brooklands Av. SW19 ....6K 13
Brooklands Cl. KT1: King T 7B 36
Brooklands Pl. TW12: Hamp H 2G 15
Brooklands Rd. KT7: T Ditt 5A 22
Brooklands Ter. TW16: Sun 1A 20
Brook La. Bus. Cen. TW8: Bford 2E 4
Brook La. Nth. TW8: Bford 2E 4
(not continuous)
Brook Mead KT19: Ewe 3B 30
Brook Rd. KT6: Surb 6F 23
TW1: Twick 3B 10
Brook Rd. Sth. TW8: Bford 3E 4
Brookside Cl. TW13: Felt 7A 8
Brookside Cres. KT4: Wor Pk 5D 24
Brooks La. W4 ....3H 5
Brooks Rd. W4 ....3H 5
Brook St. KT1: King T 4C 36 (6F 17)
Brookville Rd. SW6 ....4J 7
Brook Way KT22: Lea 7B 32
Brookwood Av. SW13 ....6C 6
Brookwood Rd. SW18 ....5J 13
Broom Cl. KT10: Esh 2G 27
TW11: Tedd 4E 16
Broome Ct. TW20: Tad 7H 35
Broome Rd. TW12: Hamp 4E 14
Broomfield TW16: Sun 5A 14
Broomfield Ride KT22: Oxs 7J 27
Broomfield Rd. KT5: Surb 5G 23
TW9: Kew 5G 5
TW11: Tedd 3D 16
Broomfields KT10: Esh 2H 27
Broomhill Rd. SW18 ....2K 13
Broomhouse La. SW6 ....6K 7
Broomhouse Rd. SW6 ....6K 7
Broomloan La. SM1: Sutt 6K 25
Broom Lock TW11: Tedd 3D 16
Broom Rd. TW11: Tedd 2C 16
Broom Water TW11: Tedd 3D 16
Broom Water W. TW11: Tedd 2D 16
Brotherstone Wlk. TW9: Kew 5J 5
Brough Cl. KT2: King T 2E 16
Broughton Av. TW10: Ham 7C 10
Browells La. TW13: Felt 6A 8
(not continuous)
Brown Bear Ct. TW13: Hanw 1C 14
Browning Av. KT4: Wor Pk 5E 24
Browning Cl. TW12: Hamp 1E 14
Browning Ct. W14 ....3J 7
(off Turneville Rd.)
Brown's Rd. KT5: Surb 4G 23
Broxholme Ho. SW6 ....5K 7
(off Harwood Rd.)
Brumfield Rd. KT19: Ewe 2K 29
Brunel Ct. SW13 ....6C 6
(off Westfields Av.)
Brunel Wlk. TW2: Whitt 4F 9
Brunswick Cl. KT7: T Ditt 5A 22
KT12: Walt T 6B 20
TW2: Twick 7J 9
Brunswick Ho. W6 ....2F 7
(off Parrs Way)
Brunswick Rd. KT2: King T 5H 17
Bryanston Av. TW2: Whitt 5G 9
Buckhold Rd. SW18 ....3K 13
Buckingham Av. KT8: W Mole 6G 15
TW14: Felt 3A 8
Buckingham Cl. TW12: Hamp 2E 14

Buckingham Ct.—Castelnau Gdns.

Buckingham Ct. SM2: Sutt . . . 5K **31**
Buckingham Gdns.
KT8: W Mole . . . 6G **15**
Buckingham Rd.
KT1: King T . . . 7E **36** (1G **23**)
TW10: Ham . . . 6E **10**
TW12: Hamp . . . 1E **14**
Buckland Rd. KT9: Chess . . . 2G **29**
SM2: Cheam . . . 6F **31**
Bucklands Rd. TW11: Tedd . . . 3D **16**
Buckland's Wharf
KT1: King T . . . 3A **36** (6E **16**)
Buckland Way KT4: Wor Pk . . . 5F **25**
Buckleigh Av. SW20 . . . 7H **19**
Bucklers All. SW6 . . . 3J **7**
Buckles Way SM7: Bans . . . 5H **35**
Bucknills Cl. KT18: Eps . . . 3K **33**
Buddleia Ho. TW13: Felt . . . 5A **8**
Budd's All. TW1: Twick . . . 2D **10**
Buer Rd. SW6 . . . 6H **7**
Buick Ho. KT2: King T . . . 6G **17**
Bull's All. SW14 . . . 6A **6**
Bunbury Way KT17: Eps D . . . 5E **34**
Burberry Cl. KT3: N Mald . . . 6B **18**
Burcham Cl. TW12: Hamp . . . 4F **15**
Burden Cl. TW8: Bford . . . 2D **4**
Burdenshott Av. TW10: Rich . . . 1J **11**
Burdett Av. SW20 . . . 5D **18**
Burdett Rd. TW9: Rich . . . 6G **5**
Burdon La. SM2: Cheam . . . 4H **31**
Burdon Pk. SM2: Cheam . . . 5J **31**
Burford Ho. KT17: Ewe . . . 7F **31**
TW8: Bford . . . 2E **4**
Burford La. KT17: Ewe . . . 7F **31**
Burford Rd. KT4: Wor Pk . . . 4C **24**
SM1: Sutt . . . 6K **25**
TW8: Bford . . . 2F **5**
Burges Gro. SW13 . . . 4E **6**
Burgess Cl. TW13: Hanw . . . 1D **14**
Burgess Rd. SM1: Sutt . . . 1K **31**
Burgh Cft. KT17: Eps . . . 4C **34**
Burghfield KT17: Eps . . . 4C **34**
BURGH HEATH . . . 7H 35
Burgh Heath Rd.
KT17: Eps, Eps D . . . 3C **34**
Burghley Av. KT3: N Mald . . . 5A **18**
Burghley Hall Cl. SW19 . . . 5H **13**
Burghley Ho. SW19 . . . 7H **13**
Burghley Rd. SW19 . . . 1G **19**
Burgh Mt. SM7: Bans . . . 4J **35**
Burgh Wood SM7: Bans . . . 4H **35**
Burgoine Quay
KT1: Hamp W . . . 2A **36** (5E **16**)
Burgoyne Ho. *TW8: Bford* . . . *2E* ***4***
(off Ealing Rd.)
BURHILL . . . 5A 26
Burhill Golf Course . . . 5A 26
Burhill Rd. KT12: Hers . . . 5A **26**
Burke Cl. SW15 . . . 1B **12**
Burlea Cl. KT12: Hers . . . 2A **26**
Burleigh Pl. SW15 . . . 2G **13**
Burleigh Rd. SM3: Sutt . . . 5H **25**
Burlington Av. TW9: Kew . . . 5H **5**
Burlington Gdns. SW6 . . . 6H **7**
W4 . . . 2K **5**
Burlington La. W4 . . . 4K **5**
Burlington M. SW15 . . . 2J **13**
Burlington Pl. SW6 . . . 6H **7**
Burlington Rd. KT3: N Mald . . . 1C **24**
SW6 . . . 6H **7**
W4 . . . 2K **5**
Burnaby Cres. W4 . . . 3K **5**
Burnaby Gdns. W4 . . . 3J **5**
Burne Jones Ho. W14 . . . 1H **7**
Burnell Av. TW10: Ham . . . 2D **16**
Burnet Gro. KT19: Eps . . . 2K **33**
Burney Av. KT5: Surb . . . 2G **23**
Burnfoot Av. SW6 . . . 5H **7**
Burnham Dr. KT4: Wor Pk . . . 6G **25**
Burnhams Gro. KT19: Eps . . . 7J **29**
Burnham St. KT2: King T . . . 5H **17**
Burnham Way W13 . . . 1C **4**
Burns Av. TW14: Felt . . . 3A **8**
Burns Dr. SM7: Bans . . . 3H **35**
Burnside KT21: Asht . . . 7G **33**
Burnside Cl. TW1: Twick . . . 3B **10**
Burnthwaite Rd. SW6 . . . 4J **7**
Burritt Rd. KT1: King T . . . 6H **17**
Burr Rd. SW18 . . . 5K **13**
Burstock Rd. SW15 . . . 1H **13**
Burston Rd. SW15 . . . 2G **13**
Burston Vs. *SW15* . . . *2G* ***13***
(off St John's Av.)
Burstow Rd. SW20 . . . 5H **19**
Burtenshaw Rd. KT7: T Ditt . . . 4B **22**
Burton Cl. KT9: Chess . . . 4E **28**
Burton Ct. KT7: T Ditt . . . 3B **22**
Burton Rd. KT2: King T . . . 1D **36** (4F **17**)
Burton's Rd. TW12: Hamp H . . . 1G **15**
Burwell *KT1: King T* . . . *6H* ***17***
(off Excelsior Cl.)
Burwood Cl. KT6: Surb . . . 5H **23**
KT12: Hers . . . 3B **26**
BURWOOD PARK
KT11 . . . 7A 26
KT12 . . . 2A 26
Burwood Pk. Rd. KT12: Hers . . . 1A **26**
Burwood Rd. KT12: Hers . . . 3A **26**
Busch Cl. TW7: Isle . . . 5C **4**
Bush Cotts. SW18 . . . 2K **13**
Bushey Ct. SW20 . . . 7E **18**
Bushey La. SM1: Sutt . . . 1K **31**
BUSHEY MEAD . . . 6G 19
Bushey Rd. SM1: Sutt . . . 1K **31**
(not continuous)
SW20 . . . 7E **18**
Bushey Shaw KT21: Asht . . . 6C **32**
Bush Rd. TW9: Kew . . . 3G **5**
Bushwood Rd. TW9: Kew . . . 3H **5**
Bushy Ct. *KT1: Hamp W* . . . *5D* ***16***
(off Beverley Rd.)
Bushy Pk. . . . 4J 15
Bushy Pk. Gdns. TW11: Tedd . . . 2J **15**
Bushy Pk. Rd. TW11: Tedd . . . 4C **16**
(not continuous)
Bushy Rd. TW11: Tedd . . . 3A **16**
Bute Av. TW10: Ham . . . 6F **11**
Bute Gdns. TW10: Ham . . . 5F **11**
W6 . . . 1G **7**
Butler Farm Cl. TW10: Ham . . . 1E **16**
Butlers Cl. TW4: Houn . . . 1E **8**
Butterfield Cl. TW1: Twick . . . 3A **10**
Buttermere Cl. SM4: Mord . . . 3G **25**
Buttermere Dr. SW15 . . . 2H **13**
Butterwick W6 . . . 1G **7**
Butts, The TW8: Bford . . . 3D **4**
TW16: Sun . . . 7B **14**
Butts Cotts TW13: Hanw . . . 7D **8**
Butts Cres. TW13: Hanw . . . 7F **9**
Buxton Cl. KT19: Eps . . . 7J **29**
Buxton Cres. SM3: Cheam . . . 1H **31**
Buxton Dr. KT3: N Mald . . . 6A **18**
Buxton Rd. SW14 . . . 7B **6**
Byatt Wlk. TW12: Hamp . . . 3D **14**
Bychurch End TW11: Tedd . . . 2A **16**
Byeway, The SW14 . . . 7K **5**
Byeways TW2: Twick . . . 7G **9**
Byeways, The KT5: Surb . . . 2H **23**
Byfeld Gdns. SW13 . . . 5D **6**
Byfield Rd. TW7: Isle . . . 7B **4**
Byron Av. KT3: N Mald . . . 2D **24**
Byron Cl. KT12: Walt T . . . 5D **20**
TW12: Hamp . . . 1E **14**
Byron Ct. *W7* . . . *1B* ***4***
(off Boston Rd.)
Byward Av. TW14: Felt . . . 3B **8**
Byway, The KT19: Ewe . . . 1C **30**
Byways, The KT21: Asht . . . 7E **32**
Bywood Cl. SM7: Bans . . . 6J **35**

C

Caci Ho. *W14* . . . *1J* ***7***
(off Kensington Village)
Cadbury Cl. TW7: Isle . . . 5B **4**
Cadman Ct. *W4* . . . *2J* ***5***
(off Chaseley Dr.)
Cadmer Cl. KT3: N Mald . . . 1B **24**
Cadnam Point SW15 . . . 5E **12**
Cadogan Cl. TW11: Tedd . . . 2K **15**
Cadogan Rd. KT6: Surb . . . 2E **22**
Caen Wood Rd. KT21: Asht . . . 7D **32**
Caerleon Cl. KT10: Clay . . . 4C **28**
Cairn Ct. KT17: Ewe . . . 6C **30**
Cairngorm Cl. TW11: Tedd . . . 2B **16**
Caithness Dr. KT18: Eps . . . 3A **34**
Caithness Rd. W14 . . . 1G **7**
Calcott Ct. *W14* . . . *1H* ***7***
(off Blythe Rd.)
Caldbeck Av. KT4: Wor Pk . . . 6D **24**
Caldecote *KT1: King T* . . . *6H* ***17***
(off Excelsior Cl.)
Caldwell Ho. *SW13* . . . *4F* ***7***
(off Trinity Chu. Rd.)
Calendar M. KT6: Surb . . . 3E **22**
California Cl. SM2: Sutt . . . 6K **31**
California Rd. KT3: N Mald . . . 1J **23**
Callington M. TW2: Twick . . . 6K **9**
Calonne Rd. SW19 . . . 1G **19**
Calverley Ct. KT19: Ewe . . . 1A **30**
Calverley Rd. KT17: Ewe . . . 3D **30**
Calvert Cl. KT19: Eps . . . 6J **29**
Calvert Ct. TW9: Rich . . . 1G **11**
Camac Rd. TW2: Twick . . . 5J **9**
Cambalt Rd. SW15 . . . 2G **13**
Camberley Av. SW20 . . . 6E **18**
Camberley Cl. SM3: Cheam . . . 7G **25**
Cambisgate SW19 . . . 2H **19**
Camborne M. SW18 . . . 4K **13**
Camborne Rd. SM2: Sutt . . . 4K **31**
SM4: Mord . . . 2G **25**
SW18 . . . 4K **13**
Cambourne Wlk. TW10: Rich . . . 3E **10**
Cambria Cl. TW3: Houn . . . 1F **9**
Cambria Ct. TW14: Felt . . . 4A **8**
Cambrian Rd. TW10: Rich . . . 3G **11**
Cambridge Av. KT3: N Mald . . . 7B **18**
(not continuous)
Cambridge Cl. SW20 . . . 5E **18**
TW4: Houn . . . 1D **8**
Cambridge Cotts. TW9: Kew . . . 3H **5**
Cambridge Ct. *W6* . . . *1F* ***7***
(off Shepherd's Bush Rd.)
Cambridge Cres. TW11: Tedd . . . 2B **16**
Cambridge Gdns.
KT1: King T . . . 6H **17**
Cambridge Gro. W6 . . . 1E **6**
Cambridge Gro. Rd.
KT1: King T . . . 7H **17**
(not continuous)
Cambridge Ho. *W6* . . . *1E* ***6***
(off Cambridge Gro.)
Cambridge Pk. TW1: Twick . . . 3D **10**
Cambridge Pk. Ct. TW1: Twick . . . 4E **10**
Cambridge Rd. KT1: King T . . . 6G **17**
KT2: King T . . . 6G **17**
KT3: N Mald . . . 1A **24**
KT8: W Mole . . . 1E **20**
KT12: Walt T . . . 3A **20**
SW13 . . . 6C **6**
SW20 . . . 5D **18**
TW1: Twick . . . 3E **10**
TW4: Houn . . . 1D **8**
TW9: Kew . . . 4H **5**
TW11: Tedd . . . 1A **16**
TW12: Hamp . . . 4E **14**
Cambridge Rd. Nth. W4 . . . 2J **5**
Cambridge Rd. Sth. W4 . . . 2J **5**
Camden Av. TW13: Felt . . . 5B **8**
Camden Gdns. SM1: Sutt . . . 2K **31**
Camden Rd. SM1: Sutt . . . 2K **31**
Camel Gro. KT2: King T . . . 2E **16**
Camellia Ho. *TW13: Felt* . . . *5A* ***8***
(off Bedfont La.)
Camellia La. KT5: Surb . . . 1J **23**
Camellia Pl. TW2: Whitt . . . 4G **9**
Camelot Cl. SW19 . . . 1J **19**
Camm Gdns. KT1: King T . . . 6G **17**
KT7: T Ditt . . . 4A **22**
Campana Rd. SW6 . . . 5K **7**
Campbell Cl. TW2: Twick . . . 5J **9**
Campbell Rd. KT8: E Mos . . . 7K **15**
TW2: Twick . . . 6J **9**
Campen Cl. SW19 . . . 6H **13**
Campion Rd. SW15 . . . 1F **13**
TW7: Isle . . . 5A **4**
Camp Rd. SW19 . . . 2E **18**
Campus Ho. TW7: Isle . . . 4A **4**
Camp Vw. SW19 . . . 2E **18**
Camrose Av. TW13: Felt . . . 1B **14**
Camrose Cl. SM4: Mord . . . 1K **25**
Canberra Pl. TW9: Rich . . . 7H **5**
Canbury Av.
KT2: King T . . . 1E **36** (5G **17**)
Canbury Bus. Cen.
KT2: King T . . . 2D **36** (5F **17**)
Canbury Bus. Pk. KT2: King T . . . 2D **36**
Canbury Ct. KT2: King T . . . 4E **16**
Canbury Pk. Rd.
KT2: King T . . . 2D **36** (5F **17**)
Canbury Pas.
KT2: King T . . . 2B **36** (5E **16**)
Candler M. TW1: Twick . . . 4B **10**
Canford Gdns. KT3: N Mald . . . 3B **24**
Canford Pl. TW11: Tedd . . . 3D **16**
Canham Gdns. TW4: Houn . . . 4E **8**
Can Hatch KT20: Tad . . . 7H **35**
Cannizaro Rd. SW19 . . . 3F **19**
Cannon Cl. SW20 . . . 7F **19**
TW12: Hamp . . . 3G **15**
Cannon Hill La. SW20 . . . 2G **25**
Cannons Health Club
Richmond . . . 1E 10
Cannon Way KT8: W Mole . . . 1F **21**
Canons La. KT20: Tad . . . 7H **35**
Canterbury Cl. KT4: Wor Pk . . . 6G **25**
Canterbury Hall KT4: Wor Pk . . . 4E **24**
Canterbury Ho. *KT19: Eps* . . . *7H 2*
(off Queen Alexandra's Wa
Canterbury Rd. TW13: Hanw . . . 6D
Capital Ho. *SW15* . . . *2H 1*
(off Plaza Gdns
Capital Interchange Way
TW8: Bford . . . 2H
Capitol Sq. KT17: Eps . . . 2B **3**
Carden Ct. KT8: W Mole . . . 1G **2**
Cardiff Rd. W7 . . . 1B
Cardigan Rd. SW13 . . . 6D
TW10: Rich . . . 3F **1**
Cardinal Av. KT2: King T . . . 2F **1**
SM4: Mord . . . 3H **2**
Cardinal Cl. KT4: Wor Pk . . . 1D **3**
SM4: Mord . . . 3H **2**
Cardinal Cres. KT3: N Mald . . . 6K **1**
Cardinal Dr. KT12: Walt T . . . 5C **2**
Cardinal Pl. SW15 . . . 1G **1**
Cardinal Rd. TW13: Felt . . . 5A
Cardinals Wlk. TW12: Hamp . . . 4H **1**
Cardington Sq. TW4: Houn . . . 1C
Cardross St. W6 . . . 1E
Carisbrooke Cl. TW4: Houn . . . 4D
Carisbrooke Ct. SM2: Cheam . . . 4J **31**
Carisbrooke Ho.
KT2: King T . . . 2C **3**
TW10: Rich . . . 2H **1**
Carlcott Cl. KT12: Walt T . . . 4A **2**
Carleton Cl. KT10: Esh . . . 5J **2**
Carlile Pl. TW10: Rich . . . 3G **1**
Carlingford Rd. SM4: Mord . . . 3G **2**
Carlisle Cl. KT2: King T . . . 5H **1**
Carlisle M. KT2: King T . . . 5H **17**
Carlisle Rd. SM1: Sutt . . . 3J **31**
TW12: Hamp . . . 4G **15**
Carlson Ct. SW15 . . . 1J **13**
Carlton Av. TW14: Felt . . . 3B **8**
Carlton Cl. KT9: Chess . . . 3E **28**
Carlton Cres. SM3: Cheam . . . 1H **31**
Carlton Dr. SW15 . . . 2G **13**
Carlton Ho. TW3: Houn . . . 3F **9**
Carlton Pk. Av. SW20 . . . 6G **19**
Carlton Rd. KT3: N Mald . . . 6B **18**
KT12: Walt T . . . 4A **20**
SW14 . . . 7K **5**
Carlton Vs. SW15 . . . 2H **13**
Carlyle Cl. KT8: W Mole . . . 6G **15**
Carlyle Ho. *KT8: W Mole* . . . *2F* ***21***
(off Down St.)
Carlyle Pl. SW15 . . . 1G **13**
Carlyle Rd. W5 . . . 1D **4**
Carmalt Gdns. KT12: Hers . . . 2B **26**
SW15 . . . 1F **13**
Carmel Lodge *SW6* . . . *3K* ***7***
(off Lillie Rd.)
Carmel Way TW9: Rich . . . 6J **5**
Carmichael Ct. *SW13* . . . *6C* ***6***
(off Grove Rd.)
Carnegie Cl. KT6: Surb . . . 6G **23**
Carnegie Pl. SW19 . . . 7G **13**
Carnforth Cl. KT19: Ewe . . . 3J **29**
Carnwath Rd. SW6 . . . 7K **7**
Caroline Ho. *W6* . . . *2F* ***7***
(off Queen Caroline St.)
Caroline Rd. SW19 . . . 4J **19**
Caroline Wlk. *W6* . . . *3H* ***7***
(off Lillie Rd.)
Caro Pl. KT3: N Mald . . . 1C **24**
Carpenter Cl. KT17: Ewe . . . 5C **30**
Carpenters Ct. TW2: Twick . . . 6K **9**
Carrara Wharf SW6 . . . 7H **7**
Carrick Cl. TW7: Isle . . . 7B **4**
Carrick Ga. KT10: Esh . . . 7H **21**
Carrick Sq. TW8: Bford . . . 4D **4**
Carrington Av. TW3: Houn . . . 2G **9**
Carrington Cl. KT2: King T . . . 2K **17**
Carrington Pl. KT10: Esh . . . 1G **27**
Carrington Rd. TW10: Rich . . . 1H **11**
Carrow Rd. KT12: Walt T . . . 7C **20**
Carslake Rd. SW15 . . . 3F **13**
Carters Cl. KT4: Wor Pk . . . 6G **25**
Carters Rd. KT17: Eps . . . 4C **34**
Carter's Yd. SW18 . . . 2K **13**
Carthew Rd. W6 . . . 1E **6**
Cartwright Way SW13 . . . 4E **6**
Carville Cres. TW8: Bford . . . 1F **5**
Cascades Ct. SW19 . . . 4J **19**
CASSEL HOSPITAL . . . 1E 16
Cassidy Rd. SW6 . . . 4K **7**
(not continuous)
Cassilis Rd. TW1: Twick . . . 2C **10**
Castello Av. SW15 . . . 2F **13**
CASTELNAU . . . 3E 6
Castelnau SW13 . . . 5D **6**
Castelnau Gdns. SW13 . . . 3E **6**

42 A-Z Kingston & Richmond

Castelnau Mans. SW13 . . . . .3E 6
  (not continuous)
Castelnau Row SW13 . . . . .3E 6
Castle Av. KT17: Ewe 5D 30
Castle Bus. Cen. TW12: Hamp . . .5G 15
  (off Castle M.)
Castle Cl. SW19 . . . . .7G 13
Castlecombe Dr. SW19 . . . . .4G 13
Castle Ct. SW15 . . . . .7H 7
  (off Brewhouse La.)
Castlegate TW9: Rich 7G 5
Castle Hill Local Nature Reserve
  . . . . .3H 29
Castle Ho. SM2: Sutt 3K 31
Castlemaine Av. KT17: Ewe 5E 30
Castle M. TW12: Hamp 5G 15
  (not continuous)
Castle Pde. KT17: Ewe 4D 30
Castle Pl. W4 . . . . .1B 6
Castle Rd. KT18: Eps 4J 33
  TW7: Isle 6A 4
Castle Row W4 . . . . .2C 6
Castle St. King T . . .3C 36 (6F 17)
Castleton Cl. SM7: Bans 4K 35
Castleton Dr. SM7: Bans 4K 35
Castletown Rd. W14 . . . . .2H 7
Castle Vw. KT18: Eps 3J 33
Castle Way KT17: Ewe 6D 30
  SW19 . . . . .7G 13
  TW3: Hanw 1B 14
Castle Yd. TW10: Rich 2E 10
Catherine Ct. SW19 . . . . .2J 19
Catherine Dr. TW9: Rich 1F 11
Catherine Gdns. TW3: Houn 1J 9
Catherine Rd. KT6: Surb 2E 22
Catherine Wheel Rd.
  TW8: Bford 4E 4
Cato's Hill KT10: Esh 1G 27
Causeway, The KT9: Chess 1F 29
  KT10: Clay 4A 28
  SW18 . . . . .1K 13
  SW19 . . . . .2F 19
  TW4: Houn 1A 8
  TW11: Tedd 3A 16
  TW4, Felt, Houn 1A 8
Cavalier Ct. KT5: Surb 3G 23
Cavalry Cres. TW4: Houn 1C 8
Cavalry Gdns. SW15 . . . . .2J 13
Cavell Way KT19: Eps 7H 29
Cavendish Av. KT3: N Mald 2D 24
Cavendish Dr. KT10: Clay 2K 27
Cavendish Ho. KT12: Hers 2B 26
Cavendish Rd. KT3: N Mald 1C 24
  W4 .5K 5
Cavendish Ter. TW13: Felt 6A 8
Cavendish Wlk. KT19: Eps 7J 29
Caverleigh Way KT4: Wor Pk 5D 24
Cave Rd. TW10: Ham 1D 16
Caversham Av. SM3: Cheam 6H 25
Caversham Ho. KT1: King T 4C 36
Caversham Rd.
  KT1: King T 3E 36 (6G 17)
Cawdor Cres. W7 . . . . .1B 4
Caxton M. TW8: Bford 3E 4
Cecil Cl. KT9: Chess 1E 28
Cecil Rd. SM1: Sutt 3J 31
  SW19 . . . . .4K 19
Cedar Av. TW2: Whitt 3G 9
Cedar Cl. KT8: E Mos 1K 21
  KT10: Esh 3E 26
  KT17: Eps 3C 34
  SW15 . . . . .1A 18
Cedar Ct. SW19 . . . . .7G 13
  TW8: Bford 3D 4
Cedarcroft Rd. KT9: Chess 1G 29
Cedar Hgts. TW10: Ham 5F 11
Cedar Hill KT18: Eps 5K 33
Cedar Ho. TW9: Kew 5J 5
Cedarland Ter. SW20 . . . . .4E 18
Cedar M. SW15 . . . . .2G 13
Cedarne Rd. SW6 . . . . .4K 7
Cedar Pk. Gdns. SW19 . . . . .2E 18
Cedar Rd. KT8: E Mos 1K 21
  TW11: Tedd 2B 16
Cedars, The TW11: Tedd 3A 16
Cedars Rd. KT1: Hamp W 5D 16
  SM4: Mord 1K 25
  SW13 . . . . .6D 6
  W4 .2K 5
Cedar Ter. TW9: Rich 1F 11
Cedar Vw. KT1: King T 6B 36
Cedar Wlk. KT10: Clay 3A 28
Celandine Rd. KT12: Hers 1D 26
Centaur Ct. TW8: Bford 2F 5
Centaurs Bus. Pk. TW7: Isle 3B 4

Central Av. KT8: W Mole 1E 20
  TW3: Houn 1H 9
Central Mall SW18 . . . . .3K 13
  (within Southside Shop. Cen.)
Central Pde. KT6: Surb 3F 23
  KT8: W Mole 1E 20
Central Rd. KT4: Wor Pk 5D 24
  SM4: Mord 3K 25
Central School Path SW14 . . . . . .7K 5
Central St. KT8: W Mole 2E 20
Central Wlk. KT19: Eps 2A 34
Central Way TW14: Felt 2A 8
Centre, The TW3: Houn 1G 9
  TW13: Felt 5A 8
Centre Ct. Shop. Cen. SW19 . . . .3J 19
Centre Sq. SW18 . . . . .2K 13
  (off Buckhold Rd.)
Century Ho. SM7: Bans 4K 35
  SW15 . . . . .1G 13
Ceylon Rd. W14 . . . . .1G 7
Chadacre Rd. KT17: Ewe 3E 30
Chadwick Av. SW19 . . . . .3K 19
Chadwick Cl. SW15 . . . . .4C 12
  TW11: Tedd 3B 16
Chadwick M. W4 . . . . .3J 5
Chadwick Pl. KT6: Surb 4D 22
Chadworth Way KT10: Clay 2J 27
Chaffers Mead KT21: Asht 5G 33
Chaffinch Cl. KT6: Surb 7H 23
Chailey Pl. KT12: Hers 1D 26
Chalcot Cl. SM2: Sutt 4K 31
Chalcott Gdns. KT6: Surb 5D 22
Chaldon Rd. SW6 . . . . .4H 7
Chalfont M. SW19 . . . . .5J 13
Chalfont Rd. TW7: Isle 6F 21
Chalfont Way W13 . . . . .1C 4
Chalford Cl. KT8: W Mole 1F 21
Chalgrove Av. SM4: Mord 2K 25
CHALKER'S CORNER 7J 5
Chalk Hill Rd. W6 . . . . .1G 7
Chalk La. KT18: Eps, Eps D 4A 34
  KT21: Asht 7H 33
Chalk Paddock KT18: Eps 4A 34
Chalk Pit Rd. KT18: Eps D 7K 33
  SM7: Bans 6K 35
Chalky La. KT9: Chess 6E 28
Challenge Ct. TW2: Twick 4K 9
Challis Rd. TW8: Bford 2E 4
Challoner Ct. W14 . . . . .2J 7
  (off Challoner St.)
Challoner Cres. W14 . . . . .2J 7
Challoner Mans. W14 . . . . .2J 7
  (off Challoner St.)
Challoners Cl. KT8: E Mos 1J 21
Challoner St. W14 . . . . .2J 7
Chalmers Way TW1: Isle 1C 10
  TW14: Felt 2A 8
Chamberlain Cl. KT19: Eps 6A 30
Chamberlain Wlk.
  TW13: Hanw 1D 14
Chamberlain Way KT6: Surb 4F 23
Chamberlens Garages W6 . . . . . .1E 6
  (off Dalling Rd.)
Chambon Pl. W6 . . . . .1D 6
Champneys Cl. SM2: Cheam 4J 31
Chancellor's Rd. W6 . . . . .2F 7
Chancellor's St. W6 . . . . .2F 7
Chancellors Wharf W6 . . . . .2F 7
Chancery Ga. Bus. Pk.
  KT6: Surb 6G 23
Chanctonbury Gdns. SM2: Sutt . .4K 31
Chandler Cl. TW12: Hamp 5F 15
Chandler Ct. TW14: Felt 3A 8
Chandlers Cl. KT8: W Mole 2G 21
Chandos Av. W5 . . . . .1D 4
Chandos Rd. KT6: Surb 2F 23
  (off Maple Rd)
Chantilly Way KT19: Eps 6J 29
Chanton Dr. KT17: Cheam 6F 31
  SM2: Cheam, Ewe 6F 31
Chantry Ho.
  KT1: King T 7D 36 (1F 23)
Chantry Hurst KT18: Eps 4A 34
Chantry Rd. KT9: Chess 2G 29
Chapel, The SW15 . . . . .3H 13
Chapel Gro. KT18: Tatt C 7F 35
Chapel Mill Rd. KT1: King T 7G 17
Chapel Rd. TW1: Twick 4C 10
  TW3: Houn 1G 9
Chapel Way KT18: Tatt C 7F 35
Chapel Yd. SW18 . . . . .2K 13
  (off Wandsworth High St.)
Chapman Sq. SW19 . . . . .6G 13
Chapter Way TW12: Hamp 1F 15

Chara Pl. W4 . . . . .3A 6
Charcot Ho. SW15 . . . . .3C 12
Chardin Rd. W4 . . . . .1B 6
CHARING CROSS HOSPITAL 3G 7
Charing Cross Sports Club 3G 7
Charles Babbage Cl.
  KT9: Chess 4D 28
Charles Harrod Ct. SW13 . . . . . . .3F 7
  (off Somerville Av.)
Charles Ho. W14 . . . . .1J 7
Charles Lesser Ho. KT9: Chess . .2E 28
Charles Rd. SW19 . . . . .5K 19
Charles St. SW13 . . . . .6B 6
Charleston Cl. TW13: Felt 7A 8
Charlesworth Pl. SW13 . . . . .7B 6
Charleville Ct. W14 . . . . .2J 7
  (off Charleville Rd.)
Charleville Mans. W14 . . . . .2H 7
  (not continuous)
Charleville M. TW7: Isle 1C 10
Charleville Rd. W14 . . . . .2H 7
Charlotte Cl. KT21: Asht 7F 33
Charlotte Ct. KT10: Esh 2H 27
  W6 .1D 6
Charlotte Ho. W6 . . . . .2F 7
  (off Queen Caroline St.)
Charlotte M. KT10: Esh 1G 27
  (off Heather Pl.)
  W14 . . . . .1H 7
Charlotte Rd. SW13 . . . . .5C 6
Charlotte Sq. TW10: Rich 3G 11
Charlotte Ter. KT10: Esh 3H 27
  (off Princess Sq.)
Charlton Av. KT12: Hers 1A 26
Charlton Ho. TW8: Bford 3F 5
Charlwood Ho. TW9: Kew 4J 5
Charlwood Rd. SW15 . . . . .1G 13
Charlwood Ter. SW15 . . . . .1G 13
Charminster Av. SW19 . . . . .6K 19
Charminster Ct. KT6: Surb 4E 22
Charminster Rd. KT4: Wor Pk 5G 25
Charmouth Ct. TW10: Rich 2G 11
Charnwood Av. SW19 . . . . .6K 19
Charnwood Cl. KT3: N Mald 1B 24
Charter Ct. KT3: N Mald 7B 18
Charter Cres. TW4: Houn 1D 8
Charter Quay KT1: King T 4B 36
Charter Rd. KT1: King T 7J 17
Charter Sq. KT1: King T 6J 17
Chartfield Av. SW15 . . . . .2E 12
Chartfield Sq. SW15 . . . . .2G 13
Chartwell Gdns. SM3: Cheam 1H 31
Chartwell Pl. KT18: Eps 3B 34
  SM3: Cheam 1H 31
Chase, The KT21: Asht 7D 32
  SW20 . . . . .5H 19
  TW16: Sun 5A 14
Chase Ct. SW20 . . . . .5H 19
  TW7: Isle 6B 4
Chase End KT19: Eps 1A 34
Chase Gdns. TW2: Whitt 4J 9
Chaseley Dr. W4 . . . . .2J 5
Chasemore Ho. SW6 . . . . .4H 7
  (off Williams Cl.)
Chase Rd. KT19: Eps 1A 34
Chase Side Av. SW20 . . . . .5H 19
Chatham Cl. SM3: Sutt 4J 25
Chatham Rd. KT1: King T 6H 17
Chatsfield KT17: Ewe 6D 30
Chatsworth Av. SW20 . . . . .5H 19
Chatsworth Cl. W4 . . . . .3K 5
Chatsworth Ct. W8 . . . . .1K 7
  (off Pembroke Rd.)
Chatsworth Cres. TW3: Houn 1J 9
Chatsworth Gdns. KT3: N Mald . .2C 24
Chatsworth Lodge W4 . . . . .2A 6
  (off Bourne Pl.)
Chatsworth Pl. TW11: Tedd 1B 16
Chatsworth Rd. SM3: Cheam 2G 31
  W4 .3K 5
Chatterton Ct. TW9: Kew 6G 5
Chaucer Av. TW9: Rich 7H 5
Chaucer Cl. SM7: Bans 3H 35
Chaucer Gdns. SM1: Sutt 7K 25
Chaucer Ho. SM1: Sutt 7K 25
  (off Chaucer Gdns.)
Chaucer Mans. W14 . . . . .3H 7
  (off Queen's Club Gdns.)
Chaucer Rd. SM1: Sutt 1K 31
Chave Cl. KT10: Esh 7F 35
Chavecroft Ter. KT18: Tatt C 7F 35
CHEAM 3H 31
Cheam Comn. Rd.
  KT4: Wor Pk 6E 24
Cheam Leisure Cen. 1G 31
Cheam Mans. SM3: Cheam 4H 31

Cheam Pk. Way SM3: Cheam 3H 31
Cheam Rd. KT17: Ewe 6D 30
  SM1: Sutt 3J 31
  SM2: Cheam 6D 30
Cheam Station (Rail) 4H 31
CHEAM VILLAGE 3H 31
Cheeseman Cl. TW12: Hamp 3D 14
Cheesemans Ter. W14 . . . . .2J 7
  (not continuous)
Chelmsford Cl. SM2: Sutt 5K 31
  W6 .3G 7
Chelsea Cl. KT4: Wor Pk 4D 24
  TW12: Hamp 2H 15
Chelsea Ct. KT18: Eps 2A 34
  (off Ashley Rd.)
Chelsea FC 4K 7
Chelsea Gdns. SM3: Cheam 1H 31
Cheltenham Av. TW1: Twick 4B 10
Cheltenham Cl. KT3: N Mald 7K 17
Chelverton Rd. SW15 . . . . .1G 13
Chelwood Cl. KT17: Eps 1C 34
Chelwood Gdns. TW9: Kew 6H 5
Chelwood Gdns. Pas.
  . . . . .6H 5
Chenies Ho. W4 . . . . .4C 6
  (off Corney Reach Way)
Chepstow Cl. SW15 . . . . .2H 13
Cherimoya Gdns.
  KT8: W Mole 7G 15
Cheriton Ct. KT12: Walt T 5B 20
Cherry Cl. SM4: Mord 1H 25
  SM7: Bans 3G 35
  W5 .1E 4
Cherry Cres. TW8: Bford 4C 4
Cherry Gth. TW8: Bford 2C 4
Cherry Orchard KT21: Asht 7J 33
Cherry Orchard Gdns.
  KT8: W Mole 7E 14
Cherry Orchard Rd.
  KT8: W Mole 7F 15
Cherry Red Records Stadium
  (Kingsmeadow) 7J 17
Cherry Way KT19: Ewe 3A 30
Cherrywood Cl. KT2: King T 4H 17
Cherrywood Ct. TW11: Tedd 2B 16
Cherrywood Dr. SW15 . . . . .2G 13
Cherrywood La. SM4: Mord 1H 25
Chertsey Cl. SW14 . . . . .7J 5
Chertsey Dr. SM3: Cheam 6H 25
Chertsey La. KT19: Eps 1H 33
Chertsey Rd. TW1: Twick 3A 10
  TW2: Twick 6G 9
Chervil Cl. TW13: Felt 7A 8
Cherwell Ct. KT19: Ewe 1K 29
Chesfield Rd. KT2: King T 4F 17
Chesham Cl. SM2: Cheam 6H 31
Chesham Ho. KT18: Eps 2A 34
  (off South St.)
Chesham Rd. KT1: King T 6H 17
Cheshire Gdns. KT9: Chess 3E 28
Chesilton Rd. SW6 . . . . .5J 7
CHESSINGTON 2F 29
Chessington Cl. KT19: Ewe 3K 29
Chessington Golf Course 4E 28
Chessington Hall Gdns.
  KT9: Chess 4E 28
Chessington Hill Pk.
  KT9: Chess 2H 29
Chessington Ho. KT17: Ewe 5C 30
  (off Spring St.)
Chessington North Station
  (Rail) 2F 29
Chessington Pde. KT9: Chess . . .3E 28
Chessington Pk. KT9: Chess 1H 29
Chessington Rd. KT17: Ewe 3J 29
  KT19: Ewe 3H 29
Chessington South Station
  (Rail) 4E 28
Chessington Sports Cen. 4E 28
Chessington Trade Pk.
  KT9: Chess 1H 29
Chessington World of Adventures
  . . . . .6D 28
Chesson Rd. W14 . . . . .3J 7
Chester Av. TW2: Whitt 5E 8
  TW10: Rich 3G 11
Chester Cl. SM1: Sutt 6K 25
  SW13 . . . . .7E 6
  TW10: Rich 3G 11
Chester Ct. W6 . . . . .1G 7
  (off Wolverton Gdns.)
Chesterfield Ct. KT5: Surb 2F 23
  (off Cranes Pk.)
Chesterfield Dr. KT10: Hin W 6B 22
Chesterfield Rd. KT19: Ewe 4A 30
  W4 .3K 5

Chesterman Ct. W4 . . . . .4B 6
(off Corney Reach Way)
Chester Rd. SW19 . . . . .3F 19
Chesters, The KT3: N Mald 5B 18
Chesterton Cl. SW18 . . . . .2K 13
Chesterton Sq. W8 . . . . .1K 7
Chesterton Ter. KT1: King T 6H 17
Chestnut All. SW6 . . . . .3J 7
Chestnut Av. KT8: E Mos 7A 16
KT10: Esh 4J 21
KT19: Ewe 1B 30
SW14 . . . . .7A 6
TW8: Bford 1E 4
TW11: Tedd 6A 16
TW12: Hamp 4F 15
Chestnut Cl. SW6 . . . . .3J 7
TW13: Hanw 2C 14
Chestnut Gro. KT3: N Mald 7A 18
TW7: Isle 1B 10
Chestnut Ho. SW15 . . . . .1C 12
W4 . . . . .1B 6
(off The Orchard)
Chestnut M. SW14 . . . . .1K 11
Chestnut Pl. KT17: Ewe 7D 30
Chestnut Rd. KT2: King T 4F 17
SW20 . . . . .6G 19
TW2: Twick 6K 9
Chestnuts, The KT12: Walt T 6A 20
Chestnut Way KT17: Eps D 5E 34
TW13: Felt 7A 8
Chetwode Dr. KT18: Tatt C 7G 35
Chetwode Rd. KT20: Tad 7G 35
Cheviot Cl. SM7: Bans 4K 35
Cheyham Gdns. SM2: Cheam 6G 31
Cheyham Way SM2: Cheam 6H 31
Cheyne Av. TW2: Whitt 5E 8
Cheyne Hill KT5: Surb 7E 36 (1G 23)
Chichester Cl. TW12: Hamp 3E 14
Chichester Ct. KT17: Ewe 5C 30
Chichester Ho. KT19: Eps 1H 33
Chichester Way TW14: Felt 4B 8
Chiddingstone Cl. SM2: Sutt 6K 31
Chiddingstone St. SW6 . . . . .6K 7
Chilcombe Ho. SW15 . . . . .4D 12
(off Fontley Way)
Childerley KT1: King T 7H 17
(off Burritt Rd.)
Childerley St. SW6 . . . . .5H 7
Child's M. SW5 . . . . .1K 7
(off Child's Pl.)
Child's Pl. SW5 . . . . .1K 7
Child's St. SW5 . . . . .1K 7
Child's Wlk. SW5 . . . . .1K 7
(off Child's St.)
Chillingworth Gdns.
TW1: Twick 7A 10
Chilmark Gdns. KT3: N Mald 3D 24
Chiltern Av. TW2: Whitt 5F 9
Chiltern Cl. KT4: Wor Pk 5F 25
Chiltern Dr. KT5: Surb 3H 23
Chilton Av. W5 . . . . .1E 4
Chilton Rd. TW9: Rich 7H 5
Chilvers Cl. TW2: Twick 6K 9
Chilworth Ct. SW19 . . . . .5G 13
Chippenham KT1: King T 6G 17
(off Excelsior Cl.)
Chipstead Rd. SM7: Bans 6J 35
Chipstead St. SW6 . . . . .5K 7
Chisholm Ct. W6 . . . . .2D 6
Chisholm Rd. TW10: Rich 3G 11
Chislehurst Rd. TW10: Rich 2F 11
CHISWICK 2A 6
Chiswick Bri. SW14 . . . . .6K 5
Chiswick Comn. Rd. W4 . . . . . . .1A 6
Chiswick Community Sports Hall
. . . . .4A 6
Chiswick Grn. Vw. W4 . . . . .1J 5
Chiswick High Rd. TW8: Bford . . .2H 5
W4 . . . . .2H 5
Chiswick House & Gdns. 3A 6
Chiswick Ho. Grounds W4 . . . . . .3B 6
Chiswick La. W4 . . . . .2B 6
Chiswick La. Sth. W4 . . . . .3C 6
Chiswick Lifeboat Station 4C 6
Chiswick Mall W4 . . . . .3C 6
W6 . . . . .3C 6
Chiswick Pk. W4 . . . . .1J 5
Chiswick Park Station
(Underground) 1K 5
Chiswick Plaza W4 . . . . .3K 5
Chiswick Quay W4 . . . . .5K 5
Chiswick Rd. W4 . . . . .1K 5
CHISWICK RDBT. 2H 5
Chiswick Sq. W4 . . . . .3B 6
Chiswick Staithe W4 . . . . .5K 5
Chiswick Station (Rail) 4K 5

Chiswick Ter. W4 . . . . .1K 5
(off Chiswick High Rd.)
Chiswick Village W4 . . . . .3H 5
Chiswick Wharf W4 . . . . .3C 6
Chivelston SW19 . . . . .5G 13
Chivenor Gro. KT2: King T 2E 16
Chobham Gdns. SW19 . . . . .6G 13
Cholmley Rd. KT7: T Ditt 3C 22
Cholmley Ter. KT7: T Ditt 4C 22
(off Portsmouth Rd.)
Cholmley Vs. KT7: T Ditt 3C 22
(off Portsmouth Rd.)
Cholmondeley Wlk. TW9: Rich . . .2D 10
Christabel Cl. TW7: Isle 7A 4
Christchurch Av. TW11: Tedd 2B 16
Christchurch Flats TW9: Rich 7F 5
Christchurch Gdns. KT19: Eps . . .7J 29
Christ Chu. Mt. KT19: Eps 1J 33
(not continuous)
Christchurch Pl. KT19: Eps 7J 29
Christ Chu. Rd. KT5: Surb 3G 23
KT19: Eps 1F 33
Christchurch Rd. SW14 . . . . .2J 11
TW2: Twick 3K 9
Chudleigh Rd. KT5: Surb 1G 23
Church Av. SW14 . . . . .7A 6
Church Cl. KT17: Eps 2B 34
Church Ct. KT10: Esh 3H 27
(off Princess Sq.)
TW9: Rich 2E 10
Church Est. Almshouses
TW9: Rich 1G 11
(off Sheen Rd.)
Church Farm La. SM3: Cheam . . .3H 31
Churchfield Mans. SW6 . . . . .6J 7
(off New Kings Rd.)
Churchfield Rd. KT12: Walt T 4A 20
Churchfields KT8: W Mole 7F 15
Churchfields Rd. TW13: Hanw 7E 8
Church Ga. SW6 . . . . .7H 7
Church Grn. KT12: Hers 3B 26
Church Gro.
KT1: Hamp W 3A 36 (5D 16)
Church Hill SW19 . . . . .2J 19
Church Hill Rd. KT6: Surb 2F 23
SM3: Cheam 7G 25
Churchill Ho. SM7: Bans 3J 35
(off Dunnymans Rd.)
Churchill Rd. KT19: Eps 7H 29
Churchlands Way KT4: Wor Pk . . .6G 25
Church La. KT7: T Ditt 3A 22
KT9: Chess 3G 29
KT18: Tad 6G 35
SW19 . . . . .5J 19
TW1: Twick 5B 10
TW10: Ham 5F 11
TW11: Tedd 5A 16
Church Mdw. KT6: Surb 6D 22
Church Pas. KT6: Surb 2F 23
TW1: Twick 5C 10
Church Path SW14 . . . . .7A 6
(not continuous)
SW19 . . . . .6J 19
W4 . . . . .1K 5
Church Ri. KT9: Chess 3G 29
Church Rd.
KT1: King T 3E 36 (6G 17)
KT4: Wor Pk 5B 24
KT6: Surb 5D 22
KT8: E Mos 1J 21
KT10: Clay 3A 28
KT17: Eps 1B 34
KT19: Ewe 4A 30
KT21: Asht 7E 32
SM3: Cheam 3H 31
SW13 . . . . .6C 6
SW19 . . . . .5J 19
TW9: Rich 1F 11
TW10: Ham 1E 16
TW10: Rich 2F 11
TW11: Tedd 1K 15
TW13: Hanw 2C 14
Church Side KT18: Eps 2J 33
Church St. KT1: King T . . .3E 36 (6E 16)
KT10: Esh 1G 27
KT17: Eps 2B 34
KT17: Ewe 5D 30
TW1: Twick 5B 10
TW7: Isle 7C 4
TW12: Hamp 5H 15
TW16: Sun 7A 14
W4 . . . . .3C 6
Church Stretton Rd. TW3: Houn . .2H 9
Church Ter. TW10: Rich 2E 10
Church Vw. TW10: Rich 2F 11
Churchview Rd. TW2: Twick 5J 9

Church Wlk. KT7: T Ditt 3A 22
SW13 . . . . .5D 6
SW15 . . . . .2E 12
SW20 . . . . .7F 19
TW8: Bford 3D 4
(not continuous)
TW9: Rich 2E 10
Churchward Ho. W14 . . . . .2J 7
(off Ivatt Pl.)
Churston Dr. SM4: Mord 2G 25
Chuter Ede Ho. SW6 . . . . .3J 7
(off Clem Attlee Ct.)
Chuters Gro. KT17: Eps 1C 34
Cineworld Cinema
Feltham 6A 8
Hammersmith 1E 6
Wandsworth 2K 13
Circle Gdns. SW19 . . . . .6K 19
City Wharf Ho. KT7: T Ditt 3C 22
Clancarty Rd. SW6 . . . . .6K 7
Clandon Cl. KT17: Ewe 3C 30
Clandon Ter. SW20 . . . . .6G 19
Clare Cres. KT22: Lea 7B 32
Clare Hill KT10: Esh 2G 27
Clare Lawn Av. SW14 . . . . .2K 11
Clare M. SW6 . . . . .4K 7
Claremont Av. KT3: N Mald 2D 24
KT10: Esh 3E 26
KT12: Hers 1C 26
TW16: Sun 5A 14
Claremont Cl. KT12: Hers 2B 26
Claremont Dr. KT10: Esh 5F 27
Claremont End KT10: Esh 3G 27
Claremont Gdns. KT6: Surb 2F 23
Claremont Gro. W4 . . . . .4B 6
Claremont Ho. SM2: Sutt 4K 31
Claremont Landscape Garden . . .4F 27
Claremont La. KT10: Esh 2G 27
CLAREMONT PARK 4G 27
Claremont Pk. Rd. KT10: Esh 3G 27
Claremont Pl. KT10: Clay 3A 28
Claremont Rd. KT6: Surb 2F 23
KT10: Clay 4K 27
TW1: Twick 3C 10
TW11: Tedd 2A 16
Claremont Ter. KT7: T Ditt 4C 22
Claremount Cl. KT18: Tatt C 6F 35
Claremount Gdns. KT18: Tatt C . . .6F 35
Clarence Av. KT3: N Mald 6K 17
Clarence Cl. KT12: Hers 1A 26
Clarence Ct. W6 . . . . .1E 6
(off Cambridge Gro.)
Clarence Ho. KT12: Hers 2A 26
(off Queens Rd.)
Clarence La. SW15 . . . . .3B 12
Clarence Rd. KT12: Hers 1A 26
SM1: Sutt 2K 31
SW19 . . . . .3K 19
TW9: Kew 5G 5
TW11: Tedd 3A 16
W4 . . . . .2H 5
Clarence St.
KT1: King T 3B 36 (6E 16)
TW9: Rich 1F 11
Clarence Ter. TW3: Houn 1G 9
Clarendon Ct. TW9: Kew 5G 5
Clarendon Cres. TW2: Twick 7J 9
Clarendon Dr. SW15 . . . . .1F 13
Clarendon Ho. KT2: King T 2D 36
Clarendon M. KT21: Asht 7G 33
(off Rectory La.)
Clare Pl. SW15 . . . . .4C 12
Clare Rd. TW4: Houn 1E 8
Clare Wood KT22: Lea 7C 32
Claridge Ct. SW6 . . . . .6J 7
Clarkes Av. KT4: Wor Pk 5G 25
Claudia Pl. SW19 . . . . .5H 13
Clavering Av. SW13 . . . . .3E 6
Clavering Cl. TW1: Twick 1B 16
Claverton KT21: Asht 6F 33
Claxton Gro. W6 . . . . .2G 7
Claybrook Rd. W6 . . . . .3G 7
Claycorn Ct. KT10: Clay 3K 27
CLAYGATE 3A 28
Claygate Common
(Local Nature Reserve) 4A 28
Claygate La. KT7: T Ditt 5B 22
KT10: Clay, Hin W 6B 22
Claygate Lodge Cl. KT10: Clay . . .4K 27
Claygate Station (Rail) 3K 27
Clayhill KT5: Surb 2H 23
Claymore Cl. SM4: Mord 4K 25
Clayponds Av. TW8: Bford 1E 4
Clayponds Gdns. W5 . . . . .1E 4
(not continuous)
CLAYPONDS HOSPITAL 1F 5

Clayponds La. TW8: Bford 2F 5
(not continuous)
Clayton Cres. TW8: Bford 2E 4
Clayton Ho. KT7: T Ditt 5C 22
SW13 . . . . .4F 7
(off Trinity Chu. Rd.)
Clayton Rd. KT9: Chess 1D 28
KT17: Eps 1B 34
TW7: Isle 1K 9
Clearwater Pl. KT6: Surb 3D 22
Cleaveland Rd. KT6: Surb 2E 22
Cleaves Almshouses
KT2: King T 3D 36
Cleeve Way SW15 . . . . .4C 12
Clem Attlee Ct. SW6 . . . . .3J 7
Clem Attlee Pde. SW6 . . . . .3J 7
(off North End Rd.)
Clement Cl. W4 . . . . .1A 6
Clement Rd. SW19 . . . . .2H 19
Clements Cl. TW4: Houn 1C 8
Clements Ho. KT22: Lea 7B 32
Clements Pl. TW8: Bford 2E 4
Clements Rd. KT12: Walt T 6A 20
Clemson M. KT17: Eps 1C 34
Clensham La. SM1: Sutt 6K 25
Clensham La. SM1: Sutt 6K 25
Clevedon Rd. KT1: King T 6H 17
TW1: Twick 3E 10
Cleveland Av. SW20 . . . . .6J 19
TW12: Hamp 4E 14
W4 . . . . .1C 6
Cleveland Cl. KT12: Walt T 7A 20
Cleveland Gdns. KT4: Wor Pk 6B 24
SW13 . . . . .6C 6
Cleveland Ri. SM4: Mord 4G 25
Cleveland Rd. KT3: N Mald 1B 24
KT4: Wor Pk 6B 24
SW13 . . . . .6C 6
TW7: Isle 1B 10
W4 . . . . .1K 5
Cleves Av. KT17: Ewe 5E 30
Cleves Cl. KT17: Eps 1C 34
Cleves Rd. TW10: Ham 7D 10
Cleves Way TW12: Hamp 4E 14
Clifden Rd. TW1: Twick 5A 10
TW8: Bford 3E 4
Clifford Av. SW14 . . . . .7J 5
Clifford Haigh Ho. SW6 . . . . .4G 7
Clifford Ho. W14 . . . . .1J 7
(off Edith Vs.)
Clifford Rd. TW10: Ham 6E 10
Clifton Av. TW13: Felt 7B 8
Clifton Cl. KT6: Surb 4G 23
KT19: Eps 1G 33
Clifton Gdns. W4 . . . . .1A 6
(not continuous)
Clifton Pde. TW13: Felt 7B 8
Clifton Pk. Av. SW20 . . . . .6F 19
Clifton Pl. SM7: Bans 4K 35
Clifton Rd. KT2: King T 4G 17
SW19 . . . . .3G 19
TW11: Tedd 1K 15
Clifton Wlk. W6 . . . . .1E 6
(off King St.)
Clinton Av. KT8: E Mos 1H 21
Clinton Ho. KT6: Surb 4E 22
(off Lovelace Gdns)
Clippesby Cl. KT9: Chess 3G 29
Clitherow Av. W7 . . . . .1B 4
Clitherow Ct. TW8: Bford 2D 4
Clitherow Pas. TW8: Bford 2D 4
Clitherow Rd. TW8: Bford 2C 4
Cliveden Rd. SW19 . . . . .5J 19
Clive Ho. KT10: Esh 1G 27
TW1: Twick 1A 16
Clockhouse, The SW19 . . . . .7F 13
Clockhouse Cl. SW19 . . . . .6F 13
Clockhouse Pl. SW15 . . . . .3H 13
Clock Twr. Ind. Est. TW1: Isle 7A 4
Clock Twr. Rd. TW7: Isle 7A 4
Cloister Cl. TW11: Tedd 2C 16
Cloisters, The TW7: Isle 7B 4
(off Pulteney Cl.)
Cloisters Mall
KT1: King T 3B 36 (6F 17)
Cloncurry St. SW6 . . . . .6G 7
Clonmel Rd. SW6 . . . . .4J 7
TW11: Tedd 1J 15
Clonmore St. SW18 . . . . .5J 13
Close, The KT3: N Mald 6K 17
KT6: Surb 3F 23
KT10: Esh 5E 26
SM3: Sutt 4J 25
TW9: Rich 7J 5
Clovelly Ct. KT17: Eps 2C 34
(off Alexandra Rd.)

Cluny M.—Cressage Ho.

Cluny M. SW5 . . . 1K 7
Clyde Flats *SW6* . . . *4J 7*
(off Rylston Rd.)
Clyde Ho. KT2: King T . . . 1B 36 (5E 16)
SW18 . . . *1K 13*
(off Enterprise Way)
Clyde Rd. SM1: Sutt . . . 2K 31
Clydesdale Cl. TW7: Isle . . . 7A 4
Clydesdale Gdns. TW10: Rich . . . 1J 11
Clymping Dene TW14: Felt . . . 4A 8
Coach Ho. La. SW19 . . . 1G 19
Coalecroft Rd. SW15 . . . 1F 13
Coates Wlk. TW8: Bford . . . 3F 5
Cobbett Rd. TW2: Whitt . . . 5F 9
Cobblers Wlk. KT1: Hamp W . . . 5B 16
KT8: E Mos . . . 5B 16
TW11: Tedd . . . 5B 16
TW12: Hamp . . . 5H 15
Cobb's Hall *SW6* . . . *3G 7*
(off Fulham Pal. Rd.)
Cobb's Rd. TW4: Houn . . . 1E 8
Cobham Av. KT3: N Mald . . . 2D 24
Cobham Rd. KT1: King T . . . 6H 17
Cochrane Rd. SW19 . . . 4H 19
COCKCROW HILL . . . 5E 22
Cocks Cres. KT3: N Mald . . . 1C 24
Coda Cen., The SW6 . . . 4H 7
Colborne Way KT4: Wor Pk . . . 7F 25
Colcokes Rd. SM7: Bans . . . 5K 35
Coldstream Gdns. SW18 . . . 3J 13
Colebrook Cl. SW15 . . . 4G 13
Cole Ct. TW1: Twick . . . 4B 10
Colehill Gdns. SW6 . . . 6H 7
Colehill La. SW6 . . . 5H 7
Coleman Ct. SW18 . . . 4K 13
COLE PARK . . . 3B 10
Cole Pk. Gdns. TW1: Twick . . . 2B 10
Cole Pk. Rd. TW1: Twick . . . 3B 10
Cole Pk. Vw. TW1: Twick . . . 3B 10
Coleridge Ct. *W14* . . . *1G 7*
(off Blythe Rd.)
Cole Rd. TW1: Twick . . . 3B 10
Coleshill Rd. TW11: Tedd . . . 3K 15
Colet Ct. *W6* . . . *1G 7*
(off Hammersmith Rd.)
Colet Gdns. W14 . . . 1G 7
Colinette Rd. SW15 . . . 1F 13
Coliston Pas. *SW18* . . . *4K 13*
(off Coliston Rd.)
Coliston Rd. SW18 . . . 4K 13
College Av. KT17: Eps . . . 3C 34
College Cl. TW2: Twick . . . 5J 9
College Ct. *W6* . . . *2F 7*
(off Queen Caroline St.)
College Dr. KT7: T Ditt . . . 4K 21
College Gdns. KT3: N Mald . . . 2C 24
College Ho. SW15 . . . 2G 13
TW7: Isle . . . 4A 4
College Rd. KT17: Eps . . . 3C 34
TW7: Isle . . . 5A 4
COLLEGE RDBT. . . . 5C 36 (7F 17)
College Wlk.
KT1: King T . . . 5D 36 (7F 17)
Collier Cl. KT19: Ewe . . . 3H 29
Collingwood Av. KT5: Surb . . . 5K 23
Collingwood Cl. TW2: Whitt . . . 4F 9
Collingwood Pl. KT12: Walt T . . . 7A 20
Collingwood Rd. SM1: Sutt . . . 7K 25
Collins Path TW12: Hamp . . . 3E 14
Collis All. TW2: Twick . . . 5K 9
Colman Cl. KT18: Tatt C . . . 6F 35
Colne Ct. KT19: Ewe . . . 1K 29
Colne Dr. KT12: Walt T . . . 7C 20
Colne Rd. TW1: Twick . . . 5K 9
TW2: Twick . . . 5K 9
Colonial Av. TW2: Whitt . . . 3H 9
Colonial Dr. W4 . . . 1K 5
Colston Rd. SW14 . . . 1K 11
Columbia Av. KT4: Wor Pk . . . 4C 24
Columbia Gdns. Nth. *SW6* . . . *3K 7*
(off Rickett St.)
Columbia Gdns. Sth. *SW6* . . . *3K 7*
(off Rickett St.)
Columbia Sq. SW14 . . . 1K 11
Colville Rd. W3 . . . 1J 5
Colwith Rd. W6 . . . 3F 7
Combemartin Rd. SW18 . . . 4H 13
Comberton *KT1: King T* . . . *6H 17*
(off Eureka Rd.)
Comeragh M. W14 . . . 2H 7
Comeragh Rd. W14 . . . 2H 7
Commerce Rd. TW8: Bford . . . 3D 4
Common, The KT21: Asht . . . 5E 32
Commondale SW15 . . . 6F 7
Commonfield Rd. SM7: Bans . . . 3K 35
Common La. KT10: Clay . . . 4B 28
Common Rd. KT10: Clay . . . 3B 28
SW13 . . . 7E 6
Common Side KT18: Eps . . . 4H 33
Commonside Cl. SM2: Sutt . . . 7K 31
Community Wlk. KT10: Esh . . . 1H 27
Compass Hill TW10: Rich . . . 3E 10
Compton Cl. KT10: Esh . . . 3J 27
Compton Cres. KT9: Chess . . . 2F 29
W4 . . . 3K 5
Compton Rd. SW19 . . . 3J 19
Conaways Cl. KT17: Ewe . . . 6D 30
Concord Ct. KT1: King T . . . 5E 36
Concord Ho. KT3: N Mald . . . 7B 18
Conifer Gdns. SM1: Sutt . . . 6K 25
Conifer Pk. KT17: Eps . . . 7B 30
Conifers Cl. TW11: Tedd . . . 4C 16
Coniger Rd. SW6 . . . 6K 7
Coniston Cl. SW13 . . . 4C 6
SW20 . . . 3G 25
W4 . . . 4K 5
Coniston Rd. TW2: Whitt . . . 3G 9
Coniston Way KT9: Chess . . . 7F 23
Connaught Av. SW14 . . . 7K 5
TW4: Houn . . . 1D 8
Connaught M. SW6 . . . 5H 7
Connaught Rd. KT3: N Mald . . . 1B 24
TW10: Rich . . . 2G 11
TW11: Tedd . . . 2J 15
Conrad Dr. KT4: Wor Pk . . . 5F 25
Consfield Av. KT3: N Mald . . . 1D 24
Consort M. TW7: Isle . . . 2J 9
Constable Ct. *W4* . . . *2J 5*
(off Chaseley Dr.)
Constable Gdns. TW7: Isle . . . 2J 9
Constance Cl. SW15 . . . 1A 18
Constance Rd. TW2: Whitt . . . 4G 9
Convent Gdns. W5 . . . 1D 4
Conway Rd. SW20 . . . 5F 19
TW4: Houn . . . 4E 8
TW13: Hanw . . . 2C 14
Conway Wlk. TW12: Hamp . . . 3E 14
Conyers Cl. KT12: Hers . . . 2C 26
Cookes La. SM3: Cheam . . . 3H 31
COOMBE . . . 4K 17
Coombe Bank KT2: King T . . . 5B 18
Coombe Cl. TW3: Houn . . . 1F 9
Coombe Cres. TW12: Hamp . . . 4E 14
Coombe End KT2: King T . . . 4A 18
Coombefield Cl. KT3: N Mald . . . 2B 24
Coombe Gdns. KT3: N Mald . . . 1C 24
SW20 . . . 6D 18
Coombe Hill Glade
KT2: King T . . . 4B 18
Coombe Hill Golf Course . . . 4A 18
Coombe Hill Rd. KT2: King T . . . 4B 18
Coombe Ho. Chase
KT3: N Mald . . . 5A 18
COOMBE LANE . . . 5C 18
Coombe La. SW20 . . . 5C 18
Coombe La. Flyover SW20 . . . 5C 18
Coombe La. W. KT2: King T . . . 5J 17
Coombe Neville KT2: King T . . . 4A 18
Coombe Pk. KT2: King T . . . 2K 17
Coombe Pl. KT2: King T . . . 2K 17
Coombe Ridings KT2: King T . . . 2K 17
Coombe Ri. KT2: King T . . . 5K 17
Coombe Rd. KT2: King T . . . 5H 17
KT3: N Mald . . . 6B 18
TW12: Hamp . . . 3E 14
W4 . . . 2B 6
Coombe Wlk. SM1: Sutt . . . 7K 25
Coombe Wood Golf Course . . . 4J 17
Coombe Wood Local Nature Reserve
. . . 4C 18
Coombe Wood Rd.
KT2: King T . . . 2K 17
Coomer M. SW6 . . . 3J 7
Coomer Pl. SW6 . . . 3J 7
Coomer Rd. SW6 . . . 3J 7
Coopers Ct. *TW7: Isle* . . . *6A 4*
(off Woodlands Rd.)
Copenhagen Way KT12: Walt T . . . 7A 20
Cope Pl. W8 . . . 1K 7
Coppard Gdns. KT9: Chess . . . 3D 28
Copperlight Apartments
SW18 . . . *2K 13*
(off Buckhold Rd.)
Copper Mill Dr. TW7: Isle . . . 6A 4
Coppice Cl. SW20 . . . 7F 19
Coppice Dr. SW15 . . . 3E 12
Coppsfield KT8: W Mole . . . 7F 15
Copse Edge Av. KT17: Eps . . . 2C 34
Copse Glade KT6: Surb . . . 4E 22
COPSE HILL . . . 4D 18
Copse Hill SW20 . . . 5D 18
Copsem Dr. KT10: Esh . . . 3G 27
Copsem La. KT10: Esh, Oxs . . . 3H 27
KT22: Oxs . . . 3H 27
Copsem Way KT10: Esh . . . 3H 27
Copsen Wood KT22: Oxs . . . 7H 27
Coptain Ho. SW18 . . . 1K 13
Copthall Gdns. TW1: Twick . . . 5A 10
Coram Ho. *W4* . . . *2B 6*
(off Wood St.)
Corban Rd. TW3: Houn . . . 1F 9
Corbet Rd. KT17: Ewe . . . 6B 30
Corbiere Ct. SW19 . . . 3G 19
Corelli Ct. *SW5* . . . *1K 7*
(off W. Cromwell Rd.)
Corfe Cl. KT21: Asht . . . 7D 32
TW4: Houn . . . 5D 8
Corkran Rd. KT6: Surb . . . 4E 22
Cormorant Pl. SM1: Sutt . . . 2J 31
Cornelia Ho. *TW1: Twick* . . . *3E 10*
(off Denton Rd.)
Cornercroft *SM3: Cheam* . . . *2G 31*
(off Wickham Av.)
Corner House Arts Cen., The . . . 5G 23
Corney Reach Way W4 . . . 4B 6
Corney Rd. W4 . . . 3B 6
Cornish Ho. TW8: Bford . . . 2G 5
Cornwall Av. KT10: Clay . . . 4A 28
Cornwall Gro. W4 . . . 2B 6
Cornwall Rd. SM2: Sutt . . . 4J 31
TW1: Twick . . . 4B 10
Coronation Ct. KT1: King T . . . 7C 36
Coronation Wlk. TW2: Whitt . . . 5F 9
Corporate Dr. TW13: Felt . . . 7A 8
Corporation Av. TW4: Houn . . . 1D 8
Corscombe Cl. KT2: King T . . . 2K 17
Corsellis Sq. *TW1: Isle* . . . *1C 10*
(off Varley Dr.)
Cortayne Ct. TW2: Twick . . . 6K 9
Cortayne Rd. SW6 . . . 6J 7
Cortis Rd. SW15 . . . 3E 12
Cortis Ter. SW15 . . . 3E 12
Cotherstone KT19: Ewe . . . 6A 30
Cotman Cl. SW15 . . . 3G 13
Cotsford Av. KT3: N Mald . . . 2K 23
Cotswold Cl. KT2: King T . . . 3K 17
KT10: Hin W . . . 6A 22
Cotswold Rd. TW12: Hamp . . . 2F 15
Cotswold Way KT4: Wor Pk . . . 6F 25
Cottage Gro. KT6: Surb . . . 3E 22
Cottage Rd. KT19: Ewe . . . 4A 30
Cottenham Dr. SW20 . . . 4E 18
Cottenham Pde. SW20 . . . 6E 18
COTTENHAM PARK . . . 5E 18
Cottenham Pk. Rd. SW20 . . . 5D 18
(not continuous)
Cottenham Pl. SW20 . . . 4E 18
Cotterill Rd. KT6: Surb . . . 6F 23
Cottimore Av. KT12: Walt T . . . 5A 20
Cottimore Cres. KT12: Walt T . . . 4A 20
Cottimore La. KT12: Walt T . . . 4A 20
Cottimore Ter. KT12: Walt T . . . 4A 20
Cottington Rd. TW13: Hanw . . . 1C 14
Couchmore Av. KT10: Hin W . . . 6K 21
Country Way TW13: Hanw . . . 3A 14
County Court
Brentford . . . 3E 4
Kingston upon Thames
. . . 4B 36 (6E 16)
Wandsworth . . . 2H 13
West London . . . *2G 7*
(off Talgarth Rd.)
County Gdns. TW7: Isle . . . 1J 9
County Pde. TW8: Bford . . . 4E 4
Court Cl. TW2: Twick . . . 7G 9
Court Cl. Av. TW2: Twick . . . 7G 9
Court Cres. KT9: Chess . . . 2E 28
Courtenay Av. SM2: Sutt . . . 5K 31
Courtenay Rd. KT4: Wor Pk . . . 7F 25
Court Farm Av. KT19: Ewe . . . 2A 30
Court Farm Gdns. KT19: Eps . . . 7K 29
Courthope Rd. SW19 . . . 2H 19
Courthope Vs. SW19 . . . 4H 19
Court Ho. Mans. KT19: Eps . . . 1A 34
Courtlands TW10: Rich . . . 2H 11
Courtlands Av. KT10: Esh . . . 3E 26
TW9: Kew . . . 6J 5
TW12: Hamp . . . 3E 14
Courtlands Cres. SM7: Bans . . . 4K 35
Courtlands Dr. KT19: Ewe . . . 3B 30
Courtlands Rd. KT5: Surb . . . 4H 23
Court La. KT19: Eps . . . 2K 33
Courtney Pl. KT11: Cobh . . . 7E 26
Court Rd. SM7: Bans . . . 5K 35
Court Royal SW15 . . . 2H 13
Court Way TW2: Twick . . . 4A 10
Coutts Av. KT9: Chess . . . 2F 29
Coval Gdns. SW14 . . . 1J 11
Coval La. SW14 . . . 1J 11
Coval Pas. SW14 . . . 1K 11
Coval Rd. SW14 . . . 1J 11
Covell Ho. KT19: Eps . . . 6J 29
Coverts Rd. KT10: Clay . . . 4A 28
Covey Rd. KT4: Wor Pk . . . 6G 25
Cowleaze Rd.
KT2: King T . . . 2D 36 (5F 17)
Cowley Cres. KT12: Hers . . . 1B 26
Cowley Rd. SW14 . . . 7B 6
Cowper Rd. KT2: King T . . . 2G 17
Coxdean KT18: Tatt C . . . 7F 35
Cox Ho. *W6* . . . *3H 7*
(off Field Rd.)
Cox La. KT9: Chess . . . 1G 29
KT19: Ewe . . . 2J 29
(not continuous)
Coxwold Path KT9: Chess . . . 4F 29
Crabtree Hall *SW6* . . . *4F 7*
(off Crabtree La.)
Crabtree La. SW6 . . . 4F 7
(not continuous)
Craddocks Av. KT21: Asht . . . 6F 33
Craddocks Cl. KT21: Asht . . . 5H 33
Craddocks Pde. KT21: Asht . . . 6F 33
Craig Rd. TW10: Ham . . . 1D 16
Crammond Cl. W6 . . . 3H 7
Cranborne Av. KT6: Surb . . . 7H 23
Cranbourne Cl. KT12: Hers . . . 3B 26
Cranbrook Ct. TW8: Bford . . . 3D 4
Cranbrook Dr. KT10: Esh . . . 5H 21
TW2: Whitt . . . 5G 9
Cranbrook Rd. SW19 . . . 4H 19
TW4: Houn . . . 1E 8
W4 . . . 2B 6
Crane Av. TW7: Isle . . . 2B 10
Cranebank M. TW1: Twick . . . 1B 10
Cranebrook TW2: Twick . . . 6H 9
Crane Ct. KT19: Ewe . . . 1K 29
SW14 . . . 1K 11
Craneford Cl. TW2: Twick . . . 4A 10
Craneford Way TW2: Twick . . . 4K 9
Crane Ho. TW13: Hanw . . . 7F 9
Crane Mead Ct. TW1: Twick . . . 4A 10
Crane Pk. Island Nature Reserve
. . . 6E 8
Crane Pk. Rd. TW2: Whitt . . . 6G 9
Crane Rd. TW2: Twick . . . 5K 9
Cranes Dr. KT5: Surb . . . 1F 23
Cranes Pk. KT5: Surb . . . 1F 23
Cranes Pk. Av.
KT5: Surb . . . 7E 36 (1F 23)
Cranes Pk. Cres. KT5: Surb . . . 1G 23
Crane Way TW2: Whitt . . . 4H 9
Cranford Cl. SW20 . . . 4E 18
Cranford Ri. KT10: Esh . . . 2H 27
Cranleigh Ct. TW9: Rich . . . 7H 5
Cranleigh Gdns. KT2: King T . . . 3G 17
Cranleigh Rd. KT10: Esh . . . 5H 21
SW19 . . . 7K 19
Cranmer Av. W13 . . . 1C 4
Cranmer Cl. SM4: Mord . . . 3G 25
Cranmer Ct. TW12: Hamp H . . . 2G 15
Cranmer Rd. KT2: King T . . . 2F 17
TW12: Hamp H . . . 2G 15
Craven Cottage . . . 6G 7
Craven Gdns. SW19 . . . 2K 19
Craven Lodge *SW6* . . . *5G 7*
(off Harbord St.)
Craven Rd.
KT2: King T . . . 1E 36 (5G 17)
Cray Av. KT21: Asht . . . 5F 33
Crayke Hill KT9: Chess . . . 4F 29
Crediton Way KT10: Clay . . . 2B 28
Creek Cotts. *KT8: E Mos* . . . *1K 21*
(off Creek Rd.)
Creek Rd. KT8: E Mos . . . 1K 21
Crefeld Cl. W6 . . . 3H 7
Creighton Rd. W5 . . . 1E 4
Cremorne Gdns. KT19: Ewe . . . 6A 30
Crescent, The KT3: N Mald . . . 7K 17
KT6: Surb . . . 2F 23
KT8: W Mole . . . 1F 21
KT18: Eps . . . 3H 33
(not continuous)
SM2: Sutt . . . 7K 31
SW13 . . . 6C 6
SW19 . . . 7K 13
Crescent Ct. KT6: Surb . . . 2E 22
Crescent Gdns. SW19 . . . 7K 13
Crescent Rd. KT2: King T . . . 4H 17
SW20 . . . 5G 19
Crescent Stables SW15 . . . 2H 13
Cresford Rd. SW6 . . . 5K 7
Cressage Ho. *TW8: Bford* . . . *3F 5*
(off Ealing Rd.)

A-Z Kingston & Richmond 45

Cressinghams, The
    KT18: Eps 2A 34
Cresswell Rd. TW1: Twick ...3E 10
    TW13: Hanw 7D 8
Cressy Ho. SW15 ....7E 6
Crest, The KT5: Surb 2H 23
Creston Way KT4: Wor Pk ...5G 25
Crestway SW15 ....3D 12
Crestwood Way TW4: Houn 2D 8
Cricketers Cl. KT9: Chess ..1E 28
Cricket La. TW12: Hamp H ...3H 15
Crieff Ct. TW11: Tedd 4D 16
Crispen Rd. TW13: Hanw 1D 14
Crispin Cl. KT21: Asht 7G 33
Crisp Rd. W6 ....2F 7
Cristowe Rd. SW6 ....6J 7
Criterion Bldgs. KT7: T Ditt ...4C 22
    (off Portsmouth Rd.)
Croft, The KT17: Eps 3C 34
Croft End Cl. KT9: Chess ...7G 23
Crofters Cl. TW7: Isle 2J 9
Crofton KT21: Asht 7F 33
Crofton Av. KT12: Walt T ...7B 20
    W4 ....4K 5
Crofton Ter. TW9: Rich 1G 11
Croftway TW10: Ham 7C 10
Cromer Hyde SM4: Mord 2K 25
Cromer Vs. Rd. SW18 ....3J 13
Cromford Rd. SW18 ....2K 13
Cromford Way KT3: N Mald ...5A 18
Cromwell Av. KT3: N Mald ...2C 24
    W6 ....2E 6
CROMWELL BUPA HOSPITAL 1K 7
Cromwell Ct. KT12: Walt T ...5A 20
    W4 ....2J 5
    (off Harvard Rd.)
Cromwell Cres. SW5 ....1K 7
Cromwell Mans. SW5 ....1K 7
    (off Cromwell Rd.)
Cromwell Pl. SW14 ....7K 5
Cromwell Rd.
    KT2: King T 2D 36 (5F 17)
    KT4: Wor Pk 7A 24
    KT12: Walt T 5A 20
    SW5 ....1K 7
    SW19 ....2K 19
    TW3: Houn 1F 9
    TW11: Tedd 3B 16
    TW13: Felt 5A 8
Cromwell Road Bus Station
    ....2D 36 (5F 17)
Cromwell St. TW3: Houn 1F 9
Crondace Rd. SW6 ....5K 7
Crondall Ho. SW15 ....4D 12
Crookham Rd. SW6 ....5J 7
Crosby Cl. TW13: Hanw 7D 8
Cross Deep TW1: Twick 6A 10
Cross Deep Gdns. TW1: Twick ...6A 10
Cross Lances Rd. TW3: Houn ...1G 9
Crosslands Rd. KT19: Ewe ...3A 30
Cross Rd. KT2: King T 4G 17
    SM2: Sutt 6K 31
    SW19 ....4K 19
    TW13: Hanw 1D 14
Cross St. SW13 ....6B 6
    TW12: Hamp H 2H 15
Crossway KT12: Walt T 6A 20
    SW20 ....1F 25
Crossways, The KT5: Surb ...5J 23
Crown Arc.
    KT1: King T 4B 36 (6E 16)
Crown Cl. KT12: Walt T 4B 20
Crown Court
    Isleworth 5A 4
    Kingston upon Thames
    ....5C 36 (7E 16)
Crown Rd. KT3: N Mald 7K 17
Crown La. SM4: Mord 1K 25
Crown M. W6 ....1D 6
Crown Pde. SM4: Mord 7K 19
Crown Pas. KT1: King T 4B 36
Crown Rd. KT3: N Mald 5K 17
    SM1: Sutt 1K 31
    SM4: Mord 1K 25
    TW1: Twick 3C 10
Crown Ter. TW9: Rich 1G 11
Crowntree Cl. TW7: Isle 3A 4
Crown Yd. SW6 ....6K 7
Crowther Av. TW8: Bford 1F 5
Crowther Cl. SW6 ....3J 7
    (off Bucklers All.)
Crowthorne Cl. SW18 ....4J 13
Croxall Ho. KT12: Walt T ...3B 20
Croylands Dr. KT6: Surb ...4F 23
Crutchfield La. KT12: Walt T ...6A 20

Crystal Pl. KT4: Wor Pk 6E 24
Cudas Cl. KT19: Ewe 1C 30
Cuddington Av. KT4: Wor Pk ...7C 24
Cuddington Cl. SM2: Cheam ...5G 31
Cuddington Glade KT19: Eps ...1H 33
Cuddington Golf Course 2H 35
Cuddington Pk. Cl. SM7: Bans ...2J 35
Cuddington Way SM2: Cheam ...1G 35
Cudham Cl. SM2: Sutt 6K 31
Cullerne Cl. KT17: Ewe 6C 30
Culsac Rd. KT6: Surb 6F 23
Culverhay KT21: Asht 5F 33
Cumberland Cl. KT19: Ewe ...6B 30
    SW20 ....4G 19
    TW1: Twick 3C 10
Cumberland Cres. W14 ....1H 7
    (not continuous)
Cumberland Dr. KT9: Chess ...7F 23
    KT10: Hin W 6B 22
Cumberland Ho. KT2: King T ...4J 17
Cumberland Pl. TW16: Sun ...1A 20
Cumberland Rd. SW13 ....5C 6
    TW9: Kew 4H 5
Cumbrae Gdns. KT6: Surb ...6E 22
Cumnor Rd. SM2: Sutt 6K 31
Cunliffe Pde. KT19: Ewe ...1C 30
Cunliffe Rd. KT19: Ewe 1C 30
Cunnington St. W4 ....1K 5
Cumnor Cl. KT6: Surb 7H 23
Currie Hill Cl. SW19 ......1J 19
Curtis Rd. KT19: Ewe 1K 29
    TW4: Houn 4E 8
Curvan Cl. KT17: Ewe 6C 30
Curzon Cinema
    Richmond 2E 10
Cusack Cl. TW1: Tedd 1A 16
Cutthroat All. TW10: Ham ...6D 10
Cyclamen Cl. TW12: Hamp ...3F 15
Cyclamen Way KT19: Ewe 2K 29
Cygnet Av. TW14: Felt 4B 8
Cygnets, The TW13: Hanw ...1D 14
Cypress Av. TW2: Whitt 4H 9
Cypress Cl. SW19 ....5A 30
Cypress Ct. SM1: Sutt 2K 31
Cypress Way SM7: Bans 3G 35

D

D'Abernon Chase KT22: Oxs ...3B 32
D'Abernon Ct. KT10: Esh ...1F 27
Daffodil Pl. TW12: Hamp ...3F 15
Dagmar Rd. KT2: King T 5G 17
Dain Ct. W8 ....1K 7
    (off Lexham Gdns.)
Dairy Cl. SW6 ....5K 7
Dairy Wlk. SW19 ....1H 19
Daisy La. SW6 ....7K 7
Dale Cl. KT2: King T 4G 17
    (off York Rd.)
Dale Rd. SM1: Sutt 1J 31
Daleside Rd. KT19: Ewe 3A 30
Dale St. W4 ....2B 6
Dalewood Gdns. KT4: Wor Pk ...6E 24
Dallas Rd. SM3: Cheam 3H 31
Dalling Rd. W6 ....1E 6
Dallington Ct. KT12: Hers ...3B 26
Dalmain Rd. TW4: Houn 4E 8
Dalmeny Av. SW16 ....1J 9
Dalmeny Cres. TW3: Houn 1J 9
Dalmeny Rd. KT4: Wor Pk ...7E 24
Dalmeny Way KT18: Eps 3K 33
Dalmore Av. KT10: Clay 3A 28
Dancer Rd. SW6 ....5J 7
    TW9: Rich 7H 5
Danbury Av. SW15 ....3B 12
Danebury TW8: Bford 4D 4
Danehurst Ct. KT17: Eps ...2C 34
Danehurst St. SW6 ....5H 7
Danemere St. SW15 ....7F 7
Danesbury Rd. TW13: Felt ...5A 8
Danesfield Cl. KT12: Walt T ...7A 20
Danesmead KT11: Cobh 7F 27
Danetree Cl. KT19: Ewe 4K 29
Danetree Rd. KT19: Ewe 4K 29
Daniel Cl. TW4: Houn 4E 8
Daniel Way SM7: Bans 3K 35
Dan Mason Dr. W4 ....6K 5
Da Palma Ct. SW6 ....3K 7
    (off Anselm Rd.)
Daphne Ct. KT4: Wor Pk 6B 24
Darby Cres. TW16: Sun 6B 14
Darby Gdns. TW16: Sun 6B 14
D'Arcy Pl. KT21: Asht 6G 33
D'Arcy Rd. KT21: Asht 6G 33
    SM3: Cheam 1G 31
Darcy Rd. TW7: Isle 5B 4
Darell Rd. TW9: Rich 7H 5

Darfur St. SW15 ....7G 7
Darlan Rd. SW6 ....4J 7
Darlaston Rd. SW19 ....4G 19
Darley Dr. KT3: N Mald 6A 18
Darling Ho. TW1: Twick ...3E 10
Dartford Ct. KT19: Eps 1F 33
Dartmouth Ho. KT2: King T ...2C 36
Dartmouth Pl. W4 ....3B 6
Darwin Rd. W5 ....2D 4
Daubeney Pl. TW12: Hamp ...5H 15
    (off High St.)
Davenport Cl. TW11: Tedd ...3B 16
David Lloyd Leisure
    Cheam 4G 31
    Epsom 6H 29
    Fulham 4K 7
    (within Fulham Broadway Shop. Cen.)
    Hampton 7F 9
    Kingston upon Thames
    ....3D 36
    (within The Rotunda Cen.)
    Raynes Park 7G 19
David Twigg Cl.
    KT2: King T 1D 36 (5F 17)
Davison Cl. KT19: Eps 7J 29
Davis Rd. KT9: Chess 1H 29
Davis Rd. Ind. Pk.
    KT9: Chess 1H 29
Davmor Ct. TW8: Bford 2D 4
Dawes Av. TW7: Isle 2B 10
Dawes Ct. KT10: Esh 1G 27
Dawes Rd. SW6 ....4H 7
Dawson Rd. KT1: King T 7G 17
Dax Ct. TW16: Sun 7B 14
Daylesford Av. SW15 ......1D 12
Daytona Sandown Pk. 7H 21
Deacon Rd.
    KT2: King T 2E 36 (5G 17)
Deacons Ct. TW1: Twick ...6A 10
Deacons Wlk. TW12: Hamp ...1F 15
Deal M. W5 ....1E 4
Dealtry Rd. SW15 ....1F 13
Deanhill Ct. SW14 ....1J 11
Deanhill Rd. SW14 ....1J 11
Dean Rd. TW3: Houn 2G 9
    TW12: Hamp 2F 15
Deans Cl. W4 ....3J 5
Deans La. W4 ....3J 5
    (off Deans Cl.)
Deans Rd. SM1: Sutt 7K 25
Debden Cl. KT2: King T 2E 16
De Brome Rd. TW13: Felt 5B 8
De Burgh Pk. SM7: Bans ...4K 35
Dee Ho. KT2: King T 1B 36
Deepdale SW19 ....1G 19
Deepdene Mans. SW6 ....5J 7
    (off Rostrevor Rd.)
Deepwell Cl. TW7: Isle 5B 4
Deerhurst Cl. TW13: Felt ...1A 14
Deerhurst Cres.
    TW12: Hamp H 2H 15
Dee Rd. TW9: Rich 1G 11
Deer Pk. Cl. KT2: King T ...4J 17
Dee Way KT19: Ewe 6B 30
Defoe Av. TW9: Kew 4H 5
Defoe Ct. KT17: Eps 1B 34
Delacy Ct. SM2: Sutt 7K 31
Delaford St. SW6 ....4H 7
Delamere Rd. SW20 ....5G 19
Delaporte Cl. KT17: Eps ...1B 34
Delcombe Av. KT4: Wor Pk ...5F 25
Delft Ho. KT2: King T 1E 36
Dell, The TW8: Bford 3D 4
    TW14: Felt 4A 8
Dellbow Rd. TW14: Felt 2A 8
Dell La. KT17: Ewe 2D 30
Dell Rd. KT17: Ewe 3D 30
Dells Cl. TW11: Tedd 3A 16
Dell Wlk. KT3: N Mald 6B 18
Delorme St. W6 ....3G 7
Delta Cl. KT4: Wor Pk 7C 24
Delta Pk. SW18 ....1K 13
Delta Rd. KT4: Wor Pk 7B 24
Delvino Rd. SW6 ....5K 7
De Mel Cl. KT19: Ewe 1J 33
Dempster Cl. KT6: Surb ...5D 22
Denbigh Cl. SM1: Sutt 2J 31
Denbigh Gdns. TW10: Rich ...2G 11
Dene, The KT8: W Mole 2E 20
    SM2: Cheam 7J 31
Dene Gdns. KT7: T Ditt 6B 22
Denehurst Gdns. TW2: Twick ...1J 9
    TW10: Rich 1H 11
Dene Rd. KT21: Asht 7G 33
Denewood KT17: Eps 2B 34

Denham Rd. KT17: Eps 1C 34
    TW14: Felt 4B 8
Denleigh Gdns. KT7: T Ditt ...3K 21
Denman Dr. KT10: Clay 2B 28
Denmark Av. SW19 ....4H 19
Denmark Ct. SM4: Mord 3K 25
Denmark Rd.
    KT1: King T 5C 36 (7F 16)
    SW19 ....3G 19
    TW2: Twick 7J 9
Denmead Ho. SW15 ....3C 12
Dennan Rd. KT6: Surb 5G 23
Denning Cl. TW12: Hamp ...2E 14
Denningtons, The KT4: Wor Pk ...6B 24
Dennis Pk. Cres. SW20 ....5H 19
Dennis Rd. KT8: E Mos 1H 21
Denton Gro. KT12: Walt T ...6D 20
Denton Rd. TW1: Twick 3E 10
Deodar Rd. SW15 ....1H 13
Depot Rd. KT17: Eps 2B 34
Derby Arms Rd. KT18: Eps D ...6C 34
Derby Cl. KT18: Tatt C 7E 34
Derby Rd. KT5: Surb 5H 23
    SM1: Sutt 3J 31
    SW14 ....1J 11
    SW19 ....4K 19
    TW3: Houn 1G 9
Derby Rd. Ind. Est. TW3: Houn ...1G 9
Derby Sq., The KT19: Eps ...2A 34
    (off High St.)
Derby Stables Rd.
    KT18: Eps D 6C 34
Dere Cl. SW6 ....5H 7
Derek Av. SW19 ....3H 29
Derek Cl. KT19: Ewe 2J 29
Derwent Av. SW15 ....1B 18
Derwent Cl. KT10: Clay ...3K 27
Derwent Ho. KT2: King T ...1B 36
Derwent Lodge KT4: Wor Pk ...6E 24
Derwent Rd. SW20 ....3G 25
    TW2: Whitt 3G 9
Desborough Ho. W14 ....3J 7
    (off North End Rd.)
Devas Rd. SW20 ....5F 19
Devereux La. SW13 ....4E 6
Devey Cl. KT2: King T 4C 18
Devitt Cl. KT21: Asht 5H 33
Devoke Way KT12: Walt T ...6C 20
Devon Av. TW2: Twick 5H 9
Devon Ct. KT18: Eps 3B 34
    (off St Martin's Av.)
    TW12: Hamp 4F 15
Devoncroft Gdns. TW1: Twick ...4B 10
Devonhurst Pl. W4 ....2A 6
Devon Rd. KT12: Hers 1B 26
    SM2: Cheam 5H 31
Devonshire Ct. TW13: Felt ...6A 8
Devonshire Dr. KT6: Surb ...5E 22
Devonshire Gdns. W4 ......4K 5
Devonshire Ho. SW15 ......2G 13
Devonshire M. W4 ....2B 6
Devonshire Pas. W4 ....2B 6
Devonshire Rd. TW13: Hanw ...7D 8
    W4 ....2B 6
Devonshires, The KT18: Eps ...3C 34
Devonshire St. W4 ....2B 6
Devon Way KT9: Chess 2D 28
    KT19: Ewe 2J 29
Dewhurst Ct. TW3: Houn 1F 9
Dewsbury Ct. W4 ....1K 5
Dewsbury Gdns. KT4: Wor Pk ...7D 24
Diana Gdns. KT6: Surb 6G 23
Diana Ho. SW13 ....5C 6
Dibdin Cl. SM1: Sutt 3K 25
Dibdin Rd. SM1: Sutt 7K 25
Diceland Lodge SM7: Bans ...5J 35
    (off Diceland Rd.)
Diceland Rd. SM7: Bans ...5J 35
Dickens Cl. TW10: Ham 6F 11
Dickenson Rd. TW13: Hanw ...2B 14
Dickerage La. KT3: N Mald ...7K 17
Dickerage Rd. KT1: King T ...5K 17
    KT3: N Mald 5K 17
Dieppe Cl. W14 ....2J 7
Digby Mans. W6 ....2E 6
    (off Hammersmith Bri. Rd.)
Digdens Ri. KT18: Eps 4K 33
Dillon Cl. KT19: Eps 1G 33
Dilton Gdns. SW15 ....5D 12
Dimes Pl. W6 ....1E 6
Dinton Rd. KT2: King T 4G 17
Dirdene Cl. KT17: Eps 1C 34
Dirdene Gdns. KT17: Eps ...1C 34
Dirdene Gro. KT17: Eps 1B 34
Disbrowe Rd. W6 ....3H 7
Disraeli Cl. W4 ....1A 6

Disraeli Gdns. SW15 1J 13
Disraeli Rd. SW15 1H 13
Distillery La. W6 2F 7
Distillery Rd. W6 2F 7
Distillery Wlk. TW8: Bford 3F 5
Distillery Wharf W6 3F 7
Ditton Cl. KT7: T Ditt 4B 22
Ditton Grange Cl. KT6: Surb 5E 22
Ditton Grange Dr. KT6: Surb 5E 22
Ditton Hill KT6: Surb 5D 22
Ditton Hill Rd. KT6: Surb 5D 22
Ditton Lawn KT7: T Ditt 5B 22
Ditton Reach KT7: T Ditt 3C 22
Ditton Rd. KT6: Surb 6E 22
Divis Way *SW15* *3E 12*
(off Dover Pk. Dr.)
Dock Rd. TW8: Bford 4E 4
Dockwell's Ind. Est. TW14: Felt 2A 8
Dolby Rd. SW6 6J 7
Dollary Pde. *KT1: King T* *7J 17*
(off Kingston Rd.)
Dolman Rd. W4 1A 6
Dolphin Cl. KT6: Surb 2E 22
Dolphin Sq. W4 4B 6
Dolphin St.
KT1: King T 3C 36 (6F 17)
Donald Woods Gdns.
KT5: Surb 6J 23
Doneraile St. SW6 6G 7
Donnelly Ct. *SW6* *4H 7*
(off Dawes Rd.)
Donnington Rd. KT4: Wor Pk 6D 24
Donovan Cl. KT19: Eps 6A 30
Doone Cl. TW11: Tedd 3B 16
Dora Rd. SW19 2K 19
Dorchester Cl. KT10: Hin W 6A 22
Dorchester Gro. W4 2B 6
Dorchester Ho. TW9: Kew 4J 5
Dorchester M. KT3: N Mald 1A 24
TW1: Twick 3D 10
Dorchester Rd. KT4: Wor Pk 5F 25
Dorey Ho. *TW8: Bford* *4D 4*
(off High St.)
Doria Rd. SW6 6J 7
Dorien Rd. SW20 6G 19
Dorking Cl. KT4: Wor Pk 6G 25
Dorking Rd. KT18: Eps 5H 33
Dorling Dr. KT17: Eps 1C 34
Dormay St. SW18 2K 13
Dorncliffe Rd. SW6 6H 7
Dorney Way TW4: Houn 2D 8
Dorset Cl. KT9: Chess 1E 28
Dorset Ct. KT17: Eps 1C 34
Dorset Mans. *SW6* *3G 7*
(off Lillie Rd.)
Dorset Rd. SM2: Sutt 6K 31
SW19 5K 19
Dorset Sq. KT19: Ewe 6A 30
Dorset Way TW2: Twick 5J 9
Dorset Wharf *W6* *4F 7*
(off Rainville Rd.)
Dorville Cres. W6 1E 6
Douai Gro. TW12: Hamp 5H 15
Douglas Av. KT3: N Mald 1E 24
Douglas Bader Ho. TW7: Isle 1J 9
Douglas Ct. KT1: King T 7D 36
Douglas Ho. KT6: Surb 5G 23
Douglas Johnstone Ho. *SW6* *3J 7*
(off Clem Attlee Ct.)
Douglas Mans. TW3: Houn 1G 9
Douglas M. SM7: Bans 5J 35
Douglas Rd. KT1: King T 6J 17
KT6: Surb 6G 23
KT10: Esh 6G 21
TW3: Houn 1G 9
Douglas Sq. SM4: Mord 3K 25
Dounesforth Gdns. SW18 5K 13
Dovecote Gdns. SW14 7A 6
Dover Ho. Rd. SW15 1D 12
Dover Pk. Dr. SW15 3E 12
Dover Ter. *TW9: Rich* *6G 5*
(off Sandycombe Rd.)
Dove Tree Cl. KT19: Eps 5A 30
Dowdeswell Cl. SW15 1B 12
Dowler Ct. KT2: King T 1D 36 (5F 17)
Downbury M. SW18 2K 13
Downes Cl. TW1: Twick 3C 10
Downe Ter. TW10: Rich 3F 11
Downfield KT4: Wor Pk 5C 24
Down Hall Rd.
KT2: King T 2B 36 (5E 16)
Downham Ct. *KT12: Walt T* *7B 20*
(off Long Lodge Dr.)
Downland Cl. KT18: Tatt C 7E 34
Downland Gdns. KT18: Tatt C 7E 34
Downland Way KT18: Tatt C 7E 34

Down Pl. W6 1E 6
Down Rd. TW11: Tedd 3C 16
Downs, The SW20 4G 19
Downs Av. KT18: Eps 3B 34
Downs Hill Rd. KT18: Eps 3B 34
Downs Ho. Rd. KT18: Eps D 7B 34
Downside KT18: Eps 3B 34
TW1: Twick 7A 10
Downside Wlk. *TW8: Bford* *3E 4*
(off Windmill Rd.)
Downs Lodge Ct. KT17: Eps 3B 34
Downs Rd. KT18: Eps, Eps D 4B 34
SM2: Sutt 6K 31
Downs Side SM2: Cheam 7J 31
Down St. KT8: W Mole 2F 21
Downs Vw. TW7: Isle 5A 4
Downs Way KT18: Eps 5C 34
Downs Wood KT18: Tatt C 6E 34
Doyle Ho. *SW13* *4F 7*
(off Trinity Chu. Rd.)
Draco Ga. SW15 7F 7
Dragonfly Cl. KT5: Surb 5K 23
Drake Ct. *KT5: Surb* *1F 23*
(off Cranes Pk. Av.)
Drake Rd. KT9: Chess 2H 29
Drake's Cl. KT10: Esh 1F 27
Drax Av. SW20 4D 18
Draxmont SW19 3H 19
Draycot Rd. KT6: Surb 5H 23
Draycott M. *SW6* *6J 7*
(off Laurel Bank Gdns.)
Draymans Way TW7: Isle 7A 4
Drayton Cl. TW4: Houn 2E 8
Drey Ct. *KT4: Wor Pk* *6D 24*
(off The Avenue)
DRIFT BRIDGE 3F 35
Driftway, The SM7: Bans 4F 35
Drive, The KT2: King T 4K 17
KT6: Surb 4F 23
KT10: Esh 5H 21
KT19: Ewe 3C 30
SM2: Cheam 1J 35
SM7: Bans 6H 35
SW6 6H 7
SW20 4F 19
TW14: Felt 4B 8
Drive Mans. *SW6* *6H 7*
(off Fulham Rd.)
Dromore Rd. SW15 3H 13
Drovers Ct. KT1: King T 3D 36
Drumaline Ridge KT4: Wor Pk 6B 24
Drummond Ct. KT19: Eps 1G 33
Drummond Gdns. KT19: Eps 7K 29
Drummond Pl. TW1: Twick 4C 10
Drummonds Pl. TW9: Rich 1F 11
Drury Cl. SW15 3D 12
Dryad St. SW15 7G 7
Dryburgh Rd. SW15 7E 6
Dryden Mans. *W14* *3H 7*
(off Queen's Club Gdns.)
Ducks Wlk. TW1: Twick 2D 10
Dudley Dr. SM4: Mord 5H 25
Dudley Gro. KT18: Eps 3K 33
Dudley Rd.
KT1: King T 5E 36 (7G 17)
KT12: Walt T 4A 20
SW19 3K 19
TW9: Rich 6G 5
Duke Ct. TW3: Houn 1E 8
Duke of Cambridge Cl.
TW2: Whitt 3J 9
Duke Rd. W4 2A 6
Duke's Av. W4 2A 6
Dukes Av. KT2: King T 1D 16
KT3: N Mald 7B 18
TW4: Houn 1D 8
TW10: Ham 1D 16
Dukes Cl. TW12: Hamp 2E 14
Dukes Ct. KT19: Ewe 5B 30
SW14 6A 6
Dukes Ga. W4 1K 5
Dukes Grn. Av. TW14: Felt 2A 8
Dukes Head Pas. TW12: Hamp 4H 15
Dukes Meadow Golf & Tennis 6A 6
Duke's Meadow Golf Course 6A 6
Duke's Meadows 6A 6
Dukes Rd. KT12: Hers 2C 26
Duke St. TW9: Rich 1E 10
Dullshot Grn. KT17: Eps 2B 34
Dumbleton Cl. KT1: King T 5J 17
Dunbar Ct. KT12: Walt T 5B 20
Dunbar Rd. KT3: N Mald 1K 23
Dunbridge Ho. SW15 3C 12
Duncan Rd. KT20: Tad 7H 35
TW9: Rich 1F 11
Dundas Gdns. KT8: W Mole 7G 15

Dundela Gdns. KT4: Wor Pk 1E 30
Dundonald Rd. SW19 4H 19
Dundonald Road Stop
(London Tramlink) 4J 19
Dungannon Ho. *SW6* *4K 7*
(off Vanston Pl.)
Dungarvan Av. SW15 1D 12
Dunhill Point SW15 5D 12
Dunleary Cl. TW4: Houn 4E 8
Dunmore Rd. SW20 5F 19
Dunmow Cl. TW13: Hanw 7D 8
Dunnymans Rd. SM7: Bans 4J 35
Dunsany Rd. W14 1G 7
Dunsford Way SW15 3E 12
Dunsmore Rd. KT12: Walt T 3A 20
Dunstable Rd. KT8: W Mole 1E 20
TW9: Rich 1F 11
Dunstall Rd. SW20 3E 18
Dunstall Way KT8: W Mole 7G 15
Dunster Av. SM4: Mord 5G 25
Dunton Cl. KT6: Surb 5F 23
Dunvegan Cl. KT8: W Mole 1F 21
Dupont Rd. SW20 6G 19
Durbin Rd. KT9: Chess 1F 29
Durford Cres. SW15 5E 12
Durham Cl. SW20 6E 18
Durham Ct. TW11: Tedd 1K 15
Durham Rd. SW20 5E 18
TW14: Felt 4B 8
W5 1E 4
Durham Wharf Dr. TW8: Bford 4D 4
Durlston Rd. KT2: King T 3F 17
Durnsford Av. SW19 6K 13
Durnsford Rd. SW19 6K 13
Durrell Rd. SW6 5J 7
Durrels Ho. *W14* *1J 7*
(off Warwick Gdns.)
Durrington Av. SW20 4F 19
Durrington Pk. Rd. SW20 5F 19
Dutch Gdns. KT2: King T 3J 17
Dutch Yd. SW18 2K 13
Duxberry Av. TW13: Felt 7B 8
Dyer Ho. TW12: Hamp 5G 15
Dyers La. SW15 1E 12
Dymes Path SW19 6G 13
Dynevor Rd. TW10: Rich 2F 11
Dysart Av. KT2: King T 2D 16

E

Ealing Pk. Gdns. W5 1D 4
Ealing Pk. Mans. *W5* *1E 4*
(off Sth. Ealing Rd.)
Ealing Rd. TW8: Bford 2E 4
Eardley Cres. SW5 2K 7
Earldom Rd. SW15 1F 13
Earle Gdns. KT2: King T 4F 17
Earl Rd. SW14 1K 11
EARL'S COURT 1K 7
Earl's Ct. Gdns. SW5 1K 7
Earl's Ct. Rd. SW5 1K 7
W8 1K 7
Earl's Ct. Sq. SW5 2K 7
Earl's Court Station
(Underground) 1K 7
Earlsfield Ho. KT2: King T 2B 36
Earls Ho. TW9: Kew 4J 5
Earls Ter. W8 1J 7
Earls Wlk. W8 1K 7
Earsby St. W14 1H 7
(not continuous)
Easedale Ho. TW7: Isle 2A 10
Eashing Point *SW15* *5E 12*
(off Wanborough Dr.)
Eastbank Rd. TW12: Hamp H 2H 15
Eastbourne Gdns. SW14 7K 5
Eastbourne Rd. TW8: Bford 2D 4
TW13: Felt 6C 8
W4 3K 5
Eastbury Gro. W4 2B 6
Eastbury Rd.
KT2: King T 1C 36 (4F 17)
Eastcote Av. KT8: W Mole 2E 20
Eastcote Ho. KT17: Eps 1B 34
Eastcott Cl. KT2: King T 2K 17
Eastcroft Rd. KT19: Ewe 4B 30
Eastdean Av. KT18: Eps 2J 33
EAST EWELL 6F 31
Eastfields Av. SW18 1K 13
Eastgate SM7: Bans 3J 35
East La. KT1: King T 5B 36 (7E 16)
Eastleigh Wlk. SW15 4D 12
Eastman Way KT19: Eps 6J 29
EAST MOLESEY 1J 21
Eastmont Rd. KT10: Hin W 6K 21

East Putney Station
(Underground) 2H 13
East Rd. KT2: King T 1D 36 (5F 17)
EAST SHEEN 1K 11
E. Sheen Av. SW14 2A 12
East St. KT17: Eps 2B 34
Eastway KT19: Eps 7A 30
SM4: Mord 2G 25
Eastwick Rd. KT12: Hers 3A 26
Eaton Dr. KT2: King T 4H 17
Eaton Rd. TW3: Houn 1J 9
Ebbas Way KT18: Eps 4J 33
Ebbisham Cen. KT19: Eps 2A 34
Ebbisham Rd. KT4: Wor Pk 6F 25
KT18: Eps 3J 33
Ebbisham Sports Club 7K 29
Ebor Cotts. SW15 7B 12
Eclipse, The KT10: Esh 6G 21
Eclipse Ind. Est. KT19: Eps 2K 33
Eddiscombe Rd. SW6 6J 7
Ede Cl. TW3: Houn 1E 8
Ede Ct. *KT17: Eps* *1C 34*
(off East St.)
Edenfield Gdns. KT4: Wor Pk 7C 24
Edenhurst Av. SW6 7J 7
Edensor Gdns. W4 4B 6
Edensor Rd. W4 4B 6
Eden St. KT1: King T 4B 36 (6E 16)
Eden Wlk. KT1: King T 4B 36 (6F 17)
Edgar Ct. KT3: N Mald 6B 18
Edgarley Ter. SW6 5H 7
Edgar Rd. TW4: Houn 4E 8
Edgar Wright Ct. *SW6* *4J 7*
(off Dawes Rd.)
Edgecombe Ho. SW19 5H 13
Edgecoombe Cl. KT2: King T 4A 18
Edge Hill SW19 4G 19
Edge Hill Ct. SW19 4G 19
Edgehill Ct. KT12: Walt T 5B 20
Edinburgh Ct. KT1: King T 5C 36
SW20 2G 25
Edith Gdns. KT5: Surb 4J 23
Edith Ho. *W6* *2F 7*
(off Queen Caroline St.)
Edith Rd. W14 1H 7
Edith Summerskill Ho. *SW6* *4J 7*
(off Clem Attlee Ct.)
Edith Vs. W14 1J 7
Edmonds Ct. KT8: W Mole 2G 21
Edmund Gro. TW13: Hanw 6E 8
Edna Rd. SW20 6G 19
Edward Cl. TW12: Hamp H 2H 15
Edwardes Pl. W8 1J 7
Edwardes Sq. W8 1J 7
Edward Ho. W14 1J 7
Edward Rd. TW12: Hamp H 2H 15
Edwards Cl. KT4: Wor Pk 6G 25
Edwin Rd. TW1: Twick 5A 10
TW2: Twick 5K 9
Edwin Stray Ho. TW13: Hanw 6F 9
Edwyn Ho. *SW18* *3K 13*
(off Neville Gill Cl.)
Eel Brook Cl. SW6 5K 7
Eel Pie Island TW1: Twick 5B 10
Effie Pl. SW6 4K 7
Effie Rd. SW6 4K 7
Effingham Lodge KT1: King T 1E 22
Effingham Rd. KT6: Surb 4C 22
Effra Rd. SW19 3K 19
Egbury Ho. *SW15* *3C 12*
(off Tangley Gro.)
Egerton Rd. KT3: N Mald 1C 24
TW2: Twick 4K 9
Egham Cl. SM3: Cheam 6H 25
SW19 6H 13
Egham Cres. SM3: Cheam 7H 25
Egleton Ho. SW15 4D 12
Egliston M. SW15 7F 7
Egliston Rd. SW15 7F 7
Egmont Av. KT6: Surb 5G 23
Egmont Ct. *KT12: Walt T* *4A 20*
(off Egmont Rd.)
Egmont M. KT19: Ewe 1A 30
Egmont Rd. KT3: N Mald 1C 24
KT6: Surb 5G 23
KT12: Walt T 4A 20
Elborough St. SW18 5K 13
Elder Cl. KT17: Eps D 4F 35
Elder Ho. KT1: King T 2B 36
Eleanor Av. KT19: Ewe 6A 30
Eleanor Gro. SW13 7B 6
Eleanor Ho. *W6* *2F 7*
(off Queen Caroline St.)
Electric Pde. KT6: Surb 3E 22
Elfin Gro. TW11: Tedd 2A 16
Elgar Av. KT5: Surb 5H 23

Elgar Ct. W14 . . . . .1H 7
(off Blythe Rd.)
Eliot Ct. SW18 . . . . .3K 13
Eliot Gdns. SW15 . . . . .1D 12
Elizabeth Cl. SM1: Sutt 1J 31
Elizabeth Ct.
KT2: King T 1C 36 (5F 17)
TW11: Tedd 2K 15
TW16: Sun 7B 14
(off Elizabeth Gdns.)
Elizabeth Gdns. TW7: Isle 1B 10
TW16: Sun 7B 14
Elizabeth Ho. SM3: Cheam 3H 31
W6 . . . . .2F 7
(off Queen Caroline St.)
Elizabeth Way TW13: Hanw 1B 14
Ellaline Rd. W6 . . . . .3G 7
Elland Rd. KT12: Walt T 6C 20
Ellenborough Pl. SW15 . . . . .1D 12
Ellen Wilkinson Ho. SW6 . . . . .3J 7
(off Clem Attlee Ct.)
Elleray Rd. TW11: Tedd 3A 16
Ellerby St. SW6 . . . . .5G 7
Ellerdine Rd. TW3: Houn 1H 9
Ellerker Gdns. TW10: Rich 3F 11
Ellerman Av. TW2: Whitt 5E 8
Ellerton Rd. KT6: Surb 6G 23
SW13 . . . . .5D 6
SW20 . . . . .4D 18
Ellesmere Ct. W4 . . . . .2A 6
Ellesmere Rd. TW1: Twick 3D 10
W4 . . . . .3K 5
Ellingham Rd. KT9: Chess 3E 28
Ellington Way KT18: Tatt C 6E 34
Elliott Rd. W4 . . . . .1B 6
Ellisfield Dr. SW15 . . . . .4D 12
Ellison Rd. SW13 . . . . .6C 6
Ellswood Ct. KT6: Surb 4E 22
Elm Bank Gdns. SW13 . . . . .6B 6
Elmbridge Av. KT5: Surb 2J 23
Elmbridge Xcel Leisure Complex
. . . . .2A 20
Elmbrook Cl. TW1: Sun 5A 14
Elmbrook Rd. SM1: Sutt 1J 31
Elm Cl. KT5: Surb 4K 23
SW20 . . . . .1F 25
TW2: Twick 6G 9
Elm Ct. KT8: W Mole 1G 21
Elm Cres. KT2: King T . . .2D 36 (5F 17)
Elmcroft Cl. KT9: Chess 7F 23
Elmcroft Dr. KT9: Chess 7F 23
Elmdene KT5: Surb 5K 23
Elm Dr. TW16: Sun 6B 14
Elmer Gdns. TW7: Isle 1J 9
Elmers Dr. TW11: Tedd 3C 16
Elmfield Av. TW11: Tedd 2A 16
Elm Gdns. KT10: Clay 3A 28
KT18: Tatt C 7F 35
Elmgate Av. TW13: Felt 7A 8
Elm Gro. KT2: King T 2D 36 (5F 17)
KT12: Walt T 5A 20
KT18: Eps 3K 33
SW19 . . . . .4H 19
Elm Gro. Rd. SW13 . . . . .5D 6
Elm Ho. KT2: King T 4G 17
(off Elm Rd.)
Elm Lodge SW6 . . . . .5F 7
Elm Rd. KT2: King T 2E 36 (5G 17)
KT3: N Mald 6A 18
KT9: Chess 1F 29
KT10: Clay 3A 28
KT17: Ewe 3C 30
SW14 . . . . .7K 5
Elm Rd. W. SM3: Sutt 4J 25
Elms, The KT10: Clay 4A 28
SW13 . . . . .7C 6
Elmshaw Rd. SW15 . . . . .2D 12
Elmshorn KT17: Eps D 5F 35
Elmsleigh Ho. TW2: Twick 6J 9
(off Staines Rd.)
Elmsleigh Rd. TW2: Twick 6J 9
Elmslie Cl. KT18: Eps 3K 33
Elmstead Cl. KT19: Ewe 2B 30
Elmstead Gdns. KT4: Wor Pk 7D 24
Elmstone Rd. SW6 . . . . .5K 7
Elm Tree Av. KT10: Esh 4J 21
Elmtree Rd. TW11: Tedd 1K 15
Elm Wlk. SW20 . . . . .1F 25
Elm Way KT4: Wor Pk 7F 25
KT19: Ewe 2A 30
Elmwood Av. TW13: Felt, Hanw 6A 8
Elmwood Cl. KT17: Ewe 4D 30
KT21: Asht 6E 32
Elmwood Ct. KT21: Asht 6E 32

Elmwood Dr. KT17: Ewe 3D 30
Elmwood Rd. W4 . . . . .3K 5
Elsenham St. SW18 . . . . .5J 13
Elsinore Ho. W6 . . . . .2G 7
(off Fulham Pal. Rd.)
Elsinore Way TW9: Rich 7J 5
Elsrick Av. SM4: Mord 2K 25
Elstead Cl. SM3: Sutt 5H 25
Elsworthy KT7: T Ditt 3K 21
Elthiron Rd. SW6 . . . . .5K 7
Elthorne Ct. TW13: Felt 5B 8
Elthorne Sports Cen. 1A 4
Elton Cl. KT1: Hamp W 4D 16
Elton Rd. KT2: King T 5G 17
Elvedon Rd. KT11: Cobh 7A 26
Ely Cl. KT3: N Mald 4C 18
Ely Ct. KT1: King T 6H 17
Elysium Pl. SW6 . . . . .6J 7
(off Elysium St.)
Elysium St. SW6 . . . . .6J 7
Emanuel Dr. TW12: Hamp 2E 14
Embankment SW15 . . . . .6G 7
Embankment, The
TW1: Twick 5B 10
Ember Cen. KT12: Walt T 6D 20
Embercourt Rd. KT7: T Ditt 3K 21
Ember Farm Av. KT8: E Mos 3J 21
Ember Farm Way
KT8: E Mos 3J 21
Ember Gdns. KT7: T Ditt 4K 21
Ember La. KT8: E Mos 4J 21
KT10: Esh 4J 21
Embleton Wlk. TW12: Hamp 2E 14
Emerald Sq. SW15 . . . . .2D 12
Emerson M. KT3: N Mald 1B 24
Emery Walker Trust 2D 6
(off Hammersmith Ter.)
Emily Davison Dr. KT18: Tatt C 7E 34
Emlyn Rd. W12 . . . . .1C 6
Emmeline Ct. KT12: Walt T 4B 20
Emms Pas.
KT1: King T 4B 36 (6E 16)
Empress App. SW6 . . . . .2K 7
Empress Pl. SW6 . . . . .2K 7
Empress State Bldg. SW6 . . . . .2K 7
Enclave, The SW13 . . . . .6C 6
Endsleigh Gdns. KT6: Surb 3D 22
KT12: Hers 2B 26
Endway KT5: Surb 4J 23
Energize Fitness Club
Hammersmith 2H 7
(off Gliddon Rd.)
Enfield Rd. TW8: Bford 2E 4
Enfield Wlk. TW8: Bford 2E 4
Engadine St. SW18 . . . . .5J 13
England Way KT3: N Mald 1J 23
Enmore Gdns. SW14 . . . . .2A 12
Enmore Rd. SW15 . . . . .1F 13
Ennerdale Cl. SM1: Sutt 1J 31
Ennerdale Rd. TW9: Kew, Rich 6G 5
Ennismore Av. W4 . . . . .1C 6
Ennismore Gdns. KT7: T Ditt 3K 21
Ennor Ct. SM3: Cheam 1F 31
Enterprise Ho. KT12: Walt T 4A 20
Enterprise Way SW18 . . . . .1K 13
TW11: Tedd 3A 16
Epirus M. SW6 . . . . .4K 7
Epirus Rd. SW6 . . . . .4J 7
Epple Rd. SW6 . . . . .5J 7
EPSOM 2A 34
Epsom Bus. Pk. KT17: Eps 7B 30
Epsom College Fitness Cen. 4D 34
Epsom Common Local Nature Reserve
. . . . .2G 33
EPSOM DAY SURGERY CENTRE
. . . . .2C 34
EPSOM DOWNS 7B 34
Epsom Downs Racecourse 7C 34
Epsom Downs Station (Rail) 4E 34
Epsom Gap KT9: Lea 4C 32
EPSOM GENERAL HOSPITAL 4K 33
Epsom Golf Course 4D 34
Epsom La. Nth.
KT18: Tad, Tatt C 7E 34
Epsom Playhouse 2A 34
Epsom Rd. KT17: Ewe 7C 30
KT21: Asht 7G 33
SM3: Sutt 4J 25
SM4: Mord 4J 25
Epsom Sports Club 4A 34
Epsom Station (Rail) 2A 34
Epsom Trade Pk. KT19: Eps 7A 30
Epworth Rd. TW7: Isle 4C 4
Equus Equestrian Cen. 6G 29
Ericcson Cl. SW18 . . . . .2K 13
Erin Cl. SW6 . . . . .4K 7

Erncroft Way TW1: Twick 3A 10
Ernest Cotts. KT17: Ewe 4C 30
Ernest Gdns. W4 . . . . .3J 5
Ernest Rd. KT1: King T 6J 17
Ernest Sq. KT1: King T 6J 17
Ernle Rd. SW20 . . . . .4E 18
Ernshaw Pl. SW15 . . . . .2H 13
Erpingham Rd. SW15 . . . . .7F 7
Erridge Rd. SW19 . . . . .6K 19
Errol Gdns. KT3: N Mald 1D 24
ESHER 1G 27
Esher Av. KT12: Walt T 4A 20
SM3: Cheam 7G 25
Esher By-Pass KT9: Chess 3D 28
KT10: Clay 6F 27
KT10: Esh 6F 27
KT11: Cobh 7A 26
KT22: Oxs 6F 27
Esher Cl. KT10: Esh 2G 27
ESHER COMMON 6H 27
Esher Common (Local Nature Reserve)
. . . . .6F 27
Esher Gdns. SW19 . . . . .6G 13
Esher Grn. KT10: Esh 1G 27
Esher Grn. Dr. KT10: Esh 7F 21
Esher Pk. Av. KT10: Esh 1G 27
Esher Pl. Av. KT10: Esh 1F 27
Esher Rd. KT8: E Mos 3J 21
KT12: Hers 2C 26
Esher RUFC 6D 20
Esher Station (Rail) 6J 21
Esmond Gdns. W4 . . . . .1A 6
Esmond Rd. W4 . . . . .1A 6
Esmond St. SW15 . . . . .1H 13
Essex Av. TW7: Isle 1K 9
Essex Cl. SM4: Mord 4G 25
Essex Ct. SW13 . . . . .6C 6
Essex Rd. W4 . . . . .1K 5
(not continuous)
Essex Pl. Sq. W4 . . . . .1A 6
Essex Rd. W4 . . . . .1A 6
Estcourt Rd. SW6 . . . . .4J 7
Estella Av. KT3: N Mald 1E 24
Estridge Cl. TW3: Houn 1F 9
Eswarah Ho. KT17: Eps 7C 30
(off Epsom Rd.)
Eternit Wlk. SW6 . . . . .5F 7
Ethel Bailey Cl. KT19: Eps 1H 33
Ethelbert Rd. SW20 . . . . .5G 19
Eton Av. KT3: N Mald 2A 24
Eton Ho. KT18: Eps 2K 33
(off Dalmeny Way)
Eton St. TW9: Rich 2F 11
Etwell Pl. KT5: Surb 3G 23
Eureka Rd. KT1: King T 6H 17
Eustace Rd. SW6 . . . . .4K 7
Evans Gro. TW13: Hanw 6F 9
Evans Ho. TW13: Hanw 6F 9
Evelyn Cl. TW2: Whitt 4G 9
Evelyn Gdns. TW9: Rich 1F 11
Evelyn Mans. W14 . . . . .3H 7
(off Queen's Club Gdns.)
Evelyn Rd. TW9: Rich 7F 5
TW10: Ham 7D 10
W4 . . . . .1A 6
Evelyn Ter. TW9: Rich 7F 5
Evelyn Way KT19: Eps 7H 29
Evenwood Cl. SW15 . . . . .2H 13
Everatt Cl. SW18 . . . . .3J 13
Everdon Rd. SW13 . . . . .3D 6
Everglades, The TW3: Houn 1H 9
Everington St. W6 . . . . .3G 7
Eve Rd. TW7: Isle 4B 4
Eversfield Rd. TW9: Kew 6G 5
Eversley Pk. SW19 . . . . .3E 18
Eversley Rd. KT5: Surb 1G 23
Evesham Cl. SM2: Sutt 4K 31
Evesham Grn. SM4: Mord 3K 25
Evesham Ter. KT6: Surb 3E 22
Ewald Rd. SW6 . . . . .6J 7
EWELL 5C 30
Ewell By-Pass KT17: Ewe 4D 30
Ewell Cl. KT17: Ewe 4D 30
Ewell Ct. Av. KT19: Ewe 2B 30
Ewell Downs Rd. KT17: Ewe 7D 30
Ewell East Station (Rail) 6E 30
Ewell Gro. Ct. KT17: Ewe 5C 30
(off West St.)
Ewell Ho. KT17: Ewe 6C 30
(off Ewell Ho. Gro.)
Ewell Ho. Gro. KT17: Ewe 6C 30
Ewell Ho. Pde. KT17: Ewe 6C 30
(off Epsom Rd.)
Ewell Pk. Gdns. KT17: Ewe 4D 30
Ewell Pk. Way KT17: Ewe 3D 30

Ewell Rd. KT6: Surb 4C 22
(Mount Holme)
KT6: Surb 3F 23
(South Ter.)
SM3: Cheam 3G 31
Ewell West Station (Rail) 5B 30
Excelsior Cl. KT1: King T 6H 17
Exeter Ct. KT6: Surb 2F 23
(off Maple Rd.)
Exeter Ho. SW15 . . . . .3F 13
TW13: Hanw 6E 8
(off Watermill Way)
Exeter M. SW6 . . . . .4K 7
Exeter Rd. TW13: Hanw 7E 8
Eyot Gdns. W6 . . . . .2C 6
Eyot Grn. W4 . . . . .2C 6

F

Fabian Rd. SW6 . . . . .4J 7
Faggs Rd. TW14: Felt 2A 8
Fairacre KT3: N Mald 7B 18
Fairacres KT11: Cobh 7C 26
SW15 . . . . .1C 12
Fairbriar Ct. KT18: Eps 2B 34
(off Hereford Cl.)
Fairburn Ct. SW15 . . . . .2H 13
Fairburn Ho. W14 . . . . .2J 7
(off Ivatt Pl.)
Faircroft Ct. TW11: Tedd 3B 16
Fairdale Gdns. SW15 . . . . .1E 12
Fairfax Av. KT17: Ewe 5E 30
Fairfax Cl. KT12: Walt T 5A 20
Fairfax Ho. KT1: King T 5E 36
Fairfax M. SW15 . . . . .1F 13
Fairfax Pl. W14 . . . . .1H 7
Fairfax Rd. TW11: Tedd 3B 16
W4 . . . . .1B 6
Fairfield KT1: King T 4E 36
Fairfield Av. TW2: Whitt 5G 9
Fairfield Cl. KT19: Ewe 2B 30
Fairfield E.
KT1: King T 3D 36 (6F 17)
Fairfield Nth.
KT1: King T 3D 36 (6F 17)
Fairfield Pl.
KT1: King T 5D 36 (7F 17)
Fairfield Rd.
KT1: King T 4D 36 (6F 17)
Fairfield Road Bus Station
. . . . .3D 36 (6F 17)
Fairfield Sth.
KT1: King T 4D 36 (6F 17)
Fairfields Rd. TW3: Houn 1H 9
Fairfield Trade Pk.
KT1: King T 7G 17
Fairfield Way KT19: Ewe 2B 30
Fairfield W.
KT1: King T 4D 36 (6F 17)
Fairford Gdns. KT4: Wor Pk 6C 24
Fairhall Ct. KT5: Surb 4G 23
Fairholme Cres. KT21: Asht 6D 32
Fairholme Rd. SM1: Sutt 3J 31
W14 . . . . .2H 7
Fairlands Av. SM1: Sutt 6K 25
Fairlawn KT2: King T 3K 17
Fairlawn Av. W4 . . . . .1K 5
Fairlawn Cl. KT2: King T 3K 17
KT10: Clay 3A 28
TW13: Hanw 1E 14
Fairlawn Dr. W4 . . . . .1K 5
Fairlawn Gro. W4 . . . . .1K 5
Fairlawn Rd. SW19 . . . . .4J 19
Fairlawns TW1: Twick 3D 10
Fairlight TW12: Hamp H 2G 15
Fairlight Cl. KT4: Wor Pk 1F 31
Fairmead KT5: Surb 5J 23
Fairmead Cl. KT3: N Mald 7A 18
Fairmead Ct. TW9: Rich 6J 5
Fairmile Golf Range 7B 26
Fairmile Ho. TW11: Tedd 1B 16
Fairmile La. KT11: Cobh 7C 26
Fairoak Cl. KT22: Oxs 7J 27
Fairoak La. KT9: Chess 7J 27
KT22: Oxs 7J 27
Fairs Rd. KT22: Lea 7B 32
Fair St. TW3: Houn 1H 9
Fairview TW17: 7F 31
Fairview Rd. KT17: Ewe 7C 30
Fairwater Ho. TW11: Tedd 1B 16
Fairway SW20 . . . . .7F 19
Fairway, The KT3: N Mald 5A 18
KT8: W Mole 7G 15
KT22: Lea 7B 32

airway Cl. KT10: Surb .7C 22
KT19: Ewe .1K 29
TW4: Houn .2B 8
(Amberley Way)
TW4: Houn .2C 8
(Islay Gdns.)
airways TW11: Tedd .4E 16
airway Trad. Est.
TW4: Houn .2B 8
alcon Cl. W4 .3K 5
alcon Rd. TW12: Hamp .4E 14
alconry Ct. KT1: King T .5D 36
alcon Way TW14: Felt .2A 8
alkland Ho. *W14* .*2J 7*
(off Edith Vs.)
allow Pl. TW11: Tedd .2K 15
almouth Ho. KT2: King T .2B 36
almouth Rd. KT12: Hers .1B 26
almouth Wlk. SW15 .3D 12
alstaff M. *TW12: Hamp H* .*2J 15*
(off High St.)
ane St. W14 .3J 7
anshawe Rd. TW10: Ham .1D 16
anthorpe St. SW15 .7F 7
araday Mans. *W14* .*3H 7*
(off Queen's Club Gdns.)
araday Pl. KT8: W Mole .1F 21
araday Rd. KT8: W Mole .1F 21
SW19 .3K 19
areham Rd. TW14: Felt .4B 8
arlington Pl. SW15 .4E 12
arlow Rd. SW15 .7G 7
arm Cl. SW6 .4K 7
arm La. KT21: Asht .6H 33
SW6 .3K 7
arm Rd. KT10: Esh .5G 21
TW4: Houn .5D 8
armside Pl. KT19: Eps .1G 33
armstead KT19: Eps .5H 29
arm Way KT4: Wor Pk .7F 25
arnborough Ho. SW15 .5D 12
arnell M. SW5 .2K 7
arnell Rd. TW7: Isle .1J 9
arnham Ct. SM3: Cheam .3H 31
arnham Gdns. SW20 .6E 18
aroe Rd. W14 .1G 7
arquhar Rd. SW19 .7K 13
arrer Ct. TW1: Twick .4E 10
arrier Pl. SM1: Sutt .7K 25
arriers Cl. KT17: Eps .1B 34
arriers Rd. KT17: Eps .7B 30
arringdon Ho. TW9: Kew .4J 5
arthings, The KT2: King T .5H 17
assett Rd.
KT1: King T .7C 36 (1F 23)
auconberg Ct. *W4* .*3K 5*
(off Fauconberg Rd.)
Fauconberg Rd. W4 .3K 5
Faulkner Ho. W6 .3F 7
Faulkners Rd. KT12: Hers .2B 26
Favart Rd. SW6 .5K 7
Fawcus Cl. KT10: Clay .3K 27
Fawe Pk. M. SW15 .1J 13
Fawe Pk. Rd. SW15 .1J 13
Fearnley Cres. TW12: Hamp .2D 14
Fee Farm Rd. KT10: Clay .4A 28
Felbridge Ct. *TW13: Felt* .*5A 8*
(off High St.)
Felcott Cl. KT12: Hers .7B 20
Felcott Rd. KT12: Hers .7B 20
Felden St. SW6 .5J 7
Felgate M. W6 .1E 6
Felix Rd. KT12: Walt T .3A 20
Fellbrook TW10: Ham .7C 10
Felsham M. *SW15* .*7G 7*
(off Felsham Rd.)
Felsham Rd. SW15 .7F 7
Felstead Rd. KT19: Eps .7A 30
FELTHAM .5A 8
Feltham Av. KT8: E Mos .1K 21
Felthambrook Ind. Est.
TW13: Felt .7A 8
Felthambrook Way TW13: Felt .7A 8
Feltham Bus. Complex
TW13: Felt .6A 8
Feltham Corporate Cen.
TW13: Felt .7A 8
FELTHAMHILL .2A 14
Feltham Station (Rail) .5A 8
Fendall Rd. KT19: Ewe .2K 29
Fenelon Pl. W14 .1J 7
Fengate Cl. KT9: Chess .3E 28
Fen La. SW13 .5E 6
Fennells Mead KT17: Ewe .5C 30
Fenn Ho. TW7: Isle .5C 4
Ferguson Av. KT5: Surb .2G 23
Fernbank Av. KT12: Walt T .4D 20
Ferndale Rd. SM7: Bans .5J 35
Ferney Meade Way TW7: Isle .6B 4
Fern Gro. TW14: Felt .4A 8
Fernhill Gdns. KT2: King T .2E 16
Fernhurst Rd. SW6 .5H 7
Fernlea Pl. KT11: Cobh .7C 26
Fernleigh Cl. KT12: Walt T .7A 20
Fernside KT7: T Ditt .5C 22
Fernside Av. TW13: Felt .1A 14
Fernwood SW19 .5J 13
Ferriers Way KT18: Tatt C .7F 35
Ferry La. SW13 .3C 6
TW8: Bford .3F 5
TW9: Kew .3G 5
Ferrymoor TW10: Ham .7C 10
Ferry Quays TW8: Bford .3F 5
(Ferry La.)
TW8: Bford .*4E 4*
(off Point Wharf La.)
Ferry Rd. KT7: T Ditt .3C 22
KT8: W Mole .7F 15
SW13 .4D 6
TW1: Twick .5C 10
TW11: Tedd .2C 16
Ferry Sq. TW8: Bford .4F 5
Ferry Wharf TW8: Bford .4F 5
Festing Rd. SW15 .7G 7
Field Cl. KT8: W Mole .2G 21
KT9: Chess .2D 28
FIELDCOMMON .4E 20
Fieldcommon La.
KT12: Walt T .5D 20
Field Ct. SW19 .7K 13
Fieldend TW1: Twick .1A 16
Fielding Av. TW2: Twick .7H 9
Fielding Ho. *W4* .*3B 6*
(off Devonshire Rd.)
Fielding M. SW13 .3E 6
Fieldings, The SM7: Bans .6J 35
Field La. TW8: Bford .4D 4
TW11: Tedd .2B 16
Field Pl. KT3: N Mald .3C 24
Field Rd. TW14: Felt .3A 8
W6 .2H 7
Fieldsend Rd. SM3: Cheam .2H 31
Fife Rd. KT1: King T .3C 36 (6F 17)
SW14 .2K 11
Fifth Cross Rd. TW2: Twick .6J 9
Filament Wlk. *SW18* .*2K 13*
(off Spectrum Way)
Filby Rd. KT9: Chess .3G 29
Filmer Chambers *SW6* .*5H 7*
(off Filmer Rd.)
Filmer Ho. *SW6* .*5J 7*
(off Filmer Rd.)
Filmer M. SW6 .5J 7
Filmer Rd. SW6 .5H 7
Finborough Rd. SW10 .2K 7
Finchdean Ho. SW15 .4C 12
Finch Dr. TW14: Felt .4C 8
Findon Cl. SW18 .3K 13
Finlays Cl. KT9: Chess .2H 29
Finlay St. SW6 .5G 7
Finney La. TW7: Isle .5B 4
Finucane Ct. *TW9: Rich* .*7G 5*
(off Lwr. Mortlake Rd.)
Fir Cl. KT12: Walt T .4A 20
Fircroft Rd. KT9: Chess .1G 29
Firdene KT5: Surb .5K 23
Fire Bell All. KT6: Surb .3F 23
Firestone Ho. TW8: Bford .2F 5
Fir Gro. KT3: N Mald .3C 24
Firle Ct. KT17: Eps .1C 34
Firman Cl. KT3: N Mald .1B 24
Fir Rd. SM3: Sutt .5J 25
TW13: Hanw .2C 14
Firs Av. SW14 .1K 11
Firs Cl. KT10: Clay .3K 27
First Av. KT8: W Mole .1E 20
KT12: Walt T .3A 20
KT19: Ewe .5B 30
SW14 .7B 6
First Cl. KT8: W Mole .7H 15
First Cross Rd. TW2: Twick .6K 9
First Quarter KT19: Eps .7B 30
First Slip KT22: Lea .7B 32
Firstway SW20 .6F 19
Firswood Av. KT19: Ewe .2B 30
Firth Gdns. SW6 .5H 7
Fir Tree Cl. KT10: Esh .2H 27
KT17: Eps D .4F 35
KT19: Ewe .1C 30
Fir Tree Rd. KT17: Eps D .5E 34
SM7: Bans .3F 35
TW4: Houn .1D 8
Fir Wlk. SM3: Cheam .3G 31
Fisher Cl. KT12: Hers .1A 26
Fisherman Cl. TW10: Ham .1C 16
Fisherman's Pl. W4 .3C 6
Fishersdene KT10: Clay .4B 28
Fisher's La. W4 .1A 6
Fitness4less
Sutton .3K 31
Fitness First
Hammersmith .1F 7
Fitrooms .*3J 7*
(off North End Rd.)
Fitzalan Ho. KT17: Ewe .6C 30
Fitzalan Rd. KT10: Clay .4K 27
Fitzgeorge Av. KT3: N Mald .5A 18
W14 .1H 7
Fitzgerald Av. SW14 .7B 6
Fitzgerald Rd. KT7: T Ditt .3B 22
SW14 .7A 6
Fitzjames Av. W14 .1H 7
Fitzroy Cres. W4 .4A 6
Fitzwilliam Av. TW9: Rich .6G 5
Fitzwilliam Ho. TW9: Rich .1E 10
Fitzwygram Cl. TW12: Hamp H .2H 15
Five Ways Bus. Cen.
TW13: Felt .7A 8
Flanders Mans. W4 .1C 6
Flanders Rd. W4 .1B 6
Flaxley Rd. SM4: Mord .4K 25
Flaxman Ho. *W4* .*2B 6*
(off Devonshire St.)
Fleece Rd. KT6: Surb .5D 22
Fleet Cl. KT8: W Mole .2E 20
Fleet La. KT8: W Mole .3E 20
Fleetside KT8: W Mole .2E 20
Fleetwood Cl. KT9: Chess .4E 28
Fleetwood Rd. KT1: King T .7J 17
Fleetwood Sq.
KT1: King T .7J 17
Fleming Way TW7: Isle .1A 10
Fleur Gates SW19 .4G 13
Flood La. TW1: Twick .5B 10
Flora Gdns. *W6* .*1E 6*
(off Albion Gdns.)
Floral Ct. KT21: Asht .7D 32
Florence Cl. KT12: Walt T .4A 20
Florence Ct. SW19 .3H 19
Florence Gdns. W4 .3K 5
Florence Ho. *KT2: King T* .*4G 17*
(off Florence Rd.)
Florence Mans. *SW6* .*5J 7*
(off Rostrevor Rd.)
Florence Rd. KT2: King T .4G 17
KT12: Walt T .4A 20
SW19 .3K 19
TW13: Felt .5A 8
Florence Ter. SW15 .7B 12
Florian Rd. SW15 .1H 13
Florys Ct. SW19 .5H 13
Floss St. SW15 .6F 7
Floyer Cl. TW10: Rich .2G 11
Foley M. KT10: Clay .3K 27
Foley Rd. KT10: Clay .4K 27
Foley Wood KT10: Clay .4A 28
Follyfield Rd. SM7: Bans .3K 35
Fontley Way SW15 .4D 12
Footpath, The SW15 .3D 12
Forbes Ho. *W4* .*2H 5*
(off Stonehill Rd.)
Fordbridge Rd. TW16: Sun .1A 20
Fordham *KT1: King T* .*6H 17*
(off Excelsior Cl.)
Fordham Cl. KT4: Wor Pk .5E 24
Foreman Ct. TW1: Twick .5A 10
Forest Cres. KT21: Asht .5H 33
Forest Rd. SM3: Sutt .5K 25
TW9: Kew .4H 5
TW13: Felt .6B 8
Forest Side KT4: Wor Pk .5C 24
Forest Way KT21: Asht .6G 33
Forge Dr. KT10: Clay .4B 28
Forge La. SM3: Cheam .4H 31
TW10: Ham .5F 11
TW13: Hanw .2D 14
TW16: Sun .7A 14
Forge M. *TW16: Sun* .*7A 14*
(off Forge La.)
Fortescue Av. TW2: Twick .7H 9
Forty Footpath SW14 .7K 5
Forum, The KT8: W Mole .1G 21
Foskett Rd. SW6 .6J 7
Foster Rd. W4 .2A 6
Foster's Way SW18 .5K 13
Foundry M. TW3: Houn .1G 9
FOUNTAIN RDBT. .1B 24
Fountains Av. TW13: Hanw .7E 8
Fountains Cl. TW13: Hanw .6E 8
(not continuous)
Four Seasons Cres. SM3: Sutt .6J 25
Four Sq. Ct. TW3: Houn .3F 9
Fourth Cross Rd.
TW2: Twick .6J 9
Foxcombe Rd. SW15 .5D 12
Foxglove La. KT9: Chess .1H 29
Fox Gro. KT12: Walt T .4A 20
Foxhollow Cl. KT12: Walt T .6C 20
Foxton M. TW10: Rich .3F 11
Foxwarren KT10: Clay .5A 28
Foxwood Cl. TW13: Felt .7A 8
Frampton Cl. SM2: Sutt .4K 31
Frampton Rd. TW4: Houn .2D 8
Francis Cl. KT19: Ewe .1A 30
Francis Ct. *KT5: Surb* .*1F 23*
(off Cranes Pk. Av.)
Francis Gro. SW19 .3J 19
Frank Beswick Ho. *SW6* .*3J 7*
(off Clem Attlee Ct.)
Franklin Cl. KT1: King T .7H 17
Franklin Sq. W14 .2J 7
Franklyn Rd. KT12: Walt T .3A 20
Franks Av. KT3: N Mald .1K 23
Frank Soskice Ho. *SW6* .*3J 7*
(off Clem Attlee Ct.)
Fraser Ho. TW8: Bford .2G 5
Fraser St. W4 .2B 6
Frederick Cl. SM1: Sutt .1J 31
Frederick Gdns. SM1: Sutt .2J 31
Frederick Rd. SM1: Sutt .2J 31
Freeman Dr. KT8: W Mole .7E 14
French St. TW16: Sun .6B 14
Frensham Dr. SW15 .7C 12
Frensham Way KT17: Eps D .5F 35
Freshmount Gdns. KT19: Eps .7J 29
Friars Av. SW15 .7C 12
Friars La. TW9: Rich .2E 10
Friars Stile Pl. TW10: Rich .3F 11
Friars Stile Rd. TW10: Rich .3F 11
Frimley Cl. SW19 .6H 13
Frimley Rd. KT9: Chess .2E 28
Friston St. SW6 .6K 7
Fritham Cl. KT3: N Mald .3B 24
Frith Knowle KT12: Hers .2A 26
Frobisher Ct. SM3: Cheam .4H 31
Frogmore SW18 .2K 13
Frogmore Cl. SM3: Cheam .7G 25
Frogmore Gdns.
SM3: Cheam .1H 31
Fromondes Rd.
SM3: Cheam .2H 31
Fulbourn *KT1: King T* .*6H 17*
(off Eureka Rd.)
Fulford Ho. KT19: Ewe .4A 30
Fulford Rd. KT19: Ewe .4A 30
FULHAM .6H 7
FULHAM BROADWAY .4K 7
Fulham B'way. SW6 .4K 7
Fulham B'way Shop. Cen.
SW6 .4K 7
Fulham Broadway Station
(Underground) .4K 7
Fulham Ct. SW6 .5K 7
Fulham FC .5G 7
Fulham High St. SW6 .6H 7
Fulham Island *SW6* .*4K 7*
(off Fulham Rd.)
Fulham Palace .6H 7
Fulham Pal. Rd. SW6 .2F 7
W6 .2F 7
Fulham Pk. Gdns. SW6 .6J 7
Fulham Pk. Rd. SW6 .6J 7
Fulham Pools
Virgin Active .3H 7
Fulham Rd. SW6 .6H 7
(not continuous)
Fullbrooks Av. KT4: Wor Pk .5C 24
Fullers Av. KT6: Surb .6G 23
Fuller's Griffin Brewery & Vis. Cen.
.3C 6
Fullers Way Nth. KT6: Surb .7G 23
Fullers Way Sth. KT9: Chess .1F 29
Fullerton Ct. TW11: Tedd .3B 16
Fulmar Cl. KT5: Surb .3G 23
Fulmer Cl. TW12: Hamp .2D 14
Fulmer Way W13 .1C 4
Fulstone Cl. TW4: Houn .1E 8
FULWELL .1J 15
Fulwell Golf Course .1J 15
Fulwell Pk. Av. TW2: Twick .6G 9
Fulwell Rd. TW11: Tedd .1J 15
Fulwell Station (Rail) .1J 15
Fulwood Gdns. TW1: Twick .3A 10
Fulwood Wlk. SW19 .5H 13

Furber St.—Grayswood Point

Furber St. W6 1E 6
Furlongs, The KT10: Esh 7G 21
Furrows, The KT12: Walt T 6B 20
Fyfield Cl. KT17: Eps 3C 34

G

Gables, The SM7: Bans 6J 35
Gables Way SM7: Bans 6J 35
Gabriel Cl. TW13: Hanw 1D 14
Gadesden Rd. KT19: Ewe 3K 29
Gainsborough Cl. KT10: Esh 5K 21
Gainsborough Ct.
KT19: Ewe 3C 30
W4 2J 5
(off Chaseley Dr.)
Gainsborough Gdns. TW7: Isle 2J 9
Gainsborough Mans. *W14 3H 7*
(off Queen's Club Gdns.)
Gainsborough Rd.
KT3: N Mald 3A 24
KT19: Eps 6K 29
TW9: Rich 6G 5
W4 1C 6
Gainsborough Ter. *SM2: Sutt 4J 31*
(off Belmont Ri.)
Gala Bingo
Feltham 6A 8
Hounslow 1F 9
Galata Rd. SW13 4D 6
Galba Ct. TW8: Bford 4E 4
Gale Cl. TW12: Hamp 3D 14
Gale Cres. SM7: Bans 6K 35
Galena Arches *W6 1E 6*
(off Galena Rd.)
Galena Rd. W6 1E 6
Galen Cl. KT19: Eps 7H 29
Galgate Cl. SW19 5G 13
Gallops, The KT10: Esh 7G 21
Galsworthy Rd. KT2: King T 4J 17
Galveston Rd. SW15 2J 13
Gamlen Rd. SW15 1G 13
Gander Grn. Cres.
TW12: Hamp 5F 15
Gander Grn. La. SM1: Sutt 7J 25
SM3: Cheam 6H 25
Gap Rd. SW19 2K 19
Garbrand Wlk. KT17: Ewe 5C 30
Garden Cl. KT3: N Mald 1B 24
SM7: Bans 4K 35
SW15 4F 13
TW12: Hamp 2E 14
Garden Ct. TW9: Kew 5G 5
TW12: Hamp 2E 14
W4 1K 5
Gardener Gro. TW13: Hanw 6E 8
Gardenfields KT20: Tad 7H 35
Garden Ho's., The *W6 3G 7*
(off Bothwell St.)
Garden Rd. KT12: Walt T 3A 20
TW9: Rich 7H 5
Garden Royal SW15 3G 13
Gardens, The KT10: Esh 1F 27
Gardner Ho. TW13: Hanw 6E 8
Gardner Pl. TW14: Felt 3A 8
Garendon Gdns. SM4: Mord 4K 25
Garendon Rd. SM4: Mord 4K 25
Gareth Cl. KT4: Wor Pk 6G 25
Garfield Rd. TW1: Twick 5B 10
Garland Ho. KT2: King T 2C 36
Garlichill Rd. KT18: Tatt C 6E 34
Garrard Rd. SM7: Bans 5K 35
Garratt La. SW18 2K 13
Garratts La. SM7: Bans 5J 35
Garraway Ct. *SW13 4F 7*
(off Wyatt Dr.)
Garrick Cl. KT12: Hers 1A 26
TW9: Rich 2E 10
Garrick Gdns. KT8: W Mole 7F 15
Garrick Ho. KT1: King T 7C 36
W4 3B 6
Garrick Rd. TW9: Rich 6H 5
Garricks Ho. KT1: King T 4B 36
Garrison Cl. TW4: Houn 2E 8
Garrison La. KT9: Chess 4E 28
Garsdale Ter. *W14 2J 7*
(off Aisgill Av.)
Garside Cl. TW12: Hamp 3G 15
Garside Ct. TW11: Hamp W 5D 16
Garson Cl. KT10: Esh 2E 26
Garson Rd. KT10: Esh 3E 26
Garth, The TW12: Hamp H 3G 15
Garth Cl. KT2: King T 2G 17
SM4: Mord 4G 25
Garth Ct. W4 2A 6
Garth Rd. KT2: King T 2G 17
SM4: Mord 3F 25
W4 2A 6
Garth Rd. Ind. Cen., The
SM4: Mord 5G 25
Garthside TW10: Ham 2F 17
Gartmoor Gdns. SW19 5J 13
Garton Bank SM7: Bans 6K 35
Gastein Rd. W6 3G 7
Gaston Bell Cl. TW9: Rich 7G 5
Gate Cen., The TW8: Bford 4B 4
Gatehouse Cl. KT2: King T 4K 17
Gateways *KT6: Surb 2F 23*
(off Surbiton Hill Rd.)
Gateways, The *TW9: Rich 1E 10*
(off Park La.)
Gatfield Gro. TW13: Hanw 6F 9
Gatfield Ho. TW13: Hanw 6E 8
Gatley Av. KT19: Ewe 2J 29
Gatwick Rd. SW18 4J 13
Gayfere Rd. KT17: Ewe 2D 30
Gay St. SW15 7G 7
Gayton Cl. KT21: Asht 7F 33
Gaywood Rd. KT21: Asht 7G 33
Geneva Rd.
KT1: King T 7D 36 (1F 23)
Genoa Av. SW15 2F 13
George Lindgren Ho. *SW6 4J 7*
(off Clem Attlee Ct.)
George Rd. KT2: King T 4J 17
KT3: N Mald 1C 24
George Sq. SW19 7K 19
George's Sq. *SW6 3J 7*
(off North End Rd.)
George St. TW9: Rich 2E 10
George Vw. Ho. *SW18 5K 13*
(off Knaresborough Dr.)
George Wyver Cl. SW19 4H 13
Georgia Rd. KT3: N Mald 1K 23
Geraldine Rd. W4 3H 5
Gerald's Gro. SM7: Bans 3G 35
Gerard Av. TW4: Houn 4F 9
Gerard Rd. SW13 5C 6
Gerrards Mead SM7: Bans 5J 35
Gibbon Rd.
KT2: King T 1D 36 (5F 17)
Gibbon Wlk. SW15 1D 12
Gibbs Grn. W14 2J 7
(not continuous)
Gibraltar Cres. KT19: Ewe 6B 30
Gibson Cl. KT9: Chess 2D 28
TW7: Isle 1K 9
Gibson Ct. KT10: Hin W 6A 22
Gibson Ho. SM1: Sutt 1K 31
Gibson M. TW1: Twick 3D 10
Gibson Rd. SM1: Sutt 2K 31
GIGGSHILL 4B 22
Giggs Hill Gdns. KT7: T Ditt 5B 22
Giggs Hill Rd. KT7: T Ditt 4B 22
Gilbert Ho. *SW13 4E 6*
(off Trinity Chu. Rd.)
Gilbert Scott Bldg. SW15 3H 13
Gilberts Lodge KT17: Eps 1B 34
Gilders Rd. KT9: Chess 4G 29
Gilesmead *KT18: Eps 3B 34*
(off Downside)
Gilhams Av. SM7: Bans 1G 35
GILLETTE CORNER 4B 4
Gillian Pk. Rd. SM3: Sutt 5J 25
Gillis Sq. SW15 3D 12
Gilpin Av. SW14 1A 12
Gilpin Cres. TW2: Whitt 4G 9
Gipsy La. SW15 7E 6
Girdler's Rd. W14 1G 7
Girdwood Rd. SW18 4H 13
Gironde Rd. SW6 4J 7
Glade, The KT17: Ewe 3D 30
SM2: Cheam 5H 31
Glade Cl. KT6: Surb 6E 22
Glades, The KT6: Surb 4F 23
Gladeside Cl. KT9: Chess 4E 28
Gladioli Cl. TW12: Hamp 3F 15
Gladsmuir Cl. KT12: Walt T 6B 20
Gladstone Av. TW2: Twick 5J 9
TW14: Felt 3A 8
Gladstone Pl. KT8: E Mos 2K 21
Gladstone Rd. KT1: King T 7H 17
KT6: Surb 6E 22
KT21: Asht 7E 32
SW19 4K 19
W4 1A 6
Gladwyn Rd. SW15 7G 7
Glamorgan Rd.
KT1: Hamp W 1A 36 (4D 16)
Glanville Way KT19: Eps 1F 33
Glasbrook Av. TW2: Whitt 5E 8
Glastonbury Rd. SM4: Mord 4K 25
Glazbury Rd. W14 1H 7
Glazebrook Rd. TW11: Tedd 4A 16
Glebe, The KT4: Wor Pk 5C 24
Glebe Cl. W4 2B 6
Glebe Cotts. *TW13: Hanw 7F 9*
(off Twickenham Rd.)
Glebe Gdns. KT3: N Mald 4B 24
Glebelands KT8: W Mole 2G 21
KT10: Clay 5A 28
Glebe Rd. KT21: Asht 7E 32
SM2: Cheam 5H 31
SW13 6D 6
Glebe Side TW1: Twick 3A 10
Glebe St. W4 2B 6
Glebe Ter. W4 2B 6
Glebe Way TW13: Hanw 7F 9
Gledstanes Rd. W14 2H 7
Glegg Pl. SW15 1G 13
Glen Albyn Rd. SW19 6G 13
Glenallan Ho. *W14 1J 7*
(off North End Cres.)
Glenavon Cl. KT10: Clay 3B 28
Glenavon Ct. KT4: Wor Pk 6E 24
Glenbuck Ct. KT6: Surb 3F 23
Glenbuck Rd. KT6: Surb 3E 22
Glendale Dr. SW19 2J 19
Glendarvon St. SW15 7G 7
Glendower Gdns. SW14 7A 6
Glendower Rd. SW14 7A 6
Glenfield Rd. SM7: Bans 4K 35
Glenhurst Rd. TW8: Bford 3D 4
Glenmill TW12: Hamp 2E 14
Glen Rd. KT9: Chess 1G 29
Glentham Gdns. SW13 3E 6
Glentham Rd. SW13 3D 6
Glenthorne Cl. SM3: Sutt 5K 25
Glenthorne Gdns. SM3: Sutt 5K 25
Glenthorne M. W6 1E 6
Glenthorne Rd.
KT1: King T 7E 36 (1G 23)
W6 1E 6
Glenthorpe Av. SW15 1D 12
Glenthorpe Rd. SM4: Mord 2G 25
Glenvern Ct. *TW7: Isle 6B 4*
(off White Lodge Cl.)
Glenville M. SW18 4K 13
Glenville M. Ind. Est. SW18 4K 13
Glenville Rd. KT2: King T 5H 17
Glen Wlk. TW7: Isle 2J 9
(not continuous)
Glenwood Rd. KT17: Ewe 3D 30
Gliddon Rd. W14 1H 7
Gloster Rd. KT3: N Mald 1B 24
Gloucester *W14 1J 7*
(off Kensington Village)
Gloucester Cl. KT7: T Ditt 5B 22
Gloucester Ct. TW9: Kew 4H 5
Gloucester Ho. TW10: Rich 2H 11
Gloucester Rd. KT1: King T 6H 17
TW2: Twick 5H 9
TW4: Houn 1D 8
TW9: Kew 4H 5
TW11: Tedd 2K 15
TW12: Hamp 4G 15
TW13: Felt 5B 8
Gloxinia Wlk. TW12: Hamp 3F 15
Glyn Cl. KT17: Ewe 5D 30
Glyndale Grange SM2: Sutt 3K 31
Glyn Mans. *W14 1H 7*
(off Hammersmith Rd.)
Glyn Rd. KT4: Wor Pk 6G 25
Goals Soccer Cen.
Gillette Corner 3A 4
Sutton 7G 25
Tolworth 6K 23
Wimbledon 7D 18
Goater's All. *SW6 4J 7*
(off Dawes Rd.)
Goat Wharf TW8: Bford 3F 5
Godfrey Av. TW2: Whitt 4J 9
Godfrey Way TW4: Houn 4D 8
Godolphin Cl. SM2: Cheam 7J 31
Godstone Rd. TW1: Twick 3C 10
Godwin Cl. KT19: Ewe 3K 29
Goldcliff Cl. SM4: Mord 4K 25
Golden Ct. TW9: Rich 2E 10
Golden Mile Ho. *TW8: Bford 2F 5*
(off Clayponds La.)
Goldhawk Rd. W6 1C 6
Goldhurst Ho. W6 3F 7
Golding Cl. KT9: Chess 3D 28
Golf Club Dr. KT2: King T 4A 18
Golf Side SM2: Cheam 7H 31
TW2: Twick 7J 9
Golfside Cl. KT3: N Mald 6B 18
Gomer Gdns. TW11: Tedd 3B 16
Gomer Pl. TW11: Tedd 3B 16
Gomshall Rd. SM2: Cheam 6F 31
Gonston Cl. SW19 6H 13
Gonville St. SW6 7H 7
Goodenough Rd. SW19 4J 19
Gooding Cl. KT3: N Mald 1K 23
Goodwood Cl. SM4: Mord 1K 25
Gordon Av. SW14 1B 12
TW1: Twick 2B 10
Gordondale Rd. SW19 6K 13
Gordon Rd.
KT2: King T 2E 36 (5G 17)
KT5: Surb 4G 23
KT10: Clay 4K 27
TW3: Houn 1H 9
TW9: Rich 6G 5
W4 3J 5
Gore Rd. SW20 6F 19
Gorleston St. W14 1H 7
(not continuous)
Gosbury Hill KT9: Chess 1F 29
Gosfield Rd. KT19: Eps 1A 34
Gostling Rd. TW2: Whitt 5F 9
Gothic Rd. TW2: Twick 6J 9
Gough Ho. KT1: King T 3C 36
Gould Rd. TW2: Twick 5K 9
Gowan Av. SW6 5H 7
Gower Rd. TW7: Isle 3A 4
Graburn Way KT8: E Mos 7J 15
Graemesdyke Av. SW14 7J 5
Grafton Cl. KT4: Wor Pk 7B 24
TW4: Houn 5D 8
Grafton Pk. Rd. KT4: Wor Pk 6B 24
Grafton Rd. KT3: N Mald 7B 18
KT4: Wor Pk 7A 24
Grafton Way KT8: W Mole 1E 20
Graham Gdns. KT6: Surb 5F 23
Graham Rd. SW19 4J 19
TW12: Hamp H 1F 15
Grainger Rd. TW7: Isle 6A 4
Granard Av. SW15 2E 12
Grand Av. KT5: Surb 2J 23
Grand Dr. SW20 6F 19
Grandfield Ct. W4 3A 6
Grandison Rd. KT4: Wor Pk 6F 25
Grand Pde. KT6: Surb 5H 23
SW14 1K 11
(off Up. Richmond Rd. W.)
Grand Pde. M. SW15 2H 13
Grandstand Rd. KT17: Eps D 6C 34
Grand Twr. *SW15 2H 13*
(off Plaza Gdns.)
Grange, The KT3: N Mald 2C 24
KT4: Wor Pk 1A 30
KT12: Walt T 6A 20
SW19 3G 19
W4 2J 5
W14 1J 7
Grange Av. TW2: Twick 6K 9
Grange Cl. KT8: W Mole 1G 21
Grange Gdns. SM7: Bans 2K 35
Grange Lodge SW19 3G 19
Grange Mans. KT17: Ewe 4C 30
Grange Pk. Pl. SW20 4E 18
Grange Pl. KT12: Walt T 6A 20
Grange Rd.
KT1: King T 5C 36 (7F 17)
KT8: W Mole 1G 21
KT9: Chess 1F 29
KT12: Hers 1D 26
SM2: Sutt 4K 31
SW13 5D 6
W4 2J 5
Grantchester *KT1: King T 6H 17*
(off St Peters Rd.)
Grantham Ct. KT2: King T 2E 16
Grantham Rd. W4 4B 6
Grantley Pl. KT10: Esh 2H 27
Grant Way TW7: Isle 3B 4
Granville Av. TW3: Houn 2F 9
Granville Rd. SW18 4J 13
SW19 4K 19
Grapsome Cl. KT9: Chess 4D 28
Grasmere Av. SW15 1A 18
SW19 7K 19
TW3: Houn 3G 9
Grasmere Ct. *SW13 3D 6*
(off Verdun Rd.)
Gratton Rd. W14 1H 7
Gravel Rd. TW2: Twick 5K 9
Grayham Cres. KT3: N Mald 1A 24
Grayham Rd. KT3: N Mald 1A 24
Gray's La. KT21: Asht 7G 33
Grayswood Gdns. SW20 6E 18
Grayswood Point SW15 5D 12

50 A-Z Kingston & Richmond

GREAT BURGH 6F 35
Gt. Chertsey Rd. TW2: Twick 7E 8
  TW13: Hanw, Twick 7E 8
  W4 .6K 5
    (not continuous)
Gt. Church La. W6 . . . . .1G 7
Great Ellshams SM7: Bans 5K 35
Greatham Wlk. SW15 . . . . .5D 12
Great Tattenhams KT18: Tatt C . . .7E 34
Gt. West Rd. TW7: Bford, Isle . . .4A 4
  TW8: Bford 4A 4
  W4 .2J 5
    (Cedars Rd.)
  W4 .2C 6
    (Dorchester Gro.)
  W6 .2C 6
Gt. West Trad. Est. TW8: Bford . .3C 4
Grebe Ct. SM3: Sutt 2J 31
Grebe Ter. KT1: King T . . .5C 36 (7F 17)
Green, The KT3: N Mald 7A 18
  KT10: Clay 3A 28
  KT12: Hers 2C 26
  KT17: Ewe 7D 30
  KT20: Tad 7H 35
  SM1: Sutt 7K 25
  SM4: Mord 1H 25
  SW14 . . . . .7K 5
  SW19 . . . . .2G 19
  TW2: Twick 5K 9
  TW9: Rich 2E 10
  TW13: Felt 6A 8
Greenacres Ho. SW18 . . . . .5K 13
    (off Knaresborough Dr.)
Greenbank Ct. TW7: Isle 6A 4
    (off Lanadron Cl.)
Green Cl. TW13: Hanw 2D 14
Green Curve SM7: Bans 3J 35
Green Dragon La. TW8: Bford 2F 5
Greenfield Av. KT5: Surb 4J 23
Greenfield Ho. SW19 . . . . .5G 13
Greenford Rd. SM1: Sutt 1K 31
    (not continuous)
Greenhayes Av. SM7: Bans 3K 35
Greenhayes Gdns. SM7: Bans . . .4K 35
Green Hedges TW1: Twick 2D 10
Greenlands KT19: Ewe 2J 29
Green La. KT3: N Mald 2K 23
  KT4: Wor Pk 5D 24
  KT8: W Mole 2G 21
  KT9: Chess 5E 28
  KT11: Cobh 7D 26
  KT12: Hers 3A 26
  KT21: Asht 6D 32
  SM4: Mord 3K 25
    (Central Rd.)
  SM4: Mord 4F 25
    (Lwr. Morden La.)
  TW4: Houn 1A 8
  TW13: Hanw 2D 14
Green La. Av. KT12: Hers 2B 26
Green Lanes KT19: Ewe 5B 30
Greenlaw Gdns. KT3: N Mald 4C 24
Greenlawn La. TW8: Bford 1E 4
Green Leas KT1: King T 5D 36
Greenlink Wlk. TW9: Kew 5J 5
Green Man La. TW14: Felt 1A 8
    (not continuous)
Green Mead KT10: Esh 3E 26
Greenoak Way SW19 . . . . .1G 19
Greenock Rd. W3 . . . . .1J 5
Green Pde. TW3: Houn 2G 9
Greenrod Pl. TW8: Bford 2F 5
    (off Clayponds La.)
Greenside Dr. KT21: Asht 7C 32
Greenslade Av. KT21: Asht 7J 33
Greenstead Gdns. SW15 . . . . . .2E 12
Green St. TW16: Sun 7A 14
Green Vw. KT9: Chess 4G 29
Greenview Dr. SW20 . . . . .7F 19
Green Wlk. TW12: Hamp 3E 14
Greenway SW20 . . . . .1F 25
Greenway, The KT18: Eps 3H 33
  TW4: Houn 1E 8
Greenways KT10: Hin W 1K 27
Greenways, The TW1: Twick 3B 10
Greenways Dr. TW4: Houn 1D 8
Greenwood Cl. KT7: T Ditt 5B 22
  SM4: Mord 1H 25
Greenwood La.
  TW12: Hamp H 2G 15
Greenwood Pk. KT2: King T 4B 18
Greenwood Pl. KT12: Hers 7D 20
Greenwood Rd. KT7: T Ditt 5B 22
  TW7: Isle 7A 4
Grena Gdns. TW9: Rich 1G 11

Grena Rd. TW9: Rich 1G 11
Grenville Cl. KT5: Surb 5K 23
Grenville M.
  TW12: Hamp H 2G 15
Gresham Rd. TW12: Hamp 3F 15
Gresham Way SW19 . . . . .7K 13
Gresham Way Ind. Est.
  SW19 . . . . .7K 13
    (off Gresham Way)
Gressenhall Rd. SW18 . . . . .3J 13
Greswell St. SW6 . . . . .5G 7
Greville Cl. KT21: Asht 7F 33
  TW1: Twick 4C 10
Greville Ct. KT21: Asht 7F 33
    (off Greville Pk. Rd.)
Greville Pk. Av. KT21: Asht 7F 33
Greville Pk. Rd. KT21: Asht 7F 33
Greville Rd. TW10: Rich 3G 11
Grey Alders SM7: Bans 3F 35
Greyhound Mans. W6 . . . . .3H 7
    (off Greyhound Rd.)
Greyhound Rd. W6 . . . . .3G 7
  W14 .3G 7
Griffin Cen. TW14: Felt 2A 8
Griffin Cen., The KT1: King T . . .4B 36
Griffin Ct. TW8: Bford 3F 5
  W4 .2C 6
Griffin Ho. W6 . . . . .1G 7
    (off Hammersmith Rd.)
Griffin Pk. 3E 4
Griffiths Cl. KT4: Wor Pk 6E 24
Griffiths Rd. SW19 . . . . .4K 19
Grimston Rd. SW6 . . . . .6J 7
Grimwood Rd. TW1: Twick 4A 10
Grogan Cl. TW12: Hamp 3E 14
Groombridge Cl.
  KT12: Hers 2A 26
Grosse Way SW15 . . . . .3E 12
Grosvenor Av. SW14 . . . . .7B 6
  TW10: Rich 2F 11
Grosvenor Ct. SM4: Mord 1K 25
  TW11: Tedd 3B 16
Grosvenor Gdns. KT2: King T . . .3E 16
  SW14 . . . . .7B 6
Grosvenor Hill SW19 . . . . .3H 19
Grosvenor Rd. KT18: Eps D 7A 34
  TW1: Twick 5B 10
  TW3: Houn 1E 8
  TW8: Bford 3E 4
  TW10: Rich 2F 11
  W4 . . . . .2J 5
Grotto Rd. TW1: Twick 6A 10
Grove, The KT12: Walt T 4A 20
  KT17: Eps 2B 34
  KT17: Ewe 6C 30
  TW1: Twick 3C 10
  TW7: Isle 5A 4
  TW11: Tedd 1B 16
Grove Av. KT17: Eps 2B 34
  SM1: Sutt 3K 31
  TW1: Twick 5A 10
Grove Cl. KT1: King T . . .7E 36 (1G 23)
  KT19: Eps 6G 29
  TW13: Hanw 1D 14
Grove Cotts. W4 . . . . .3B 6
Grove Ct. KT1: King T 6C 36
  KT8: E Mos 2J 21
  TW3: Houn 1F 9
Grove Cres.
  KT1: King T 6C 36 (7F 17)
  KT12: Walt T 4A 20
  TW13: Hanw 1D 14
Grove End La. KT10: Esh 5J 21
Grove Gdns. TW10: Rich 3G 11
  TW11: Tedd 1B 16
Grove Ho. KT17: Eps 1E 22
    (off The Grove)
  KT8: W Mole 1F 21
Grove La. KT1: King T . . .7D 36 (1F 23)
Grove La. KT1: King T 5K 5
Grove Pk. Bri. W4 . . . . .4K 5
Grove Pk. Gdns. W4 . . . . .4J 5
Grove Pk. M. W4 . . . . .4K 5
Grove Pk. Rd. W4 . . . . .4J 5
Grove Pk. Ter. W4 . . . . .4J 5
Grove Rd. KT6: Surb 2E 22
  KT8: E Mos 1J 21
  KT17: Eps 2B 34
  KT21: Asht 7G 33
  SM1: Sutt 3K 31
  SW13 . . . . .6C 6
  TW2: Twick 7J 9

Grove Rd. TW3: Houn 1F 9
  TW7: Isle 5A 4
  TW8: Bford 2D 4
  TW10: Rich 3G 11
Grove Ter. TW11: Tedd 1B 16
Grovewood TW9: Kew 5H 5
Grove Way KT10: Esh 4H 21
Grovewood TW9: Kew 5H 5
Guilford Av. KT5: Surb 2G 23
Guinness Trust Bldgs. W6 . . . . . .2G 7
    (off Fulham Pal. Rd.)
Guion Rd. SW6 . . . . .6J 7
Gumleigh Rd. W5 . . . . .1D 4
Gumley Gdns. TW7: Isle 7B 4
GUNNERSBURY 2J 5
Gunnersbury Av. W3 . . . . .1H 5
  W4 .1H 5
Gunnersbury Cl. W4 . . . . .2J 5
Gunnersbury M. W4 . . . . .2J 5
Gunnersbury Pk. Mus. 1H 5
Gunnersbury Station
  (Underground & Overground) . . .2J 5
Gunnersbury Triangle Nature Reserve
   . . . . .1K 5
Gunters Mead KT10: Esh 7H 27
    (not continuous)
  KT22: Oxs 7H 27
Gunterstone Rd. W14 . . . . .1H 7
Gwalior Rd. SW15 . . . . .1G 13
Gwendolen Av. SW15 . . . . .1G 13
Gwendolen Cl. SW15 . . . . .2G 13
Gwendwr Rd. W14 . . . . .2H 7
Gwynne Cl. W4 . . . . .3C 6

H

Haarlem Rd. W14 . . . . .1G 7
Haddon Cl. KT3: N Mald 2C 24
Haddon Rd. SM1: Sutt 1K 31
    (not continuous)
Hadleigh Cl. SW20 . . . . .6J 19
Hadleigh Dr. SM2: Sutt 5K 31
Hadley Gdns. W4 . . . . .2A 6
Hadrian Cl. SM2: Sutt 4K 31
Haggard Rd. TW1: Twick 4C 10
Haig Pl. SM4: Mord 3K 25
Hailsham Cl. KT6: Surb 4E 22
Haining Cl. W4 . . . . .2H 5
Halcyon Cl. SW13 . . . . .7D 6
Haldane Rd. SW6 . . . . .4J 7
Haldon Rd. SW18 . . . . .3J 13
Halesowen Rd. SM4: Mord 4K 25
Half Acre TW8: Bford 3E 4
Halford Rd. SW6 . . . . .3K 7
  TW10: Rich 2F 11
Halfway Grn. KT12: Walt T 7A 20
Haliburton Rd. TW1: Twick 2B 10
Halifax Cl. TW11: Tedd 3K 15
Hallam Rd. SW13 . . . . .7E 6
Hall Ct. TW11: Tedd 2A 16
Hall Farm Dr. TW2: Whitt 4J 9
Halliford Rd. TW16: Sun 1A 20
Hallmead Rd. SM1: Sutt 7K 25
Hall Rd. TW7: Isle 2J 9
HAM 7D 10
Ham, The TW8: Bford 4D 4
Hambledon Hill KT18: Eps 5K 33
Hambledon Rd. SW18 . . . . .4J 13
Hambledon Va. KT18: Eps 5K 33
Hambleton Cl. KT4: Wor Pk 6F 25
Ham Cl. TW10: Ham 7D 10
    (not continuous)
Ham Comn. TW10: Ham 7E 10
Ham Common (Nature Reserve)
   . . . . .1F 17
Ham Farm Rd. TW10: Ham 1E 16
Ham Flds. TW10: Ham 7C 10
Ham Ga. Av. TW10: Ham 7E 10
Ham House & Garden 5D 10
Hamilton Av. KT6: Surb 6H 23
  SM3: Cheam 6H 25
Hamilton Cl. KT19: Eps 1K 33
  TW11: Tedd 3C 16
Hamilton Cres. SW15 . . . . .7H 7
  TW3: Houn 1G 9
    (off Hanworth Rd.)
Hamilton Ho. W4 . . . . .3B 6
Hamilton M. SW18 . . . . .5K 13
  SW19 . . . . .4K 19
Hamilton Pl. TW16: Sun 4A 14
Hamilton Rd. TW2: Twick 5K 9
  TW8: Bford 3E 4
Ham Lands Nature Reserve 6B 10
Hamlet Cl. W6 . . . . .1D 6

Hamlet Gdns. W6 . . . . .1D 6
Hamlyn Ho. TW13: Felt 5A 8
HAMMERSMITH 1F 7
Hammersmith Apollo 2F 7
Hammersmith Bri. SW13 . . . . . . .3E 6
Hammersmith Bri. Rd. W6 . . . . . .2F 7
HAMMERSMITH BROADWAY . . .1F 7
Hammersmith B'way. W6 . . . . . . .1F 7
Hammersmith Bus Station 1F 7
Hammersmith Emb. W6 . . . . .3F 7
Hammersmith Fitness & Squash Cen.
   . . . . .1G 7
    (off Chalk Hill Rd.)
HAMMERSMITH FLYOVER 2F 7
Hammersmith Flyover W6 . . . . . .2F 7
Hammersmith Gro. W6 . . . . .1F 7
Hammersmith Rd. W6 . . . . .1G 7
  W14 . . . . .1G 7
Hammersmith Station
  (Underground) 1F 7
Hammersmith Ter. W6 . . . . .2D 6
Hammond Cl. TW12: Hamp 5F 15
Hampden Rd. KT1: King T 7H 17
Hampshire Hog La. W6 . . . . .2D 6
HAMPTON 5G 15
Hampton & Richmond Borough FC
   . . . . .5G 15
Hampton Bus. Pk.
  TW13: Hanw 7D 8
Hampton Cl. SW20 . . . . .4F 19
HAMPTON COURT 1K 21
HAMPTON COURT 7K 15
Hampton Ct. Av. KT8: E Mos 3J 21
Hampton Ct. Bri. KT8: E Mos 1K 21
Hampton Ct. Cres.
  KT8: E Mos 7J 15
Hampton Ct. Est. KT7: T Ditt 1K 21
Hampton Ct. M. KT8: E Mos 1K 21
    (off Feltham Av.)
Hampton Court Palace 1A 22
Hampton Court Palace Golf Course
   . . . . .2D 22
Hampton Ct. Pde.
  KT8: E Mos 1K 21
Hampton Ct. Rd.
  KT1: Hamp W 7K 15
  KT8: E Mos 3A 36 (7K 15)
  TW12: E Mos, Hamp
   . . . . .6H 15
Hampton Court Station (Rail) 1K 21
Hampton Ct. Way KT7: T Ditt 6K 21
  KT8: E Mos 6K 21
  KT10: T Ditt 6K 21
Hampton Golf Course 7F 9
Hampton Gro. KT17: Ewe 7C 30
HAMPTON HILL 2H 15
Hampton Hill Bus. Pk.
  TW12: Hamp H 2H 15
    (off High St.)
Hampton Hill Playhouse Theatre
   . . . . .2H 15
Hampton La. TW13: Hanw 1D 14
Hampton Open Air Pool 4H 15
Hampton Rd. KT4: Wor Pk 6D 24
  TW2: Twick 7J 9
  TW11: Tedd 2J 15
  TW12: Hamp H 2J 15
Hampton Rd. E. TW13: Hanw 1E 14
Hampton Rd. W. TW13: Hanw 7D 8
Hampton Sports & Fitness Cen.
   . . . . .2F 15
Hampton Station (Rail) 5F 15
HAMPTON WICK 2A 36 (5D 16)
Hampton Wick Station
  (Rail) 2A 36 (5D 16)
Hampton Youth Project (Sports Hall)
   . . . . .3E 14
Ham Ridings TW10: Ham 2G 17
Ham St. TW10: Ham 5C 10
Hanah Ct. SW19 . . . . .4G 19
Handel Mans. SW13 . . . . .4F 7
Handside Cl. KT4: Wor Pk 5G 25
Hanford Cl. SW18 . . . . .5K 13
Hanford Row SW19 . . . . .3F 19
Hannay Ho. SW15 . . . . .3H 13
Hannell Rd. SW6 . . . . .4H 7
Hanover Cl. SM3: Cheam 1H 31
  TW9: Kew 4H 5
Hanover Ct. SW15 . . . . .1C 12
Hanover Ter. TW7: Isle 5B 4
Hansa Cl. SW19 . . . . .5H 13
    (off Princes Way)
Hansler Gro. KT8: E Mos 1J 21
Hanson Cl. SW14 . . . . .7K 5
HANWORTH 1C 14
Hanworth Air Pk. Leisure Cen. . . .6C 8

Hanworth Rd.—High St.

Hanworth Rd. TW3: Houn 5D **8**
TW4: Houn 5D **8**
TW12: Hamp 1E **14**
TW13: Felt 5A **8**
TW16: Sun 4A **14**
(not continuous)
Hanworth Ter. TW3: Houn 1G **9**
Hanworth Trad. Est.
TW13: Hanw 7D **8**
Harbledown Rd. SW6 . . . . .5K **7**
Harbord St. SW6 . . . . .5G **7**
Harbourfield Rd. SM7: Bans 4K **35**
Harbridge Av. SW15 . . . . .4C **12**
Harcourt Cl. TW7: Isle 7B **4**
Harcourt Rd. SW19 . . . . .4K **19**
Harding Ho. *SW13* *3E* **6**
(off Wyatt Dr.)
Harding Rd. KT18: Eps D 7B **34**
Harding's Cl.
KT2: King T 1E **36** (5G **17**)
Hardman Rd.
KT2: King T 3D **36** (6F **17**)
Hardwicke Rd. TW10: Ham 1D **16**
W4 . . . . .1K **5**
Hardwicks Sq. SW18 . . . . .2K **13**
Hardy's M. KT8: E Mos 1K **21**
Harefield KT10: Hin W 7K **21**
Harefield Av. SM2: Cheam 5H **31**
Hare La. KT10: Clay 2J **27**
Harewood Rd. TW7: Isle 4A **4**
Harfield Rd. TW16: Sun 6C **14**
Harkness Cl. KT17: Eps D 5F **35**
Harlequin Av. TW8: Bford 3B **4**
Harlequin Cl. TW7: Isle 2K **9**
Harlequin Rd. TW11: Tedd 4C **16**
Harlequins RUFC 4K **9**
Harlington Rd. E. TW13: Felt 4A **8**
TW14: Felt 4A **8**
Harlington Rd. W.
TW14: Felt 3A **8**
Harold Wilson Ho. *SW6* *3J* **7**
(off Clem Attlee Ct.)
Harpers Yd. *TW7: Isle* *6A* **4**
(off Rennels Way)
Harrier Cen., The 3A **30**
Harriott's La. KT21: Asht 7D **32**
Harrow Cl. KT9: Chess 4E **28**
Harrowdene Gdns.
TW11: Tedd 3B **16**
Harrow Gdns. KT8: E Mos 7J **15**
Hartfield Cres. SW19 . . . . .4J **19**
Hartfield Rd. KT9: Chess 2E **28**
SW19 . . . . .4J **19**
Hartford Rd. KT19: Ewe 3J **29**
Hartham Cl. TW7: Isle 5B **4**
Hartham Rd. TW7: Isle 5A **4**
Hartington Ct. W4 . . . . .4J **5**
Hartington Rd. TW1: Twick 4C **10**
W4 . . . . .4J **5**
Hartismere Rd. SW6 . . . . .4J **7**
Hartland Rd. SM4: Mord 4K **25**
TW7: Isle 7B **4**
TW12: Hamp H 1G **15**
Hartland Way SM4: Mord 4J **25**
Hartop Point *SW6* *4H* **7**
(off Pellant Rd.)
Hart Sq. SM4: Mord 3K **25**
Hartswood Gdns. W12 . . . . .1C **6**
Harvard Hill W4 . . . . .3J **5**
Harvard La. W4 . . . . .2K **5**
Harvard Rd. W4 . . . . .2J **5**
Harvest Ct. KT10: Esh 6F **21**
Harvester Rd. KT19: Eps 6A **30**
Harvesters Cl. TW7: Isle 2J **9**
Harvest La. KT7: T Ditt 3B **22**
Harvey Ct. KT19: Eps 5J **29**
Harvey Dr. TW12: Hamp 5G **15**
Harvey Ho. TW8: Bford 2F **5**
Harvey Rd. TW4: Houn 4E **8**
Harwood Ct. SW15 . . . . .1F **13**
Harwood M. SW6 . . . . .4K **7**
Harwood Rd. SW6 . . . . .4K **7**
Haslam Av. SM3: Sutt 5H **25**
Haslemere Av. SW18 . . . . .6K **13**
W7 . . . . .1B **4**
W13 . . . . .1B **4**
Haslemere Cl. TW12: Hamp 2E **14**
Hastings Ct. TW11: Tedd 2J **15**
Hastings Dr. KT6: Surb 3D **22**
Hatch Pl. KT2: King T 2G **17**
Hatfeild Mead SM4: Mord 2K **25**
Hatfield Cl. SM2: Sutt 5K **31**
Hatfield Rd. KT21: Asht 7G **33**
Hatherleigh Cl. KT9: Chess 2E **28**
SM4: Mord 1K **25**
Hatherley Rd. TW9: Kew 5G **5**
Hatherop Rd. TW12: Hamp 4E **14**
Hatton Ho. *KT1: King T* *6G* **17**
(off Victoria Rd.)
Hauteville Ct. Gdns. *W6* *1C* **6**
(off South Side)
Havana Rd. SW19 . . . . .6K **13**
Haven, The TW9: Rich 7H **5**
Haven Cl. KT10: Esh 6K **21**
SW19 . . . . .7G **13**
Haven Ct. KT5: Surb 3G **23**
KT10: Esh 6K **21**
Haven Dr. KT19: Eps 6J **29**
Haven Pl. KT10: Esh 6K **21**
Haven Way KT19: Eps 7J **29**
Haverfield Gdns. TW9: Kew 4H **5**
Havers Av. KT12: Hers 2C **26**
Haversham Cl. TW1: Twick 3E **10**
Haweswater Ho. TW7: Isle 2A **10**
Hawker Ct. *KT1: King T* *6G* **17**
(off Church Rd.)
Hawkesbury Rd. SW15 . . . . .2E **12**
Hawkesley Cl. TW1: Twick 1B **16**
Hawkes Yd. KT7: T Ditt 3A **22**
Hawkewood Rd. TW16: Sun 7A **14**
Hawkfield Ct. TW7: Isle 6A **4**
Hawkhurst Gdns. KT9: Chess 1F **29**
Hawkhurst Way KT3: N Mald 2A **24**
Hawkins Rd. TW11: Tedd 3C **16**
Hawkshill Cl. KT10: Esh 3F **27**
Hawkshill Pl. KT10: Esh 3F **27**
Hawkshill Way KT10: Esh 3E **26**
Hawksmoor St. W6 . . . . .3G **7**
Hawks Pas. KT1: King T 3E **36**
Hawks Rd.
KT1: King T 4E **36** (6G **17**)
Hawley Cl. TW12: Hamp 3E **14**
Hawthorn Cl. SM7: Bans 3H **35**
TW12: Hamp 2F **15**
Hawthorn Ct. TW9: Kew 5J **5**
Hawthorne Ct. KT12: Walt T 5C **20**
Hawthorne Pl. KT17: Eps 1B **34**
Hawthorn Gdns. W5 . . . . .1E **4**
Hawthorn Hatch TW8: Bford 4C **4**
Hawthorn Rd. TW8: Bford 4C **4**
TW13: Felt 5A **8**
Hawthorns, The KT17: Ewe 4C **30**
Haycroft Rd. KT6: Surb 6E **22**
Haydon Pk. Rd. SW19 . . . . .2K **19**
Hayes Cres. SM3: Cheam 1G **31**
Haygarth Pl. SW19 . . . . .2G **19**
Haygreen Cl. KT2: King T 3J **17**
Haylands Ct. TW8: Bford 3D **4**
Haylett Gdns. KT1: King T 1E **22**
Hayling Ct. SM3: Cheam 1F **31**
Haymeads Dr. KT10: Esh 3H **27**
Haymer Gdns. KT4: Wor Pk 7D **24**
Haynt Wlk. SW20 . . . . .7H **19**
Hays Wlk. SM2: Cheam 6G **31**
Hayward Gdns. SW15 . . . . .3F **13**
Hayward Rd. KT7: T Ditt 5A **22**
Hazelbank KT5: Surb 5K **23**
Hazelbury Cl. SW19 . . . . .6K **19**
Hazel Cl. KT19: Eps 6A **30**
TW2: Whitt 4H **9**
TW8: Bford 4C **4**
Hazel La. TW10: Ham 6F **11**
Hazel Mead KT17: Ewe 6D **30**
Hazelwood Ct. KT6: Surb 3F **23**
Hazledene Rd. W4 . . . . .3K **5**
Hazlemere Gdns. KT4: Wor Pk . . .5D **24**
Hazlewell Rd. SW15 . . . . .2F **13**
Hazlitt Cl. TW13: Hanw 1D **14**
Hazlitt M. W14 . . . . .1H **7**
Hazlitt Rd. W14 . . . . .1H **7**
Hazon Way KT19: Eps 1K **33**
Headley Cl. KT19: Ewe 3H **29**
Headley Rd. KT18: Eps, Eps D 7J **33**
Headway, The KT17: Ewe 5C **30**
Headway Cl. TW10: Ham 1D **16**
Hearne Rd. W4 . . . . .3H **5**
Heatham Pk. TW2: Twick 4A **10**
Heath Bus. Cen. TW3: Houn 1H **9**
Heathcote Ga. SW6 . . . . .7K **7**
Heathcote Rd. KT18: Eps 3A **34**
TW1: Twick 3C **10**
Heath Ct. TW4: Houn 1E **8**
Heathdale Av. TW4: Houn 1D **8**
Heathdene KT20: Tad 7H **35**
Heath Dr. SW20 . . . . .1F **25**
Heatherbank Cl. KT11: Cobh 7C **26**
Heather Cl. TW7: Isle 2J **9**
TW12: Hamp 5E **14**
Heatherdale Cl. KT2: King T 3H **17**
Heather Gdns. SM2: Sutt 3K **31**
Heatherlea Gro. KT4: Wor Pk 5E **24**
Heather Pl. KT10: Esh 1G **27**
Heatherset Cl. KT10: Esh 2H **27**
Heatherside Rd. KT19: Ewe 4A **30**
Heather Wlk. *TW2: Whitt* *4F* **9**
(off Stephenson Rd.)
Heathfield Ct. W4 . . . . .2A **6**
Heathfield Gdns. W4 . . . . .2K **5**
Heathfield Nth. TW2: Twick 4K **9**
Heathfield Rd. KT12: Hers 1D **26**
Heathfields Cl. KT21: Asht 7D **32**
Heathfields Ct. TW4: Houn 2D **8**
Heathfield Sth. TW2: Twick 4A **10**
Heathfield Ter. W4 . . . . .2K **5**
Heath Gdns. TW1: Twick 5A **10**
Heathland M. KT18: Tatt C 7G **35**
Heathlands Cl. TW1: Twick 6A **10**
Heathlands Way
TW4: Houn 2D **8**
Heathmans Rd. SW6 . . . . .5J **7**
Heath Mead SW19 . . . . .7G **13**
Heath Ri. SW15 . . . . .3G **13**
Heath Rd. KT22: Oxs 7H **27**
TW1: Twick 5A **10**
TW2: Twick 5A **10**
TW3: Houn, Isle 1G **9**
TW7: Isle 1G **9**
Heathrow Causeway Cen.
TW4: Houn 1A **8**
Heathrow Gateway TW4: Houn 4D **8**
Heathrow Intl. Trad. Est.
TW4: Houn 1A **8**
Heath Royal SW15 . . . . .3G **13**
Heathside KT10: Hin W 7K **21**
TW4: Houn 4E **8**
Heathside Cl. KT10: Hin W 7K **21**
Heathside Pl. KT18: Tatt C 7G **35**
Heathview Gdns. SW15 . . . . .4F **13**
Heber Mans. *W14* *3H* **7**
(off Queen's Club Gdns.)
Hebron Rd. W6 . . . . .1F **7**
Heckets Ct. KT10: Esh 6H **27**
Heckfield Pl. SW6 . . . . .4K **7**
Heddon Cl. TW7: Isle 1B **10**
Hedera Pl. TW4: Houn 1E **8**
Hedges Cl. TW14: Felt 3A **8**
Hedingham Ho. KT2: King T 2C **36**
Hedley Rd. TW2: Whitt 4F **9**
Heidegger Cres. SW13 . . . . .4E **6**
Heights Cl. SM7: Bans 5H **35**
SW20 . . . . .4E **18**
Heldmann Cl. TW3: Houn 1J **9**
Helen Av. TW14: Felt 4A **8**
Helen Cl. KT8: W Mole 1G **21**
Helix Ter. SW19 . . . . .6G **13**
Helm Cl. KT19: Eps 1H **33**
Helme Cl. SW19 . . . . .2J **19**
Hemingford Rd. SM3: Cheam 1F **31**
Hemming Cl. TW12: Hamp 5F **15**
Hemmings Mead KT19: Ewe 3K **29**
Hemsby Rd. KT9: Chess 3G **29**
Hendon Gro. KT19: Eps 5H **29**
Henfield Rd. SW19 . . . . .5J **19**
Hengest Av. KT10: Surb 7B **22**
Henley Av. SM3: Cheam 7H **25**
Henley Cl. TW7: Isle 5A **4**
Henley Dr. KT2: King T 4C **18**
Henley Way TW13: Hanw 2C **14**
Henlow Pl. TW10: Ham 6E **10**
Henrietta Ct. *TW1: Twick* *4D* **10**
(off Richmond Rd.)
Henrietta Ho. *W6* *2F* **7**
(off Queen Caroline St.)
Henry Chester Bldg. SW15 . . . . . . .6F **7**
Henry Jackson Rd. SW15 . . . . .7G **7**
Henry Lodge KT12: Hers 3B **26**
Henry Macaulay Av.
KT2: King T 2B **36** (5E **16**)
Henry Peters Dr. *TW11: Tedd* *2K* **15**
(off Somerset Gdns.)
Henty Wlk. SW15 . . . . .2E **12**
Hepple Cl. TW7: Isle 6C **4**
Hepplestone Cl. SW15 . . . . .3E **12**
Hepworth Ct. SM3: Sutt 5K **25**
Herbert Gdns. W4 . . . . .3J **5**
Herbert Morrison Ho. *SW6* *3J* **7**
(off Clem Attlee Ct.)
Herbert Rd.
KT1: King T 6E **36** (7G **17**)
SW19 .4J **19**
(not continuous)
Hereford Cl. KT18: Eps 2A **34**
Hereford Ct. SM2: Sutt 4K **31**
Hereford Gdns.
TW2: Twick 5H **9**
Hereford Rd. TW13: Felt 5B **8**
W5 . . . . .1D **4**
Hereford Way KT9: Chess 2D **28**
Hermitage, The
KT1: King T 7B **36** (1E **22**)
SW13 .5C **6**
TW10: Rich 2F **11**
Hermitage Cl. KT10: Clay 3B **28**
Hermitage Vs. *SW6* *3K* **7**
(off Lillie Rd.)
Herne Rd. KT6: Surb 6E **22**
Heron Cl. SM1: Sutt 2J **31**
Heron Ct. KT1: King T 6C **36** (7F **17**)
KT17: Eps 3D **34**
Heron Rd. TW1: Twick 1B **10**
Heronry, The KT12: Hers 3A **26**
Heron's Pl. TW7: Isle 7C **4**
Heron Sq. TW9: Rich 2E **10**
Heron Vw. *TW8: Bford* *4D* **4**
(off Commerce Rd.)
Heron Way TW14: Felt 1A **8**
HERSHAM 2C **26**
Hersham By-Pass KT12: Hers 2A **26**
Hersham Cl. SW15 . . . . .4D **12**
Hersham Gdns. KT12: Hers 1A **26**
Hersham Golf Course 7D **20**
HERSHAM GREEN 2C **26**
Hersham Grn. Shop. Cen.
KT12: Hers 2C **26**
Hersham Pl. KT12: Hers 2C **26**
Hersham Rd.
KT12: Hers, Walt T 5A **20**
Hersham Station (Rail) 7D **20**
Hersham Trad. Est.
KT12: Walt T 6D **20**
Hershell Ct. SW14 . . . . .1J **11**
Hertford Av. SW14 . . . . .2A **12**
Hessle Gro. KT17: Ewe 7C **30**
Hestercombe Av. SW6 . . . . .6H **7**
Hester Ter. TW9: Rich 7H **5**
Hever Pl. KT8: E Mos 7H **15**
Hexham Gdns. TW7: Isle 4B **4**
Hexham Rd. SM4: Mord 5K **25**
Heyford Av. SW20 . . . . .7J **19**
Heythorp St. SW18 . . . . .5J **13**
Hibernia Gdns. TW3: Houn 1F **9**
Hibernia Rd. TW3: Houn 1F **9**
Hibiscus Ho. TW13: Felt 5A **8**
Hickey's Almshouses
TW9: Rich 1G **11**
Hicks Gallery 2K **19**
Hidcote Gdns. SW20 . . . . .7E **18**
Hidden Cl. KT8: W Mole 1H **21**
Higgins Wlk. *TW12: Hamp* *3D* **14**
(off Abbott Cl.)
High Ashton KT2: King T 4J **17**
High Beeches SM7: Bans 3F **35**
Highbury Cl. KT3: N Mald 1K **23**
Highbury Rd. SW19 . . . . .2H **19**
High Cedar Dr. SW20 . . . . .4F **19**
Highclere Rd. KT3: N Mald 7A **18**
Highcliffe Dr. SW15 . . . . .3C **12**
High Coombe Pl. KT2: King T 3A **18**
Highcross Way SW15 . . . . .5D **12**
Highdown KT4: Wor Pk 6B **24**
Highdown Cl. SM7: Bans 5J **35**
Highdown Rd. SW15 . . . . .3E **12**
High Dr. KT3: N Mald 5K **17**
Higher Dr. SM7: Bans 1G **35**
Higher Grn. KT17: Eps 2D **34**
Highfield Cl. KT6: Surb 5D **22**
KT22: Oxs 7J **27**
Highfield Dr. KT19: Ewe 3C **30**
Highfield Rd. KT5: Surb 4K **23**
KT12: Walt T 5A **20**
TW7: Isle 5A **4**
TW13: Felt 6A **8**
Highfields KT21: Asht 7E **32**
SM1: Sutt 6K **25**
High Foleys KT10: Clay 4C **28**
High Garth KT10: Esh 3H **27**
Highgrove Ct. SM1: Sutt 3K **31**
Highlands Heath SW15 . . . . .4F **13**
High Pk. Av. TW9: Kew 5H **5**
High Pk. Rd. TW9: Kew 5H **5**
Highridge Cl. KT18: Eps 3B **34**
High St. KT1: Hamp W . . .2A **36** (5D **16**)
KT1: King T 5B **36** (7E **16**)
KT3: N Mald 1B **24**
KT7: T Ditt 3B **22**
KT8: W Mole 1F **21**
KT10: Clay 3A **28**
KT10: Esh 1G **27**
KT17: Eps 2A **34**
KT17: Ewe 5C **30**
KT19: Eps 2A **34**
SM3: Cheam 3H **31**
SM7: Bans 4K **35**
SW19 . . . . .2G **19**

High St. TW2: Whitt 4H 9
TW3: Houn 1G 9
TW8: Bford 4D 4
TW11: Tedd 2A 16
TW12: Hamp, Hamp H 5H 15
TW13: Felt 6A 8
High St. M. SW19 . . . . .2H 19
High Vw. SM2: Cheam 7J 31
Highview Path SM7: Bans 4K 35
Hilbert Rd. SM3: Cheam 7G 25
Hilda Ct. KT6: Surb 4E 22
Hilderley Ho. KT1: King T 5E 36
Hilders, The KT21: Asht 6J 33
Hildyard Rd. SW6 . . . . .3K 7
Hillary Cres. KT12: Walt T 5B 20
Hillary Dr. TW7: Isle 2A 10
Hillbrow KT3: N Mald 7C 18
Hillbrow Rd. KT10: Esh 7H 21
Hill Cl. KT11: Cobh 7F 27
Hill Cres. KT4: Wor Pk 6F 25
KT5: Surb 2G 23
Hill Crest KT6: Surb 4F 23
Hillcrest Cl. KT18: Eps 4C 34
Hillcrest Gdns. KT10: Hin W 7A 22
Hillcross Av. SM4: Mord 3G 25
Hilldale Rd. SM1: Sutt 1J 31
Hillersdon Av. SW13 . . . . .6D 6
Hillfield Ct. KT10: Esh 2G 27
Hill Fld. Rd. TW12: Hamp 4E 14
Hill Gro. TW13: Hanw 6E 8
Hill Ho. Dr. TW12: Hamp 5F 15
Hillier Lodge TW11: Tedd 2J 15
Hillier Pl. KT9: Chess 3E 28
Hillmont Rd. KT10: Hin W 7K 21
Hill Ri. KT10: Hin W 6C 22
TW10: Rich 2E 10
Hillside KT10: Esh 2G 27
SM7: Bans 4H 35
SW19 . . . . .3G 19
Hillside Cl. SM4: Mord 1H 25
SM7: Bans 5H 35
Hillside Rd. KT5: Surb 1G 23
KT17: Ewe 6F 31
KT21: Asht 6G 33
SM2: Sutt 4J 31
Hill St. TW9: Rich 2E 10
Hill Top SM3: Sutt 4J 25
SM4: Mord 3K 25
Hillview SW20 . . . . .4E 18
Hill Vw. Rd. KT10: Clay 4B 28
TW1: Twick 3B 10
Hilsea Point SW15 . . . . .5E 12
Hinchley Cl. KT10: Hin W 1A 28
Hinchley Dr. KT10: Hin W 7A 22
Hinchley Mnr. KT10: Hin W 7A 22
Hinchley Way KT10: Hin W 7B 22
HINCHLEY WOOD 7A 22
Hinchley Wood Station (Rail) . . .7A 22
Hindhead Point SW15 . . . . .5E 12
Hine Cl. KT17: Eps 7J 29
Hinton Av. TW4: Houn 1C 8
Hippisley Ct. TW7: Isle 7A 4
Hobart Pl. TW10: Rich 4G 11
Hobart Rd. KT4: Wor Pk 7E 24
Hobbes Wlk. SW15 . . . . .3E 12
Hobill Wlk. KT5: Surb 3G 23
Hogarth Bus. Pk. W4 . . . . .3B 6
Hogarth Health Club, The 1C 6
Hogarth La. W4 . . . . .3B 6
Hogarth Pl. SW5 . . . . .1K 7
(off Hogarth Rd.)
Hogarth Rd. SW5 . . . . .1K 7
HOGARTH RDBT. 3B 6
Hogarth's House 3B 6
(off Hogarth La.)
Hogarth Ter. W4 . . . . .3B 6
Hogarth Way TW12: Hamp 5H 15
Hogsmill Ho. KT1: King T 5E 36
Hogsmill La. KT1: King T 7G 17
Hogsmill Local Nature Reserve
. . . . .2J 29
Hogsmill Way KT19: Ewe 2K 29
Holbrooke Pl. TW10: Rich 2E 10
Holcombe St. W6 . . . . .1E 6
Holdernesse Ct. TW7: Isle 5B 4
Holford Way SW15 . . . . .3D 12
Holland Av. SM2: Sutt 5K 31
SW20 . . . . .5C 18
Holland Cl. KT19: Eps 7K 29
Holland Ct. KT6: Surb 4E 22
Holland Gdns. TW8: Bford 3F 5
Holland Rd. W14 . . . . .1J 7
Hollands, The KT4: Wor Pk 5C 24
TW13: Hanw 1C 14
Hollies Cl. TW12: Hamp 3F 15

Hollies Cl. TW1: Twick 6A 10
Hollies Rd. W5 . . . . .1D 4
Hollingsworth Ct. KT6: Surb 4E 22
Hollington Cres. KT3: N Mald . . .3C 24
Hollingworth Cl. KT8: W Mole . . .1E 20
Hollows, The TW8: Bford 3G 5
Holly Av. KT12: Walt T 5C 20
Hollybank Cl. TW12: Hamp 2F 15
Holly Bush La. TW12: Hamp 4E 14
Hollybush Rd. KT2: King T 2F 17
Holly Cl. KT19: Eps 5A 30
TW13: Hanw 2D 14
TW16: Sun 7A 14
SM2: Sutt 4K 31
Hollyfield Rd. KT5: Surb 4G 23
Hollygrove Cl. TW3: Houn 1E 8
Holly Hill Dr. SM7: Bans 5K 35
Holly Hill Pk. SM7: Bans 6K 35
Holly Ho. TW8: Bford 3D 4
Holly La. SM7: Bans 5K 35
Holly La. E. SM7: Bans 5K 35
Holly La. W. SM7: Bans 6K 35
Hollymoor La. KT19: Ewe 6A 30
Holly Rd. TW1: Twick 5A 10
TW3: Houn 1G 9
TW12: Hamp H 3H 15
W4 . . . . .1A 6
Holly Tree Cl. SW19 . . . . .5G 13
Holly Vs. W6 . . . . .1E 6
(off Wellesley Av.)
Hollywood Bowl
Tolworth 6J 23
Holman Ct. KT17: Ewe 5D 30
Holman Hunt Ho. W6 . . . . .2H 7
(off Field Rd.)
Holman Rd. KT19: Ewe 2K 29
Holmbush Rd. SW15 . . . . .3H 13
Holme Ct. TW7: Isle 7B 4
Holmesdale Av. SW14 . . . . .7J 5
Holmesdale Rd. TW9: Kew 5G 5
TW11: Tedd 4D 16
Holmes Rd. TW1: Twick 6A 10
Holmewood Sq. SM2: Sutt 3K 31
Holm Oak Cl. SW15 . . . . .3J 13
Holmsley Cl. KT3: N Mald 3C 24
Holmsley Ho. SW15 . . . . .4C 12
(off Tangley Gro.)
Holmwood Cl. SM2: Cheam 5G 31
Holmwood Rd. KT9: Chess 2E 28
SM2: Cheam 5F 31
Holne Chase SM4: Mord 3J 25
Holroyd Cl. KT10: Clay 5A 28
Holroyd Rd. KT10: Clay 5A 28
SW15 . . . . .1F 13
Holst Mans. SW13 . . . . .3F 7
Holsworthy Way KT9: Chess 2D 28
Holt, The SM4: Mord 1K 25
Holwood Cl. KT12: Walt T 6B 20
Holybourne Av. SW15 . . . . .4D 12
Holycross Cl. SM4: Mord 4K 25
Holyhead Ct. KT1: King T 7B 36
Holyport Rd. SW6 . . . . .4G 7
Home Ct. KT6: Surb 2E 22
Home Farm Cl. KT7: T Ditt 4A 22
KT10: Esh 3G 27
KT20: Tad 6G 35
Home Farm Gdns.
KT12: Walt T 6B 20
Homefield SM4: Mord 1K 25
Homefield Av. KT12: Hers 1C 26
Homefield Rd. KT12: Walt T 4D 20
SW19 . . . . .3G 19
W4 . . . . .2C 6
Homeland Dr. SM2: Sutt 5K 31
Home Mdw. SM7: Bans 5K 35
Home Pk. Ct. KT1: King T 1E 22
(off Palace Rd.)
Home Pk. Pde. KT1: Hamp W . . .3A 36
Home Pk. Rd. SW19 . . . . .1J 19
Home Pk. Ter. KT1: Hamp W 3A 36
Home Pk. Wlk. KT1: King T 1E 22
Homersham Rd. KT1: King T 6H 17
Homestead Gdns. KT10: Clay . . .2K 27
Homestead Rd. SW6 . . . . .4J 7
Homewater Ho. KT17: Eps 2B 34
Homewood Cl. TW12: Hamp 3E 14
Honeysuckle Pl. KT17: Eps D . . .5E 34
Honeywood Rd. TW7: Isle 1B 10
Hood Av. SW14 . . . . .2J 11
Hood Rd. SW20 . . . . .4C 18
HOOK 1E 28
Hookfield KT19: Eps 2K 33
Hookfield M. KT19: Eps 2K 33
HOOK JUNC. 7F 23
Hook Ri. Nth. KT6: Surb 7F 23
Hook Ri. Sth. KT6: Surb 7F 23

Hook Ri. Sth. Ind. Pk.
KT6: Surb 7G 23
Hook Rd. KT6: Surb 6F 23
KT9: Chess 2E 28
KT19: Eps, Ewe 4K 29
Hope Cl. TW8: Bford 2F 5
Hoppingwood Av. KT3: N Mald . .7B 18
Hopton Gdns. KT3: N Mald 3D 24
Horace Rd.
KT1: King T 6E 36 (7G 17)
Horatio Ho. W6 . . . . .2G 7
(off Fulham Pal. Rd.)
Horatio Pl. SW19 . . . . .5K 19
Horder Rd. SW6 . . . . .5H 7
Horizon Ct. SM2: Cheam 4H 31
(off Up. Mulgrave Rd.)
Horizon Ho. KT17: Eps 2B 34
Hornbeam Cres. TW8: Bford 4C 4
Hornbeam Gdns. KT3: N Mald . .3D 24
Hornbeam Wlk. TW10: Rich 6G 11
Hornchurch Cl. KT2: King T 1E 16
Horndean Cl. SW15 . . . . .5D 12
Horne Way SW15 . . . . .6F 7
Horsecroft SM7: Bans 6J 35
Horsecroft Mdws. SM7: Bans . . .5J 35
Horse Fair KT1: King T 3A 36 (6E 16)
Horseshoe, The SM7: Bans 4J 35
Horsley Cl. KT19: Eps 2A 34
Horsley Dr. KT2: King T 2E 16
Horticultural Pl. W4 . . . . .2A 6
HORTON 7K 29
Horton Country Pk. 6G 29
Horton Country Pk.
Local Nature Reserve 5G 29
Horton Cres. KT19: Eps 7H 29
Horton Footpath KT19: Eps 7K 29
Horton Gdns. KT19: Eps 7K 29
Horton Hill KT19: Eps 7K 29
Horton Ho. W6 . . . . .2H 7
(off Field Rd.)
Horton La. KT19: Eps 1H 33
Horton Pk. Children's Farm 6H 29
Horton Pk. Golf Course 4K 29
Hospital Bri. Rd.
TW2: Twick, Whitt 4G 9
HOSPITAL BRIDGE RDBT. 6G 9
Hospital Rd. TW3: Houn 1F 9
Hotham Cl. KT8: W Mole 7F 15
Hotham Rd. SW15 . . . . .7F 7
Houblon Cl. TW12: Hamp 3D 14
Houghton Cl. TW12: Hamp 3D 14
HOUNSLOW 1G 9
Hounslow Av. TW3: Houn 2G 9
Hounslow Bus. Pk. TW3: Houn . .1F 9
Hounslow Gdns. TW3: Houn 2G 9
Hounslow Heath Golf Course 2B 8
Hounslow Heath Nature Reserve
. . . . .3D 8
Hounslow Rd. TW2: Whitt 3G 9
TW13: Hanw 1C 14
TW14: Felt 5A 8
Hounslow Station (Rail) 2G 9
HOUNSLOW WEST 1C 8
Houston Pl. KT10: Esh 5K 21
Houston Rd. KT6: Surb 3C 22
Howard Av. KT17: Ewe 6D 30
Howard Cl. KT21: Asht 7G 33
TW12: Hamp 4H 15
Howard Rd. KT3: N Mald 7B 18
KT5: Surb 3G 23
TW7: Isle 7A 4
Howard's La. SW15 . . . . .1E 12
Howard St. KT7: T Ditt 4C 22
Howell Hill SM2: Cheam 6F 31
Howell Hill Cl. KT17: Ewe 7F 31
Howell Hill Gro. KT17: Ewe 7F 31
Howell Hill Nature Reserve 7G 31
Howgate Rd. SW14 . . . . .7A 6
Howitts Cl. KT10: Esh 3F 27
Howsman Rd. SW13 . . . . .3D 6
Howson Ter. TW10: Rich 3F 11
Hubbard Dr. KT9: Chess 3E 28
Hudson Rd. KT19: Eps 2A 34
Hugh Dalton Av. SW6 . . . . .3J 7
Hughenden Rd. KT4: Wor Pk 4D 24
Hugh Gaitskell Cl. SW6 . . . . .3J 7
Hugh Herland Ho.
KT1: King T 6D 36 (7F 17)
Hugon Rd. SW6 . . . . .7K 7
Hulverston Cl. SM2: Sutt 6K 31
Humbolt Rd. W6 . . . . .3H 7
Hunston Rd. SM4: Mord 5K 25
Hunter Ct. KT19: Eps 6H 29
Hunter Ho. SW5 . . . . .2K 7
(off Old Brompton Rd.)
Hunter Rd. SW20 . . . . .5F 19

Hunters Cl. KT19: Eps 2K 33
Hunters Ct. TW9: Rich 2E 10
Hunter's Rd. KT9: Chess 7F 23
Hunting Cl. KT10: Esh 1F 27
Huntingdon Gdns. KT4: Wor Pk . .7F 25
W4 . . . . .4K 5
Huntingfield Rd. SW15 . . . . .1D 12
Hunting Ga. Dr. KT9: Chess 4F 29
Hunting Ga. M. TW2: Twick 5K 9
Huntley Way SW20 . . . . .6D 18
Huntsmans Cl. TW13: Felt 1A 14
Huntsmoor Rd. KT19: Ewe 2A 30
Hurley Cl. KT12: Walt T 6A 20
SM7: Bans 5J 35
Hurlingham Bus. Pk. SW6 . . . . . .7K 7
Hurlingham Club, The 7K 7
Hurlingham Ct. SW6 . . . . .7J 7
Hurlingham Gdns. SW6 . . . . .7J 7
Hurlingham Pk. 6J 7
Hurlingham Rd. SW6 . . . . .6J 7
Hurlingham Sq. SW6 . . . . .7K 7
Hurlingham Yacht Club 7H 7
Hurstbourne KT10: Clay 3A 28
Hurstbourne Ho. SW15 . . . . .3C 12
(off Tangley Gro.)
Hurst Cl. KT9: Chess 2H 29
Hurstcourt Rd. SM1: Sutt 6K 25
Hurstfield Rd. KT8: W Mole 7F 15
Hurst La. KT8: E Mos 1H 21
HURST PARK 6H 15
Hurst Pool 7G 15
Hurst Rd. KT8: W Mole, E Mos . . .7G 15
KT12: Walt T 2B 20
KT19: Eps 7A 30
Hurtwood Rd. KT12: Walt T 4E 20
Hussars Cl. TW4: Houn 1D 8
Hutton Cl. KT12: Hers 2A 26
Hutton M. SW15 . . . . .2E 12
Hyacinth Cl. TW12: Hamp 3F 15
Hyacinth Rd. SW15 . . . . .5D 12
Hyde Ho. TW3: Houn 1H 9
Hyde Rd. TW10: Rich 2G 11
Hyde Wlk. SM4: Mord 4K 25
Hylands Cl. KT18: Eps 4K 33
Hylands M. KT18: Eps 4K 33
Hylands Rd. KT18: Eps 4K 33
Hyperion Pl. KT19: Ewe 5A 30
Hythe Ho. W6 . . . . .1F 7
(off Shepherd's Bush Rd.)

I

Ibberton Ho. W14 . . . . .1H 7
(off Russell Rd.)
Ibis La. W4 . . . . .5K 5
Idmiston Rd. KT4: Wor Pk 4C 24
Idmiston Sq. KT4: Wor Pk 4C 24
Iffley Rd. W6 . . . . .1E 6
Ilex Cl. TW16: Sun 6B 14
Illumina Ho. SW18 . . . . .2K 13
(off Broomhill Rd.)
Imber Cl. KT10: Esh 5J 21
Imber Court 4J 21
Imber Ct. Trad. Est.
KT8: E Mos 3J 21
Imber Cross KT7: T Ditt 3A 22
Imber Gro. KT10: Esh 4J 21
Imber Pk. Rd. KT10: Esh 5J 21
India Way SW15 . . . . .3D 12
Inglethorpe St. SW6 . . . . .5G 7
Inglewood M. KT6: Surb 5H 23
Ingram Cl. KT17: Hers 2B 26
Ingress St. W4 . . . . .2B 6
Inkerman Ter. W8 . . . . .1K 7
(off Allen St.)
Inner Pk. Rd. SW19 . . . . .5G 13
Innes Cl. SW20 . . . . .6H 19
Innes Gdns. SW15 . . . . .3E 12
Interface Ho. TW3: Houn 1F 9
(off Staines Rd.)
International Ho. TW8: Bford 2F 5
(off Gt. West Rd.)
Inver Ct. W6 . . . . .1D 6
Inveresk Gdns. KT4: Wor Pk 7D 24
Invermead Cl. W6 . . . . .1D 6
Inverness Rd. KT4: Wor Pk 5G 25
TW3: Houn 1E 8
In View Ct. KT12: Hers 1A 26
Inwood Av. TW3: Houn 1H 9
Inwood Bus. Pk. TW3: Houn 1G 9
Inwood Cl. KT12: Walt T 6B 20
Inwood Rd. TW3: Houn 1G 9
Iona Cl. SM4: Mord 4K 25
Irene Rd. SW6 . . . . .5K 7

Ireton Ho. SW15 . . . . .2H 13
(off Stamford Sq.)
Iris Cl. KT6: Surb 4G 23
Iris Gdns. KT7: T Ditt 4K 21
Iris M. TW4: Houn 3F 9
Iris Rd. TW19: Ewe 2J 29
Ironside Ct. TW11: Hamp W . . .5D 16
Irving Mans. W14 . . . . .3H 7
(off Queen's Club Gdns.)
Isabel Hill Cl. TW12: Hamp . . .5G 15
Isabella Ct. TW10: Rich 3G 11
(off Kingsmead)
Isabella Ho. W6 . . . . .2F 7
(off Queen Caroline St.)
Isabella Pl. KT2: King T 2G 17
Isabella Plantation Garden 7J 11
Isis Cl. SW15 . . . . .1F 13
Isis Ct. W4 . . . . .4J 5
Island, The KT7: T Ditt 3B 22
3G 21
Island Barn Reservoir Sailing Club
Island Farm Av. KT8: W Mole . . .2E 20
Island Farm Rd.
KT8: W Mole 2E 20
Islay Gdns. TW4: Houn 2C 8
ISLEWORTH 7B 4
Isleworth Ait Nature Reserve . . .7C 4
Isleworth Bus. Complex
TW7: Isle 6A 4
Isleworth Prom. TW1: Twick . . .1C 10
Isleworth Recreation Cen. 1A 10
Isleworth Station (Rail) 6A 4
Issa Rd. TW3: Houn 1E 8
Ivatt Pl. W14 . . . . .2J 7
Ivybridge Cl. TW1: Twick 4B 10
Ivy Bri. Retail Pk. TW7: Isle . . .2A 10
Ivy Cl. TW16: Sun 6B 14
Ivy Cres. W4 . . . . .1K 5
Ivydene KT8: W Mole 2E 20
Ivy La. TW4: Houn 1E 8
Ivy Rd. KT6: Surb 5H 23
TW3: Houn 1G 9

J

Jacaranda Cl. KT3: N Mald 7B 18
Jack Goodchild Way
KT1: King T 7J 17
Jackson Cl. KT18: Eps 3A 34
Jackson Way KT19: Eps 5H 29
Jacobs M. SW15 . . . . .1H 13
James's Cotts. TW9: Kew 4H 5
James St. TW3: Houn 1J 9
James Ter. SW14 . . . . .7A 6
(off Church Path)
Jamieson Ho. TW4: Houn 3E 8
Jasmine Cl. SW19 . . . . .2K 19
Jasmine Way KT8: E Mos 1K 21
Jasmin Rd. KT19: Ewe 2J 29
Jeal Oakwood Cl. KT18: Eps 3B 34
Jefferson Cl. W13 . . . . .1C 4
Jefferson Ho. TW8: Bford 3F 5
Jeffs Cl. TW12: Hamp 3G 15
Jeffs Rd. SM1: Sutt 1J 31
Jemmett Cl. KT2: King T 5J 17
Jenner Pl. SW13 . . . . .3E 6
Jenner Way KT19: Eps 5H 29
Jennings Cl. KT6: Surb 4D 22
Jephtha Rd. SW18 . . . . .3K 13
Jerdan Ho. SW6 . . . . .4K 7
(off North End Rd.)
Jerdan Pl. SW6 . . . . .4K 7
Jerome Ho. KT1: Hamp W 3A 36
Jerome Pl. KT1: King T 4B 36
Jersey Rd. TW7: Isle 3A 4
Jervis Rd. SW6 . . . . .3J 7
Jessel Mans. W14 . . . . .3H 7
(off Queen's Club Gdns.)
Jessop Ho. W4 . . . . .1A 6
(off Kirton Cl.)
Jillian Cl. TW12: Hamp 4F 15
Jim Griffiths Ho. SW6 . . . . .3J 7
(off Clem Attlee Ct.)
Joanna Ho. W6 . . . . .2F 7
(off Queen Caroline St.)
Jocelyn Rd. TW9: Rich 7F 5
Jodrell Cl. TW7: Isle 5B 4
John Austin Cl.
KT2: King T 2E 36 (5G 17)
John Bull Pl. W4 . . . . .1K 5
John Gale Ct. KT17: Ewe 5C 30
(off West St.)
John Goddard Way TW13: Felt . . .6A 8
John Knight Lodge SW6 . . . . . . .4K 7
John Smith Av. SW6 . . . . .4J 7

Johnson Mans. W14 . . . . .3H 7
(off Queen's Club Gdns.)
Johnsons Dr. TW12: Hamp 5H 15
John Strachey Ho. SW6 . . . . .3J 7
(off Clem Attlee Ct.)
John Watkin Cl. KT19: Eps 5J 29
John Wesley Ct. TW1: Twick 5B 10
John Wheatley Ho. SW6 . . . . . . .3J 7
(off Clem Attlee Ct.)
John Williams Cl.
KT2: King T 1B 36 (5E 16)
Jones M. SW15 . . . . .1H 13
Jones Wlk. TW10: Rich 3G 11
Jonquil Gdns. TW12: Hamp 3F 15
Jordan Cl. SW15 . . . . .1G 13
Jordans Cl. TW7: Isle 5A 4
Jordans M. TW2: Twick 6K 9
Joseph Locke Way KT10: Esh . . .6F 21
Jubilee Av. TW2: Whitt 5H 9
Jubilee Cl.
KT1: Hamp W 2A 36 (5D 16)
Jubilee Ct. TW3: Houn 1G 9
(off Bristow Rd.)
Jubilee Rd. SM3: Cheam 4G 31
Jubilee Vs. KT10: Esh 5J 21
Jubilee Way KT9: Chess 1H 29
Jubilee Way Training Track 7J 23
Judge Wlk. KT10: Clay 3K 27
Julien Rd. W5 . . . . .1D 4
Junction Rd. TW8: Bford 1D 4
W5 . . . . .1D 4
Juniper Ct. KT9: Chess 2G 29
KT19: Eps 5A 30
TW13: Felt 7A 8
Juniper Ct. KT8: W Mole 1G 21
TW3: Houn 1G 9
(off Grove Rd.)
Juniper Ho. TW9: Kew 5J 5
Juniper Pl. KT17: Bans 4F 35
Jurassic Encounter 7D 18
Justin Cl. TW8: Bford 4E 4

K

Katherine Rd. TW1: Twick 5B 10
Kathleen Godfree Ct. SW19 . . . .3K 19
Kavanagh Ct. KT18: Eps 3B 34
(off Martin's Av.)
Kean Ho. TW1: Twick 3E 10
(off Arosa Rd.)
Keble Cl. KT4: Wor Pk 5C 24
Keble Pl. SW13 . . . . .3E 6
Kedeston Cl. SM1: Sutt 5K 25
Keep, The KT2: King T 3G 17
Keepers M. TW11: Tedd 3D 16
Keevil Dr. SW19 . . . . .4G 13
Keir, The SW19 . . . . .2F 19
Keir Hardie Ho. W6 . . . . .3G 7
(off Fulham Pal. Rd.)
Kelmscott House 2E 6
Kelmscott Pl. KT21: Asht 6D 32
Kelsall M. TW9: Kew 5J 5
Kelsey Cl. KT9: Chess 4E 28
Kelvedon Cl. KT2: King T 3H 17
Kelvedon Rd. SW6 . . . . .4J 7
Kelvinbrook KT8: W Mole 7G 15
Kelvin Cl. KT19: Ewe 3H 29
Kelvin Ct. TW7: Isle 6A 4
Kelvin Dr. TW1: Twick 3C 10
Kelvin Gro. KT9: Chess 7E 22
Kelway Ho. W14 . . . . .2J 7
Kempsford Gdns. SW5 . . . . .5K 7
Kempson Rd. SW6 . . . . .5K 7
Kempton Av. TW16: Sun 5A 14
Kempton Cl. TW16: Sun 5A 14
Kempton Ga. TW12: Hamp 5E 14
Kempton Nature Reserve 3C 14
Kempton Pk. Racecourse 4B 14
Kempton Park Station (Rail) 4A 14
Kenbrook Ho. W14 . . . . .1J 7
Kendall Rd. TW7: Isle 6B 4
Kendal Pl. SW15 . . . . .2J 13
Kendor Av. KT19: Eps 7K 29
Kendrey Gdns. TW2: Whitt 4K 9
Kenilworth Av. SW19 . . . . .2K 19
Kenilworth Cl. SM7: Bans 5K 35
Kenilworth Ct. SW15 . . . . .7H 7
(off Lwr. Richmond Rd.)
Kenilworth Dr. KT12: Walt T 7C 20
Kenilworth Rd. KT17: Ewe 2D 30
Kenley Rd. KT1: King T 6J 17
SW19 . . . . .6K 19
TW1: Twick 3C 10
Kenley Wlk. SM3: Cheam 1G 31

Kenmore Cl. TW9: Kew 4H 5
Kennet Ho. SW18 . . . . .1K 13
(off Enterprise Way)
Kenneth Younger Ho. SW6 . . . . .3J 7
(off Clem Attlee Ct.)
Kennet Rd. TW7: Isle 7A 4
Kennett Ct. W4 . . . . .4J 5
Kensington Cen. W14 . . . . .1H 7
(not continuous)
Kensington Gdns.
KT1: King T 6B 36 (7E 16)
Kensington Hall Gdns. W14 . . . .2J 7
Kensington High St. W8 . . . . . . .1J 7
W14 . . . . .1J 7
Kensington Mans. SW5 . . . . . . .2K 7
(not continuous)
Kensington Olympia Station
(Rail, Underground & Overground)
. . . . .1H 7
Kensington Village W14 . . . . . . .1H 7
Kensington W. W14 . . . . .1H 7
Kent Dr. TW11: Tedd 2K 15
Kent Ho. W4 . . . . .2B 6
(off Devonshire St.)
Kenton Av. TW16: Sun 6C 14
Kenton Cl. TW1: Twick 3E 10
W14 . . . . .1J 7
Kent Rd. KT1: King T 5B 36 (7E 16)
KT8: E Mos 1H 21
TW9: Kew 4H 5
W4 . . . . .1K 5
Kent's Pas. TW12: Hamp 5E 14
Kent Way KT6: Surb 7F 23
Kentwode Grn. SW13 . . . . .4D 6
Kenway Rd. SW5 . . . . .1K 7
Kenwood Dr. KT12: Hers 3A 26
Kenwyn Rd. SW20 . . . . .5F 19
Kenyngton Dr. TW16: Sun 2A 14
Kenyon Mans. W14 . . . . .3H 7
(off Queen's Club Gdns.)
Kenyon St. SW6 . . . . .5G 7
Kersfield Ho. SW15 . . . . .3G 13
Kersfield Rd. SW15 . . . . .3G 13
Keston Ct. KT5: Surb 2G 23
(off Cranes Pk.)
Kestrel Cl. KT2: King T 1E 16
KT19: Eps 1H 33
Keswick Av. SW15 . . . . .2B 18
SW19 . . . . .6K 19
Keswick B'way. SW15 . . . . .2J 13
(off Up. Richmond Rd.)
Keswick Rd. SW15 . . . . .2H 13
TW2: Whitt 3H 9
KEW .5H 5
KEW BRIDGE 2G 5
Kew Bri. TW8: Bford 3H 5
Kew Bri. Arches TW9: Kew 3H 5
Kew Bri. Ct. W4 . . . . .2H 5
Kew Bri. Distribution Cen.
TW8: Bford 2G 5
Kew Bri. Rd. TW8: Bford 3G 5
Kew Bridge Station (Rail) 2G 5
Kew Cres. SM3: Cheam 7H 25
Kew Ct. KT2: King T 1C 36 (5F 17)
Kew Foot Rd. TW9: Rich 1F 11
Kew Gdns. 4F 5
Kew Gdns. Rd. TW9: Kew 4G 5
Kew Gardens Station
(Underground & Overground)
. . . . .5H 5
KEW GREEN 4H 5
Kew Grn. TW9: Kew 3G 5
Kew Mdw. Path TW9: Kew 5H 5
(Clifford Av.)
TW9: Kew 5J 5
(Magnolia Ct.)
Kew Retail Pk. TW9: Kew 5J 5
Kew Riverside Pk. TW9: Kew 4J 5
Kew Rd. TW9: Kew, Rich 3H 5
Keynsham Rd. SM4: Mord 5K 25
Kilcorral Cl. KT17: Eps 3D 34
Killester Gdns. KT4: Wor Pk 1E 30
Killick Ho. SM1: Sutt 1K 31
Killick M. SM3: Cheam 3H 31
Kilmaine Rd. SW6 . . . . .4H 7
Kilmarsh Rd. W6 . . . . .1F 7
Kilmington Rd. SW13 . . . . .3D 6
Kilmorey Gdns. TW1: Twick 2C 10
Kilmorey Rd. TW1: Twick 1C 10
Kilmuir Ho. KT17: Eps 2B 34
(off Depot Rd.)
Kiln La. KT17: Eps 7B 30
Kilnside KT10: Clay 4B 28
Kilsha Rd. KT12: Walt T 3B 20
Kimbell Gdns. SW6 . . . . .5H 7
Kimberley Wlk. KT12: Walt T 4A 20

Kimber Pl. TW4: Houn 4E 8
(Conway Rd.)
TW4: Houn 1E 8
(Marryat Cl.)
Kimber Rd. SW18 . . . . .4K 13
Kimpton Ho. SW15 . . . . .4D 12
Kimpton Ind. Est. SM3: Sutt 6J 25
Kimpton Link Bus. Cen.
SM3: Sutt 6J 25
Kimpton Pk. Way SM1: Sutt 6H 25
SM3: Sutt 6H 25
Kimpton Rd. SM3: Sutt 6J 25
Kimpton Trade & Bus. Cen.
SM3: Sutt 6J 25
Kincha Lodge KT2: King T 1E 36
King Charles Cres. KT5: Surb . . .4G 23
King Charles Rd. KT5: Surb 2G 23
King Charles Wlk. SW19 . . . . . . .5H 13
King Edward Dr. KT9: Chess 7F 23
King Edward M. SW13 . . . . .5D 6
King Edwards Gro.
TW11: Tedd 3C 16
King Edwards Mans. SW6 . . . . . .4K 7
(off Fulham Rd.)
Kingfisher Cl. KT12: Hers 2D 26
Kingfisher Ct. KT8: E Mos 1K 21
SM1: Sutt 2J 31
SW19 . . . . .6G 13
TW3: Houn 2G 9
Kingfisher Dr. TW10: Ham 1C 16
Kingfisher Leisure Cen.
Kingston upon Thames
. . . . .4D 36 (6F 17)
King George Av. KT12: Walt T . . .5C 20
King George Sq. TW10: Rich 3G 11
King George's Trad. Est.
KT9: Chess 1H 29
King Georges Wlk. KT10: Esh . . .1H 27
King Henry's Reach W6 . . . . .3F 7
King Henry's Rd. KT1: King T 7J 17
King's Arms All. TW8: Bford 3E 4
Kings Av. KT3: N Mald 1B 24
Kingsbridge Rd. KT12: Walt T . . .4A 20
SM4: Mord 3G 25
Kingsbrook KT22: Lea 7B 32
Kings Chase KT8: E Mos 7H 15
Kingsclere Cl. SW15 . . . . .4D 12
Kingscliffe Gdns. SW19 . . . . . . .5J 13
Kings Cl. KT7: T Ditt 3B 22
KT12: Walt T 5A 20
King's Club, The 3F 19
Kingscote Rd. KT3: N Mald 7A 18
W4 . . . . .1A 6
Kings Ct. KT12: Walt T 7A 20
W6 . . . . .1D 6
Kings Ct. Mans. SW6 . . . . .5J 7
(off Fulham Rd.)
Kings Ct. M. KT8: E Mos 2J 21
Kingsdowne Rd. KT6: Surb 4F 23
Kingsdown Rd. KT17: Eps 2D 34
SM3: Cheam 2H 31
Kings Dr. KT5: Surb 4H 23
KT7: T Ditt 4C 22
TW11: Tedd 2J 15
Kings Farm Av. TW10: Rich 1H 11
Kings Gdns. KT12: Walt T 5A 20
Kingsgate Bus. Cen.
KT2: King T 2C 36
Kingsgate Rd.
KT1: King T 2C 36 (5F 17)
KT2: King T 2C 36 (5F 17)
Kingshill Av. KT4: Wor Pk 4D 24
Kings Keep KT1: King T 1F 23
SW15 . . . . .2G 13
Kingslawn Cl. SW15 . . . . .2E 12
Kingsleigh Cl. TW8: Bford 3E 4
Kingsley Av. SM7: Bans 4K 35
Kingsley Ct. KT4: Wor Pk 6C 24
(off The Avenue)
KT12: Walt T 1A 20
(off Ashley Pk. Rd.)
Kingsley Dr. KT4: Wor Pk 6C 24
Kingsley Ho. W14 . . . . .1H 7
(off Avonmore Pl.)
Kingsley Mans. W14 . . . . .3H 7
(off Greyhound Rd.)
Kings Mall W6 . . . . .1F 7
Kingsmead TW10: Rich 3G 11
Kingsmead Av. KT4: Wor Pk 6E 24
KT6: Surb 6H 23
TW16: Sun 6B 14
Kingsmead Cl. KT19: Ewe 4A 30
TW11: Tedd 3C 16
Kingsmeadow 7H 17
Kingsmeadow Athletics Cen. . . .7H 17
Kings Mead Pk. KT10: Clay 4K 27

Kingsmere Cl. SW15 . . . . .7G **7**
Kingsmere Rd. SW19 . . . . .6G **13**
Kingsmill Bus. Pk.
   KT1: King T 7G **17**
Kingsnympton Pk. KT2: King T . . .4J **17**
Kingspark Bus. Cen.
   KT3: N Mald 1K **23**
King's Pas.
   KT2: King T 1B **36** (5E **16**)
Kings Pas. KT1: King T . .4B **36** (6E **16**)
King's Pl. W4 . . . . .2K **5**
Kings Ride Ga. TW10: Rich 1H **11**
Kingsridge SW19 . . . . .6H **13**
King's Rd. KT2: King T . . .1C **36** (4F **17**)
   KT6: Surb 5D **22**
   SM2: Sutt 6K **31**
   SW19 . . . . .3K **19**
   TW11: Tedd 2J **15**
Kings Rd. KT12: Walt T 6A **20**
   SW14 . . . . .7A **6**
   TW1: Twick 3C **10**
   TW10: Rich 3G **11**
   TW13: Felt 5B **8**
King's Ter. TW7: Isle 1B **10**
Kingston Av. SM3: Cheam 7H **25**
Kingston Bri.
   KT1: King T 3A **36** (6E **16**)
Kingston Bus. Cen. KT9: Chess . . .7F **23**
Kingston By-Pass KT3: N Mald . . .2B **24**
   KT6: Surb 7E **22**
   SW15 . . . . .1B **18**
   SW20 . . . . .6D **18**
Kingston By-Pass Rd.
   KT6: Surb 6K **21**
   KT10: Hin W, Surb 6K **21**
Kingston Cl. TW11: Tedd 3C **16**
Kingston Crematorium
   KT1: King T 7H **17**
Kingston Hall Rd.
   KT1: King T 5B **36** (7E **16**)
Kingston Hill KT2: King T 5H **17**
Kingston Hill Pl. KT2: King T 1K **17**
KINGSTON HOSPITAL 5J **17**
Kingston Ho. KT1: King T 7B **36**
Kingston Ho. Est. KT6: Surb 3C **22**
Kingstonian FC 7H **17**
Kingston La. TW11: Tedd 2B **16**
Kingston Lodge KT3: N Mald 1B **24**
Kingston Rd. KT1: King T 7J **17**
   KT3: N Mald 7J **17**
   KT4: Wor Pk 6J **23**
   KT5: Surb 6J **23**
   KT17: Ewe 5C **30**
   KT19: Ewe 6J **23**
   KT22: Lea 7B **32**
   (not continuous)
   SW15 . . . . .6D **12**
   SW19 . . . . .6D **12**
   (Norstead Pl.)
   SW19 . . . . .6D **12**
   (Watery La.)
   SW20 . . . . .6G **19**
   TW11: Tedd 2C **16**
Kingston Station
   (Rail) 2C **36** (5F **17**)
Kingston University
   Kingston Hill Campus 2A **18**
   Knights Pk. Campus
   . . . . .6D **36** (7F **17**)
   Penrhyn Road Campus
   . . . . .7C **36** (1F **23**)
   Roehampton Vale Cen. 7C **12**
KINGSTON UPON THAMES
   . . . . .4B **36** (6E **16**)
Kingston upon Thames
   Art Gallery & Mus.
   . . . . .3D **36** (6F **17**)
Kingston upon Thames
   (Park & Ride) 5D **28**
KINGSTON VALE 1B **18**
Kingston Va. SW15 . . . . .1A **18**
King St. TW1: Twick 5B **10**
   TW9: Rich 2E **10**
   W6 .1D **6**
King St. Cloisters W6 . . . . .1E **6**
   (off King St.)
King St. Pde. TW1: Twick 5B **10**
   (off King St.)
Kings Warren KT22: Oxs 7H **27**
Kingsway KT3: N Mald 1F **25**
   SW14 . . . . .7J **5**
Kingsway, The KT17: Ewe 7B **30**
Kingsway Bus. Pk.
   TW12: Hamp 5E **14**

Kingsway Rd. SM3: Cheam 4H **31**
Kingswood Av. TW12: Hamp 3G **15**
Kingswood Cl. KT3: N Mald 3C **24**
   KT6: Surb 4F **23**
Kings Wood Ct.
   TW10: Rich 2G **11**
Kingswood Dr. SM2: Sutt 6K **31**
Kingswood Rd. SW19 . . . . .4J **19**
   W4 .1K **5**
Kingsworthy Cl. KT1: King T 7G **17**
Kings Yd. SW15 . . . . .7F **7**
   (off Lwr. Richmond Rd.)
Kingwood Rd. SW6 . . . . .5H **7**
Kinnaird Av. W4 . . . . .4K **5**
Kinnoul Rd. W6 . . . . .3H **7**
Kinross Av. KT4: Wor Pk 6D **24**
Kinsella Gdns. SW19 . . . . .2E **18**
Kinsheron Pl. KT8: E Mos 1H **21**
Kirby Cl. KT19: Ewe 2C **30**
Kirby Way KT12: Walt T 3B **20**
Kirkgate, The KT17: Eps 2B **34**
Kirkleas Rd. KT6: Surb 5F **23**
Kirkley Rd. SW19 . . . . .5K **19**
Kirksted Rd. SM4: Mord 5K **25**
Kirrane Ct. KT3: N Mald 2C **24**
Kirton Cl. W4 . . . . .1A **6**
Kitson Rd. SW13 . . . . .5D **6**
Kittiwake Pl. SM1: Sutt 2J **31**
Knaresborough Dr. SW18 . . . . . . .5K **13**
Kneller Gdns. TW7: Isle 3J **9**
Kneller Rd. KT3: N Mald 4B **24**
   TW2: Whitt 3H **9**
Knevett Ter. TW3: Houn 1F **9**
Knightly Wlk. SW18 . . . . .1K **13**
Knights Ct.
   KT1: King T 5C **36** (7F **17**)
Knight's Ho. W14 . . . . .2J **7**
   (off Baron's Ct. Rd.)
Knight's Pk.
   KT1: King T 5D **36** (7F **17**)
Knight's Pl. TW2: Twick 5K **9**
Knightwood Cres.
   KT3: N Mald 3B **24**
Knockholt Cl. SM2: Sutt 6K **31**
Knollmead KT5: Surb 5K **23**
Knolls, The KT17: Eps D 5F **35**
Knolls Cl. KT4: Wor Pk 7E **24**
Knowle Rd. TW2: Twick 5K **9**
Knowles Ho. SW18 . . . . .3K **13**
   (off Neville Gill Cl.)
Kramer M. SW5 . . . . .2K **7**
Kreisel Wlk. TW9: Kew 3G **5**
Kristina Ct. SM2: Sutt 3K **31**
   (off Overton Rd.)
Kurdish Mus. 1D **6**

L

Laburnum Cres. TW16: Sun 5A **14**
Laburnum Gro. KT3: N Mald 6A **18**
   TW3: Houn 1E **8**
Laburnum Rd. KT18: Eps 2B **34**
Lacey Dr. TW12: Hamp 5E **14**
Lacy Rd. SW15 . . . . .1G **13**
Ladbroke Rd. KT18: Eps 3A **34**
Ladderstile Ride KT2: King T 2J **17**
Lady Booth Rd.
   KT1: King T 4C **36** (7F **17**)
Lady Elizabeth Ho. SW14 . . . . . . .7K **5**
Lady Forsdyke Way
   KT19: Ewe 5H **29**
Lady Harewood Way
   KT19: Eps 5H **29**
Lady Hay KT4: Wor Pk 6C **24**
Lady Jane Ct. KT2: King T 6G **17**
   (off Cambridge Rd.)
Ladygrowd Rd. KT6: Surb 6H **23**
Lafone Av. TW13: Felt 6B **8**
Lainson St. SW18 . . . . .4K **13**
Lake Cl. SW19 . . . . .2J **19**
Lake Gdns. TW10: Ham 6C **10**
Lakehurst Rd. KT19: Ewe 2B **30**
Lakeland Cl. SW19 . . . . .2J **19**
Laker Pl. SW15 . . . . .3H **13**
Lakeside Cl. KT2: King T 4J **17**
   KT19: Ewe 3B **30**
Lakeside Dr. KT10: Esh 3H **27**
Lakewood Cl. KT10: Esh 7E **26**

Lalor St. SW6 . . . . .6H **7**
Lambert Av. TW9: Rich 7H **5**
Lambert Lodge TW8: Bford 2E **4**
   (off Layton Rd.)
Lambert Rd. SM7: Bans 3K **35**
Lamberts Rd. KT5: Surb 2F **23**
Lambourne Av. SW19 . . . . .1J **19**
Lambourn Gro. KT1: King T 6J **17**
Lambrook Ter. SW6 . . . . .5H **7**
Lambton Rd. SW20 . . . . .5F **19**
LAMDA 2G **7**
Lamington St. W6 . . . . .1E **6**
Lammas Hill KT10: Esh 1G **27**
Lammas La. KT10: Esh, Hers 1E **26**
Lammas Rd. TW10: Ham 1D **16**
Lampeter Sq. W6 . . . . .3H **7**
Lampton Ho. Cl. SW19 . . . . .1G **19**
Lampton Rd. TW3: Houn 1G **9**
Lanadron Cl. TW7: Isle 6A **4**
Lancaster Av. SW19 . . . . .2G **19**
Lancaster Cl. KT2: King T 2E **16**
   KT12: Walt T 4A **20**
Lancaster Cotts. TW10: Rich 3F **11**
Lancaster Ct. KT12: Walt T 4A **20**
   KT19: Ewe 6A **30**
   SM2: Sutt 4K **31**
   (off Mulgrave Rd.)
   SM7: Bans 3J **35**
   SW6 . . . . .4J **7**
   SW19 . . . . .2H **19**
Lancaster Ho. TW7: Isle 4A **4**
   TW10: Rich 3F **11**
Lancaster M. TW10: Rich 2F **11**
Lancaster Pk. TW10: Rich 2F **11**
Lancaster Pl. SW19 . . . . .2G **19**
   TW1: Twick 3B **10**
Lancaster Rd. SW19 . . . . .2G **19**
   TW1: Twick 3B **10**
Lancaster Way KT4: Wor Pk 4E **24**
Landford Rd. SW15 . . . . .7F **7**
Landgrove Rd. SW19 . . . . .2K **19**
Landmark Arts Cen. 2C **16**
Landmark Ho. W6 . . . . .2F **7**
   (off Hammersmith Br. Rd.)
Landridge Rd. SW6 . . . . .6J **7**
Landseer Rd. KT3: N Mald 4A **24**
   SM1: Sutt 3K **31**
Lane End KT18: Eps 3J **33**
Lane Gdns. KT10: Clay 4A **28**
Laneway SW15 . . . . .2E **12**
Lanfrey Pl. W14 . . . . .2J **7**
Langbourne Way KT10: Clay 3B **28**
Langdale Cl. SW14 . . . . .1J **11**
Langdon Pk. TW11: Tedd 4D **16**
Langdon Pl. SW14 . . . . .7K **5**
Langham Ct. SW20 . . . . .6F **19**
Langham Gdns. TW10: Ham 1D **16**
Langham Ho. Cl. TW10: Ham 1E **16**
Langham Mans. SW5 . . . . .2J **7**
   (off Earl's Ct. Sq.)
Langham Pl. W4 . . . . .3B **6**
Langham Rd. SW20 . . . . .5F **19**
   TW11: Tedd 2C **16**
Langhorn Dr. TW2: Twick 4K **9**
Langlands Ri. KT19: Eps 2K **33**
Langley Av. KT4: Wor Pk 5G **25**
   KT6: Surb 5E **22**
Langley Gro. KT3: N Mald 6B **18**
Langley Rd. KT6: Surb 4F **23**
   SW19 . . . . .5J **19**
   TW7: Isle 6A **4**
LANGLEY VALE 7B **34**
Langley Va. Rd. KT18: Eps D 7A **34**
Langport Ct. KT12: Walt T 5B **20**
Langridge M. TW12: Hamp 3E **14**
Langside Av. SW15 . . . . .1D **12**
Langthorne St. SW6 . . . . .4G **7**
Langton Av. KT17: Ewe 7C **30**
Langton Pl. SW18 . . . . .5K **13**
Langton Rd. KT8: W Mole 1H **21**
Langtry Ct. TW7: Isle 6A **4**
Langtry Ho. KT2: King T 5H **17**
   (off London Rd.)
Langtry Pl. SW6 . . . . .3K **7**
Langwood Chase TW11: Tedd 3D **16**
Langwood Cl. KT21: Asht 6H **33**
Lanigan Dr. TW3: Houn 2G **9**
Lannoy Point SW6 . . . . .4H **7**
   (off Pellant Rd.)
Lansbury Av. TW14: Felt 3K **8**
Lansdown Cl. KT12: Walt T 5B **20**
Lansdowne Cl. KT6: Surb 6J **23**
   SW20 . . . . .4G **19**
   TW1: Twick 5A **10**
Lansdowne Rd. KT4: Wor Pk 6D **24**
Lansdowne Rd. KT18: Eps 3K **33**
   (off Dalmeny Way)

Lansdowne Rd. KT19: Ewe 4K **29**
   SW20 . . . . .4F **19**
Lantern Cl. SW15 . . . . .1D **12**
Lapwing Ct. KT6: Surb 7H **23**
Lara Cl. KT9: Chess 4F **29**
Larby Pl. KT17: Ewe 6B **30**
Larch Cres. KT19: Ewe 3J **29**
Larch Dr. W4 . . . . .2H **5**
Larches Av. SW14 . . . . .1A **12**
Larchwood Cl. SM7: Bans 4H **35**
Larcombe Ct. SM2: Sutt 4K **31**
   (off Worcester Rd.)
Largewood Av. KT6: Surb 6H **23**
Larkfield Rd. TW9: Rich 1F **11**
Larkhall Cl. KT12: Hers 3B **26**
Larkspur Way KT19: Ewe 2K **29**
Larnach Rd. W6 . . . . .3G **7**
Larpent Av. SW15 . . . . .2F **13**
Lascar Cl. TW3: Houn 1E **8**
Latchmere Cl. TW10: Ham 2F **17**
Latchmere La. KT2: King T 3G **17**
   TW10: Ham 3G **17**
Latchmere Rd. KT2: King T 4F **17**
Lateward Rd. TW8: Bford 3E **4**
Latham Cl. TW1: Twick 4B **10**
Latham Cl. SW5 . . . . .1K **7**
   (off W. Cromwell Rd.)
Latham Rd. TW1: Twick 4A **10**
Latimer Cl. KT4: Wor Pk 1E **30**
Latimer Rd. TW11: Tedd 2A **16**
Lattimer Pl. W4 . . . . .4B **6**
Latton Cl. KT10: Esh 1G **27**
   KT12: Walt T 4D **20**
Latymer Ct. W6 . . . . .1G **7**
Laubin Cl. TW1: Twick 1C **10**
Lauderdale Dr. TW10: Ham 7E **10**
Laundry Rd. W6 . . . . .3H **7**
Laurel Av. TW1: Twick 5A **10**
Laurel Bank Gdns. SW6 . . . . .6J **7**
Laurel Gdns. TW4: Houn 1D **8**
Laurel Rd. SW13 . . . . .6D **6**
   SW20 . . . . .5E **18**
   TW12: Hamp H 2J **15**
Laurels, The SM7: Bans 6J **35**
Lauriston Rd. SW19 . . . . .3G **19**
Laval Ho. TW8: Bford 2F **5**
   (off Ealing Rd.)
Lavender Av. KT4: Wor Pk 7F **25**
Lavender Cl. KT8: W Mole 7G **15**
   TW14: Felt 3A **8**
Lavender Ho. TW9: Kew 5J **5**
Lavender Rd. KT19: Ewe 2J **29**
Lavenham Rd. SW18 . . . . .6J **13**
Laverstoke Gdns. SW15 . . . . .4C **12**
Lawford Rd. W4 . . . . .4K **5**
Lawley Ho. TW1: Twick 3E **10**
Lawn Cl. KT3: N Mald 6B **18**
Lawn Cres. TW9: Kew 6H **5**
Lawns, The SM2: Cheam 4H **31**
   SW19 . . . . .2J **19**
Lawrence Av. KT3: N Mald 3A **24**
Lawrence Est. TW4: Houn 1B **8**
Lawrence M. SW15 . . . . .1F **13**
Lawrence Pde. TW7: Isle 7C **4**
   (off Lower Sq.)
Lawrence Rd. TW4: Houn 1B **8**
   TW10: Ham 1D **16**
   TW12: Hamp 4E **14**
   W5 .1E **4**
Lawrence Weaver Cl.
   SM4: Mord 3K **25**
Lawson Cl. SW19 . . . . .7G **13**
Lawson Ct. KT6: Surb 4E **22**
Layton Cl. TW8: Bford 2E **4**
Layton Pl. TW9: Kew 5H **5**
Layton Rd. TW3: Houn 1G **9**
   TW8: Bford 2E **4**
Lea Cl. TW2: Whitt 4E **8**
Leaf Cl. KT7: T Ditt 2K **21**
Leafield Rd. SM1: Sutt 6K **25**
   SW20 . . . . .7J **19**
Leamington Av. SM4: Mord 1H **25**
Leamington Cl. TW3: Houn 2H **9**
Leamore St. W6 . . . . .1E **6**
   (off Lower Sq.)
Leander Ct. KT6: Surb 4E **22**
Leas Cl. KT9: Chess 4G **29**
Leatherhead Bus. Pk.
   KT22: Lea 7A **32**
LEATHERHEAD COMMON 7B **32**
Leatherhead Golf Course 5B **32**
Leatherhead Rd. KT9: Chess 3C **32**
   KT21: Asht 7F **33**
Lebanon Av. TW13: Hanw 2C **14**
Lebanon Cl. TW1: Twick 4C **10**
Lebanon Gdns. SW18 . . . . .3K **13**
Lebanon Pk. TW1: Twick 4C **10**

Lebanon Rd. SW18 . . . . .2K 13
Leconfield Av. SW13 . . . . .7C 6
Leeson Ho. TW1: Twick 4C 10
Leeward Gdns. SW19 . . . . .2H 19
Leeways, The
   SM3: Cheam 3H 31
Legion Ct. SM4: Mord 3K 25
Leg O'Mutton Local Nature Reserve
   . . . . .4C 6
Leicester Cl. KT4: Wor Pk 1F 31
Leicester Ct. TW1: Twick 3E 10
   (off Clevedon Rd.)
Leigh, The KT2: King T 4B 18
Leigham Dr. TW7: Isle 4A 4
Leigh Cl. KT3: N Mald 1K 23
Leigh Cl. Ind. Est.
   KT3: N Mald 1A 24
Leigh Ct. W14 . . . . .1J 7
   (off Avonmore Pl.)
Leigh Pl. TW13: Felt 5B 8
Leigh Rd. TW3: Houn 1J 9
Leighton Mans. W14 . . . . .3H 7
   (off Greyhound Rd.)
Leighton Way KT18: Eps 3A 34
Leinster Av. SW14 . . . . .7K 5
Leisure W. TW13: Felt 6A 8
Leith Rd. KT17: Eps 1B 34
Lena Gdns. W6 . . . . .1F 7
Lendy Pl. TW16: Sun 1A 20
Lenelby Rd. KT6: Surb 5H 23
Len Freeman Pl. SW6 . . . . .3J 7
   W6 . . . . .1C 6
   (off Goldhawk Rd.)
Lennox Ho. TW1: Twick 3E 10
   (off Clevedon Rd.)
Lenton Ri. TW9: Rich 7F 5
Leo Ct. TW8: Bford 4E 4
Leopold Av. SW19 . . . . .2J 19
Leopold Cl. KT10: Esh 3H 27
   (off Princess Sq.)
Leopold Rd. SW19 . . . . .1J 19
Leopold Ter. SW19 . . . . .2J 19
Lerry Cl. W14 . . . . .3J 7
Leslie Gdns. SM2: Sutt 3K 31
Letterstone Rd. SW6 . . . . .4J 7
Lettice St. SW6 . . . . .5J 7
Levana Cl. SW19 . . . . .5H 13
Lewesdon Cl. SW19 . . . . .5G 13
Lewin Rd. SW14 . . . . .7A 6
Lewins Rd. KT18: Eps 3J 33
Lewis Rd. TW10: Rich 2E 10
Lewiston Cl. KT4: Wor Pk 4E 24
Lexham Gdns. W8 . . . . .1K 7
Lexham M. W8 . . . . .1K 7
Lexington Pl.
   KT1: Hamp W 1A 36 (4E 16)
Leyborne Pk. TW9: Kew 5H 5
Leyfield KT4: Wor Pk 5B 24
Leylands SW18 . . . . .3J 13
Leys, The KT12: Hers 1E 26
Liberty Cl. KT4: Wor Pk 5F 25
Library M. TW12: Hamp H 3H 15
Library Way TW2: Whitt 4H 9
Lichfield Cl. KT6: Surb 2F 23
   (off Claremont Rd.)
   TW9: Rich 2F 11
Lichfield Gdns. TW9: Rich 1F 11
Lichfield La. TW2: Whitt 5H 9
Lichfield Rd. TW4: Houn 1B 8
   TW9: Kew 5G 5
Lichfield Ter. TW9: Rich 2F 11
   (off Sheen Rd.)
Lickey Ho. W14 . . . . .3J 7
   (off North End Rd.)
Liffords Pl. SW13 . . . . .6C 6
Lifford St. SW15 . . . . .1G 13
Lighterage Ct. TW8: Bford 3F 5
Lightermans Wlk. SW18 . . . . . . .1K 13
Lilian Rd. SW13 . . . . .3D 6
Lillie Bri. Dpt. W14 . . . . .2J 7
Lillie Mans. SW6 . . . . .2J 7
   (off Lillie Rd.)
Lillie Rd. SW6 . . . . .3H 7
Lillie Road Fitness Cen. 4G 7
Lillie Sq. SW6 . . . . .3K 7
Lillie Yd. SW6 . . . . .3K 7
Lilliot's La. KT22: Lea 7B 32
Lily Cl. W14 . . . . .1G 7
Lilyville Rd. SW6 . . . . .5J 7
Lime Cres. TW16: Sun 6B 14
Limecroft Cl. KT19: Ewe 4A 30
Lime Gro. KT3: N Mald 7A 18
   TW1: Twick 3A 10
Lime Ho. TW9: Kew 5J 5
Lime Rd. TW9: Rich 1G 11

Limes, The KT8: W Mole 1G 21
   KT19: Eps 6J 29
Limes Av. SW13 . . . . .3K 13
   SW13 .6C 6
Limes Fld. Rd. SW13 . . . . .7B 6
Limes Gdns. SW18 . . . . .3K 13
Lime Tree Av. KT7: T Ditt 5J 21
   KT10: Esh 5J 21
Lime Tree Ct. KT21: Asht 7F 33
Lime Wlk. KT8: E Mos 1A 22
Limewood Ho. KT19: Eps 5A 30
Limpsfield Av. SW19 . . . . .6G 13
Linacre Ct. W6 . . . . .2G 7
Lincoln Av. SW19 . . . . .7G 13
   TW2: Twick 6H 9
Lincoln Ho. TW8: Bford 2E 4
   (off Ealing Rd.)
Lincoln Rd. KT3: N Mald 7K 17
   KT4: Wor Pk 5E 24
   TW13: Hanw 7E 8
Lincoln Ter. SM2: Sutt 4K 31
Lincoln Wlk. KT19: Ewe 6A 30
Linden Av. TW3: Houn 2G 9
Linden Cl. KT7: T Ditt 4A 22
Linden Cres. KT1: King T 6G 17
Linden Gdns. W4 . . . . .2B 6
Linden Gro. KT3: N Mald 7D 18
   TW11: Tedd 2A 16
Linden Ho. TW12: Hamp 3F 15
Linden Pl. KT17: Eps 1B 34
Linden Rd. TW12: Hamp 4F 15
Lindens, The W4 . . . . .5K 5
Lindisfarne Rd. SW20 . . . . .4D 18
Lindley Cl. KT1: Hamp W 5D 16
Lindley Pl. TW9: Kew 5H 5
Lindley Rd. KT12: Walt T 7C 20
Lindsay Cl. KT9: Chess 4F 29
   KT19: Eps 2K 33
Lindsay Rd. KT4: Wor Pk 6E 24
   TW12: Hamp H 1G 15
Lindsey Ho. W5 . . . . .1E 4
Lindum Rd. TW11: Tedd 4D 16
Linfield Cl. KT12: Hers 2A 26
Lingfield Av.
   KT1: King T 7D 36 (1F 23)
Lingfield Rd. KT4: Wor Pk 7F 25
   SW19 .2G 19
Linkenholt Mans. W6 . . . . .1C 6
   (off Stamford Brook Av.)
Linkfield KT8: W Mole 7G 15
Linkfield Rd. TW7: Isle 6A 4
Links Av. SM4: Mord 1K 25
Linkside KT3: N Mald 6B 18
Links Pl. KT21: Asht 6E 32
Links Rd. KT17: Eps 2D 34
   KT21: Asht 7D 32
Linksview Ct. TW12: Hamp H 1J 15
Links Vw. Rd. TW12: Hamp H 2H 15
Linkway SW20 . . . . .7E 18
   TW10: Ham 6C 10
Linnet Ct. SW15 . . . . .3F 13
Linsdale Cl. TW4: Houn 2D 8
Linstead Way SW18 . . . . .4H 13
Lintaine Cl. W6 . . . . .3H 7
Lintons La. KT17: Eps 1B 34
Linver Rd. SW6 . . . . .6J 7
Lion Av. TW1: Twick 5A 10
Lionel Mans. W14 . . . . .1H 7
   (off Haarlem Rd.)
Lionel Rd. Nth. TW8: Bford 1F 5
Lionel Rd. Sth. TW8: Bford 2G 5
Lion Ga. Gdns. TW9: Rich 7G 5
Lion Ga. M. SW18 . . . . .4K 13
Lion Pk. Av. KT9: Chess 1H 29
Lion Rd. TW1: Twick 5A 10
Lion Way TW8: Bford 4E 4
Lion Wharf Rd. TW7: Isle 7C 4
Lisbon Av. TW2: Twick 6H 9
Lisgar Ter. W14 . . . . .1J 7
Lismore SW19 . . . . .5H 13
   (off Woodside)
Lismore Cl. TW7: Isle 6B 4
Lissant Cl. KT6: Surb 4E 22
Listergate Ct. SW15 . . . . .1F 13
Litchfield Av. SM4: Mord 4J 25
Littlecombe Cl. SW15 . . . . .3G 13
Littlecote Cl. SW19 . . . . .4H 13
Littlefield Cl.
   KT1: King T 4D 36 (6F 17)
Littlefield Ho. KT1: King T 4C 36
Little Green TW9: Rich 1E 10

Littlemead KT10: Esh 1J 27
Lit. Orchard Pl. KT10: Esh 7H 21
Little Orchards KT18: Eps 3B 34
   (off Worple Rd.)
Lit. Park Dr. TW13: Felt 6D 8
Lit. Park La. KT17: Ewe 7F 31
Lit. Queen's Rd. TW11: Tedd 3A 16
Lit. St Leonard's SW14 . . . . .7K 5
Littlewood Cl. W13 . . . . .1C 4
Lit. Wood St.
   KT1: King T 3B 36 (6E 16)
Littleworth Av. KT10: Esh 2J 27
Littleworth Comn. Rd.
   KT10: Esh 7J 21
Littleworth La. KT10: Esh 1J 27
Littleworth Pl. KT10: Esh 1J 27
Littleworth Rd. KT10: Esh 2J 27
Liverpool Rd. KT2: King T 4H 17
Livesey Cl.
   KT1: King T 5E 36 (7G 17)
Livingstone Ho. KT17: Eps 1B 34
   (off Winter Cl.)
Livingstone Mans. W14 . . . . .3H 7
   (off Queen's Club Gdns.)
Livingstone Rd. TW3: Houn 1H 9
Lizmans Ter. W8 . . . . .1K 7
   (off Earl's Ct. Rd.)
Llewellyn Mans. W14 . . . . .1H 7
   (off Hammersmith Rd.)
Lloyd Rd. KT4: Wor Pk 7F 25
Lloyds Lanes Raynes Pk. 7G 19
Lochaline St. W6 . . . . .3F 7
Locksley Sq. KT6: Surb 3E 22
Lock Rd. TW10: Ham 1D 16
Locksmeade Rd.
   TW10: Ham 1D 16
Lockwood Way KT9: Chess 2H 29
Lockyer Ho. SW15 . . . . .7G 7
Locomotive Dr. TW14: Felt 5A 8
Lodge Av. SW14 . . . . .7B 6
Lodge Cl. KT17: Ewe 6F 31
   TW7: Isle 5C 4
Lofthouse Pl. KT9: Chess 3D 28
Logan Cl. TW4: Houn 1E 8
Logan M. W8 . . . . .1K 7
Logan Pl. W8 . . . . .1K 7
London Rd.
   KT2: King T 3E 36 (6G 17)
   KT17: Ewe 5C 30
   SM3: Cheam 7G 25
   SM4: Mord 2K 25
   TW1: Twick 4B 10
   TW7: Bford, Isle 6A 4
   TW7: Isle, Twick 6A 4
   TW8: Bford 6A 4
LONDON ROAD RDBT. 3B 10
London Scottish & Richmond Rugby
   Football Ground 7E 4
London Scottish Golf Course 7E 12
London Stile W4 . . . . .2H 5
London Wetland Cen. 5E 6
London Wetland Cen. Vis. Cen.
   . . . . .5E 6
LONG DITTON 5D 22
Longdown La. Nth. KT17: Eps 3D 34
Longdown La. Sth.
   KT17: Eps, Eps D 3D 34
Longdown Rd. KT17: Eps 3D 34
Longfellow Rd. KT4: Wor Pk 6D 24
Longfield Dr. SW14 . . . . .2J 11
Longfield St. SW18 . . . . .4K 13
Longford Cl. TW12: Hamp H 1F 15
   TW13: Hanw 7D 8
Longford Ct. KT19: Ewe 1K 29
   TW12: Hamp H 3G 15
Longford Ho. TW12: Hamp H 1F 15
Longford Ind. Est.
   TW12: Hamp 3G 15
Longford Rd. TW2: Whitt 5F 9
Long Gro. Rd. KT19: Eps 7K 29
Longland Pl. KT17: Eps 1F 33
Long Lodge Dr. KT12: Walt T 7B 20
Longmead Bus. Pk.
   KT19: Eps 7A 30
Longmead Rd. KT7: T Ditt 4K 21
   KT19: Eps, Ewe 7A 30
Longmoor Point SW15 . . . . .5E 12
   (off Norley Va.)
Longmore Rd. KT12: Hers 1D 26
Longridge Rd. SW5 . . . . .1K 7
Longs Ct. TW9: Rich 1G 11
Longshott Ct. SW5 . . . . .1K 7
   (off W. Cromwell Rd.)
Longstaff Cres. SW18 . . . . .3K 13
Longstaff Rd. SW18 . . . . .3K 13
Longthorpe Ct. W6 . . . . .1D 6

Long Wlk. KT3: N Mald 7K 17
   KT18: Tatt C 7F 35
   SW13 .6B 6
Longwater Ho. KT1: King T 6B 36
Longwood Dr. SW15 . . . . .3D 12
Lonsdale Ct. KT6: Surb 4E 22
Lonsdale M. TW9: Kew 5H 5
Lonsdale Rd. SW13 . . . . .5C 6
   W4 . . . . .1C 6
Loop Rd. KT18: Eps 5K 33
Lorac Ct. SM2: Sutt 4K 31
Loraine Gdns. KT21: Asht 6F 33
Loraine Rd. W4 . . . . .3J 5
Lord Chancellor Wlk.
   KT2: King T 5K 17
Lordell Pl. SW19 . . . . .3F 19
Lord Napier Pl. W6 . . . . .2D 6
Lord Roberts M. SW6 . . . . .4K 7
Lord Rosebery Lodge
   KT18: Eps 3K 33
Lords Cl. TW13: Hanw 6D 8
Loring Rd. TW7: Isle 6A 4
Lorne Rd. TW10: Rich 2G 11
Loseberry Rd. KT10: Clay 2J 27
Louisa Ct. TW2: Twick 6K 9
Lovekyn Cl.
   KT2: King T 3D 36 (6F 17)
Lovelace Gdns. KT6: Surb 4E 22
   KT12: Hers 2B 26
Lovelace Rd. KT6: Surb 4D 22
Lovelace Vs. KT7: T Ditt 4C 22
   (off Portsmouth Rd.)
Love La. KT6: Surb 6D 22
   SM1: Sutt 3J 31
   SM3: Cheam, Sutt 3H 31
   SM4: Mord 4K 25
Lovell Rd. TW10: Ham 7D 10
LOWER ASHTEAD 7E 32
Lwr. Common Sth. SW15 . . . . .7E 6
Lower Ct. Rd. KT19: Eps 7K 29
Lwr. Downs Rd. SW20 . . . . .5G 19
Lower Dunnymans SM7: Bans 3J 35
Lwr. George St. TW9: Rich 2E 10
LOWER GREEN 6G 21
Lower Grn. Gdns.
   KT4: Wor Pk 5D 24
Lower Grn. Rd. KT10: Esh 6G 21
Lwr. Grn. Rd. TW10: Rich 3G 11
Lwr. Hampton Rd. TW16: Sun 7B 14
Lwr. Ham Rd.
   KT2: King T 1C 36 (2E 16)
Lwr. Hill Rd. KT19: Eps 1J 33
Lwr. King's Rd.
   KT1: King T 1C 36 (5F 17)
Lower Mall W6 . . . . .2E 6
Lwr. Marsh La.
   KT1: King T 7E 36 (1G 23)
Lower Mill KT17: Ewe 4C 30
Lwr. Morden La. SM4: Mord 3F 25
Lwr. Mortlake Rd. TW9: Rich 1F 11
Lwr. Northfield SM7: Bans 3J 35
Lwr. Richmond Rd. SW14 . . . . . . .7H 5
   SW15 .7E 6
   TW9: Rich 7H 5
Lwr. Sand Hills KT6: Surb 4D 22
Lwr. Sawley Wood SM7: Bans 3J 35
Lower Sq. TW7: Isle 7C 4
Lwr. Sunbury Rd. TW12: Hamp 6E 14
Lwr. Teddington Rd.
   KT1: Hamp W 1A 36 (5E 16)
Lwr. Wood Rd. KT10: Clay 3C 28
Lowther Rd. KT2: King T 5G 17
   SW13 .5C 6
Loxford Rd. KT17: Eps 1B 34
Loxley Rd. TW12: Hamp 1E 14
Lucent Ho. SW18 . . . . .2K 13
   (off Hardwicks Sq.)
Lucien Rd. SW19 . . . . .6K 13
Ludovick Wlk. SW15 . . . . .1B 12
Lulworth Pl. KT19: Eps 1F 33
Lumley Gdns. SM3: Cheam 2H 31
Lumley Rd. SM3: Cheam 2H 31
Lurgan Av. W6 . . . . .3G 7
Lushington Ho. KT12: Walt T 3B 20
Luther M. TW11: Tedd 2A 16
Luther Rd. TW11: Tedd 2A 16
Luttrell Av. SW15 . . . . .2E 12
Lux Apartments SW18 . . . . .2K 13
   (off Broomhill Rd.)
Luxemburg Gdns. W6 . . . . .1G 7
Lydia Ct. KT1: King T 6C 36
Lydney Cl. SW19 . . . . .6H 13
Lygon Ho. SW6 . . . . .4H 7
   (off Fulham Pal. Rd.)
Lymbourne Cl. SM2: Sutt 6K 31
Lyme Regis Rd. SM7: Bans 6J 35

Lymescote Gdns. SM1: Sutt ...6K 25
Lymington Gdns. KT19: Ewe ...2C 30
Lyncroft Gdns. KT17: Ewe ...5C 30
　　TW3: Houn ...2H 9
Lyndale KT7: T Ditt ...4K 21
Lynde Ho. KT12: Walt T ...3B 20
Lyndhurst Av. KT5: Surb ...5J 23
　　TW2: Whitt ...5E 8
Lyndhurst Ct. SM2: Sutt ...4K 31
　　(off Grange Rd.)
Lyndhurst Dr. KT3: N Mald ...4B 24
Lyndhurst Way SM2: Sutt ...5K 31
Lynmouth Av. SM4: Mord ...3G 25
Lynne Wlk. KT10: Esh ...2H 27
Lynton Cl. KT9: Chess ...1F 29
　　TW7: Isle ...1A 10
Lynton Ct. KT17: Ewe ...7C 30
Lynton Rd. KT3: N Mald ...2A 24
Lynwood Av. KT17: Eps ...3C 34
Lynwood Ct. KT1: King T ...6J 17
　　KT17: Eps ...2C 34
Lynwood Dr. KT4: Wor Pk ...6D 24
Lynwood Rd. KT7: T Ditt ...6A 22
　　KT17: Eps ...3C 34
Lyon Cl. KT12: Walt T ...6D 20
Lyon Rd. KT12: Walt T ...6D 20
Lyons Wlk. W14 ...1H 7
Lyric Rd. SW13 ...5C 6
Lyric Sq. W6 ...1F 7
　　(off King St.)
Lyric Theatre
　　Hammersmith ...1F 7
Lysander Gdns. KT6: Surb ...3G 23
Lysia Ct. SW6 ...4G 7
　　(off Lysia St.)
Lysia St. SW6 ...4G 7
Lysons Wlk. SW15 ...1D 12
Lytcott Dr. KT8: W Mole ...7E 14
Lytton Gro. SW15 ...2G 13

M

Mablethorpe Rd. SW6 ...4H 7
Macaulay Av. KT10: Hin W ...6A 22
Macbeth St. W6 ...2E 6
McCarthy Rd. TW13: Hanw ...2C 14
McDonough Cl. KT9: Chess ...1F 29
McDougall Ct. TW9: Rich ...6H 5
Mace Ho. TW7: Isle ...5C 4
Macfarlane La. TW7: Isle ...3A 4
McKay Rd. SW20 ...4E 18
McKenzie Way KT19: Eps ...5H 29
Maclaren M. SW15 ...1F 13
Maclise Rd. W14 ...1H 7
Macmillan Ho. SM7: Bans ...3J 35
　　(off Basing Rd.)
MacOwan Theatre ...1K 7
Madans Wlk. KT18: Eps ...4A 34
　　(not continuous)
Maddison Cl. TW11: Tedd ...3A 16
Madrid Rd. SW13 ...5D 6
Mafeking Av. TW8: Bford ...3F 5
Magdala Rd. TW7: Isle ...7B 4
Magistrates' Court
　　Feltham ...5A 8
　　Hammersmith ...2G 7
　　Richmond-upon-Thames ...1E 10
　　Wimbledon ...3K 19
Magna Sq. SW14 ...7K 5
　　(off Moore Cl.)
Magnolia Cl. KT2: King T ...3J 17
Magnolia Ct. SM2: Sutt ...4K 31
　　(off Grange Rd.)
　　TW9: Kew ...5J 5
Magnolia Dr. SM7: Bans ...5J 35
Magnolia Rd. W4 ...3J 5
Magnolia Way KT19: Ewe ...2K 29
Magnolia Wharf W4 ...3H 5
Maguire Dr. TW10: Ham ...1D 16
Maidenshaw Rd. KT19: Eps ...1A 34
Maids of Honour Row
　　TW9: Rich ...2E 10
Main St. TW13: Hanw ...2C 14
Maisonettes, The SM1: Sutt ...2J 31
Maitland Cl. KT12: Walt T ...6D 20
Malbrook Rd. SW15 ...1E 12
Malcolm Dr. KT6: Surb ...5F 23
Malcolm Rd. SW19 ...3H 19
Malden Cl. KT3: N Mald ...7E 18
Malden Golf Course ...6B 18
MALDEN GREEN ...5D 24
Malden Grn. Av. KT4: Wor Pk ...5C 24
Malden Grn. M.
　　KT4: Wor Pk ...5D 24
Malden Hill KT3: N Mald ...7C 18

Malden Hill Gdns.
　　KT3: N Mald ...7C 18
MALDEN JUNC. ...2C 24
Malden Manor Station (Rail) ...4B 24
Malden Pk. KT3: N Mald ...3C 24
Malden Rd. KT3: N Mald ...2B 24
　　KT4: Wor Pk ...3C 24
　　SM3: Cheam ...1G 31
MALDEN RUSHETT ...7D 28
Malden Way KT3: N Mald ...4A 24
Maldon District Society of
　　Model Engineers, The ...5B 22
Mall, The KT6: Surb ...2E 22
　　KT12: Hers ...2C 26
　　(off Hersham Grn. Shop. Cen.)
　　SW14 ...2K 11
　　TW8: Bford ...3E 4
Mallard Cl. TW2: Whitt ...4F 9
Mallard Pl. TW1: Twick ...7B 10
Mall Rd. W6 ...2E 6
Mall Vs. W6 ...2E 6
　　(off Mall Rd.)
Maltby Rd. KT9: Chess ...3H 29
Malthouse Ct. TW8: Bford ...3F 5
　　(off Hight St.)
Malthouse Dr. TW13: Hanw ...2C 14
　　W4 ...3C 6
Malthouse Pas. SW13 ...6C 6
　　(off Clevelands Gdns.)
Maltings, The W4 ...2H 5
　　(off Spring Gro.)
Maltings Cl. SW13 ...6C 6
Maltings Lodge W4 ...3B 6
　　(off Corney Reach Way)
Malting Way TW7: Isle ...7A 4
Malvern Cl. KT6: Surb ...5F 23
Malvern Ct. KT18: Eps ...3A 34
　　SM2: Sutt ...4K 31
Malvern Dr. TW13: Hanw ...2C 14
Malvern Rd. KT6: Surb ...6F 23
　　TW12: Hamp ...4F 15
Manbre Rd. W6 ...3F 7
Mandel Ho. SW18 ...1K 13
Mandeville Cl. SW20 ...4H 19
Mandeville Dr. KT6: Surb ...5E 22
Mandeville Rd. TW7: Isle ...6B 4
Manfred Rd. SW15 ...2J 13
Manning Pl. TW10: Rich ...3G 11
Manningtree Cl. SW19 ...5H 13
Mann's Cl. TW7: Isle ...2A 10
Manny Shinwell Ho. SW6 ...3J 7
　　(off Clem Attlee Ct.)
Manoel Rd. TW2: Twick ...6H 9
Manor Av. SM1: Sutt ...2K 31
Maria Theresa Cl.
　　KT3: N Mald ...2A 24
Marina Av. KT3: N Mald ...2E 24
Marina Pl.
　　KT1: Hamp W ...3A 36 (5E 16)
Marina Way TW11: Tedd ...4E 16
Mariner Gdns. TW10: Ham ...7D 10
Market Dr. W4 ...4B 6
Market Pde. KT17: Ewe ...5C 30
　　(off High St.)
　　TW13: Hanw ...7D 8
Market Pl. KT1: King T ...3B 36 (6E 16)
　　TW8: Bford ...4D 4
Market Rd. TW9: Rich ...7H 5
Market Sq. KT1: King T ...4B 36
　　(off Market Pl.)
Market Ter. TW8: Bford ...3F 5
　　(off Albany Rd.)
Markhole Cl. TW12: Hamp ...4E 14
Marksbury Av. TW9: Rich ...7H 5
Markway TW16: Sun ...6B 14
Marlborough SW19 ...5G 13
　　(off Inner Pk. Rd.)
Marlborough Cl. KT12: Hers ...7C 20
Marlborough Cl. W8 ...1K 7
　　(off Pembroke Rd.)
Marlborough Cres. W4 ...1A 6
Marlborough Gdns.
　　KT6: Surb ...4E 22
Marlborough M. SM7: Bans ...4K 35
Marlborough Rd. SM1: Sutt ...7K 25
　　TW7: Isle ...5C 4
　　TW10: Rich ...3G 11
　　TW12: Hamp ...3G 11
　　TW13: Felt ...6C 8
　　W4 ...1A 6
Marld, The KT21: Asht ...7G 33
Marl Fld. Cl. KT4: Wor Pk ...5D 24
Marling Ct. TW12: Hamp ...3E 14
Marlingdene Cl. TW12: Hamp ...3F 15
MARLING PARK ...4E 14
Marlin Pk. TW14: Felt ...2A 8

Manor Way KT4: Wor Pk ...5B 24
Mansel Rd. SW19 ...3H 19
Mansfield Rd. SW19 ...2D 28
Mansions, The SW5 ...2K 7
　　(off Old Brompton Rd.)
Manston Gro. KT2: King T ...2E 16
Manston Ho. W14 ...1H 7
　　(off Russell Rd.)
Mantle Ct. SW18 ...3K 13
　　(off Mapleton Rd.)
Maple Cl. KT1: Eps ...5A 30
　　TW12: Hamp ...3E 14
Maple Ct. KT3: N Mald ...7A 18
Maple Gdns. KT17: Eps ...2B 34
　　(off Up. High St.)
Maple Gro. TW8: Bford ...4C 4
Maple Gro. Bus. Cen.
　　TW4: Houn ...1B 8
Maple Ho. KT1: King T ...2F 23
　　(off Maple Rd.)
　　TW9: Kew ...5J 5
Maplehurst Cl.
　　KT1: King T ...7C 36 (1F 23)
Maple Ind. Est. TW13: Felt ...7A 8
Maple Pl. SM7: Bans ...3G 35
Maple Rd. KT6: Surb ...3E 22
　　KT21: Asht ...7E 32
Maples, The KT1: Hamp W ...4D 16
　　KT10: Clay ...4B 28
Mapleton Cres. SW18 ...3K 13
Mapleton Rd. SW18 ...3K 13
　　(not continuous)
Maple Way TW11: Felt ...7A 8
Marble Hill Cl. TW1: Twick ...4C 10
Marble Hill Gdns.
　　TW1: Twick ...4C 10
Marble Hill House ...4D 10
Marchbank Rd. W14 ...3J 7
March Cl. SW15 ...1E 12
Marchmont Gdns. TW10: Rich ...2G 11
Marchmont Rd. TW10: Rich ...2G 11
March Rd. TW1: Twick ...4B 10
Marco Rd. W6 ...1F 7
Margaret Herbison Ho. SW6 ...3J 7
　　(off Clem Attlee Ct.)
Margaret Ho. W6 ...2F 7
　　(off Queen Caroline St.)
Margaret Ingram Cl. SW6 ...3J 7
Margaret Lockwood Cl.
　　KT1: King T ...1G 23
Margin Dr. SW19 ...2G 19
Margravine Gdns. W6 ...2G 7
Margravine Rd. W6 ...2G 7
Marian Cl. SM1: Sutt ...2K 31

Marloes Rd. W8 ...1K 7
Marlow Cres. TW1: Twick ...3A 10
Marlow Dr. SM3: Cheam ...6G 25
Marlowe Rd. KT1: King T ...7B 36
Marlow Ho. KT5: Surb ...2F 23
　　(off Cranes Pk.)
　　TW11: Tedd ...1B 16
Marncrest Cl. KT12: Hers ...2A 26
Marnell Way TW4: Houn ...1C 8
Marneys Ct. KT18: Eps ...4H 33
Marquis Ct. KT1: King T ...7B 36
　　KT19: Eps ...2A 34
Marrick Cl. SW15 ...1D 12
Marryat Cl. TW4: Houn ...1E 8
Marryat Pl. SW19 ...1H 19
Marryat Rd. SW19 ...2G 19
Marryat Sq. SW6 ...5H 7
Marshall Cl. TW4: Houn ...2E 8
Marshalls Cl. KT19: Eps ...2K 33
Marsh Av. KT19: Ewe ...6B 30
Marsh Farm Rd. TW2: Twick ...5A 10
Marshgate La. TW19: Eps ...7K 29
Marston Av. KT9: Chess ...3F 29
Marston Cl. KT12: Walt T ...5A 20
Marston Rd. TW11: Tedd ...2C 16
Martindale SW14 ...2K 11
Martindale Rd. TW4: Houn ...1D 8
Martineau Cl. KT10: Esh ...1J 27
Martineau Dr. TW1: Twick ...1C 10
Martingales Cl. TW10: Ham ...7E 10
Martin Gro. SM4: Mord ...7K 19
Martin Way SM4: Mord ...6G 19
　　SW20 ...6G 19
Marville Rd. SW6 ...4J 7
Mary Adelaide Cl. SW15 ...1B 18
Mary Ho. W6 ...2F 7
　　(off Queen Caroline St.)
Maryland Way TW16: Sun ...6A 14
Marylebone Gdns. TW9: Rich ...1H 11
Mary Macarthur Ho. W6 ...3H 7
Mary Rose Ct. TW12: Hamp ...5F 15
Mary Seacole Ho. W6 ...1D 6
　　(off Invermead Cl.)
Mary Smith Ct. SW5 ...1K 7
　　(off Trebovir Rd.)
Mary's Ter. TW1: Twick ...4B 10
Mary Wallace Theatre
　　Twickenham ...5B 10
Marzell Ho. W14 ...2J 7
　　(off North End Rd.)
Marzena Ct. TW3: Houn ...3H 9
Masault Ct. TW9: Rich ...1F 11
　　(off Kew Foot Rd.)
Masbro' Rd. W14 ...1G 7
Mascotte Rd. SW15 ...1G 13
Masefield Ct. KT6: Surb ...4E 22
Masefield Rd. TW12: Hamp ...1E 14
Mason Cl. SW20 ...5G 19
　　TW12: Hamp ...5E 14
Masons Yd. SW19 ...2G 19
Masson Ho. TW8: Bford ...3G 5
Maswell Pk. Cres. TW3: Houn ...2H 9
Maswell Pk. Rd. TW3: Houn ...2H 9
Matcham Ct. TW1: Twick ...3E 10
　　(off Clevedon Rd.)
Matham Rd. KT8: E Mos ...2J 21
Matheson Rd. W14 ...1J 7
Mathias Cl. KT18: Eps ...2K 33
Matlock Cres. SM3: Cheam ...1H 31
Matlock Gdns. SM3: Cheam ...1H 31
Matlock Pl. SM3: Cheam ...1H 31
Matlock Way KT3: N Mald ...5A 18
Maton Ho. SW6 ...4J 7
　　(off Estcourt Rd.)
Matthias Ct. TW10: Rich ...2F 11
Maudsley Ho. TW8: Bford ...2F 5
Maurice Ct. TW8: Bford ...4E 4
Mauveine Gdns. TW3: Houn ...1F 9
Mavis Av. KT19: Ewe ...2B 30
Mavis Cl. KT19: Ewe ...2B 30
Mawson Cl. SW20 ...6H 19
Mawson La. W4 ...3C 6
May Bate Av.
　　KT2: King T ...1B 36 (5E 16)
Mayberry Pl. KT5: Surb ...4G 23
May Cl. KT9: Chess ...3G 29
Maycross Av. SM4: Mord ...1J 25
Mayfair Av. KT4: Wor Pk ...5D 24
　　TW2: Whitt ...4H 9
Mayfair Cl. KT6: Surb ...5F 23
Mayfield Av. W4 ...1B 6
Mayfield Cl. KT7: T Ditt ...5C 22
　　KT12: Hers ...1A 26
Mayfield Gdns. KT12: Hers ...1A 26
Mayfield Mans. SW15 ...2J 13

Mayfield Rd.—Mountcombe Cl.

Mayfield Rd. KT12: Hers 1A **26**
SW19 5J **19**
Mayo Ct. W13 1C **4**
May Rd. TW2: Twick 5K **9**
Mayroyd Av. KT6: Surb 6H **23**
Mays Rd. TW11: Tedd 2J **15**
May St. W14 2J **7**
(Kelway Ho.)
W14 2J **7**
(Orchard Sq.)
Maze Rd. TW9: Kew 4H **5**
Mead, The KT21: Asht 7F **33**
Meade Cl. W4 3H **5**
Mead End KT21: Asht 6G **33**
Meadlands Dr. TW10: Ham 6E **10**
Meadowbank KT5: Surb 3G **23**
Meadowbank Cl. SW6 4F **7**
Meadowbrook Ct. TW7: Isle 7A **4**
Meadow Cl. KT10: Hin W 7A **22**
KT12: Hers 1E **26**
SW20 1F **25**
TW4: Houn 3F **9**
TW10: Ham 5F **11**
Meadow Ct. KT18: Eps 2K **33**
TW3: Houn 3G **9**
Meadowcroft *W4* *2H 5*
(off Brooks Rd.)
Meadow Ga. KT21: Asht 6F **33**
Meadow Hill KT3: N Mald 3B **24**
Meadow Pl. W4 4B **6**
Meadow Rd. KT10: Clay 3K **27**
KT21: Asht 6F **33**
TW13: Felt 6D **8**
Meadowside KT12: Walt T 6B **20**
TW1: Twick 4E **10**
Meadowside Rd.
SM2: Cheam 5H **31**
Meadowsweet Cl. SW20 1F **25**
Meadow Vw. Rd. SW20 1F **25**
Meadowview Rd. KT19: Ewe 5B **30**
Meadow Wlk. KT17: Ewe 4C **30**
KT19: Ewe 3B **30**
Meadow Way KT9: Chess 2F **29**
KT20: Tad 6H **35**
Mead Rd. KT12: Hers 1D **26**
TW10: Ham 7D **10**
Meads, The SM3: Cheam 7H **25**
Meadside *KT18: Eps* *3A 34*
(off South St.)
Meadway KT5: Surb 5K **23**
KT10: Esh 5G **27**
KT19: Eps 1K **33**
SW20 1F **25**
TW2: Twick 5J **9**
Meadway Ct. TW11: Tedd 2D **16**
Medcroft Gdns. SW14 1K **11**
Medfield St. SW15 4D **12**
Medina Av. KT10: Hin W 7K **21**
Medina Sq. KT19: Eps 5H **29**
Medway Ho.
KT2: King T 1B **36** (5E **16**)
Melancholy Wlk. TW10: Ham 6D **10**
Melbourne Mans. *W14* *3H 7*
(off Musard Rd.)
Melbourne Rd. SW19 5K **19**
TW11: Tedd 3D **16**
Melbourne Ter. *SW6* *4K 7*
(off Moore Pk. Rd.)
Melbray M. SW6 6J **7**
Melbury Cl. KT10: Clay 3C **28**
Melbury Gdns. SW20 5E **18**
Meldone Cl. KT5: Surb 4J **23**
Melford Cl. KT9: Chess 2G **29**
Melina Ct. SW15 7D **6**
Melliss Av. TW9: Kew 5J **5**
Mellor Cl. KT12: Walt T 4E **20**
Melrose Av. SW19 6J **13**
TW2: Whitt 4G **9**
Melrose Gdns. KT3: N Mald 7A **18**
KT12: Hers 2B **26**
Melrose Rd. SW13 6C **6**
SW18 3J **13**
SW19 6K **19**
Melton Flds. KT19: Ewe 5A **30**
Melton Pl. KT19: Ewe 5A **30**
Melville Av. SW20 4D **18**
Melville Ct. *W4* *2H 5*
(off Haining Cl.)
Melville Rd. SW13 5D **6**
Mendez Way SW15 3D **12**
Mendip Cl. KT4: Wor Pk 5F **25**
Mendora Rd. SW6 4H **7**
Mentmore Ho. *KT18: Eps* *3K 33*
(off Dalmeny Way)
Mercer Cl. KT7: T Ditt 4A **22**
Mercers Pl. W6 1G **7**
Merchant Cl. KT19: Ewe 2A **30**
Mercier Rd. SW15 2H **13**
Mercury Ho. *KT17: Ewe* *6D 30*
(off Cheam Rd.)
TW8: Bford *3D 4*
(off Glenhurst Rd.)
Mercury Rd. TW8: Bford 3D **4**
Mere Cl. SW15 4G **13**
Meredyth Rd. SW13 6D **6**
Mereway Rd. TW2: Twick 5J **9**
Merideth Ct. KT1: King T 6G **17**
Merivale Rd. SW15 1H **13**
Merland Ri. KT18: Tatt C 7F **35**
Merling Cl. KT9: Chess 2D **28**
Merrilands Rd. KT4: Wor Pk 5F **25**
Merrilyn Cl. KT10: Clay 3B **28**
Merrington Rd. SW6 3K **7**
Merritt Gdns. KT9: Chess 3D **28**
Merrow Rd. SM2: Cheam 5G **31**
Merryweather Ct. KT3: N Mald 2B **24**
Mersey Ct. KT2: King T 1B **36**
Merthyr Ter. SW13 3E **6**
Merton Av. W4 1C **6**
Merton Hall Gdns. SW20 5H **19**
Merton Hall Rd. SW19 4H **19**
Merton Mans. SW20 6G **19**
MERTON PARK 6K **19**
Merton Pk. Pde. SW19 5J **19**
Merton Park Stop
(London Tramlink) 5K **19**
Merton Rd. SW18 3K **13**
Merton Wlk. KT22: Lea 7B **32**
Merton Way KT8: W Mole 1G **21**
KT22: Lea 7B **32**
Metcalf Wlk. TW13: Hanw 1D **14**
Metro Ind. Cen. TW7: Isle 6A **4**
Metropolitan Ho. TW8: Bford 3G **5**
Metropolitan Police FC 3J **21**
Metropolitan Sta. Bldgs. *W6* *1F 7*
(off Beadon Rd.)
Mews, The KT10: Clay 3K **27**
TW1: Twick 3C **10**
TW12: Hamp H 3H **15**
Mexfield Rd. SW15 2J **13**
Michaelmas Cl. SW20 7F **19**
Michael Stewart Ho. *SW6* *3J 7*
(off Clem Attlee Ct.)
Michelham Gdns. TW1: Twick 7A **10**
Michelsdale Dr. TW9: Rich 1F **11**
Michel's Row *TW9: Rich* *1F 11*
(off Michelsdale Dr.)
Mickleham Gdns.
SM3: Cheam 3H **31**
Micklethwaite Rd. SW6 3K **7**
Midas Metropolitan Ind. Est.
SM4: Mord 4F **25**
Middle Cl. KT17: Eps 1B **34**
Middle Grn. Cl. KT5: Surb 3G **23**
Middle La. KT17: Eps 1B **34**
TW11: Tedd 3A **16**
Middle Mill Halls of Residence
KT1: King T 6D **36** (7G **17**)
Middlesex Ct. *TW8: Bford* *2D 4*
(off Glenhurst Rd.)
W4 1C **6**
Middleton Rd. KT19: Ewe 6A **30**
SM4: Mord 3K **25**
Midhurst Rd. W13 1C **4**
Midleton Rd. KT3: N Mald 7K **17**
Midmoor Rd. SW19 5G **19**
Midsummer Av. TW4: Houn 1E **8**
Midway KT12: Walt T 6A **20**
SM3: Sutt 4J **25**
Miena Way KT21: Asht 6E **32**
Milbourne Ho. *KT1: King T* *5H 17*
(off Coombe Rd.)
Milbourne La. KT10: Esh 3H **27**
Milbourne Pl. KT19: Ewe 1A **30**
Milbrook KT10: Esh 3H **27**
Milburn Wlk. KT18: Eps 4B **34**
Miles Pl. KT5: Surb 7E **36** (1G **23**)
Miles Rd. KT19: Eps 1A **34**
MILESTONE GREEN 1K **11**
Milestone Ho. KT1: King T 6B **36**
Millais Cres. KT19: Ewe 2B **30**
Millais Rd. KT3: N Mald 4B **24**
Millais Way KT19: Ewe 1K **29**
Millbourne Ho. *KT10: Esh* *3H 27*
(off Princess Sq.)
Millbourne Rd. TW13: Hanw 1D **14**
Millbrooke Ct. *SW15* *2H 13*
(off Keswick Rd.)
Millennium Ho. *SW15* *2H 13*
(off Plaza Gdns.)
Miller Pl. KT19: Eps 1F **33**
Millers Cl. KT12: Hers 1B **26**
Mill Farm Bus. Pk. TW4: Houn 4D **8**
Mill Farm Cres. TW4: Houn 5D **8**
Millfield KT1: King T 5E **36** (7G **17**)
Millfield Rd. TW4: Houn 5D **8**
Mill Hill SW13 6D **6**
Mill Hill Rd. SW13 6D **6**
Milliners Ho. SW18 1K **13**
Mill La. KT17: Ewe 5C **30**
Millmead KT10: Esh 6F **21**
Mill Pl. KT1: King T 5D **36** (7G **17**)
Mill Plat TW7: Isle 6B **4**
(not continuous)
Mill Plat Av. TW7: Isle 6B **4**
Mill Rd. KT10: Esh 6F **21**
KT17: Eps 1C **34**
TW2: Twick 6H **9**
Millshott Cl. SW6 5F **7**
Millside Pl. TW7: Isle 6C **4**
Mills Rd. KT12: Hers 2B **26**
Mills Row W4 1A **6**
Mill St. KT1: King T 5D **36** (7F **17**)
Mill Vw. Cl. KT17: Ewe 4C **30**
Mill Way TW14: Felt 2A **8**
Millwood Rd. TW3: Houn 2H **9**
Milner Dr. KT11: Cobh 7E **26**
TW2: Whitt 4J **9**
Milner Rd. KT1: King T 6B **36** (7E **16**)
SW19 5K **19**
Milnthorpe Rd. W4 3A **6**
Milton Ct. SW18 2K **13**
TW2: Twick 7K **9**
Milton Gdns. KT18: Eps 3B **34**
Milton Ho. SM1: Sutt 7K **25**
Milton Lodge TW1: Twick 4A **10**
Milton Mans. *W14* *3H 7*
(off Queen's Club Gdns.)
Milton Rd. KT12: Walt T 7C **20**
SM1: Sutt 7K **25**
SW14 7A **6**
TW12: Hamp 4F **15**
Mimosa St. SW6 5J **7**
Mina Rd. SW19 5K **19**
Minden Rd. SM3: Sutt 6H **25**
Minerva Rd.
KT1: King T 3E **36** (6G **17**)
Minima Yacht Club 5A **36**
Minniedale KT5: Surb 2G **23**
MINOR INJURIES UNIT
ROEHAMPTON 3D **12**
Minstead Gdns. SW15 4C **12**
Minstead Way KT3: N Mald 3B **24**
Minster Av. SM1: Sutt 6K **25**
Minster Gdns. KT8: W Mole 1E **20**
Minstrel Gdns. KT5: Surb 1G **23**
Mintwater Cl. KT17: Ewe 6D **30**
Mirabel Rd. SW6 4J **7**
Mission Sq. TW8: Bford 3F **5**
Mistley Ct. *KT18: Eps* *2A 34*
(off Ashley Rd.)
Misty's Fld. KT12: Walt T 5B **20**
Mitford Bldgs. *SW6* *4K 7*
(off Dawes Rd.)
Mitford Cl. KT9: Chess 3D **28**
Moat, The KT3: N Mald 5B **18**
Moat Ct. KT21: Asht 6F **33**
Moat La. KT8: E Mos 7A **16**
Moat Side TW13: Hanw 1B **14**
Modder Pl. SW15 1G **13**
Model Cotts. SW14 1K **11**
Moffat Ct. SW19 2K **19**
Mogden La. TW7: Isle 2K **9**
Mole Abbey Gdns.
KT8: W Mole 7G **15**
Mole Ct. KT19: Ewe 1K **29**
Molember Ct. KT8: E Mos 1K **21**
Molember Rd. KT8: E Mos 2K **21**
Mole Pl. KT8: W Mole 1G **21**
Mole Rd. KT12: Hers 2C **26**
Molesey Av. KT8: W Mole 2E **20**
Molesey Cl. KT12: Hers 1D **26**
Molesey Dr. SM3: Cheam 6H **25**
Molesey Heath Local Nature Reserve
3F **21**
MOLESEY HOSPITAL 2F **21**
Molesey Pk. Av. KT8: W Mole 2G **21**
Molesey Pk. Cl. KT8: E Mos 2H **21**
Molesey Pk. Rd.
KT8: W Mole, E Mos 2G **21**
Molesey Road 6D **20**
Molesey Rd. KT8: W Mole 4D **20**
KT12: Hers, Walt T 2C **26**
Molesford Rd. SW6 5K **7**
Molesham Cl. KT8: W Mole 7G **15**
Molesham Way KT8: W Mole 7G **15**
Moles Hill KT22: Oxs 7J **27**
Monaveen Gdns. KT8: W Mole 7G **15**
Moncks Row SW18 3J **13**
Mongers La. KT17: Ewe 6C **30**
(not continuous)
Monkleigh Rd. SM4: Mord 7H **19**
Monks Av. KT8: W Mole 2E **20**
Monks Cres. KT12: Walt T 5A **20**
Monks Rd. SM7: Bans 6K **35**
Monmouth Av.
KT1: Hamp W 1A **36** (4D **16**)
Monmouth Cl. W4 1K **5**
Monmouth Gro. TW8: Bford 1F **5**
Mono La. TW13: Felt 6A **8**
Monroe Dr. SW14 2J **11**
Monro Pl. KT19: Eps 5H **29**
Montague Cl. KT12: Walt T 4A **20**
Montague Rd. SW19 4K **19**
TW3: Houn 1G **9**
TW10: Rich 3F **11**
Montana Rd. SW20 5F **19**
Montem Rd. KT3: N Mald 1B **24**
Montford Rd. TW16: Sun 1A **20**
Montfort Pl. SW19 5G **13**
Montgomery Av. KT10: Hin W 6K **21**
Montgomery Ct. W4 4K **5**
Montgomery Rd. W4 1K **5**
Montolieu Gdns. SW15 2E **12**
Montpelier Row TW1: Twick 4D **10**
Montpellier Ct. KT12: Walt T 3A **20**
Montrose Av. TW2: Whitt 4G **9**
Montrose Gdns. KT22: Oxs 7J **27**
Montrouge Cres. KT17: Eps D 5F **35**
Montserrat Rd. SW15 1H **13**
Moore Cl. SW14 7K **5**
Moore Pk. Rd. SW6 4K **7**
Moore Place Golf Course 2F **27**
Moore Way SM2: Sutt 5K **31**
Moorfield Rd. KT9: Chess 2F **29**
Moorings Ho. TW8: Bford 4D **4**
Moorland Cl. TW2: Whitt 4F **9**
Moorlands *KT12: Walt T* *7A 20*
(off Ashley Pk. Rd.)
Moor La. KT9: Chess 1F **29**
Moormead Dr. KT19: Ewe 2B **30**
Moor Mead Rd. TW1: Twick 3B **10**
Moor Pk. Gdns. KT2: King T 4B **18**
MORDEN 2K **25**
Morden Ct. SM4: Mord 1K **25**
Morden Ct. Pde. SM4: Mord 1K **25**
Morden Ho. SM4: Mord 1K **25**
MORDEN PARK 3H **25**
Morden Pk. Pools 3J **25**
Morden South Station (Rail) 2K **25**
Morden Station
(Underground) 7K **19**
Morden Way SM3: Sutt 4K **25**
More Cl. W14 1G **7**
Morecoombe Cl. KT2: King T 4J **17**
More La. KT10: Esh 6G **21**
Moresby Av. KT5: Surb 4J **23**
Moreton Rd. KT4: Wor Pk 6D **24**
Morland Cl. TW12: Hamp 2E **14**
Morley Rd. SM3: Sutt 5J **25**
TW1: Twick 3E **10**
Morningside Rd. KT4: Wor Pk 6F **25**
Mornington Av. W14 1J **7**
Mornington Av. Mans. *W14* *1J 7*
(off Mornington Av.)
Mornington Wlk. TW10: Ham 1D **16**
Morris Gdns. SW18 4K **13**
Morris Rd. TW7: Isle 7A **4**
Mortimer Cres. KT4: Wor Pk 7A **24**
Mortimer Ho. *W14* *1H 7*
(off North End Rd.)
MORTLAKE 7A **6**
Mortlake Crematorium
TW9: Kew 6J **5**
Mortlake High St. SW14 7A **6**
Mortlake Rd. TW9: Kew, Rich 4H **5**
Mortlake Station (Rail) 7K **5**
Mortlake Ter. *TW9: Kew* *4H 5*
(off Mortlake Rd.)
Moscow Mans. *SW5* *1K 7*
(off Cromwell Rd.)
Mospey Cres. KT17: Eps 4C **34**
Mossville Gdns. SM4: Mord 7J **19**
Mostyn Rd. SW19 5J **19**
MOTSPUR PARK 3D **24**
Motspur Pk. KT3: N Mald 3C **24**
Motspur Park Station (Rail) 2E **24**
Mount, The KT3: N Mald 7C **18**
KT4: Wor Pk 1E **30**
KT10: Esh 3F **27**
KT17: Ewe 6C **30**
Mt. Angelus Rd. SW15 4C **12**
Mt. Ararat Rd. TW10: Rich 2F **11**
Mountcombe Cl. KT6: Surb 4F **23**

Mount Ct.—Oak Glade

Mount Ct. SW15 7H 7
Mount Holme KT7: T Ditt 4C 22
Mount M. TW12: Hamp 5G 15
Mt. Pleasant KT17: Ewe 6C 30
Mt. Pleasant Rd.
KT3: N Mald 7K 17
Mount Rd. KT3: N Mald 7A 18
KT9: Chess 2G 29
SW19 6K 13
TW13: Hanw 7D 8
Mountstuart Ct.
TW11: Hamp W 5C 16
Mount Vw. Rd. KT10: Clay 4C 28
Mountwood KT8: W Mole 7G 15
Mowat Ct. *KT4: Wor Pk 6C 24*
(off The Avenue)
Mowbray Rd. TW10: Ham 7D 10
Moylan Rd. W6 3H 7
Muirdown Av. SW14 1A 12
Mulberry Cl. KT19: Eps 5K 29
TW13: Felt 7A 8
Mulberry Ct. KT6: Surb 4E 22
TW1: Twick 7A 10
Mulberry Cres. TW8: Bford 4C 4
Mulberry Ga. SM7: Bans 5J 35
Mulberry Pl. W6 2D 6
Mulgrave Rd. SM2: Sutt 4J 31
SW6 3J 7
Mullins Path SW14 7A 6
Munden St. W14 1H 7
Mund St. W14 2J 7
Munnings Gdns. TW7: Isle 2J 9
Munro Ho. KT11: Cobh 7C 26
Munster Av. TW4: Houn 2D 8
Munster Ct. SW6 6J 7
TW11: Tedd 3D 16
Munster M. SW6 4H 7
Munster Rd. SW6 4H 7
TW11: Tedd 3C 16
Murfett Cl. SW19 6H 13
Murray Av. TW3: Houn 2G 9
Murray Ct. TW2: Twick 6J 9
Murray Rd. SW19 3G 19
TW10: Ham 6C 10
W5 1D 4
Murray Ter. W5 1E 4
Murreys, The KT21: Asht 7D 32
Murreys Ct. KT21: Asht 7E 32
Musard Rd. W6 3H 7
W14 3H 7
Muscal *W6 3H 7*
(off Field Rd.)
Mus. of Richmond 2E 10
Mus. of Water & Steam 2G 5
Mus. of Wimbledon 3H 19
Musgrave Cres. SW6 4K 7
Musgrave Rd. TW7: Isle 5A 4
Musical Mus., The 3F 5
Mustow Pl. SW6 6J 7
Muybridge Rd. KT3: N Mald 6K 17
Muybridge Yd. KT5: Surb 4G 23
Mylne Cl. W6 2D 6
Mynn's Cl. KT18: Eps 3J 33
Myrtle Gro. KT3: N Mald 6K 17
Myrtle Rd. TW12: Hamp H 3H 15

N

Nallhead Rd. TW13: Hanw 2B 14
Napier Av. SW6 7J 7
Napier Ct. *SW6 7J 7*
(off Ranelagh Gdns.)
Napier Pl. W14 1J 7
Napier Rd. TW7: Isle 1B 10
W14 1J 7
Napoleon Rd. TW1: Twick 4C 10
Narborough St. SW6 6K 7
Narrowboat Av. TW8: Bford 4D 4
Narwhal Inuit Art Gallery 1A 6
Naseby Cl. TW7: Isle 5A 4
Naseby Ct. KT12: Walt T 6B 20
Nasmyth St. W6 1E 6
Nassau Rd. SW13 5C 6
Natalie M. TW2: Twick 7J 9
National Archives, The 4J 5
National Tennis Cen. 2B 12
National Works TW4: Houn 1E 8
Nella Rd. W6 3G 7
Nell Gwynne Cl. KT19: Eps 7H 29
Nelson Cl. KT12: Walt T 5A 20
Nelson Gdns. TW3: Houn 3F 9
NELSON HOSPITAL 6J 19
Nelson Rd. KT3: N Mald 2A 24
TW2: Whitt 4G 9
TW3: Houn 3F 9
Nelson Trad. Est. SW19 5K 19
Nelson Wlk. KT19: Eps 5H 29
Nene Gdns. TW13: Hanw 7E 8
Nepean St. SW15 3D 12
Nero Ct. TW8: Bford 4E 4
Nescot Sports Cen. 7D 30
Netheravon Rd. W4 1C 6
Netheravon Rd. Sth. W4 2C 6
Netherbury Rd. W5 1E 4
Netherton Rd. TW1: Twick 2B 10
Netley Cl. SM3: Cheam 2G 31
Netley Dr. KT12: Walt T 4E 20
Netley Rd. TW8: Bford 3F 5
Nevada Cl. KT3: N Mald 1K 23
Nevern Mans. *SW5 2K 7*
(off Warwick Rd.)
Nevern Pl. SW5 1K 7
Nevern Rd. SW5 1K 7
Nevern Sq. SW5 1K 7
Neville Av. KT3: N Mald 5A 18
Neville Cl. KT10: Esh 3E 26
SM7: Bans 3K 35
Neville Gill Cl. SW18 3K 13
Neville Ho. Yd.
KT1: King T 3C 36 (6F 17)
Neville Rd. KT1: King T 6H 17
TW10: Ham 7D 10
Newark Ct. KT12: Walt T 5B 20
New Berry La. KT12: Hers 2C 26
Newbolt Av. SM3: Cheam 2F 31
Newborough Grn.
KT3: N Mald 1A 24
New Broadway
TW12: Hamp H 2J 15
Newbury Gdns. KT19: Ewe 1C 30
New Chapel Sq. TW13: Felt 5A 8
New Chiswick Pool 4B 6
New Cl. TW13: Hanw 2D 14
Newcombe Gdns. TW4: Houn 1E 8
NEW EPSOM & EWELL
COTTAGE HOSPITAL 7F 29
Newfield Cl. TW12: Hamp 5F 15
Newgate Cl. TW13: Hanw 6D 8
Newhall Gdns. KT12: Walt T 6B 20
New Horizons Ct. TW8: Bford 3B 4
Newhouse Cl. KT3: N Mald 4B 24
New Kelvin Av. TW11: Tedd 3K 15
New Kings Rd. SW6 6J 7
Newlands, The KT7: T Ditt 5K 21
Newlands Av. KT7: T Ditt 5K 21
Newlands Cl. KT12: Hers 1D 26
Newlands Way KT9: Chess 2D 28
NEW MALDEN 1B 24
New Malden Station (Rail) 7B 18
Newmans La. KT6: Surb 3E 22
Newnes Path SW15 1E 12
Newport Rd. SW13 5D 6
New Rd. KT2: King T 4H 17
KT8: W Mole 1F 21
KT10: Esh 7H 21
KT22: Oxs 7A 28
TW3: Houn 1G 9
TW8: Bford 3E 4
TW10: Ham 1D 16
TW13: Hanw 2D 14
TW14: Felt 5A 8
Newry Rd. TW1: Twick 2B 10
Newstead Way SW19 1G 19
Newton Gro. W4 1B 6
Newton Mans. *W14 3H 7*
(off Queen's Club Gdns.)
Newton Rd. SW19 4H 19
TW7: Isle 6A 4
Newton's Yd. SW18 2K 13
Newton Wood Rd. KT21: Asht 5G 33
NEW VICTORIA HOSPITAL 5B 18
Nexus Cl. TW14: Felt 2A 8
NHS WALK-IN CENTRE
PARSONS GREEN 5K 7
TEDDINGTON 3K 15
Niagara Av. W5 1D 4
Nicholas Ct. *W4 3B 6*
(off Corney Reach Way)
Nicholas Lodge KT10: Esh 6F 21
Nicholas M. W4 3B 6
Nicholes Rd. TW3: Houn 1F 9
Nichols Cl. KT9: Chess 3D 28
Nicholson M.
KT1: King T 7D 36 (1F 23)
Nickols Wlk. SW18 1K 13
Nicol Cl. TW1: Twick 3C 10
Nigel Fisher Way KT9: Chess 4D 28
Nigel Playfair Av. W6 1E 6
Nightingale Cl. KT11: Cobh 7C 26
KT19: Eps 1H 33
W4 3K 5
Nightingale Dr. KT19: Ewe 3J 29
Nightingale Ho. *KT17: Eps 1B 34*
(off Winter Cl.)
KT17: Eps 1B 34
(East St.)
Nightingale La. TW10: Rich 4F 11
Nightingale M. KT1: King T 5B 36
Nightingale Rd.
KT8: W Mole 2G 21
KT10: Esh 2E 26
KT12: Walt T 4B 20
TW12: Hamp 2F 15
Nimbus Rd. KT19: Eps 6A 30
Nipper All. KT1: King T 3C 36
Niton Rd. TW9: Rich 7H 5
Niton St. SW6 4G 7
Noble St. KT12: Walt T 7B 20
Nonsuch Ct. Av. KT17: Ewe 6E 30
Nonsuch Ind. Est. KT17: Eps 7B 30
Nonsuch Pl. *SM3: Cheam 4G 31*
(off Ewell Rd.)
Nonsuch Wlk. SM2: Cheam 6F 31
(not continuous)
NORBITON 6H 17
Norbiton Av. KT1: King T 5H 17
Norbiton Comn. Rd.
KT1: King T 7J 17
Norbiton Hall KT2: King T 6G 17
Norbiton Station (Rail) 5H 17
Norbury Av. TW3: Houn 1J 9
Norcutt Rd. TW2: Twick 5K 9
Norfolk Cl. TW1: Twick 3C 10
Norfolk Rd. KT10: Clay 2K 27
TW13: Felt 5B 8
Norfolk Ter. W6 2H 7
NORK 4G 35
Nork Gdns. SM7: Bans 3H 35
Nork Ri. SM7: Bans 5G 35
Nork Way SM7: Bans 5F 35
Norley Va. SW15 5D 12
Norman Av. KT17: Eps 1C 34
TW1: Twick 4D 10
TW13: Hanw 6D 8
Normanby Cl. SW15 2J 13
Norman Colyer Ct. KT19: Eps 6A 30
Normand Gdns. *W14 3H 7*
(off Greyhound Rd.)
Normand Mans. *W14 3H 7*
(off Normand M.)
Normand M. W14 3H 7
Normand Rd. W14 3J 7
Norman Ho. *TW13: Hanw 6E 8*
(off Watermill Way)
Normanhurst Dr. TW1: Twick 2B 10
Normanhurst Rd. KT12: Walt T 6C 20
Norman Rd. SM1: Sutt 2K 31
Normansfield Av. TW11: Tedd 4D 16
Normanton Av. SW19 6K 13
Norris Cl. KT19: Eps 7J 29
Norris Ho. TW7: Isle 6B 4
Norroy Rd. SW15 1G 13
Norstead Pl. SW15 6D 12
North Acre SM7: Bans 5J 35
North Av. TW9: Kew 5H 5
NORTH CHEAM 7F 25
Northcliffe Cl. KT4: Wor Pk 7B 24
North Cl. SM4: Mord 1H 25
Northcote Av. KT5: Surb 4J 23
TW7: Isle 2B 10
Northcote Rd. KT3: N Mald 7K 17
TW1: Twick 2B 10
Northcroft Rd. KT19: Ewe 4B 30
Northdown Rd. SM2: Sutt 6K 31
Nth. E. Surrey Crematorium
SM4: Mord 3F 25
Nth. End Cres. W14 1J 7
Nth. End Ho. W14 1H 7
Nth. End Pde. *W14 1H 7*
(off North End Rd.)
Nth. End Rd. SW6 1H 7
W14 1H 7
Northernhay Wlk. SM4: Mord 1H 25
Northey Av. SM2: Cheam 6G 31
Nth. Eyot Gdns. W6 2C 6
NORTH FELTHAM 3A 8
Nth. Feltham Trad. Est.
TW14: Felt 2A 8
Northfield Av. W5 1D 4
Northfield Cres. SM3: Cheam 1H 31
NORTHFIELDS 1C 4
Northfields KT17: Eps 7B 30
KT21: Asht 7F 33
(not continuous)
SW18 1K 13
Northfields Prospect Bus. Cen.
SW18 1K 13
Northfields Station
(Underground) 1D 4
North La. TW11: Tedd 3A 16
Nth. Lodge Cl. SW15 2G 13
NORTH LOOE 2F 35
North Mall *SW18 2K 13*
(off Southside Shop. Cen.)
North Pde. KT9: Chess 2G 29
North Pas. SW18 2K 13
North Pl. TW11: Tedd 3A 16
North Rd. KT6: Surb 3E 22
KT12: Hers 2B 26
TW8: Bford 3F 5
TW9: Kew, Rich 7H 5
W5 1E 4
NORTH SHEEN 7H 5
North Sheen Station (Rail) 1H 11
Northspur Rd. SM1: Sutt 7K 25
North St. TW7: Isle 7B 4
Northumberland Av. TW7: Isle 5A 4
Northumberland Gdns.
TW7: Isle 4B 4
Northumberland Pl.
TW10: Rich 2E 10
Nth. Verbena Gdns. W6 2D 6
North Vw. SW19 2F 19
North Vw. Cres. KT18: Tatt C 6F 35
Northway SM4: Mord 7H 19
Northweald La. KT2: King T 2E 16
Nth. Weylands Ind. Est.
KT12: Walt T 6D 20
Northwood Ho. *KT2: King T 6H 17*
(off Coombe Rd.)
Nth. Worple Way SW14 7A 6
Norton Av. KT5: Surb 4J 23
Norwood Cl. TW2: Twick 6J 9
Norwood Farm La.
KT11: Cobh 7A 26
KT12: Cobh 7A 26
Nottingham Rd. TW7: Isle 6A 4
Nova M. SM3: Sutt 5H 25
Novello St. SW6 5K 7
Novellus Ct. *KT18: Eps 3A 34*
(off South St.)
Nowell Rd. SW13 3D 6
Nuffield Health
Cheam 4H 31
Fulham 5G 7
Surbiton 3D 22
Twickenham 4K 9
Wandsworth 4K 13
Wimbledon 3J 19
Numa Ct. TW8: Bford 4E 4
Nursery Cl. KT17: Ewe 6B 30
SW15 1G 13
TW14: Felt 4A 8
(not continuous)
Nursery Gdns. TW4: Houn 2E 8
TW12: Hamp 1E 14
Nursery Rd. SW19 4H 19
Nuthatch Row KT10: Clay 3A 28
Nye Bevan Ho. *SW6 4J 7*
(off St Thomas's Way)
Nylands Av. TW9: Kew 5H 5
Nymans Gdns. SW20 7E 18

O

Oak Av. TW12: Hamp 2D 14
Oak Avenue Local Nature Reserve
2D 14
Oakbank Av. KT12: Walt T 4E 20
Oakbark Ho. *TW8: Bford 4D 4*
(off High St.)
Oakcombe Cl. KT3: N Mald 5B 18
Oakcroft Bus. Cen. KT9: Chess 1G 29
Oakcroft Rd. KT9: Chess 1G 29
Oakcroft Vs. KT9: Chess 1G 29
Oakdale Rd. KT19: Ewe 5A 30
Oakdene Av. KT7: T Ditt 5B 22
Oakdene Ct. KT12: Walt T 7A 20
Oakdene Dr. KT5: Surb 4K 23
Oakdene M. SM3: Sutt 5J 25
Oake Ct. SW15 2H 13
Oakeford Ho. *W14 1H 7*
(off Russell Rd.)
Oaken Coppice KT21: Asht 7H 33
Oaken Dr. KT10: Clay 3A 28
Oaken La. KT10: Clay 1K 27
Oakenshaw Cl. KT6: Surb 4F 23
Oakfield Cl. KT3: N Mald 2C 24
Oakfield Rd. KT21: Asht 6E 32
SW19 7G 13
Oakfields KT12: Walt T 5A 20
Oak Glade KT19: Eps 1H 33

A-Z Kingston & Richmond 59

Oak Gro. TW16: Sun 4A 14
Oak Hill KT6: Surb 4F 23
  KT18: Eps 5A 34
Oakhill KT10: Clay 3B 28
Oakhill Cl. KT21: Asht 7D 32
Oakhill Ct. SW19 .....4G 19
Oak Hill Cres. KT6: Surb 4F 23
Oakhill Dr. KT6: Surb 4F 23
Oak Hill Gro. KT6: Surb 3F 23
Oak Hill Path KT6: Surb 3F 23
Oakhill Pl. SW15 .....2K 13
Oak Hill Rd. KT6: Surb 3F 23
Oakhill Rd. KT21: Asht 7D 32
  SW15 .....2J 13
Oak Ho. KT19: Eps 6K 29
  TW9: Kew 5J 5
Oakhurst Cl. KT2: King T 3G 17
  TW11: Tedd 2K 15
Oakhurst Rd. KT19: Ewe 3K 29
Oakington Cl. TW16: Sun 6B 14
Oakington Dr. TW16: Sun 6B 14
Oaklands Av. KT10: Esh 5J 21
  TW7: Isle 3A 4
Oaklands Cl. KT9: Chess 1D 28
Oaklands Dr. TW2: Whitt 4H 9
Oaklands SW14 .....7A 6
Oakland Way KT19: Ewe 3B 30
Oak La. TW1: Twick 4B 10
  TW7: Isle 1K 9
Oaklawn Rd. KT22: Lea 6A 32
Oak Leaf Cl. KT19: Eps 1K 33
Oaklea Pas.
  KT1: King T 5B 36 (7E 16)
Oakleigh KT18: Eps 3B 34
Oakleigh Av. KT6: Surb 5H 23
Oakleigh Way KT6: Surb 5H 23
Oakley Gdns. SM7: Bans 4K 35
Oakley Wlk. W6 .....3G 7
Oak Lock M. W4 .....2B 6
Oak Lodge Cl. KT12: Hers 2B 26
Oakman Ho. SW19 .....5G 13
Oakmead Grn.
  KT18: Eps 4K 33
Oak Pk. Gdns. SW19 .....5G 13
Oak Rd. KT3: N Mald 6A 18
  KT22: Lea 7B 32
Oaks, The KT18: Eps 3C 34
  SM4: Mord 1H 25
  TW13: Felt 6C 8
Oaks Av. KT4: Wor Pk 7E 24
  TW13: Felt 6D 8
Oaks Cvn. Pk., The
  KT9: Chess 7D 22
Oaksend Cl. KT22: Oxs 7H 27
Oaks Sq., The KT19: Eps 2A 34
  (off High St.)
Oaks Way KT6: Surb 5E 22
  KT18: Tatt C 7E 34
Oak Tree Cl. KT19: Ewe 3J 29
Oak Tree Pl. KT10: Esh 6G 21
Oak Way KT21: Asht 5H 33
Oakway SW20 .....1F 25
Oakwood KT18: Eps 3B 34
  (off Worple Rd.)
Oakwood Av. KT19: Eps 5H 29
Oakwood Gdns. SM1: Sutt 6K 25
Oakwood Rd. SW20 .....5D 18
Oarsman Pl. KT8: E Mos 1K 21
Oast Lodge W4 .....4B 6
  (off Corney Reach Way)
Observatory Rd. SW14 .....1K 11
Occupation La. W5 .....1E 4
Occupation Rd. KT19: Ewe 4A 30
Octavia Rd. TW7: Isle 7A 4
Odard Rd. KT8: W Mole 1F 21
Odeon Cinema
  Epsom 2B 34
  Esher 1G 27
  Kingston upon Thames 3D 36
  Putney 7H 7
  Richmond upon Thames -
    Hill Street 2E 10
    Red Lion Street 2E 10
  Wimbledon 3J 19
Offers Ct. KT1: King T 5E 36 (7G 17)
Office Pk., The KT22: Lea 7A 32
Ogden Ho. TW13: Hanw 7D 8
Oil Mill La. W6 .....2D 6
Old Barn Cl. SM2: Cheam 4H 31
Old Barn La. KT6: Surb 6K 33
OLD BRENTFORD 4E 4
Old Bridge La. KT17: Eps 1C 34
Old Bridge St.
  KT1: Hamp W 3A 36 (6E 16)
Old Brompton Rd. SW5 .....2K 7
Old Chestnut Av. KT10: Esh 3F 27

Old Chiswick Yd. W4 .....3B 6
  (off Pumping Sta. Rd.)
Old Church Path KT10: Esh 1G 27
Old Claygate La. KT10: Clay 3B 28
Old Common Rd. KT11: Cobh 7A 26
Old Courthouse, The
  KT18: Eps 2A 34
  (off The Parade)
Old Deer Pk. 6D 4
Old Deer Pk. Gdns. TW9: Rich 7F 5
Old Dock Cl. TW9: Kew 3H 5
Old Esher Cl. KT12: Hers 2C 26
Old Esher Rd. KT12: Hers 2C 26
Old Farm Cl. TW4: Houn 1E 8
Old Farm La. SW19 .....2K 19
Old Farm Pas. TW12: Hamp 5H 15
Old Farm Rd. TW12: Hamp 3E 14
Oldfield Ct. KT5: Surb 1G 23
  (off Cranes Pk. Cres.)
Oldfield Gdns. KT21: Asht 7E 32
Oldfield Ho. W4 .....2B 6
  (off Devonshire Rd.)
Oldfield Rd. SW19 .....3H 19
  TW12: Hamp 5E 14
Oldfields Rd. SM1: Sutt 7J 25
Old Highwayman Pl. SW15 .....5E 12
Old Ho. Cl. KT17: Ewe 6C 30
  SW19 .....2H 19
Old Ho. Gdns. TW1: Twick 3D 10
Old Kingston Rd.
  KT4: Wor Pk 6K 23
Old Lodge Pl. TW1: Twick 3C 10
Old London Rd.
  KT2: King T 3D 36 (6F 17)
  KT18: Eps D 7D 34
  (not continuous)
OLD MALDEN 5B 24
Old Malden La. KT4: Wor Pk 6A 24
Old Manor Dr. TW7: Isle 3H 9
Old Manor Yd. SW5 .....1K 7
Old Oak Cl. KT9: Chess 1G 29
Old Orchard TW16: Sun 6B 14
Old Palace La. TW9: Rich 2D 10
Old Palace Ter. TW9: Rich 2E 10
Old Palace Yd. TW9: Rich 2D 10
Old Post Office Wlk. KT6: Surb 3E 22
  (off Victoria Rd.)
Old Pound Cl. TW7: Isle 5B 4
Old Rope Wlk. TW16: Sun 7A 14
Old School Cl. SW19 .....6K 19
Old School La. KT17: Ewe 5C 30
Old School Sq. KT7: T Ditt 3A 22
Old School Ter. SM3: Cheam 4G 31
Old Station Gdns. TW11: Tedd 3B 16
  (off Victoria Rd.)
Old Station Pas. TW9: Rich 1E 10
  (off Little Green)
Old Stede Cl. KT21: Asht 6G 33
Olde Haines Lodge SW15 .....2J 13
Oliver Cl. W4 .....3J 5
Oliver Rd. KT3: N Mald 1E 4
Olivette St. SW15 .....7G 7
Olympia 1H 7
Olympia Way W14 .....1H 7
Ongar Rd. SW6 .....3K 7
Onslow Av. SM2: Cheam 6J 31
Onslow Cl. KT7: T Ditt 5K 21
Onslow Gdns. KT7: T Ditt 5K 21
Onslow Ho. KT2: King T 1E 36
Onslow Rd. KT3: N Mald 1D 24
  KT12: Hers 3A 26
  TW10: Rich 2F 11
Onslow Way KT7: T Ditt 5K 21
Ophelia Ho. W6 .....2G 7
  (off Fulham Pal. Rd.)
Orangery, The TW10: Ham 6D 10
Orange Tree Theatre 1F 11
Orbain Rd. SW6 .....4H 7
Orchard, The KT17: Ewe 4C 30
  (Meadow Wlk.)
  KT17: Ewe 4C 30
  (Tayles Hill Dr.)
  SM7: Bans 4K 35
  W4 .....1A 6
Orchard Av. KT3: N Mald 6B 18
  KT7: T Ditt 5B 22
  KT12: Walt T 4A 20
  KT19: Ewe 3J 29
  SW20 .....1F 25
Orchard Cotts. KT2: King T 5G 17
Orchard Ct. KT4: Wor Pk 5D 24
  TW2: Twick 6J 9

Orchard Gdns. KT9: Chess 1F 29
  KT18: Eps 3K 33
  SM1: Sutt 2K 31
Orchard Ga. KT10: Esh 5J 21
Orchard Ho. SW6 .....4J 7
  (off Varna Rd.)
Orchard La. KT8: E Mos 3J 21
  SW20 .....5E 18
Orchard Pl. W4 .....1B 6
Orchard Ri. KT2: King T 5K 17
  TW10: Rich 1J 11
Orchard Rd.
  KT1: King T 4C 36 (6F 17)
  KT9: Chess 1F 29
  SM1: Sutt 2K 31
  TW1: Twick 3A 10
  TW4: Houn 2E 8
  TW8: Bford 3D 4
  TW9: Rich 7H 5
  TW12: Hamp 4E 14
  TW16: Sun 4A 14
Orchard Sq. W14 .....2J 7
Orchard Studios W6 .....1G 7
  (off Brook Grn.)
Orchard Wlk. KT2: King T 5H 17
  (off Gordon Rd.)
Orchard Way KT10: Esh 3H 27
Orchid Cl. KT9: Chess 4D 28
Orchid Gdns. TW3: Houn 1E 8
Ordnance Cl. TW13: Felt 6A 8
Oregon Cl. KT3: N Mald 1K 23
Orford Gdns. TW1: Twick 6A 10
ORGAN CROSSROADS 4D 30
Oriel Dr. SW13 .....3F 7
Orion M. SM4: Mord 1K 25
Orlando Gdns. KT19: Ewe 6A 30
Orleans Cl. KT10: Esh 6J 21
Orleans Ct. KT12: Walt T 6B 20
  TW1: Twick 4C 10
Orleans House Gallery 5C 10
Orleans Pk. School Sports Cen.
  .....4C 10
Orleans Rd. TW1: Twick 4C 10
Orme Rd. KT1: King T 6J 17
Ormond Av. TW10: Rich 2E 10
  TW12: Hamp 5G 15
Ormond Cres.
  TW12: Hamp 5G 15
Ormond Dr. TW12: Hamp 4E 14
Ormonde Av. KT19: Ewe 6A 30
Ormonde Cl. SW15 .....1F 13
Ormonde Rd. SW14 .....7K 5
Orpen Ho. SW5 .....1K 7
  (off Trebovir Rd.)
Orpwood Cl. TW12: Hamp 3E 14
Osborne Cl. TW13: Hanw 2C 14
Osborne Rd. KT2: King T 4F 17
  KT12: Walt T 5A 20
  TW3: Houn 1E 8
Osborne Way KT9: Chess 2G 29
  KT19: Eps 1F 33
Osborne Ho.
  TW2: Twick 6H 9
Osier Cl. TW8: Bford 3F 5
  (off Ealing Rd.)
Osier M. W4 .....3B 6
Osiers Cl. KT1: King T 2B 36
Osiers Ct. SW18 .....1K 13
Osiers Twr. SW18 .....1K 13
  (off Enterprise Way)
Osier Way SM7: Bans 3H 35
Osprey Cl. SM1: Sutt 2J 31
Osprey Dr. KT18: Tatt C 6E 34
Osram Ct. W6 .....1F 7
Osterley Cres. TW7: Isle 5A 4
Osterley Sports & Athletics Cen.
  .....4A 4
Otho Ct. TW8: Bford 4E 4
Otterburn Gdns. TW7: Isle 4B 4
Ottway's Av. KT21: Asht 7F 33
Oval, The SM7: Bans 3K 35
Overdale KT21: Asht 4F 33
Overdale Av.
  KT3: N Mald 6K 17
Overstone Rd. W6 .....1F 7
Overton Cl. TW7: Isle 5A 4
Overton Ct. SM2: Sutt 4K 31
Overton Ho. SW15 .....7F 7
  (off Tangley Gro.)
Overton Rd. SM2: Sutt 3K 31
Owen Ho. TW1: Twick 4C 10
Owen Mans. W14 .....3H 7
  (off Queen's Club Gdns.)
Oxberry Av. SW6 .....6H 7
Oxford Av. SW20 .....6H 19

Oxford Ct. KT6: Surb 2F 23
  (off Avenue Elmers)
  KT18: Eps 3B 34
  TW13: Hanw 1C 14
  W4 .....2J 5
Oxford Cres. KT3: N Mald 3A 24
Oxford Gdns. W4 .....2H 5
Oxford Ga. W6 .....1G 7
Oxford Rd. SW15 .....1H 13
  TW11: Tedd 2J 15
Oxford Rd. Nth. W4 .....2J 5
Oxford Rd. Sth. W4 .....2H 5
Oxford Row TW16: Sun 7B 14
Oxford Way TW13: Hanw 1C 14
Ox La. KT17: Ewe 5D 30
Oxleigh Cl. KT3: N Mald 2B 24
OXSHOTT 7K 27
Oxshott Rd. KT22: Lea 5A 32

P

Pachesham Dr. KT22: Lea 5A 32
PACHESHAM PARK 5B 32
Pachesham Pk. KT22: Lea 5B 32
Pachesham Pk. Golf Course
  .....7A 32
Packham Ct. KT4: Wor Pk 7F 25
Paddenswick Rd. W6 .....1D 6
Paddock Cl. KT4: Wor Pk 5B 24
Paddocks, The W5 .....1E 4
  (off Popes La.)
Paddocks Cl. KT21: Asht 7F 33
Paddock Rd. KT21: Asht 7F 33
Paddock Way SW15 .....4F 13
Padley Cl. KT9: Chess 2G 29
Page Cl. TW12: Hamp 3D 14
Pages Yd. W4 .....3C 6
Paget Cl. TW12: Hamp H 1J 15
Paget La. TW7: Isle 1J 9
Paget Pl. KT2: King T 3K 17
  KT7: T Ditt 5A 22
Pagoda Av. TW9: Rich 7G 5
Palace Mans. KT1: King T 1E 22
  (off Palace Rd.)
  W14 .....1H 7
  (off Hammersmith Rd.)
Palace M. SW6 .....4J 7
Palace Rd. KT1: King T 1E 22
  KT8: E Mos 7H 15
Palace Wharf W6 .....4F 7
  (off Rainville Rd.)
Palemead Cl. SW6 .....5G 7
Palewell Comn. Dr. SW14 .....2A 12
Palewell Pk. SW14 .....2A 12
Palgrave Ct. TW11: Hamp W 4D 16
Palgrave Ho. TW2: Whitt 4H 9
Palgrave Rd. W12 .....1C 6
Palladio Ct. SW18 .....3K 13
  (off Mapleton Rd.)
Palliser Ct. W14 .....2H 7
  (off Palliser Rd.)
Palliser Rd. W14 .....2H 7
Pallister Ter. SW15 .....7C 12
Palmer Av. SM3: Cheam 1F 31
Palmer Cres.
  KT1: King T 5C 36 (7F 17)
Palmersfield Rd. SM7: Bans 3K 35
Palmers Grn. KT6: W Mole 1F 21
Palmers Pas. SW14 .....7K 5
  (off Little St Leonard's)
Palmers Rd. SW14 .....7K 5
Palmerston Cl. KT6: Surb 4E 22
Palmerston Gro. SW19 .....4K 19
Palmerston Rd. SM7: Bans 4J 35
  (off Basing Rd.)
Palmerston Mans. W14 .....3H 7
  (off Queen's Club Gdns.)
Palmerston Rd. SW14 .....1K 11
  SW19 .....4K 19
  TW2: Twick 3K 9
Pams Way KT19: Ewe 2A 30
Pankhurst Cl. TW7: Isle 7A 4
Pankhurst Rd.
  KT12: Walt T 4B 20
Panmuir Rd. SW20 .....5E 18
Parabola Ct. KT8: E Mos 1H 21
Parade, The KT2: King T 3D 36
  KT10: Clay 3K 27
  KT17: Eps 2B 34
  KT18: Eps 3A 34
  (off Spa Dr.)
  KT18: Eps 2A 34
  (Ashley Rd.)

Parade, The KT20: Tad 7H 35
SM1: Sutt 7J 25
TW12: Hamp H 2J 15
Paradise Rd. TW9: Rich 2E 10
Paragon TW8: Bford 2D 4
(off Boston Pk. Rd.)
Paragon Gro. KT5: Surb 3G 23
Paragon Pl. KT5: Surb 3G 23
Parbury Rd. KT9: Chess 3F 29
Parfrey St. W6 . . . . .3F 7
Parish Ct. KT6: Surb 2F 23
Parison Cl. TW9: Rich 7H 5
Park & Ride
Kingston upon Thames 5D 28
TW3: Houn 3G 9
Park Av. SW14 . . . . .1A 12
Park Av. E. KT17: Ewe 3D 30
Park Av. W. KT17: Ewe 3D 30
Park Cl. KT2: King T 5H 17
KT10: Esh 3F 21
TW3: Houn 2H 9
TW12: Hamp 5H 15
W4 . . . . .3A 6
Park Ct. KT1: Hamp W 5D 16
KT3: N Mald 1A 24
W6 . . . . .1D 6
Park Cres. TW2: Twick 5J 9
Parkdale Cres. KT4: Wor Pk 7A 24
Park Dr. KT21: Asht 7H 33
SW14 . . . . .2A 12
W3 . . . . .1H 5
Parke Rd. SW13 . . . . .5D 6
TW16: Sun 1A 20
Parker's Cl. KT21: Asht 7F 33
Parker's La. KT21: Asht 7F 33
Park Farm Rd. KT2: King T 4F 17
Parkfield Av. SW14 . . . . .1B 12
Parkfield Cres. TW13: Felt 7A 8
Parkfield Rd. TW13: Felt 7A 8
Parkfields KT22: Oxs 7J 27
SW15 . . . . .1F 13
Parkfields Av. SW20 . . . . .5E 18
Parkfields Rd. KT2: King T 2G 17
Park Gdns. KT2: King T 2G 17
Parkgate Cl. KT2: King T 3J 17
Park Ga. Ct. TW12: Hamp H 3H 15
Parkgate Gdns. SW14 . . . . .2A 12
Park Hgts. KT18: Eps 3A 34
Park Hill TW10: Rich 3G 11
Parkhill KT10: Esh 1H 27
Park Hill Rd. KT17: Ewe 7C 30
Park Ho. Gdns. TW1: Twick 2D 10
Parkhurst KT19: Eps 6K 29
Parkland Gdns. SW19 . . . . .5G 13
Parklands KT5: Surb 2G 23
Parklands Cl. SW14 . . . . .2K 11
Parklands Ct. KT19: Eps 1F 33
Parklands Gro. TW7: Isle 5A 4
Parklands Way KT4: Wor Pk 6B 24
Park La. KT21: Asht 7G 33
SM3: Cheam 3H 31
TW9: Rich 1E 10
TW11: Tedd 3A 16
Parklawn Av. KT18: Eps 2J 33
Parkleys TW10: Ham 1E 16
Parkleys Pde. TW10: Ham 1E 16
Parkmead SW15 . . . . .3E 12
Park Pl. TW12: Hamp H 3H 15
W3 . . . . .1H 5
Park Pl. Dr. W3 . . . . .1H 5
Park Rd.
KT1: Hamp W 2A 36 (5D 16)
KT2: King T 2G 17
KT3: N Mald 1A 24
KT5: Surb 3G 23
KT8: E Mos 1H 21
KT10: Esh 1G 27
KT21: Asht 7F 33
SM3: Cheam 3H 31
TW1: Twick 3D 10
TW3: Houn 2G 9
TW7: Isle 5C 4
TW10: Rich 3G 11
TW11: Tedd 3A 16
TW12: Hamp H 1G 15
TW13: Hanw 1C 14
TW16: Sun 4A 14
W4 .4K 5
Park Rd. KT2: King T 4H 17
Park Rd. Nth. W4 . . . . .2A 6
Parkshot TW9: Rich 1E 10
Parkside SM3: Cheam 3H 31
SW19 . . . . .7G 13
TW12: Hamp H 2J 15
Parkside Av. SW19 . . . . .5J 13
Parkside Cres. KT5: Surb 3K 23
Parkside Gdns. SW19 . . . . .1G 19
PARKSIDE HOSPITAL 7G 13
Parkside Rd. TW3: Houn 2G 9
Park Sq. KT10: Esh 1G 27
Parkstead Rd. SW15 . . . . .2D 12
Park St. TW11: Tedd 3K 15
Park Ter. KT4: Wor Pk 5D 24
Park Vw. KT3: N Mald 7C 18
KT12: Hers 2B 26
Parkview Ct. SW6 . . . . .6H 7
SW18 . . . . .3K 13
Parkview Cres. KT4: Wor Pk 4F 25
Parkview Way KT19: Eps 6A 30
Parkville Rd. SW6 . . . . .4J 7
Park Wlk. KT21: Asht 7G 33
Park Way KT8: W Mole 7G 15
TW14: Felt 4A 8
W3 . . . . .1H 5
Parkway SW20 . . . . .1G 25
Parkwood Av. KT10: Esh 5H 21
Parkwood Cl. SM7: Bans 4G 35
Parkwood Rd. SM7: Bans 4G 35
SW19 . . . . .2J 19
TW7: Isle 5A 4
Parkwood Vw. SM7: Bans 5F 35
Parliament M. SW4 . . . . .6K 5
Parr Av. KT17: Ewe 5E 30
Parr Ct. TW13: Hanw 1B 14
Parrs Pl. TW12: Hamp 4F 15
Parrs Way W6 . . . . .3F 7
Parry Cl. KT17: Ewe 4E 30
Parsonsfield Cl. SM7: Bans 4G 35
Parsonsfield Rd. SM7: Bans 5G 35
Parsons Ga. M. SW6 . . . . .6K 7
PARSONS GREEN 6J 7
Parson's Grn. SW6 . . . . .5K 7
Parson's Grn. La. SW6 . . . . .5K 7
Parsons Green Station
(Underground) 5K 7
Parsons Mead KT8: E Mos 7H 15
Parthenia Dr. TW7: Isle 7B 4
Parthenia Rd. SW6 . . . . .5K 7
Partridge Mead SM7: Bans 4F 35
Partridge Rd. TW12: Hamp 3E 14
Passage, The TW9: Rich 2F 11
Passfields W14 . . . . .2H 7
(off Star Rd.)
Patricia Gdns. SM2: Sutt 7K 31
Patten All. TW10: Rich 2E 10
Pauline Cres. TW2: Whitt 5H 9
Paul Robeson Theatre, The 1G 9
Paul's Pl. KT21: Asht 7J 33
Paul Vanson Ct. KT12: Hers 3C 26
Paved Ct. TW9: Rich 2E 10
Pavement, The SW19 . . . . .3J 19
(off Worple Rd.)
TW7: Isle 7B 4
(off South St.)
TW11: Tedd 4C 16
W5 . . . . .1F 5
Pavilion Sports & Fitness Club, The
. . . . .7H 15
Paxton Cl. TW12: Walt T 4B 20
TW9: Kew 6G 5
Paxton Rd. W4 . . . . .3B 6
Paynesfield Av. SW14 . . . . .7A 6
Paynes Wlk. W6 . . . . .3H 7
Peabody Est. SW6 . . . . .3K 7
(off Lillie Rd.)
W6 . . . . .2J 7
(off Mornington Av.)
Peaches Cl. SM2: Cheam 4H 31
Peacock Cl. KT19: Eps 1G 33
Pearing Cl. KT4: Wor Pk 6G 25
Pears Rd. TW3: Houn 1H 9
Pear Tree Cl. KT9: Chess 2H 29
KT19: Eps 5A 30
Peek Cres. SW19 . . . . .2G 19
Peel Pl. SW6 . . . . .3K 7
Pegasus Ct.
KT1: King T 6B 36 (7E 16)
SM7: Bans 4K 35
TW8: Bford 2G 5
Pegasus Pl. SW6 . . . . .4H 7
Pelabon Ho. TW1: Twick 3E 10
(off Clevedon Rd.)
Peldon Ct. TW9: Rich 1G 11
Peldon Pas. TW10: Rich 1G 11
Pelham Av. W14 . . . . .1J 7
(off Mornington Av.)
Pelham Rd. SW19 . . . . .4K 19
Pelham's Cl. KT10: Esh 1F 27
Pelham's Wlk. KT10: Esh 1F 27
Pellant Rd. SW6 . . . . .4H 7
Pelling Ho. W14 . . . . .1J 7
(off Mornington Av.)
Pelman Way KT19: Eps 6J 29

Pemberley Chase KT19: Ewe 2J 29
Pemberley Cl. KT19: Ewe 2J 29
Pemberley Ho. KT19: Ewe 2J 29
(off Pemberley Chase)
Pemberton Pl. KT10: Esh 7H 21
Pemberton Rd. KT8: E Mos 1H 21
Pembridge Av. TW2: Whitt 5E 8
Pembridge Pl. SW15 . . . . .2K 13
Pembroke W14 . . . . .1J 7
(off Kensington Village)
Pembroke Av. KT5: Surb 2J 23
KT12: Hers 1C 26
Pembroke Cl. SM7: Bans 5K 35
Pembroke Cotts. W8 . . . . .1K 7
(off Pembroke Sq.)
Pembroke Ct. W8 . . . . .1K 7
(off Sth. Edwardes Sq.)
Pembroke Gdns. SW14 . . . . .1J 11
W8 . . . . .1J 7
Pembroke Gdns. Cl. W8 . . . . .1K 7
Pembroke M. W8 . . . . .1K 7
Pembroke Pl. W8 . . . . .1K 7
Pembroke Rd. W8 . . . . .1J 7
Pembroke Sq. W8 . . . . .1K 7
Pembroke Studios W8 . . . . .1K 7
W8 . . . . .1K 7
Pembroke Vs. TW9: Rich 1E 10
W8 . . . . .1K 7
Pembroke Wlk. W8 . . . . .1K 7
Pembury Av. KT4: Wor Pk 5D 24
Penates KT10: Esh 1J 27
Pendarves Rd. SW20 . . . . .5F 19
Penderel Rd. TW3: Houn 2F 9
Pendlebury Ct. KT5: Surb 1F 23
(off Cranes Pk.)
Penhurst Mans. SW6 . . . . .5J 7
(off Rostrevor Rd.)
Pennant M. W8 . . . . .1K 7
Pennards, The TW16: Sun 7B 14
Penner Cl. SW19 . . . . .6H 13
Penners Gdns. KT6: Surb 4F 23
Pennington Lodge KT5: Surb 2F 23
(off Cranes Dr.)
Pennymead Pl. KT10: Esh 3E 26
Penrhyn Cres. SW14 . . . . .1K 11
Penrhyn Gdns.
KT1: King T 7B 36 (1E 22)
Penrhyn Rd.
KT1: King T 7C 36 (1F 23)
Penrith Cl. SW15 . . . . .2H 13
Penrith Rd. KT3: N Mald 1A 24
Penrose Dr. KT19: Eps 7H 29
Pensford Av. TW9: Kew 6H 5
Penshurst Way SM2: Sutt 4K 31
Pentlow St. SW15 . . . . .7F 7
Pentney Rd. SW19 . . . . .5H 19
Penwith Rd. SW18 . . . . .6K 13
Penwood Ho. SW15 . . . . .3C 12
Penywern Rd. SW5 . . . . .2K 7
Pepys Cl. KT21: Asht 6H 33
Pepys Rd. SW20 . . . . .5F 19
Percheron Cl. TW7: Isle 7A 4
Percival Cl. KT22: Oxs 7G 27
Percival Rd. SW14 . . . . .1K 11
Percival Way KT19: Ewe 1A 30
Percy Gdns. KT4: Wor Pk 5A 24
TW7: Isle 7C 4
Percy Laurie Ho. SW15 . . . . .1G 13
(off Nursery Cl.)
Percy Rd. TW2: Whitt 5G 9
TW7: Isle 1B 10
TW12: Hamp 4F 15
Percy Way TW2: Whitt 5H 9
Peregrine Way SW19 . . . . .4F 19
Perham Rd. W14 . . . . .2H 7
Perkin Cl. TW3: Houn 1F 9
Perran Wlk. TW8: Bford 2F 5
Perrers Rd. W6 . . . . .1E 6
Perry Ct. KT1: King T 3D 36
Perryfield Way KT10: Ham 7C 10
Perry How KT4: Wor Pk 5C 24
Perrymead St. SW6 . . . . .5K 7
Perryn Ct. TW1: Twick 3B 10
Perseverance Pl. TW9: Rich 1F 11
Persfield Cl. KT17: Ewe 6C 30
Persfield M. KT17: Ewe 6C 30
Perth Cl. SW20 . . . . .6C 18
Petavel Rd. TW11: Tedd 3K 15
Peterborough M. SW6 . . . . .6K 7
Peterborough Rd. SW6 . . . . .6K 7
Peterborough Vs. SW6 . . . . .5K 7
Petersfield Ri. SW15 . . . . .5E 12
Petersgate KT2: King T 3K 17
(off Warren Rd.)
PETERSHAM 5F 11
Petersham Cl. SM1: Sutt 2K 31
TW10: Ham 6E 10

Petersham Rd.
TW10: Rich, Ham 3E 10
Peterstow Cl. SW19 . . . . .6H 13
Petley Rd. W6 . . . . .3G 7
Petters Rd. KT21: Asht 5G 33
Pettiward Cl. SW15 . . . . .1F 13
Petworth Gdns. SW20 . . . . .7E 18
Pevensey Rd. TW13: Felt 5D 8
Peveril Dr. TW11: Tedd 2J 15
Pheasantry Welcome Cen., The
. . . . .5A 16
Philbeach Gdns. SW5 . . . . .2K 7
Phoenix Cl. KT19: Eps 1H 33
Phoenix Ct. KT3: N Mald 7C 18
KT17: Eps 2B 34
(off Depot Rd.)
TW3: Houn 1F 9
TW4: Houn 2C 8
TW8: Bford 2F 5
Phoenix Lodge Mans. W6 . . . . . . .1G 7
(off Brook Grn.)
Phoenix Trad. Pk. TW8: Bford 2E 4
Phyllis Av. KT3: N Mald 2E 24
Pickering Ho. W5 . . . . .1D 4
(off Windmill Rd.)
Pickwick Cl. TW4: Houn 2D 8
Picquets Way SM7: Bans 5H 35
Picton Cl. KT6: Surb 5H 23
Pieris Ho. TW13: Felt 6A 8
(off High St.)
Pier Rd. TW14: Felt 2A 8
Pigeon La. TW12: Hamp 1F 15
Pikemans Ct. SW5 . . . . .1K 7
(off W. Cromwell Rd.)
Pikes Hill KT17: Eps 2B 34
Pilsdon Cl. SW19 . . . . .5G 13
Pine Cl. KT19: Eps 5K 29
Pine Gdns. KT5: Surb 3H 23
Pine Gro. SW19 . . . . .2J 19
Pine Hill KT18: Eps 4A 34
Pine Pl. SM7: Bans 3G 35
Pines, The KT9: Chess 7F 23
TW16: Sun 7A 14
Pine Wlk. KT5: Surb 3H 23
Pine Wood TW16: Sun 5A 14
Pinewood Pl. KT19: Ewe 1A 30
Pinewood Rd. TW13: Felt 7A 8
Pinkcoat Cl. TW13: Felt 7A 8
Pinkham Mans. W4 . . . . .2H 5
Piper Bldg., The SW6 . . . . .7K 7
Pipit Dr. KT1: King T 7H 17
Pippin Cl. TW13: Hanw 7E 8
Pirbright Rd. SW18 . . . . .5J 13
Pitcairn Rd. KT21: Asht 7J 33
Pitt Cres. SW19 . . . . .1K 19
Pitt Pl. KT17: Eps 3B 34
Pitt Rd. KT17: Eps 3B 34
Planetree Ct. W6 . . . . .1G 7
(off Brook Grn.)
Plane Tree Cres. TW13: Felt 7A 8
Plantagenet Cl. KT4: Wor Pk 1A 30
Platt, The SW15 . . . . .7G 7
Platt's Eyot TW12: Hamp 6F 15
Playfair Mans. W14 . . . . .3H 7
(off Queen's Club Gdns.)
Playfair St. W6 . . . . .2F 7
Plaza Gdns. SW15 . . . . .2H 13
Pleasance, The SW15 . . . . .1E 12
Pleasance Rd. SW15 . . . . .2E 12
Pleasant Pl. KT12: Hers 3B 26
Pleasure Pit Rd. KT21: Asht 7J 33
Plevna Rd. TW12: Hamp 5G 15
Pleydell Av. W6 . . . . .1C 6
Plough La. TW11: Tedd 2B 16
Ploughmans End TW7: Isle 2J 9
Plough Rd. KT19: Ewe 5A 30
Plum Gth. TW8: Bford 1E 4
Plymen Ho. KT8: W Mole 2F 21
Plymouth Ct. KT5: Surb 1F 23
(off Cranes Pk. Av.)
Pocklington Ct. SW15 . . . . .5D 12
Pointers Cotts. TW10: Ham 6D 10
Point Pleasant SW18 . . . . .1K 13
Point Wharf TW8: Bford 4F 5
Point Wharf La. TW8: Bford 4E 4
Polehamptons, The
TW12: Hamp 4H 15
Polesden Gdns. SW20 . . . . .6E 18
Police Sta. Rd. KT12: Hers 3B 26
Polka Theatre for Children 3K 19
Pollard Ho. KT4: Wor Pk 1F 31
Pomeroy Cl. TW1: Twick 1C 10
Pond Hill Gdns. SM3: Cheam 3H 31
Pond Pl. KT21: Asht 6F 33
Pondside Av. KT4: Wor Pk 5F 25
Pond Way TW11: Tedd 3D 16

Ponsonby Rd.—Rainville Rd.

Ponsonby Rd. SW15 .....4E 12
Pontes Av. TW3: Houn 1E 8
Pool Cl. KT8: W Mole 2E 20
Poole Rd. KT19: Ewe 3A 30
Pooles Cotts. TW10: Ham 6E 10
Pooley Dr. SW14 .....7K 5
Pool Rd. KT8: W Mole 2E 20
Pools on the Pk. 1E 10
Popes Av. TW2: Twick 6K 9
Popes Ct. TW2: Twick 6K 9
Popes Gro. TW1: Twick 6K 9
TW2: Twick 6K 9
Popes La. W5 .....1E 4
Popham Cl. TW13: Hanw 7E 8
Popham Gdns. TW9: Rich 7H 5
Popinjays Row SM3: Cheam 2G 31
(off Netley Cl.)
Poplar Cl. KT17: Eps D 4E 34
Poplar Ct. SW19 .....2K 19
TW1: Twick 3D 10
Poplar Cres. KT19: Ewe 3K 29
Poplar Dr. SM7: Bans 3G 35
Poplar Farm Cl. KT19: Ewe 3K 29
Poplar Gdns. KT3: N Mald 6A 18
Poplar Gro. KT3: N Mald 6A 18
Poplar Ho. KT19: Eps 5A 30
Poplar Rd. KT10: Surb 7C 22
SM3: Sutt 5J 25
SW19 .....6K 19
Poplar Rd. Sth. SW19 .....7K 19
Poplar Way TW13: Felt 7A 8
Porchester Rd.
KT1: King T 6J 17
Porten Ho's. W14 .....1H 7
(off Porten Rd.)
Porten Rd. W14 .....1H 7
Portinscale Rd. SW15 .....2H 13
Portland Av. KT3: N Mald 4C 24
Portland Cl. KT4: Wor Pk 4E 24
Portland Ho. SW15 .....2G 13
Portland Ho. M. KT18: Eps 3A 34
(off Caithness Dr.)
Portland Mans. W14 .....1J 7
(off Addison Bri. Pl.)
Portland Pl. KT17: Eps 1B 34
Portland Rd.
KT1: King T 6D 36 (7F 17)
Portland Ter. TW9: Rich 1E 10
Portman Av. SW14 .....7A 6
Portman Rd. KT1: King T 6G 17
Porton Ct. KT6: Surb 3D 22
Portsmouth Av. KT7: T Ditt 4B 22
Portsmouth Rd. KT1: King T 4B 22
KT6: Surb 7B 36 (4B 22)
KT7: T Ditt 7B 36 (4B 22)
KT10: Esh 7C 26
(Fairmile La.)
KT10: Esh 3F 27
(Hawkshill Cl.)
KT10: Esh 1H 27
(Sandown Rd.)
KT11: Cobh 7C 26
SW15 .....4E 12
Portswood Pl. SW15 .....3C 12
Portugal Gdns. TW2: Twick 6H 9
Portway KT17: Ewe 5D 30
Portway Cres. KT17: Ewe 5D 30
POSK 1D 6
(off King St.)
Post La. TW2: Twick 5J 9
Post Office All. W4 .....3J 5
(off Thames Rd.)
Potterne Cl. SW19 .....4G 13
Potters Ct. SM1: Sutt 3J 31
(off Rosebery Rd.)
Potters Gro. KT3: N Mald 1K 23
Pottery Rd. TW8: Bford 3F 5
Poulett Gdns. TW1: Twick 5B 10
Pound Cl. KT6: Surb 5D 22
KT19: Eps 7A 30
Pound Ct. KT21: Asht 7G 33
Pound Farm Cl. KT10: Esh 5J 21
Pound La. KT19: Eps 1K 33
Pound Rd. SM7: Bans 6J 35
Powder Mill La. TW2: Whitt 4E 8
Powell Cl. KT9: Chess 2E 28
Powell's Wlk. W4 .....3B 6
Power Rd. W4 .....1H 5
Powers Ct. TW1: Twick 4E 10
Pownall Gdns. TW3: Houn 1G 9
Pownall Rd. TW3: Houn 1G 9
Prado Path TW1: Twick 5A 10
(off Laurel Av.)
Pratts La. KT12: Hers 1C 26
Pratts Pas.
KT1: King T 4C 36 (6F 17)
Prebend Gdns. W4 .....1C 6
W6 .....1C 6
(not continuous)
Prebend Mans. W4 .....1C 6
(off Chiswick High Rd.)
Precincts, The SM4: Mord 3K 25
Premier Pl. SW15 .....1H 13
Prentice Ct. SW19 .....2J 19
Presburg Rd. KT3: N Mald 2B 24
Preston Cl. TW2: Twick 7K 9
Preston Ct. KT12: Walt T 5B 20
Preston Dr. KT19: Ewe 3B 30
Preston Gro. KT21: Asht 6D 32
Preston Pl. TW10: Rich 2F 11
Preston Rd. SW20 .....4C 18
Price Way TW12: Hamp 3D 14
Priest Cl. TW12: Hamp 1F 15
Priest Hill Cl. KT17: Eps 2E 34
Priests Bri. SW14 .....7B 6
SW15 .....7B 6
Primrose Ho. KT18: Eps 2K 33
(off Dalmeny Way)
Primrose Pl. TW7: Isle 6A 4
Primrose Rd. KT12: Hers 2B 26
Primrose Wlk. KT17: Ewe 4C 30
Prince George's Av. SW20 .....6F 19
Prince of Wales Ter. W4 .....2B 6
Princes Av. KT6: Surb 5H 23
W3 .....1H 5
Prince's Cl. TW11: Tedd 1J 15
Prince's Dr. KT22: Oxs 7K 27
Princes M. TW3: Houn 1F 9
W6 .....2E 6
(off Down Pl.)
Prince's Rd. SW19 .....3K 19
TW11: Tedd 1J 15
Princes Rd. KT2: King T 4H 17
SW14 .....7A 6
TW9: Kew 5G 5
TW10: Rich 2G 11
PRINCESS ALICE HOSPICE 2F 27
Princess Ct. KT1: King T 6E 36
Princess M.
KT1: King T 6E 36 (7G 17)
Princess Sq. KT10: Esh 3H 27
Princes St. TW9: Rich 1F 11
Princes Way SW19 .....4G 13
W3 .....1H 5
Princeton Ct. SW15 .....7G 7
Princeton M. KT2: King T 5H 17
Prior Ct. KT8: W Mole 2E 20
Priors Wood KT10: Hin W 6A 22
Priory Av. SM3: Cheam 1G 31
W4 .....1B 6
Priory Cl. TW12: Hamp 5E 14
TW16: Sun 4A 14
Priory Ct. KT1: King T 5C 36
KT17: Ewe 5C 30
SM3: Cheam 1H 31
Priory Cres. SM3: Cheam 1G 31
Priory Gdns. SW13 .....7C 6
TW12: Hamp 4E 14
W4 .....1B 6
Priory La. KT8: W Mole 1G 21
SW15 .....3B 12
Priory Lodge W4 .....2H 5
(off Kew Bri. Ct.)
Priory Pl. KT12: Walt T 7A 20
Priory Rd. KT9: Chess 7F 23
SM3: Cheam 1G 31
TW3: Houn 2H 9
TW9: Kew 3H 5
TW12: Hamp 4E 14
W4 .....1A 6
Priory Ter. TW16: Sun 4A 14
Priory Wlk. TW16: Sun 4A 14
Profumo Rd. KT12: Hers 2C 26
Prologis Pk. TW4: Houn 1B 8
Promenade, The W4 .....6B 6
Promenade App. Rd. W4 .....4B 6
Prospect Cotts. SW18 .....1K 13
Prospect Cres. TW2: Whitt 3H 9
Prospect Ho. KT19: Eps 5J 29
Prospect Pl. KT17: Eps 1B 34
SW20 .....4E 18
W4 .....2A 6
Prospect Quay SW18 .....1K 13
(off Lightermans Wlk.)
Prospect Rd. KT6: Surb 3D 22
Prothero Rd. SW6 .....4H 7
Providence Pl. KT17: Eps 1B 34
Pugin Cl. SW19 .....1K 19
Pulborough Rd. SW18 .....4J 13
Pulborough Way TW4: Houn 1B 8
Pullman Gdns. SW15 .....3F 13
Pulteney Cl. TW7: Isle 7B 4
Pulton Pl. SW6 .....4K 7
Pump All. TW8: Bford 4E 4
Pump Ho. Rd.
TW8: Bford 2F 5
Pumping Station Rd. W4 .....4B 6
Purbeck Av. KT3: N Mald 3C 24
Purberry Gro. KT17: Ewe 6C 30
Purberry Shot KT17: Ewe 6C 30
Purcell Cres. SW6 .....4G 7
Purcell Mans. W14 .....3H 7
(off Queen's Club Gdns.)
Purcell's Cl. KT21: Asht 7G 33
Purdy Ct. KT4: Wor Pk 6D 24
Pursers Cross Rd. SW6 .....5J 7
PUTNEY 1G 13
Putney Arts Theatre 1G 13
Putney Bri. SW15 .....7H 7
Putney Bri. App. SW6 .....7H 7
Putney Bri. Rd. SW15 .....1H 13
SW18 .....1H 13
Putney Bridge Station
(Underground) 7J 7
Putney Comn. SW15 .....7F 7
Putney Exchange (Shop. Cen.)
SW15 .....1G 13
PUTNEY HEATH 3F 13
Putney Heath SW15 .....4E 12
Putney Heath La. SW15 .....3G 13
Putney High St. SW15 .....1G 13
Putney Hill SW15 .....4G 13
(not continuous)
Putney Leisure Cen. 1F 13
Putney Pk. Av. SW15 .....1D 12
Putney Pk. La. SW15 .....1E 12
(not continuous)
Putney Pier (River Bus) 7H 7
Putney Station (Rail) 1H 13
PUTNEY VALE 7D 12
Putney Va. Crematorium
SW19 .....6E 12
Putney Wharf SW15 .....7H 7
Putt in the Pk. 1J 13
Pylbrook Rd. SM1: Sutt 7K 25
Pyne Rd. KT6: Surb 5H 23
Pyramid Ct. KT1: King T 6G 17
(off Cambridge Rd.)
Pyrland Rd. TW10: Rich 3G 11
Pyrmont Rd. W4 .....3H 5

Q

Quadrangle, The SW6 .....4H 7
Quadrant, The KT17: Eps 2B 34
SW20 .....5H 19
TW9: Rich 1E 10
Quadrant Rd. TW9: Rich 1E 10
Quain Mans. W14 .....3H 7
(off Queen's Club Gdns.)
Quakers La. TW7: Isle 4B 4
Quantock Dr. KT4: Wor Pk 6F 25
Quarrendon St. SW6 .....6K 7
Quarry Pk. Rd. SM1: Sutt 3J 31
Quarry Ri. SM1: Sutt 3J 31
Quayside Wlk. KT1: King T 4B 36
Queen Alexandra's Ct. SW19 .....2J 19
Queen Alexandra's Way
KT19: Eps 7H 29
Queen Anne Dr. KT10: Clay 4K 27
Queen Anne's Cl. TW2: Twick 7J 9
Queen Anne's Gdns. W4 .....1B 6
Queen Anne's Gro. W4 .....1B 6
Queen Caroline St. W6 .....2F 7
Queen Elizabeth Gdns.
SM4: Mord 1K 25
Queen Elizabeth Rd.
KT2: King T 3E 36 (6G 17)
Queen Elizabeth Wlk. SW13 .....5D 6
Queen Mary Av. SM4: Mord 2G 25
Queen Mary Cl. KT6: Surb 7H 23
QUEEN MARY'S HOSPITAL,
ROEHAMPTON 3D 12
Queen Mary's Ho. SW15 .....3D 12
Queens Acre SM3: Cheam 4G 31
Queens Av. TW13: Hanw 1B 14
Queensberry Ho. TW9: Rich 2D 10
Queensberry Pl. TW9: Rich 2E 10
(off Friars La.)
Queensbridge Pk. TW7: Isle 2K 9
Queen's Cl. KT10: Esh 1G 27
Queen's Club Gdns. W14 .....3H 7
Queen's Club, The (Tennis Courts)
.....2H 7
Queens Club Ter. W14 .....3J 7
(off Normand Rd.)
Queen's Ct. SM2: Sutt 7K 31
Queens Ct. KT19: Ewe 6B 30
TW10: Rich 3G 11
Queen's Cres. TW10: Rich 2G 11
Queen's Dr. KT5: Surb 4H 23
KT7: T Ditt 3B 22
KT22: Oxs 7H 27
Queensfield Ct.
SM3: Cheam 1F 31
Queens Ga. Gdns. SW15 .....1E 12
Queens Ho. TW11: Tedd 3A 16
Queen's Keep TW1: Twick 3D 10
Queensland Av. SW19 .....5K 19
Queen's Mans. W6 .....1G 7
(off Brook Grn.)
Queensmead KT22: Oxs 7H 27
Queensmead Av. KT17: Ewe 6E 30
Queensmere Cl. SW19 .....6G 13
Queensmere Ct. SW13 .....4C 6
Queensmere Rd. SW19 .....6G 13
Queensmill Rd. SW6 .....4G 7
Queens Pl. SM4: Mord 1K 25
Queen's Prom.
KT1: King T, Surb 7A 36 (1E 22)
Queens Reach
KT1: King T 4A 36 (6E 16)
KT8: E Mos 1K 21
Queens Ride SW13 .....7D 6
SW15 .....7D 6
Queens Ri. TW10: Rich 3G 11
Queen's Rd. KT7: T Ditt 2A 22
SM2: Sutt 6K 31
SW14 .....7A 6
TW10: Rich 4G 11
TW11: Tedd 3A 16
TW12: Hamp H 1G 15
TW13: Felt 5A 8
Queens Rd. KT2: King T 4H 17
KT3: N Mald 1C 24
KT12: Hers 1A 26
SM4: Mord 1K 25
SW19 .....3J 19
TW1: Twick 5B 10
Queens Ter. KT7: T Ditt 3B 22
(off Queens Dr.)
TW7: Isle 1B 10
Queens Way TW13: Hanw 1B 14
Queensway TW16: Sun 6A 14
Queensway Nth. KT12: Hers 1B 26
Queensway Sth. KT12: Hers 2B 26
Queens Wharf W6 .....2F 7
Queenswood Av. TW12: Hamp 3G 15
Queenswood Ct. KT2: King T 5H 17
QUEEN VICTORIA 1G 31
Quennell Cl. KT21: Asht 7G 33
Quiberon Ct. TW16: Sun 7A 14
Quick Rd. W4 .....2B 6
Quill La. SW15 .....1G 13
Quintain Ho. KT1: King T 2B 36
Quintin Av. SW20 .....5J 19
Quinton Rd. KT7: T Ditt 5B 22

R

Raby Rd. KT3: N Mald 1A 24
RAC Golf Course 6K 33
Racton Rd. SW6 .....3K 7
Radbourne Av. W5 .....1D 4
Radcliffe M. TW12: Hamp H 2H 15
Radcliffe Sq. SW15 .....3G 13
Radipole Rd. SW6 .....5J 7
Radley M. W8 .....1K 7
Radnor Gdns. TW1: Twick 6A 10
Radnor Rd. TW1: Twick 5A 10
Radnor Ter. SM2: Sutt 4K 31
W14 .....1J 7
Raeburn Av. KT5: Surb 5J 23
Raeburn Cl. KT1: Hamp W 4E 16
Raglan Cl. TW4: Houn 2E 8
Railshead Rd. TW1: Isle 1C 10
TW7: Isle 1C 10
Railway App. TW1: Twick 4B 10
Railway Arches W6 .....1F 7
Railway Cotts. SW19 .....1K 19
Railway Pas. TW11: Tedd 3B 16
Railway Rd. TW11: Tedd 1K 15
Railway Side SW13 .....7B 6
Railway Ter. TW13: Felt 5A 8
Railway Wharf KT1: King T 2B 36
Rainbow Ind. Est. SW20 .....6E 18
Rainbow Leisure Cen.
Epsom 1B 34
Rainsborough Ho. SW15 .....2H 13
(off Stamford Sq.)
Rainsborough Sq. SW6 .....3K 7
Rainville Rd. W6 .....3F 7

62 A-Z Kingston & Richmond

Raleigh Dr.—Roehampton

Raleigh Dr. KT5: Surb 5K 23
KT10: Clay 2J 27
Raleigh Rd. TW9: Rich 7G 5
Raleigh Way TW13: Hanw 2B 14
Ramillies Rd. W4 . . . . .1A 6
Ramornie Cl. KT12: Hers 1E 26
Ram Pas.
KT1: King T 4B 36 (6E 16)
Ram St. SW18 . . . . .2K 13
Ram Twr. SW18 . . . . .2K 13
Randle Rd. TW10: Ham 1D 16
Randolph Cl. KT2: King T 2K 17
Randolph Ho. *KT18: Eps 3K 33*
(off Dalmeny Way)
Randolph Rd. KT17: Eps 3C 34
Ranelagh Av. SW6 . . . . .7J 7
SW13 . . . . .6D 6
Ranelagh Dr. TW1: Twick 1C 10
Ranelagh Gdns. SW6 . . . . .7H 7
(not continuous)
W4 .4K 5
W6 .1C 6
Ranelagh Gdns. Mans. *SW6 . . . . .7H 7*
(off Ranelagh Gdns.)
Ranelagh Pl. KT3: N Mald 2B 24
Ranfurly Rd. SM1: Sutt 6K 25
Ranmore Ct. KT6: Surb 2E 22
Ranmore Rd. SM2: Cheam 5G 31
Rannoch Rd. W6 . . . . .3F 7
Ranyard Cl. KT9: Chess 7G 23
Raphael Cl.
KT1: King T 7B 36 (1E 22)
Raphael Dr. KT7: T Ditt 4A 22
Ravenna Rd. SW15 . . . . .2G 13
Raven's Ait 2E 22
Ravensbourne Rd. TW1: Twick . . .3D 10
Ravensbury Rd. SW18 . . . . .6K 13
Ravenscar Rd. KT6: Surb 6G 23
Ravens Cl. KT6: Surb 3E 22
Ravens Ct. *KT1: King T 2E 22*
(off Uxbridge Rd.)
Ravenscourt Av. W6 . . . . .1D 6
Ravenscourt Gdns. W6 . . . . .1D 6
Ravenscourt Pk. W6 . . . . .1D 6
Ravenscourt Pk. Mans. *W6 . . . . . .1E 6*
(off Paddenswick Rd.)
Ravenscourt Park Station
(Underground) 1E 6
Ravenscourt Pl. W6 . . . . .1E 6
Ravenscourt Rd. W6 . . . . .1E 6
Ravenscourt Sq. W6 . . . . .1D 6
Ravenscroft Rd. W4 . . . . .1K 5
Ravensfield Gdns. KT19: Ewe 2B 30
Ravenside *KT1: King T 2E 22*
(off Portsmouth Rd.)
Ravensmede Way W4 . . . . .1C 6
Ravenswood Av. KT6: Surb 6G 23
Ravenswood Ct. KT2: King T 3J 17
Ravensworth Ct. *SW6 . . . . .4K 7*
(off Fulham Rd.)
Rawchester Cl. SW18 . . . . .5J 13
Rawsthorne Ct. TW4: Houn 1E 8
Raybell Ct. TW7: Isle 6A 4
Ray Cl. KT9: Chess 3D 28
Rayleigh Av. TW11: Tedd 3K 15
Rayleigh Ct. KT1: King T 6H 17
Rayleigh Rd. SW19 . . . . .5J 19
Raymond Av. W13 . . . . .1B 4
Raymond Rd. SW19 . . . . .3H 19
Raymond Way KT10: Clay 3B 28
Rayners Rd. SW15 . . . . .2H 13
RAYNES PARK 1F 25
Raynes Pk. Bri. SW20 . . . . .6F 19
Raynes Pk. School Sports Cen.
. . . . .7E 18
Raynes Park Station (Rail) 6F 19
Raynham Rd. W6 . . . . .1E 6
Ray Rd. KT8: W Mole 2G 21
Read Cl. KT7: T Ditt 4B 22
Read Rd. KT21: Asht 6E 32
Reapers Way TW7: Isle 2J 9
Reckitt Rd. W4 . . . . .2B 6
Rectory Cl. KT6: Surb 5D 22
KT21: Asht 7G 33
SW20 . . . . .7F 19
Rectory Ct. TW13: Felt 1B 14
Rectory Gro. TW12: Hamp 1E 14
Rectory La. KT6: Surb 5C 22
KT21: Asht 7G 33
Rectory Orchard SW19 . . . . .1H 19
Rectory Rd. SM1: Sutt 7K 25
SW13 . . . . .6D 6
Redcliffe Cl. *SW5 . . . . .2K 7*
(off Old Brompton Rd.)
Redcliffe Gdns. W4 . . . . .4J 5
Redclose Av. SM4: Mord 2K 25
Redenham Ho. *SW15 . . . . .4D 12*
(off Ellisfield Dr.)
Redesdale Gdns. TW7: Isle 4B 4
Redfern Av. TW4: Houn 4F 9
Redfield La. SW5 . . . . .1K 7
Redfield M. SW5 . . . . .1K 7
Redgate Ter. SW15 . . . . .3G 13
Redgrave Rd. SW15 . . . . .7G 7
Red Ho. La. KT12: Walt T 6A 20
Redknap Ho. TW10: Ham 7D 10
Redland Gdns.
KT8: W Mole 1E 20
Redlands TW11: Tedd 3B 16
Red La. KT10: Clay 3B 28
Redlees Cl. TW7: Isle 1B 10
Red Lion Bus. Pk. KT6: Surb 7G 23
Red Lion Rd. KT6: Surb 6G 23
Red Lion Sq. SW18 . . . . .2K 13
Red Lion St. TW9: Rich 2E 10
Red Lion Wlk. *TW3: Houn 1G 9*
(off High St.)
Redmore Rd. W6 . . . . .1E 6
RED ROVER 1D 12
Redruth Gdns. KT10: Clay 4A 28
Redway Dr. TW2: Whitt 4H 9
Redwood Ct. KT6: Surb 4E 22
KT17: Ewe 7C 30
Redwood Dr. KT19: Eps 6K 29
Redwood Gro. W5 . . . . .1C 4
Redwoods SW15 . . . . .5D 12
Redwood Wlk. KT6: Surb 5E 22
Regal Ct. *SW6 . . . . .4K 7*
(off Dawes Rd.)
Regatta Ho. TW11: Tedd 1B 16
Regatta La. W6 . . . . .3F 7
Regatta Point TW8: Bford 3G 5
Regency Cl. TW12: Hamp 2E 14
Regency Ct. TW11: Tedd 3C 16
Regency Gdns. KT12: Walt T 5B 20
Regency M. TW7: Isle 2K 9
Regency Wlk. *TW10: Rich 2F 11*
(off The Vineyard)
Regent Ho. KT17: Eps 7B 30
W14 . . . . .1H 7
(off Windsor Way)
Regent Pk. KT22: Lea 7B 32
Regent Rd. KT5: Surb 2G 23
Regents Ct. KT2: King T 2C 36
Regents Pl. KT12: Walt T 7B 20
Regent St. W4 . . . . .2H 5
Reigate Av. SM1: Sutt 5K 25
Reigate Rd.
KT17: Eps, Ewe, Eps D 6C 30
KT18: Tatt C 6G 35
KT20: Tad 6G 35
Relko Ct. KT19: Eps 7A 30
Rembrandt Ct. KT19: Ewe 3C 30
Rembrandt Way KT12: Walt T 6A 20
Renaissance Ho. *KT17: Eps 2B 34*
(off Up. High St.)
Renfrew Rd. KT2: King T 4J 17
Renmans, The KT21: Asht 5G 33
Rennels Way TW7: Isle 6A 4
Replingham Rd. SW18 . . . . .5J 13
Reporton Rd. SW6 . . . . .4H 7
Restormel Cl. TW3: Houn 2F 9
Retreat, The KT4: Wor Pk 6E 24
KT5: Surb 3G 23
SW14 . . . . .7B 6
Retreat Rd. TW9: Rich 2E 10
Reubens Ct. *W4 . . . . .2J 5*
(off Chaseley Dr.)
Revell Rd. KT1: King T 6J 17
SM1: Sutt 3J 31
Revelstoke Rd. SW18 . . . . .6J 13
Revere Way KT19: Ewe 5B 30
Reydon Pl. KT12: Walt T 6A 20
Reynard Bus. Pk. TW8: Bford 2D 4
Reynolds Av. KT9: Chess 4F 29
Reynolds Pl. TW10: Rich 3G 11
Reynolds Rd. KT3: N Mald 4A 24
Rhodes Moorhouse Ct.
SM4: Mord 3K 25
Rhodrons Av. KT9: Chess 2F 29
Ricards Rd. SW19 . . . . .2J 19
Richard Burbidge Mans. *SW13 . . . .3F 7*
(off Brasenose Dr.)
Richard Challoner Sports Cen.
. . . . .4A 24
Richards Fld. KT19: Ewe 5A 30
Richbell Cl. KT21: Asht 7E 32
Richlands Av. KT17: Ewe 1D 30
RICHMOND 2E 10
Richmond, The American International
University in London
Richmond Hill Campus 4F 11
Richmond & London Scottish RUFC
. . . . .7E 4
Richmond Athletic Ground 7E 4
Richmond Av. SW20 . . . . .5H 19
Richmond Bri. TW1: Twick 3E 10
RICHMOND CIRCUS 1F 11
Richmond Cl. KT18: Eps 3B 34
Richmond Cotts. *W14 . . . . .1H 7*
(off Hammersmith Rd.)
Richmond Ct. *W14 . . . . .1H 7*
(off Hammersmith Rd.)
Richmond Cres. KT19: Eps 1F 33
Richmond Cricket Ground 7F 5
Richmond Golf Course 6F 11
Richmond Gro. KT5: Surb 3G 23
Richmond Hill TW10: Rich 3F 11
Richmond Hill Ct. TW10: Rich . . .3F 11
Richmond Mans. TW1: Twick 3E 10
Richmond M. TW11: Tedd 2A 16
Richmond Pde. *TW1: Twick 3D 10*
(off Richmond Rd.)
Richmond Pk. Golf Course 4B 12
Richmond Pk.
(National Nature Reserve)
. . . . .5H 11
Richmond Pk. Rd.
KT2: King T 1C 36 (5F 17)
SW14 . . . . .2K 11
Richmond Rd.
KT2: King T 1C 36 (2E 16)
SW20 . . . . .5E 18
TW1: Twick 4C 10
TW7: Isle 7B 4
RICHMOND ROYAL HOSPITAL 7F 5
Richmond Station
(Rail, Underground & Overground)
. . . . .1F 11
Richmond Theatre 1E 10
Rickards Cl. KT6: Surb 6F 23
Rickett St. SW6 . . . . .3K 7
Ride, The TW8: Bford 2C 4
Ridge, The KT5: Surb 2H 23
KT18: Eps 7K 33
TW2: Whitt 4J 9
Ridge Rd. SM3: Sutt 5H 25
(not continuous)
Ridge Way TW13: Hanw 7D 8
Ridgeway KT19: Eps 1K 33
Ridgeway Rd. TW7: Isle 5A 4
Ridgway SW19 . . . . .4F 19
TW10: Rich 3F 11
Ridgway Ct. SW19 . . . . .3G 19
Ridgway Gdns. SW19 . . . . .4G 19
Ridgway Pl. SW19 . . . . .3H 19
Ridings, The KT5: Surb 2H 23
KT11: Cobh 7F 27
KT17: Ewe 5C 30
KT18: Eps 4B 34
KT21: Asht 6E 32
Ridley Av. W13 . . . . .1C 4
Rifle Butts All. KT18: Eps 3C 34
Rigault Rd. SW6 . . . . .6H 7
Riley Cl. KT19: Eps 7J 29
Ringford Rd. SW18 . . . . .2J 13
Ringmer Av. SW6 . . . . .5H 7
Ringmore Rd. KT12: Walt T 7B 20
Ringwood Gdns. SW15 . . . . .5D 12
Ringwood Way TW12: Hamp H . . .1F 15
Ripley Gdns. SW14 . . . . .7A 6
Ripley Rd. TW12: Hamp 4F 15
Ripley Way KT19: Eps 7H 29
Ripon Gdns. KT9: Chess 2E 28
Risborough Dr. KT4: Wor Pk 4D 24
Rise, The KT17: Ewe 6C 30
River Av. KT7: T Ditt 4B 22
River Bank KT7: T Ditt 2A 22
KT8: E Mos 7K 15
TW12: Hamp 7F 15
Riverbank Way TW8: Bford 3D 4
River Brent Bus. Pk. W7 . . . . .1A 4
River Ct. *KT6: Surb 2E 22*
(off Portsmouth Rd.)
Rivercourt Rd. W6 . . . . .1E 6
River Crane Way *TW13: Hanw 6E 8*
(off Watermill Way)
Riverdale Dr. SW18 . . . . .5K 13
Riverdale Gdns. TW1: Twick 3D 10
Riverdale Rd. TW1: Twick 3D 10
TW13: Hanw 1D 14
Riverdene Ind. Est.
KT12: Hers 2C 26
River Gdns. TW14: Felt 2A 8
River Gdns. Bus. Cen.
TW14: Felt 2A 8
Riverhead Dr. SM2: Sutt 6K 31
Riverhill KT4: Wor Pk 6A 24
Riverhill M. KT4: Wor Pk 7A 24
Riverhill Mobile Home Pl.
KT4: Wor Pk 6A 24
Riverholme Dr. KT19: Ewe 5A 30
River La. TW10: Ham 4E 10
Rivermead KT1: King T 2E 22
KT8: E Mos 7H 15
Rivermead Cl. TW11: Tedd 2C 16
Rivermead Ct. SW6 . . . . .7J 7
Rivermead Ho. *TW16: Sun 7B 14*
(off Thames St.)
River Meads Av. TW2: Twick 7F 9
River Mole Bus. Pk.
KT10: Esh 6F 21
Rivernook Cl. KT12: Walt T 2B 20
River Reach TW11: Tedd 2D 16
Riversdale Rd. KT7: T Ditt 2B 22
Rivers Ho. *TW7: Isle 1C 10*
(off Richmond Rd.)
TW8: Bford 2H 5
(off Aitman Dr.)
Riverside TW1: Twick 5C 10
TW9: Rich 2E 10
TW10: Rich 2E 10
TW16: Sun 6C 14
W6 . . . . .3F 7
Riverside, The KT8: E Mos 7J 15
Riverside Arts Cen. 7B 14
Riverside Av. KT8: E Mos 2J 21
Riverside Bus. Cen. SW18 . . . . . .5K 13
Riverside Cl.
KT1: King T 7B 36 (1E 22)
Riverside Ct. *TW7: Isle 6A 4*
(off Woodlands Rd.)
Riverside Dr. KT10: Esh 1F 27
TW10: Ham 7C 10
W4 .4A 6
Riverside Gdns. W6 . . . . .2E 6
Riverside Rd. KT12: Hers 1C 26
Riverside Studios 2F 7
Riverside Vs. KT6: Surb 3D 22
Riverside Wlk.
KT1: King T 3A 36 (7E 16)
SW6 .7H 7
TW7: Isle 7A 4
W4 . . . . .3C 6
(off Chiswick Wharf)
Riverstone Ct.
KT2: King T 2E 36 (5G 17)
River Ter. W6 . . . . .2F 7
River Thames Vis. Cen. 3E 10
River Vw. Gdns. TW1: Twick 6A 10
Riverview Gdns. SW13 . . . . .3E 6
Riverview Gro. W4 . . . . .3J 5
Riverview Rd. KT19: Ewe 1K 29
W4 . . . . .4J 5
River Wlk. KT12: Walt T 3A 20
W6 . . . . .4F 7
River Way KT19: Ewe 2A 30
TW2: Twick 6G 9
Robert Cl. KT12: Hers 2A 26
Robert Gentry Ho. *W14 . . . . .2H 7*
(off Gledstanes Rd.)
Robert Owen Ho. SW6 . . . . .5G 7
Roberts Cl. SM3: Cheam 4G 31
Roberts Ct. KT9: Chess 2E 28
Robin Cl. TW12: Hamp 2D 14
Robin Gro. TW8: Bford 3D 4
ROBIN HOOD 7B 12
Robin Hood La. SM1: Sutt 2K 31
SW15 . . . . .7B 12
Robin Hood Rd. SW19 . . . . .2D 18
Robin Hood Way SW15 . . . . .7B 12
SW20 . . . . .1B 18
Robinson Ct. TW9: Rich 1G 11
Robinsway KT12: Hers 1B 26
Robinwood Pl. SW15 . . . . .1A 18
Rochester M. W5 . . . . .1D 4
Rock Av. SW14 . . . . .7A 6
Rockingham Cl. SW15 . . . . .1C 12
Rockland Rd. SW15 . . . . .1H 13
Rocks La. SW13 . . . . .5D 6
Rocque Ho. *SW6 . . . . .4J 7*
(off Estcourt Rd.)
Rodney Cl. KT3: N Mald 2B 24
KT12: Walt T 5B 20
Rodney Grn. KT12: Walt T 6B 20
Rodney Rd. KT3: N Mald 2B 24
KT12: Walt T 6B 20
TW2: Whitt 3F 9
Rodway Rd. SW15 . . . . .4D 12
Rodwell Ct. KT12: Walt T 7A 20
Roebuck Cl. TW13: Felt 1A 14
Roebuck Rd. KT9: Chess 2H 29
Roedean Cres. SW15 . . . . .3B 12
ROEHAMPTON 4D 12

A-Z Kingston & Richmond 63

Roehampton Cl. SW15 . . . . . .1D 12
Roehampton Ga. SW15 . . . . . .3B 12
Roehampton Golf Course 1C 12
Roehampton High St. SW15 . . .4D 12
ROEHAMPTON HUNTERCOMBE
HOSPITAL 4D 12
ROEHAMPTON LANE 5E 12
Roehampton La. SW15 . . . . . .1D 12
ROEHAMPTON PRIORY HOSPITAL
. . . . .1C 12
Roehampton Sport & Fitness Cen.
. . . . .4D 12
Roehampton University 3C 12
Roehampton Va. SW15 . . . . . .7C 12
Rokeby Pl. SW20 . . . . .4E 18
Rollesby Rd. KT9: Chess 3H 29
Rollit Cres. TW3: Houn 2F 9
Roman Cl. TW14: Felt 2B 8
Roman Rd. W4 . . . . .1B 6
Romany Gdns. SM3: Sutt 4K 25
Roma Read Cl. SW15 . . . . . . .4E 12
Romily Ct. SW6 . . . . .6J 7
Romney Cl. KT9: Chess 1F 29
Romney Rd. KT3: N Mald 3A 24
Romulus Ct. TW8: Bford 4E 4
Rona Maclean Cl.
KT19: Eps 1H 33
Ronelean Rd. KT6: Surb 6G 23
Rookeries Cl. TW13: Felt 7A 8
Rookery Hill KT21: Asht 7H 33
Rookwood Av. KT3: N Mald 1D 24
Rope Wlk. TW16: Sun 7B 14
Rosaline Rd. SW6 . . . . .4H 7
Rosaline Ter. SW6 . . . . .4H 7
(off Rosaline Rd.)
Rosaville Rd. SW6 . . . . .4J 7
Rose & Crown M. TW7: Isle 5B 4
Rosebank KT18: Eps 3K 33
SW6 . . . . .4F 7
Rosebank Cl. TW11: Tedd 3B 16
Rosebery Av. KT3: N Mald 6C 18
KT17: Eps 3B 34
Rosebery Cl. SM4: Mord 3G 25
Rosebery Rd. KT1: King T 6J 17
KT18: Eps D 7A 34
SM1: Sutt 3J 31
TW3: Houn 2H 9
Roseberys, The KT18: Eps 3B 34
Rosebery Sq. KT1: King T 6J 17
Rosebine Av. TW2: Twick 4J 9
Rosebriars KT10: Esh 2R 27
(not continuous)
Rose Bushes KT17: Eps D 5E 34
Rosecroft Gdns. TW2: Twick . . .5J 9
Rosedale KT21: Asht 7D 32
Rosedale Rd. KT17: Ewe 2D 30
TW9: Rich 7F 5
Rosedale Ter. W6 . . . . .1E 6
(off Dalling Rd.)
Rosedene Av. SM4: Mord 2K 25
Rosedew Rd. W6 . . . . .3G 7
Rose End KT4: Wor Pk 5G 25
Rose Gdns. W5 . . . . .1E 4
Roseheath Rd. TW4: Houn 2E 8
Rosehill KT10: Clay 3B 28
TW12: Hamp 5F 15
Roseleigh Cl. TW1: Twick 3E 10
Rosemary Av. KT8: W Mole 7F 15
Rosemary Gdns. KT9: Chess . . .1F 29
SW14 . . . . .7K 5
Rosemary Ga. KT10: Esh 2H 27
Rosemary La. SW14 . . . . .7K 5
Rosemead Cl. KT6: Surb 5H 23
Rosemont Rd. KT3: N Mald 7K 17
TW10: Rich 3F 11
Rose Theatre Kingston
. . . . .4B 36 (6E 16)
Rosetree Pl. TW12: Hamp 4F 15
Roseville Av. TW3: Houn 2F 9
Rosevine Rd. SW20 . . . . .5F 19
Rosewood KT7: T Ditt 6B 22
Rosewood Ct. KT2: King T 4H 17
Roskeen Ct. SW20 . . . . .4F 19
Roskell Rd. SW15 . . . . .7G 7
Ross Ct. SW15 . . . . .4G 13
Rossdale Rd. SW15 . . . . .1F 13
Rossindel Rd. TW3: Houn 2F 9
Rosslyn Av. SW13 . . . . .7B 6
TW14: Felt 3A 8
Rosslyn Rd. TW1: Twick 3D 10
Ross Rd. TW2: Whitt 5G 9
Rostrevor Mans. SW6 . . . . .5J 7
(off Rostrevor Rd.)
Rostrevor M. SW6 . . . . .5J 7

Rostrevor Rd. SW6 . . . . .5J 7
SW19 . . . . .2K 19
Rothbury Gdns. TW7: Isle 4B 4
Rotherwood Cl. SW20 . . . . . . .5H 19
Rotherwood Rd. SW15 . . . . . . .7G 7
Rothesay Av. SW20 . . . . .6H 19
TW10: Rich 1J 11
Rothschild Rd. W4 . . . . .1K 5
Rotunda Cen., The 3D 36 (6F 17)
Rougemont Av. SM4: Mord 3K 25
Roundacre SW19 . . . . .6G 13
Roundhill Way KT11: Cobh 7G 27
Roundway, The KT10: Clay 3A 28
Roundwood Vw. SM7: Bans 4G 35
Roundwood Way SM7: Bans 4G 35
Roupell Ho. KT2: King T 4G 17
(off Florence Rd.)
Rowallan Rd. SW6 . . . . .4H 7
Rowan Cl. KT3: N Mald 6B 18
SM7: Bans 4G 35
Rowan Rd. TW8: Bford 4C 4
W6 . . . . .1G 7
Rowan Ter. SW6 . . . . .4H 19
W6 . . . . .1G 7
Rowden Rd. KT19: Ewe 1J 29
Rowhurst Av. KT22: Lea 6A 32
Rowlls Rd. KT1: King T 7G 17
Rowntree Rd. TW2: Twick 5K 9
Roxborough Av. TW7: Isle 4A 4
Royal Av. KT4: Wor Pk 6B 24
Royal Botanic Gdns.
Kew 5F 5
Royal Cl. KT4: Wor Pk 6B 24
SW19 . . . . .7G 13
Royal Dr. KT18: Tatt C 7E 34
Royal Gdns. W7 . . . . .1K 5
ROYAL HOSPITAL FOR
NEURO-DISABILITY 3H 13
Royal M. KT8: E Mos 7K 15
Royal Mid-Surrey Golf Course . . .7E 4
Royal Oak M. TW11: Tedd 2B 16
Royal Orchard Cl. SW18 . . . . . .4H 13
Royal Pde. SW6 . . . . .4H 7
TW9: Kew 5F 5
(off Station App.)
Royal Quarter
KT2: King T 2B 36 (5F 17)
Royal Rd. TW11: Tedd 2J 15
Royal Wimbledon Golf Course
. . . . .2E 18
Roydon Ct. KT12: Hers 1A 26
Roy Gro. TW12: Hamp 3G 15
Roymount Ct. TW2: Twick 7K 9
Roy Richmond Way KT19: Eps . .6B 30
Royston Cl. KT12: Walt T 5A 20
Royston Ct. KT10: Hin W 6A 22
TW9: Kew 5G 5
Royston Rd. TW10: Rich 2F 11
Roystons, The KT5: Surb 2J 23
RO33 SW18 . . . . .1K 13
Ruden Way KT17: Eps D 5E 34
Ruffetts Way KT20: Tad 7H 35
Rugby La. SM2: Cheam 5G 31
Rugby Mans. W14 . . . . .1H 7
(off Bishop King's Rd.)
Rugby Rd. TW1: Twick 2K 9
Rumsey Cl. TW12: Hamp 3E 14
Running Horse Yd. TW8: Bford . . .3F 5
Runnymede Cl. TW2: Whitt 3G 9
Runnymede Ct. SW15 . . . . .5D 12
Runnymede Gdns. TW2: Whitt . . .3G 9
Runnymede Rd. TW2: Whitt 3G 9
Rupert Ct. KT8: W Mole 1F 21
(off St Peter's Rd.)
Rupert Ho. SW5 . . . . .1H 7
(off Nevern Sq.)
Rupert Rd. W4 . . . . .1B 6
Rush, The SW19 . . . . .5J 19
(off Watery La.)
Rushbury Ct. TW12: Hamp 5F 15
Rushett Cl. KT7: T Ditt 5C 22
Rushett La. KT9: Chess 7D 28
KT18: Eps 7D 28
Rushett Rd. KT7: T Ditt 4C 22
Rushey Cl. KT3: N Mald 1A 24
Rushlight M. KT9: Chess 1D 32
Rushmead TW10: Ham 7C 10
Rushmere Cl. KT4: Wor Pk 6D 24
Rushmere Pl. SW19 . . . . .2G 19
Rushmon Gdns. KT12: Walt T . . .7A 20
Rushmon Pl. SM3: Cheam 3H 31
Rushmon Vs. KT3: N Mald 1C 24
Rushmore Ho. SW15 . . . . .4D 12
W14 . . . . .1H 7
(off Russell Rd.)

Rusholme Rd. SW15 . . . . .3G 13
Ruskin Av. TW9: Kew 4H 5
Ruskin Dr. KT4: Wor Pk 6E 24
Ruskin Mans. W14 . . . . .3H 7
(off Queen's Club Gdns.)
Ruskin Rd. TW7: Isle 7A 4
Russell Cl. W4 . . . . .3C 6
Russell Gdns. TW10: Ham 6D 10
Russell Kerr Cl. W4 . . . . .4K 5
Russell Rd. KT12: Walt T 3A 20
SW19 . . . . .4K 19
TW2: Twick 3A 10
W14 . . . . .1H 7
Russell Wlk. TW10: Rich 3G 11
Russell Way SM1: Sutt 2K 31
Russell Yd. SW15 . . . . .1H 13
Russet Cl. KT12: Hers 7C 20
Rusthall Av. W4 . . . . .1A 6
Rustington Wlk. SM4: Mord 4J 25
Ruston Av. KT5: Surb 4J 23
Ruthen Cl. KT18: Eps 3J 33
Rutherwyke Cl. KT17: Ewe 3D 30
Rutland Cl. KT9: Chess 3G 29
KT19: Ewe 6A 30
KT21: Asht 6F 33
SW14 . . . . .7J 5
Rutland Ct. KT1: King T 1E 22
(off Palace Rd.)
Rutland Dr. SM4: Mord 3J 25
TW10: Ham 5E 10
Rutland Gro. W6 . . . . .2E 6
Rutland Rd. TW2: Twick 6J 9
Rutlish Rd. SW19 . . . . .5K 19
Ruvigny Gdns. SW15 . . . . .7G 7
Ruxley Cl. KT19: Ewe 2J 29
Ruxley Ct. KT19: Ewe 2K 29
Ruxley Cres. KT10: Clay 3C 28
Ruxley La. KT19: Ewe 3J 29
Ruxley M. KT19: Ewe 2J 29
Ruxley Ridge KT10: Clay 4B 28
Ruxley Towers KT10: Clay 4B 28
Ryan Dr. TW8: Bford 3B 4
Rybrook Dr. KT12: Walt T 6B 20
Rydal Gdns. SW15 . . . . .2B 18
TW3: Houn 3G 9
RYDENS 7B 20
Rydens Av. KT12: Walt T 6A 20
Rydens Cl. KT12: Walt T 6B 20
Rydens Gro. KT12: Hers 1C 26
Rydens Pk. KT12: Walt T 6C 20
Rydens Rd. KT12: Walt T 7A 20
Ryde Pl. TW1: Twick 3E 10
Rydon M. SW19 . . . . .4F 19
Ryebridge Cl. KT22: Lea 7B 32
Ryebrook Rd. KT22: Lea 7B 32
Ryecroft Av. TW2: Whitt 4G 9
Ryecroft St. SW6 . . . . .5K 7
Rye Fld. KT21: Asht 5E 32
Ryefield Path SW15 . . . . .5D 12
Ryelands Ct. KT22: Lea 7B 32
Rye Wlk. SW15 . . . . .2G 13
Ryfold Rd. SW19 . . . . .7K 13
Rylston Rd. SW6 . . . . .3J 7
Rythe, The KT10: Esh 6G 27
Rythe Bank Cl. KT7: T Ditt 4C 22
Rythe Cl. KT9: Chess 4D 28
KT10: Clay 2K 27
Rythe Ct. KT7: T Ditt 4B 22
Rythe Rd. KT10: Clay 2J 27

Sackville Rd. SM2: Sutt 4K 31
Saddlers Ct. KT18: Eps 2K 33
Saddlers M.
KT1: Hamp W 2A 36 (5D 16)
Sadlers Ga. M. SW15 . . . . .7F 7
Sadlers Ride KT8: W Mole 6H 15
Saffron Ho. SM2: Sutt 4K 31
TW9: Kew 5J 5
Saffron M. SW19 . . . . .4H 19
Saffron Way KT6: Surb 5E 22
Sage Yd. KT6: Surb 5G 23
St Agatha's Dr. KT2: King T 3G 17
St Alban's Av. W4 . . . . .1A 6
St Albans Av. TW13: Hanw 2C 14
St Albans Farm TW14: Houn 2B 8
St Alban's Gdns. TW11: Tedd . . .2B 16
St Alban's Rd. KT2: King T 3F 17
SM1: Sutt 1J 31
St Albans Ter. W6 . . . . .3H 7
St Andrews Cl. KT7: T Ditt 5C 22
St Andrews Ho. KT17: Eps 2A 34
(off High St.)

St Andrews Mans. W14 . . . . . . .3H 7
(off St Andrew's Rd.)
St Andrew's Rd. KT6: Surb 3E 22
W14 . . . . .3H 7
St Andrew's Sq. KT6: Surb 3E 22
St Annes M. SW20 . . . . .4G 19
St Ann's Pas. SW13 . . . . .7B 6
St Ann's Rd. SW13 . . . . .6C 6
ST ANTHONY'S HOSPITAL 5G 25
St Aubyn's Av. SW19 . . . . .2J 19
TW3: Houn 2F 9
St Barnabas Gdns.
KT8: W Mole 2F 21
St Catherine's Cl. SW20 . . . . . . .2F 25
St Catherines Cl. KT9: Chess . . .3E 28
St Catherine's Ct. W4 . . . . .1B 6
St Cecilia's Cl. SM3: Sutt 5H 25
St Chads Cl. KT6: Surb 4D 22
St Christophers Ct.
KT12: Walt T 6B 20
(off Rydens Av.)
St Clair Dr. KT4: Wor Pk 7E 24
St Clare Bus. Pk.
TW12: Hamp H 3H 15
St Clements Mans. SW6 . . . . . . .3G 7
(off Lillie Rd.)
St Dionis Rd. SW6 . . . . .6J 7
ST DUNSTAN'S 3J 31
St Dunstan's Hill
SM1: Sutt 2H 31
St Dunstan's Rd. W6 . . . . .2G 7
ST EBBA'S 5K 29
St Ebbas Way KT19: Eps 5K 29
St Edith Cl. KT18: Eps 3K 33
St Edmund's La. TW2: Whitt 4G 9
St Edmunds Sq. SW13 . . . . .3F 7
St Elizabeth Dr. KT18: Eps 3K 33
St George's Cl. SW15 . . . . .1J 13
St George's Gdns. KT6: Surb 6J 23
KT17: Eps 3C 34
St George's Ind. Est.
KT2: King T 2E 16
St George's Pl. TW1: Twick 5B 10
St Georges Pl. KT10: Esh 1H 27
St George's Rd. KT2: King T 4H 17
SW19 . . . . .4J 19
(not continuous)
TW1: Twick 2C 10
TW13: Hanw 1C 14
St Georges Rd. TW9: Rich 7G 5
St George's Sq. KT3: N Mald 7B 18
St Helena Ter. TW9: Rich 2E 10
St Helens KT7: T Ditt 4A 22
St Helen's Cl. KT4: Wor Pk 5D 24
St Helier's Av. TW3: Houn 2F 9
St Helier Station (Rail) 3K 25
St Hilda's Rd. SW13 . . . . .3E 6
St James Av. KT17: Ewe 7C 30
SM1: Sutt 2K 31
St James Cl. KT3: N Mald 2C 24
KT18: Eps 3K 33
St James Rd. KT21: Asht 6E 32
St James Rd. SM1: Sutt 2K 31
St James' Rd. KT6: Surb 3E 22
St James's Av. TW12: Hamp H . . .2H 15
St James's Cotts. TW9: Rich 2E 10
St James's Ct.
KT1: King T 6C 36 (7F 17)
St James's Rd.
KT1: King T 4B 36 (6E 16)
TW12: Hamp H 2G 15
St James St. W6 . . . . .2F 7
St John's Av. KT17: Eps 1D 34
SW15 . . . . .2G 13
St John's Cl. SW6 . . . . .4K 7
St John's Ct. KT1: King T 7D 36
TW7: Isle 6A 4
W6 . . . . .1E 6
(off Glenthorne Rd.)
St John's Dr. KT12: Walt T 5B 20
St John's Gro. SW13 . . . . .6C 6
TW9: Rich 1F 11
St John's M.
KT1: Hamp W 3A 36 (6D 16)
St John's Rd.
KT1: Hamp W 3A 36 (6D 16)
KT3: N Mald 7K 17
KT8: E Mos 1J 21
SM1: Sutt 6K 25
SW19 . . . . .4H 19
TW7: Isle 6A 4
TW9: Rich 1F 11
TW13: Hanw 1D 14
St John's Ter. SW15 . . . . .7B 12
(off Kingston Va.)

St Josephs Almshouses W6 .....1G 7
(off Brook Grn.)
St Joseph's Ho. W6 .....1G 7
(off Brook Grn.)
St Lawrence Bus. Cen.
  TW13: Felt 6A 8
St Leonards Ct. SW14 .....7K 5
St Leonard's Rd. KT6: Surb 2E 22
  KT7: T Ditt 3B 22
  KT10: Clay 3A 28
  KT18: Tatt C 7F 35
  SW14 .....7J 5
St Leonards Sq. KT6: Surb 2E 22
St Luke's Pas.
  KT2: King T 1E 36 (5G 17)
St Margaret Dr. KT18: Eps 3K 33
ST MARGARETS 3C 10
St Margaret's KT2: King T 2K 17
St Margaret's Av. SM3: Cheam 7H 25
St Margarets Bus. Cen.
  TW1: Twick 3C 10
St Margarets Ct. SW15 .....1E 12
St Margaret's Cres. 2E 12
St Margaret's Dr. TW1: Twick 2C 10
St Margaret's Gro. TW1: Twick 3B 10
St Margaret's La. W8 .....1K 7
St Margaret's M. KT2: King T 2K 17
St Margarets Rd. TW1: Twick 3C 10
  TW7: Isle, Twick 1C 10
ST MARGARETS RDBT. 3C 10
St Margarets Station
  (Rail) 3C 10
St Marks Cl. SW6 .....5K 7
St Mark's Hill KT6: Surb 3F 23
St Mark's Pl. SW19 .....3J 19
St Mark's Rd. KT18: Tatt C 7F 35
  TW11: Tedd 4C 16
St Martin's Av. KT18: Eps 3B 34
St Martins Ct. KT17: Eps 2C 34
St Martins Dr. KT12: Walt T 7B 20
St Mary Abbot's Ct. W14 .....1J 7
(off Warwick Gdns.)
St Mary Abbot's Pl. W8 .....1J 7
St Mary Abbot's Ter. W14 .....1J 7
St Mary's Av. TW11: Tedd 3A 16
St Mary's Cl. KT9: Chess 4G 29
  KT17: Ewe 4C 30
St Mary's Copse KT4: Wor Pk 6B 24
St Mary's Ct. KT3: N Mald 7B 18
St Mary's Gro. SW13 .....7E 6
  TW9: Rich 1G 11
  W4 .....3J 5
St Marys M. TW10: Ham 6D 10
St Mary's Rd. KT4: Wor Pk 6B 24
  KT6: Surb 4D 22
  (St Chads Cl.)
  KT6: Surb 3E 22
  (Victoria Rd.)
  KT8: E Mos 2J 21
  SW19 .....2H 19
St Mary's University College 7A 10
St Mary's University College
  Sports Cen. 1A 16
St Matthew's Av. KT6: Surb 5F 23
St Maur Rd. SW6 .....5J 7
St Michael's Cl. KT4: Wor Pk 6C 24
  KT12: Walt T 6B 20
St Nicholas Cl. KT1: King T 7C 36
St Nicholas M. KT7: T Ditt 3A 22
St Nicholas Rd. KT7: T Ditt 3A 22
St Normans Way KT17: Ewe 6D 30
St Olaf's Rd. SW6 .....4H 7
St Oswalds Studios SW6 .....3K 7
(off Sedlescombe Rd.)
St Paul's Cl. KT9: Chess 1E 28
St Paul's Rd. TW8: Bford 3E 4
  TW9: Rich 7G 5
St Paul's Studios W14 .....2D 6
(off Talgarth Rd.)
St Paul's Wlk. KT1: King T 4H 17
St Peters Ct. KT8: W Mole 1F 21
St Peter's Gro. W6 .....1D 6
St Peter's Rd. KT1: King T 6H 17
  KT8: W Mole 1F 21
  TW1: Twick 2C 10
  W6 .....2D 6
St Peter's Sq. W6 .....1C 6
St Peter's Ter. SW6 .....4J 7
St Peter's Vs. W6 .....1D 6
St Peter's Wharf W4 .....2D 6
St Philip's Av. KT4: Wor Pk 6E 24
St Philip's Ga. KT4: Wor Pk 6E 24
St Philips Rd. KT6: Surb 3E 22
ST RAPHAEL'S HOSPICE 6G 25
St Simon's Av. SW15 .....2F 13
St Stephen's Av. KT21: Asht 5F 33

St Stephen's Gdns. SW15 .....2J 13
  TW1: Twick 3D 10
St Stephen's Pas. TW1: Twick 3D 10
St Stephen's Rd. TW3: Houn 3F 9
St Theresa Cl. KT18: Eps 3K 33
St Thomas Cl. KT6: Surb 5G 23
St Thomas M. SW18 .....2K 13
St Thomas Rd. W4 .....3K 5
St Thomas's Way SW6 .....4J 7
St Vincent Rd. KT12: Walt T 7A 20
  TW2: Whitt 3H 9
St Winifred's Rd. 3C 16
Salamander Cl. KT2: King T 2D 16
Salamander Quay
  KT1: Hamp W 2A 36 (5E 16)
Salcombe Dr. SM4: Mord 5G 25
Salcombe Vs. TW10: Rich 2F 11
Salisbury Av. SM1: Sutt 3J 31
Salisbury Cl. KT4: Wor Pk 7C 24
Salisbury Gdns. SW19 .....4H 19
Salisbury M. SW6 .....4J 7
Salisbury Pas. SW6 .....4J 7
(off Dawes Rd.)
Salisbury Pavement SW6 .....4J 7
(off Dawes Rd.)
Salisbury Rd. KT3: N Mald 7A 18
  KT4: Wor Pk 1A 30
  SW19 .....4H 19
  TW4: Houn 1B 8
  TW9: Rich 1F 11
  TW13: Felt 5B 8
Salix Cl. TW16: Sun 4A 14
Salliesfield TW2: Whitt 3J 9
Salmons Rd. KT9: Chess 3F 29
Saltash Cl. SM1: Sutt 1J 31
Salvin Rd. SW15 .....7G 7
Samels Ct. W6 .....2D 6
Samuel Gray Gdns.
  KT2: King T 1B 36 (5E 16)
Samuel Lewis Trust Dwellings
  SW6 .....4K 7
  (off Vanston Pl.)
  W14 .....1J 7
  (off Lisgar Ter.)
Samuel Richardson Ho. W14 .....1J 7
(off Nth. End Cres.)
Samuel's Cl. W6 .....1F 7
Sanctuary, The SM4: Mord 3K 25
Sandal Rd. KT3: N Mald 2A 24
Sandalwood Mans. W8 .....1K 7
(off Stone Hall Gdns.)
Sandalwood Rd. TW13: Felt 7A 8
Sanders Cl. TW12: Hamp H 2H 15
Sandersfield Gdns. SM7: Bans 4K 35
Sandersfield Rd. SM7: Bans 4K 35
Sanders La. TW4: Houn 2E 8
Sandersons La. W4 .....2A 6
(off Chiswick High Rd.)
Sandes Pl. KT22: Lea 7B 32
Sandhurst Av. KT5: Surb 4J 23
Sandiford Rd. SM3: Sutt 6J 25
Sandon Cl. KT10: Esh 4J 21
Sandown Av. KT10: Esh 2H 27
Sandown Cl. SM2: Sutt 4K 31
Sandown Ind. Pk. KT10: Esh 6F 21
Sandown Lodge KT18: Eps 3A 34
Sandown Pk. Golf Course 7G 21
Sandown Pk. Racecourse 6H 21
Sandown Rd. KT10: Esh 1H 27
Sandown Sports Club 7G 21
Sandpiper Rd. SM1: Sutt 2J 31
Sandpits Rd. TW10: Ham 6E 10
Sandra Cl. TW3: Houn 2G 9
Sandringham Av. SW20 .....5H 19
Sandringham Cl. SW19 .....5G 13
  SM2: Sutt 5K 31
Sandringham Ct. KT2: King T 1B 36
  KT8: W Mole 1F 21
Sandringham Ho. W14 .....1H 7
(off Windsor Way)
Sandringham M. TW12: Hamp 5E 14
Sandringham Rd. KT11: Cobh 7F 27
  KT4: Wor Pk 7D 24
Sandycombe Rd.
  TW9: Kew, Rich 7G 5
  TW14: Felt 5A 8
Sandycoombe Rd.
  TW1: Twick 3D 10
Sandy Cft. KT17: Ewe 6F 31
Sandy Dr. KT11: Cobh 7F 27

Sandy La. KT1: Hamp W 4B 16
  KT11: Cobh 7E 26
  KT12: Walt T 3A 20
  KT22: Oxs 7E 26
  SM2: Cheam 4H 31
  TW10: Ham 6D 10
  TW11: Hamp W, Tedd 4B 16
Sandy Mead KT19: Eps 6H 29
Sandy Way KT11: Cobh 7F 27
Sanger Av. KT9: Chess 2F 29
Santos Rd. SW18 .....2K 13
Sarjant Path SW19 .....6G 13
(off Blincoe Cl.)
Satis Ct. KT17: Ewe 7C 30
Savery Dr. KT6: Surb 4C 22
Savile Cl. KT3: N Mald 2B 24
  KT7: T Ditt 5A 22
Saville Cl. KT19: Eps 7J 29
Saville Rd. TW1: Twick 5A 10
Savill Gdns. SW20 .....7D 18
Savona Cl. SW19 .....4G 19
Savoy Ct. SW5 .....1K 7
(off Cromwell Rd.)
Sawkins Cl. SW19 .....6H 13
Sawyer's Hill TW10: Rich 4G 11
Saxon Av. TW13: Hanw 6D 8
Saxonbury Av. TW16: Sun 7A 14
Saxonbury Gdns. KT6: Surb 5D 22
Saxon Cl. KT6: Surb 3E 22
Saxon Ho. KT1: King T 1G 23
  TW13: Hanw 6E 8
Saxon Rd.
  KT2: King T 1C 36 (5F 17)
  KT12: Walt T 7C 20
Saxton Pl. KT8: W Mole 1E 20
Sayer's Wlk. TW10: Rich 4G 11
Scarborough Cl. SM2: Cheam 7J 31
Scarsdale Studios W8 .....1K 7
(off Stratford Rd.)
Scarsdale Vs. W8 .....1K 7
Scarth Rd. SW13 .....7C 6
SCC Smallholdings Rd.
  KT17: Eps 3F 35
  (not continuous)
Scholars Rd. KT12: Walt T 5B 20
School All. TW1: Twick 5B 10
School Ho. La. TW11: Tedd 4C 16
School La.
  KT1: Hamp W 2A 36 (5D 16)
  KT6: Surb 5G 23
School Pas. KT1: King T 6G 17
School Rd. KT1: Hamp W 5D 16
  KT8: E Mos 1J 21
  TW12: Hamp H 3H 15
School Rd. Av.
  TW12: Hamp H 3H 15
Schubert Rd. SW15 .....2J 13
Schurlock Pl. TW2: Twick 6K 9
SCILLY ISLES 6K 21
Scope Way
  KT1: King T 7D 36 (1F 23)
Scotsdale Cl. SM3: Cheam 4H 31
Scott Av. SW15 .....3H 13
Scott Cl. KT19: Ewe 2K 29
Scott Farm Cl. KT7: T Ditt 5C 22
Scott Ho. KT17: Eps 1B 34
(off Winter Cl.)
Scotts Dr. TW12: Hamp 4G 15
Scotts Farm Rd. KT19: Ewe 3K 29
Scotts La. KT12: Hers 1C 26
Seaforth Av. KT3: N Mald 2E 24
Seaforth Gdns. KT19: Ewe 1C 30
Seagrave Lodge SW6 .....3K 7
(off Seagrave Rd.)
Seagrave Rd. SW6 .....3K 7
Seaton Cl. SW15 .....5E 12
  TW2: Whitt 3J 9
Seaton Rd. TW2: Whitt 3H 9
Secombe Theatre
  Sutton 2K 31
Second Av. KT12: Walt T 3A 20
  SW14 .....7B 6
Second Cl. KT8: W Mole 1H 21
Second Cross Rd. TW2: Twick 6K 9
Sedleigh Rd. SW18 .....3J 13
Sedlescombe Rd. SW6 .....3K 7
SEETHING WELLS 3D 22
Seething Wells La. KT6: Surb 3D 22
Sefton Rd. KT19: Ewe 6A 30
Sefton St. SW15 .....7F 7
Sekhon Ter. TW13: Hanw 7F 9
Selborne Rd. KT3: N Mald 6B 18
Selbourne Av. KT6: Surb 6G 23
Selby Cl. KT9: Chess 4F 29
Selhurst Cl. SW19 .....5G 13
Selkirk Rd. TW2: Twick 6H 9

Selsdon Cl. KT6: Surb 2F 23
Selwin Ct. KT12: Walt T 5B 20
Selwood Rd. KT9: Chess 1E 28
  SM3: Sutt 5J 25
Selwyn Av. TW9: Rich 7F 5
Selwyn Cl. TW4: Houn 1D 8
Selwyn Ct. TW10: Rich 2G 11
(off Church Rd.)
Selwyn Rd. KT3: N Mald 2A 24
Senhouse Rd. SM3: Cheam 7G 25
Sergeant Ind. Est. SW18 .....3K 13
Servite Ho. KT4: Wor Pk 6C 24
(off The Avenue)
Servius Ct. TW8: Bford 4E 4
Settrington Rd. SW6 .....6K 7
Seven Kings Way
  KT2: King T 1C 36 (5F 17)
Sevenoaks Cl. SM2: Sutt 6K 31
Severn Cl. KT2: King T 1B 36
Severn Dr. KT10: Hin W 6B 22
  KT12: Walt T 6C 20
Severn Ho. SW18 .....1K 13
(off Enterprise Way)
Seymour Av. KT17: Ewe 5E 30
  SM4: Mord 4G 25
Seymour Cl. KT8: E Mos 2H 21
Seymour Ct.
  KT1: Hamp W 1A 36 (5E 16)
  KT19: Ewe 5B 30
Seymour Gdns. KT5: Surb 2G 23
  TW1: Twick 4C 10
  TW13: Hanw 1B 14
Seymour M. KT17: Ewe 6D 30
Seymour Rd.
  KT1: Hamp W 2A 36 (5E 16)
  KT8: W Mole, E Mos 2H 21
  SW18 .....4J 13
  SW19 .....7G 13
  TW12: Hamp H 2H 15
  W4 .....1K 5
Shacklegate La. TW11: Tedd 1K 15
Shadbolt Cl. KT4: Wor Pk 6C 24
Shael Way TW11: Tedd 4B 16
Shaftesbury Av. TW14: Felt 3A 8
Shaftesbury Pl. W14 .....1J 7
(off Warwick Rd.)
Shaftesbury Rd. TW9: Rich 7F 5
Shaftesbury Way KT2: Twick 7J 9
Shakespeare Way
  TW13: Hanw 1B 14
Shalden Ho. SW15 .....3C 12
Shaldon Dr. SM4: Mord 2H 25
Shaldon Way KT12: Walt T 7B 20
Shalstone Rd. SW14 .....7J 5
Shalston Vs. KT6: Surb 3G 23
Shannon Commercial Cen.
  KT3: N Mald 1D 24
SHANNON CORNER 1D 24
Shannon Cnr. Retail Pk.
  KT3: N Mald 1D 24
Shanti Cl. SW18 .....5K 13
Sharnbrook Ho. W14 .....3K 7
Sharon Cl. KT6: Surb 5D 22
  KT19: Eps 2K 33
Sharon Rd. W4 .....2A 6
Sharp Ho. TW1: Twick 3E 10
Shaw Cl. KT17: Ewe 7C 30
Shaw Dr. KT12: Walt T 4B 20
Shawford Cl. SW15 .....4D 12
Shawford Rd. KT19: Ewe 3A 30
Shawley Cres. KT18: Tatt C 7F 35
Shawley Way KT18: Tatt C 7E 34
Shaws Path KT1: Hamp W 5D 16
(off Bennett Cl.)
Sheaf Cotts. KT7: T Ditt 5K 21
(off Weston Grn.)
Shearwater Rd. SM1: Sutt 2J 31
Sheath Cotts. KT7: T Ditt 3C 22
(off Ferry Rd.)
Sheen Comn. Dr.
  TW10: Rich 1H 11
Sheen Ct. TW10: Rich 1H 11
Sheen Ct. Rd. TW10: Rich 1H 11
Sheendale Rd. TW9: Rich 1G 11
Sheen Ga. Gdns. SW14 .....1K 11
Sheengate Mans. SW14 .....1A 12
Sheen La. SW14 .....2K 11
Sheen Pk. TW9: Rich 1G 11
Sheen Rd. TW9: Rich 2F 11
  TW10: Rich 2F 11
Sheen Wood SW14 .....2K 11
Sheephouse Way
  KT3: N Mald 5A 24
Sheep Wlk. M. SW19 .....3G 19
Shelburne Dr. TW4: Houn 3F 9

Shelley Cl. SM7: Bans 4G 35
Shelton Rd. SW19 . . . . .5K 19
Shene Sports & Fitness Cen.
. . . . .1B 12
Shepherd Cl. TW13: Hanw . . .1D 14
Shepherd's Bush Rd. W6 . . . . . .1F 7
Sheppard Cl.
KT1: King T 7D 36 (1F 23)
Sheraton Dr. KT19: Eps 2K 33
Sherborne Cl. KT18: Tatt C 6F 35
Sherborne Rd. KT9: Chess 2F 29
SM3: Sutt 6K 25
Sherbourne Ct. SW5 . . . . .1K 7
(off Cromwell Rd.)
Sherbrooke Rd. SW6 . . . . .4H 7
Sherbrooke Ter. SW6 . . . . .4H 7
(off Sherbrooke Rd.)
Sherbrooke Way KT4: Wor Pk . .4E 24
Shere Av. SM2: Cheam 6F 31
Shere Cl. KT9: Chess 2E 28
Sherfield Cl. KT3: N Mald 1J 23
Sherfield Gdns. SW15 . . . . .3C 12
Sheridan Ct. TW4: Houn 2D 8
Sheridan Pl. SW13 . . . . .7C 6
TW12: Hamp 5G 15
Sheridan Rd. SW19 . . . . .5J 19
TW10: Ham 7D 10
Sheringham Av. TW2: Whitt 5E 8
Sherland Rd. TW1: Twick 5A 10
Sherriff Cl. KT10: Esh 6G 21
Sherwood KT6: Surb 6E 22
Sherwood Cl. SW13 . . . . .7E 6
Sherwood Pk. Rd. SM1: Sutt . . .2K 31
Sherwood Rd. SW19 . . . . .4J 19
TW12: Hamp H 2H 15
Sherwood Way KT19: Eps 1G 33
Shield Dr. TW8: Bford 3B 4
Shillingstone Ho. W14 . . . . .1H 7
(off Russell Rd.)
Ship All. W4 . . . . .3H 5
Ship La. SW14 . . . . .7K 5
Shire Ct. KT17: Ewe 4C 30
Shire Horse Way TW7: Isle 7A 4
Shire M. TW2: Whitt 3H 9
Shire Pl. TW8: Bford 4E 4
Shires, The TW10: Ham 1F 17
Shires Cl. KT21: Asht 7E 32
Shirley Av. SM2: Cheam 5J 31
Shirley Cl. TW3: Houn 2H 9
Shirley Dr. TW3: Houn 2H 9
SHOOTING STAR HOUSE,
CHILDREN'S HOSPICE . . .3E 14
Shore Cl. TW12: Hamp 3D 14
Shore Gro. TW13: Hanw 6F 9
Shorrold's Rd. SW6 . . . . .4J 7
Shortcroft Rd. KT17: Ewe 4C 30
Shortlands W6 . . . . .1G 7
Shortlands Rd. KT2: King T 4G 17
Short Rd. W4 . . . . .3B 6
Short Way TW2: Whitt 4H 9
Shottendane Rd. SW6 . . . . .5K 7
Shottfield Av. SW14 . . . . .1B 12
Shrewsbury Av. SW14 . . . . .1K 11
Shrewsbury Cl. KT6: Surb 6F 23
Shrewsbury Wlk. TW7: Isle 7B 4
(off Magdala Rd.)
Shrubbery, The KT6: Surb 5F 23
Shrubland Ct. SM7: Bans 5J 35
(off Garratts La.)
Shrubland Gro. KT4: Wor Pk . . .7F 25
Shrubland Rd. SM7: Bans 5J 35
Shuters Sq. W14 . . . . .2J 7
Sidbury St. SW6 . . . . .5H 7
Sidney Gdns. TW8: Bford 3E 4
Sidney Rd. KT12: Walt T 4A 20
TW1: Twick 3B 10
Sienna Cl. KT9: Chess 3E 28
Sigrist Sq. KT2: King T . . .2D 36 (5F 17)
Silver Cres. W4 . . . . .1J 5
Silverdale Cl. SM1: Sutt 1J 31
Silverdale Dr. TW16: Sun 6A 14
Silvergate KT19: Ewe 2K 29
Silverglade Bus. Pk.
KT9: Chess 1D 32
Silverhall St. TW7: Isle 7B 4
Silverton Rd. W6 . . . . .3G 7
Simmil Rd. KT10: Clay 2K 27
Simmonds Ct. SW5 . . . . .1K 7
(off Earl's Ct. Gdns.)
Simmonds Ho. TW8: Bford 2F 5
(off Clayponds La.)
Simmons Cl. KT9: Chess 3D 28
Simmons Ga. KT10: Esh 2H 27
Simpson Rd. TW4: Houn 3E 8
TW10: Ham 1D 16
Simpson Way KT6: Surb 3D 22

Simrose Ct. SW18 . . . . .2K 13
Sinclair Dr. SM2: Sutt 5K 31
Sinclair Rd. W14 . . . . .1H 7
Sion Ct. TW1: Twick 5C 10
Sion Rd. TW1: Twick 5C 10
Sir Abraham Dawes Cotts.
SW15 . . . . .1H 13
Sir Cyril Black Way SW19 . . . .4K 19
Sir Oswald Stoll Foundation, The
SW6 .4K 7
(off Fulham Rd.)
Sir Oswald Stoll Mans. SW6 . . .4K 7
(off Fulham Rd.)
Sir William Atkins Ho.
KT18: Eps 2A 34
Sir William Powell's Almshouses
SW6 .6H 7
Sispara Gdns. SW18 . . . . .3J 13
Sixth Cross Rd. TW2: Twick 7H 9
Skeena Hill SW18 . . . . .4H 13
Skelgill Rd. SW15 . . . . .1H 13
Skelwith Rd. W6 . . . . .3F 7
Skerne Rd.
KT2: King T 2B 36 (5E 16)
Skerne Wlk.
KT2: King T 1B 36 (5E 16)
Skinners La. KT21: Asht 7E 32
Skylark Ct. SW15 . . . . .3F 13
Slade Ho. TW4: Houn 3E 8
Slattery Rd. TW13: Felt 5C 8
Smallberry Av. TW7: Isle 6A 4
Smeaton Cl. KT9: Chess 3E 28
Smeaton Rd. SW18 . . . . .4K 13
Smith Hill TW8: Bford 3F 5
Smith St. KT5: Surb 3G 23
Smithwood Cl. SW19 . . . . .5H 13
Smoothfield Ct. TW3: Houn 1F 9
Snakey La. TW13: Felt 1A 14
Snellings Rd. KT12: Hers 2B 26
Snowdrop Cl. TW12: Hamp 3F 15
Snowy Fielder Waye TW7: Isle . .6C 4
Soames Wlk. KT3: N Mald 5B 18
Soap Ho. La. TW8: Bford 4F 5
Sobraon Ho. KT2: King T 1E 36
Solna Av. SW15 . . . . .2F 13
Sombourne Ho. SW15 . . . . .4D 12
(off Fontley Way)
Somer Ct. SW6 . . . . .3K 7
(off Anselm Rd.)
Somerfield Cl. KT20: Tad 7H 35
Somerset Av. KT9: Chess 1E 28
SW20 . . . . .6E 18
Somerset Cl. KT3: N Mald 3B 24
KT12: Hers 2A 26
KT19: Ewe 5A 30
SM3: Wor Pk 1F 31
Somerset Ct. TW11: Tedd 2K 15
Somerset Gdns. TW11: Tedd . . .2K 15
Somerset Ho. SW19 . . . . .7G 13
Somerset Lodge TW8: Bford 3E 4
Somerset Rd. KT1: King T 6G 17
SW19 . . . . .7G 13
TW8: Bford 3D 4
TW11: Tedd 2K 15
Somerton Av. TW9: Rich 7J 5
Somerville Av. SW14 . . . . .3E 6
Sonning Gdns. TW12: Hamp . . .3D 14
Sontan Ct. TW2: Twick 5J 9
Sophia Ho. W6 . . . . .2F 7
(off Queen Caroline St.)
Soprano Way KT10: Surb 7C 22
Sopwith Av. KT9: Chess 2F 29
Sopwith Cl. KT2: King T 2G 17
Sopwith Way
KT2: King T 2C 36 (5F 17)
Sorrento Rd. SM1: Sutt 7K 25
Souldern Rd. W14 . . . . .1G 7
South Av. TW9: Kew 6H 5
South Bank KT6: Surb 5F 23
Sth. Bank Ter. KT6: Surb 5F 23
Sth. Black Lion La. W6 . . . . .2D 6
SOUTHBOROUGH 5F 23
Southborough Cl. KT6: Surb 5E 22
Southborough Rd. KT6: Surb . . .5E 22
South Cl. SM4: Mord 3K 25
TW2: Twick 7F 9
Southcombe St. W14 . . . . .1H 7
Southcote Av. KT5: Surb 4J 23
Southcott Rd.
TW11: Hamp W 5D 16
Southdean Gdns. SW19 . . . . . . .6J 13
Southdown Av. W7 . . . . .1B 4
Southdown Dr. SW20 . . . . .4G 19
Southdown Rd. KT12: Hers 1D 26
SW20 . . . . .5G 19

South Dr. SM2: Cheam 6H 31
Sth. Ealing Rd. W5 . . . . .1E 4
Sth. Edwardes Sq. W8 . . . . .1J 7
Southerton Rd. W6 . . . . .1F 7
Southey Rd. SW19 . . . . .4K 19
Southfield Gdns.
TW1: Twick 1A 16
SOUTHFIELDS 5J 13
Southfields KT8: E Mos 3K 21
Southfields Ct. SM1: Sutt 6K 25
Southfields M. SW18 . . . . .3K 13
Southfields Pas. SW18 . . . . .3K 13
Southfields Rd. SW18 . . . . .3K 13
Southfields Station
(Underground) 5J 13
Southlands Dr. SW19 . . . . .6G 13
Southland Way TW3: Houn 2J 9
South La.
KT1: King T 6B 36 (7E 16)
KT3: N Mald 1A 24
South La. W. KT3: N Mald 1A 24
South Lodge TW2: Whitt 3H 9
Sth. Lodge Rd. KT12: Hers 5A 26
South Mall SW18 . . . . .3K 13
South Mead KT19: Ewe 4C 30
Southmead Gdns. TW11: Tedd . .3B 16
Southmead Rd. SW19 . . . . .5H 13
South Merton Station (Rail) 7J 19
Southmont Rd. KT10: Hin W 6K 21
South Pde. W4 . . . . .1A 6
South Pk. Gro. KT3: N Mald 1K 23
South Pk. M. SW6 . . . . .7K 7
South Pk. Rd. SW19 . . . . .3K 19
Sth. Pk. Ter. KT6: Surb 4G 23
Southridge Pl. SW20 . . . . .4G 19
South Rd. TW2: Twick 7J 9
TW12: Hamp 3D 14
TW13: Hanw 2C 14
W5 . . . . .1E 4
Southsea Rd.
KT1: King T 7C 36 (1F 23)
South Side W6 . . . . .1C 6
Southside Comn. SW19 . . . . . . .3F 19
Southside House 3F 19
Southside Shop. Cen. SW18 . . . .3K 13
South St. KT18: Eps 2A 34
TW7: Isle 7B 4
Sth. Ter. KT6: Surb 3F 23
South Vw. KT19: Eps 6H 29
SW19 . . . . .3G 19
South Vw. Rd. KT21: Asht 7E 32
Southville Cl. KT19: Ewe 5A 30
Southville Rd. KT7: T Ditt 4B 22
Southway SW20 . . . . .2F 25
Sth. Western Rd. TW1: Twick . . .3B 10
SOUTH WEST LONDON ELECTIVE
ORTHOPAEDIC CENTRE 4K 33
(within Epsom General Hospital)
Sth. W. Middlesex Crematorium
TW13: Felt 5D 8
SOUTH WIMBLEDON 3K 19
Southwood Av. KT2: King T 5K 17
Southwood Cl. KT4: Wor Pk 5G 25
Southwood Dr. KT5: Surb 4K 23
Southwood Gdns. KT10: Hin W . .7B 22
Sth. Worple Av. SW14 . . . . .7B 6
Sth. Worple Way SW14 . . . . .7A 6
Sovereign Ct. KT8: W Mole 1E 20
TW3: Houn 1F 9
Space Waye TW14: Felt 2A 8
Spa Dr. KT18: Eps 3H 33
Sparks Cl. TW12: Hamp 3D 14
Sparrow Cl. TW12: Hamp 3D 14
Sparrow Farm Dr. TW14: Felt . . .4B 8
Sparrow Farm Rd.
KT17: Ewe 1D 30
Spear M. SW5 . . . . .1K 7
Spectrum Way SW18 . . . . .2K 13
Speer Rd. KT7: T Ditt 3A 22
Speirs Cl. KT3: N Mald 3C 24
Spencer Cl. SW20 . . . . .5E 18
Spencer Gdns. SW14 . . . . .2K 11
Spencer Hill SW19 . . . . .3H 19
Spencer Hill Rd. SW19 . . . . .4H 19
Spencer Mans. W14 . . . . .3H 7
(off Queen's Club Gdns.)
Spencer M. W6 . . . . .3H 7
Spencer Pk. KT8: E Mos 2H 21
Spencer Rd. KT8: E Mos 1H 21
SW20 . . . . .5E 18
TW2: Twick 7K 9
W4 . . . . .4K 5
Spencer Wlk. SW15 . . . . .1G 13
Spicer Cl. KT12: Walt T 3B 20
Spindle Cl. KT19: Eps 5A 30
Spinnaker Ct. KT1: Hamp W 2A 36

Spinney, The KT18: Tatt C 7E 34
KT22: Oxs 7H 27
SM3: Cheam 1F 31
SW13 . . . . .4E 6
TW16: Sun 5A 14
Spinney Cl. KT3: N Mald 2B 24
KT4: Wor Pk 6C 24
KT11: Cobh 7F 27
Spinney Gdns. KT10: Esh 7F 21
Sports Village, The 5K 25
Spray La. TW2: Whitt 3K 9
Spread Eagle Wlk. KT19: Eps . . .2A 34
Spreighton Rd. KT8: W Mole 1G 21
Springclose La. SM3: Cheam . . .3H 31
Spring Cotts. KT6: Surb 2E 22
Spring Ct. KT17: Ewe 5C 30
Springfield Av. SW20 . . . . .7J 19
TW12: Hamp 3G 15
Springfield Cl. KT1: King T 6C 36
Springfield Pl. KT3: N Mald 1K 23
Springfield Rd.
KT1: King T 6D 36 (7F 17)
KT17: Ewe 6F 31
KT22: Lea 7A 32
SW19 . . . . .2J 19
TW2: Whitt 5F 9
TW11: Tedd 2B 16
Spring Gdns. KT8: W Mole 2G 21
SPRING GROVE 5A 4
Spring Gro. TW12: Hamp 5G 15
W4 . . . . .2H 5
Spring Gro. Rd. TW10: Rich 2G 11
SpringHealth Leisure Club
Richmond 1E 10
(within Pools on the Park)
Spring M. KT17: Ewe 5C 30
TW9: Rich 1F 11
(off Rosedale Rd.)
Spring Pas. SW15 . . . . .7G 7
Spring St. KT17: Ewe 5C 30
Spring Ter. TW9: Rich 2F 11
Springvale Av. TW8: Bford 2E 4
Spur, The KT12: Walt T 6B 20
Spurfield KT8: W Mole 7G 15
Spur Rd. TW7: Isle 4C 4
TW14: Felt 1A 8
Square, The TW9: Rich 2E 10
W6 . . . . .2F 7
Squires Ct. SW19 . . . . .1J 19
Squirrels Ct. KT4: Wor Pk 6C 24
(off The Avenue)
Squirrels Grn. KT4: Wor Pk 6C 24
Squirrels Way KT18: Eps 3A 34
Stable Cl. KT2: King T 3G 17
Stable M. TW1: Twick 5A 10
Stable Yd. SW18 . . . . .3K 13
Stable Yd. SW15 . . . . .7F 7
Stableyard M. TW11: Tedd 3A 16
Stafford Cl. SM3: Cheam 3H 31
Stafford Cripps Ho. SW6 . . . . . . .3J 7
(off Clem Attlee Ct.)
Stafford Mans. W14 . . . . .1G 7
(off Haarlem Rd.)
Stafford Pl. TW10: Rich 4G 11
Stafford Rd. KT3: N Mald 7K 17
(off Coombe Rd.)
Stag Ct. KT2: King T 5H 17
(off Coombe Rd.)
STAG LANE 6C 12
Stag La. SW15 . . . . .7C 12
Stags Way TW7: Isle 3A 4
Staines Av. SM3: Cheam 6G 25
Staines Rd. TW2: Twick 7F 9
TW3: Houn 3A 8
TW4: Houn 3A 8
TW14: Felt 3A 8
Staines Rd. E. TW16: Sun 4A 14
Stamford Bridge 4K 7
Stamford Brook Arches W6 . . . .1D 6
Stamford Brook Av. W6 . . . . .1C 6
Stamford Brook Gdns. W6 . . . . .1C 6
Stamford Brook Mans. W6 . . . . .1C 6
(off Goldhawk Rd.)
Stamford Brook Rd. W6 . . . . . . .1C 6
Stamford Brook Station
(Underground) 1C 6
Stamford Ct. W6 . . . . .1D 6
STAMFORD GREEN 2J 33
Stamford Grn. Rd. KT18: Eps . . .2J 33
Stamford Rd. KT12: Walt T 7C 20
Stamford Sq. SW15 . . . . .2H 13
Stanborough Cl. TW12: Hamp . . .3E 14
Stanbridge Pl. SW15 . . . . .7F 7
Standard Rd. TW4: Houn 1C 8
Standen Rd. SW18 . . . . .4J 13
Standish Ho. W6 . . . . .1D 6
(off St Peter's Gro.)

Standish Rd. W6 . . . . .1D 6
Stane Way KT17: Ewe 6D 30
Stanford Cl. TW12: Hamp 3E 14
Stanfords, The KT12: Eps 1C 34
(off East St.)
Stanhope Ter. TW2: Twick 4A 10
Stanier Cl. W14 . . . . .2J 7
Stanley Av. KT3: N Mald 2D 24
Stanley Cl. SM2: Sutt 4K 31
Stanley Gdns. KT12: Hers 3B 26
Stanley Gdns. Rd.
TW11: Tedd 2K 15
Stanley Picker Gallery 6D 36
(off Springfield Rd.)
Stanley Rd. SM2: Sutt 3K 31
SM4: Mord 1K 25
SW14 . . . . .1J 11
SW19 . . . . .3K 19
TW2: Twick 7J 9
TW3: Houn 1H 9
TW11: Tedd 1K 15
Stanmore Gdns. TW9: Rich 7G 5
Stanmore Rd. TW9: Rich 7G 5
Stanstead Mnr. SM1: Sutt 3K 31
Stanton Av. TW11: Tedd 3K 15
Stanton Cl. KT4: Wor Pk 5G 25
KT19: Ewe 2J 29
Stanton Rd. SW13 . . . . .6C 6
SW20 . . . . .5G 19
Stanwick Rd. W14 . . . . .1J 7
Stapleford Cl. KT1: King T 6H 17
SW19 . . . . .1H 19
Star & Garter Hill TW10: Rich . . .5F 11
Star Apartments KT12: Hers . . .3B 26
Starling Wlk. TW12: Hamp 2D 14
Star Rd. W14 . . . . .3J 7
Staten Gdns. TW1: Twick 5A 10
Station App. KT1: King T 5H 17
KT4: Wor Pk 5D 24
KT10: Hin W 7A 22
KT17: Ewe 5C 30
(Fennells Mead)
KT17: Ewe 5C 30
(Nonsuch Ct. Av.)
KT19: Eps 2A 34
KT19: Ewe 2D 30
SM2: Cheam 4H 31
SM2: Sutt 6K 31
SW6 . . . . .7H 7
SW14 . . . . .7K 5
SW20 . . . . .6E 18
TW8: Bford 3D 4
(off Sidney Gdns.)
TW9: Kew 5H 5
TW12: Hamp 5F 15
Station App. Rd. W4 . . . . .4K 5
Station Av. KT3: N Mald 7B 18
KT12: Walt T 7A 20
KT19: Ewe 5B 30
TW9: Kew 5H 5
Station Bldgs. KT1: King T 3C 36
Station Cl. TW12: Hamp 5G 15
Station Est. Rd. TW14: Felt 5A 8
Station Gdns. W4 . . . . .4K 5
Station Pde. TW9: Kew 5H 5
TW14: Felt 5A 8
W4 . . . . .4K 5
Station Path SW6 . . . . .7J 7
Station Rd.
KT1: Hamp W 1A 36 (5D 16)
KT2: King T 5H 17
KT3: N Mald 2E 24
KT7: T Ditt 4A 22
KT9: Chess 2F 29
KT10: Clay 3K 27
KT10: Esh 6J 21
SM2: Sutt 6K 31
SW13 . . . . .6C 6
TW1: Twick 5A 10
TW3: Houn 1G 9
TW11: Tedd 3B 16
TW12: Hamp 5F 15
Station Way KT10: Clay 3K 27
KT19: Eps 2A 34
SM3: Cheam 3H 31
Station Yd. TW1: Twick 4B 10
Staunton Rd. KT2: King T 3F 17
Staveley Gdns. W4 . . . . .5A 6
Staveley Rd. W4 . . . . .3K 5
Stayton Rd. SM1: Sutt 7K 25
Steadfast Rd.
KT1: King T 2B 36 (5E 16)
Steele Cl. TW11: Tedd 4D 16
Steele Rd. TW7: Isle 1B 10
Steeple Cl. SW6 . . . . .6H 7
SW19 . . . . .2H 19

Stephen Fox Ho. W4 . . . . .2B 6
(off Chiswick La.)
Stephenson Ct. SM2: Cheam . . .4H 31
(off Station App.)
Stephenson Rd. TW2: Whitt 4F 9
Sterling Pl. W5 . . . . .1F 5
Sterndale Rd. W14 . . . . .1G 7
Sterry Dr. KT7: T Ditt 3K 21
KT19: Ewe 1B 30
Steve Biko Way TW3: Houn 1F 9
Stevenage Rd. SW6 . . . . .4G 7
Stevens Cl. KT17: Eps 1B 34
TW12: Hamp 3E 14
Stevens La. KT10: Clay 4B 28
Stewart Cl. TW12: Hamp 3D 14
Stewart Ho.
KT1: King T 6E 36 (7G 17)
Steyning Way TW4: Houn 1B 8
Stile Hall Gdns. W4 . . . . .2H 5
Stile Hall Mans. W4 . . . . .2H 5
(off Wellesley Rd.)
Stile Hall Pde. W4 . . . . .2H 5
Stile Path TW16: Sun 7A 14
Stillingfleet Rd. SW13 . . . . .3D 6
Stirling Cl. SM7: Bans 6J 35
Stirling Rd. TW2: Whitt 4F 9
W3 .1J 5
Stirling Wlk. KT5: Surb 3J 23
Stockfield Rd. KT10: Clay 2K 27
Stockhurst Cl. SW15 . . . . .6F 7
Stockenchurch St. SW6 . . . . . . .5K 7
Stoford Cl. SW19 . . . . .4H 13
Stoke Rd. KT2: King T 4K 17
KT12: Walt T 7B 20
Stokesby Rd. KT9: Chess 3G 29
Stokes Field (Local Nature Reserve)
. . . . .6C 22
Stokesheath Rd.
KT22: Oxs 7H 27
Stokes M. TW11: Tedd 2B 16
Stonecrat M. SW15 . . . . .1D 12
Stonecot Cl. SM3: Sutt 5H 25
Stonecot Hill SM3: Sutt 5H 25
Stone Hall Gdns. W8 . . . . .1K 7
Stonehill Cl. SW14 . . . . .2A 12
Stonehill Rd. SW14 . . . . .2K 11
W4 .2H 5
STONELEIGH 2D 30
Stoneleigh Av. KT4: Wor Pk 1D 30
KT19: Ewe 2D 30
Stoneleigh B'way. KT17: Ewe . . .2D 30
Stoneleigh Cres. KT19: Ewe 2C 30
Stoneleigh Pk. Rd.
KT4: Wor Pk 3C 30
KT19: Ewe 3C 30
Stoneleigh Station (Rail) 2D 30
Stone Pl. KT4: Wor Pk 6D 24
Stone's Rd. KT17: Eps 1B 34
Stoneydeep TW11: Tedd 1B 16
Stonny Cft. KT21: Asht 6G 33
Stonor Rd. W14 . . . . .1J 7
Stony Hill KT10: Esh 4E 26
Stormont Way KT9: Chess 2D 28
Stoughton Av. SM3: Cheam 2G 31
Stoughton Cl. SW15 . . . . .5D 12
Stourhead Cl. SW19 . . . . .4G 13
Stourhead Gdns. SW20 . . . . . . .7D 18
Stourton Av. TW13: Hanw 1E 14
Strachan Pl. SW19 . . . . .3F 19
Strafford Rd. TW1: Twick 4B 10
TW3: Houn 1E 8
Straight Mile PL. KT18: Tatt C . . .7F 35
Strand Dr. TW9: Kew 4J 5
STRAND ON THE GREEN 3H 5
Strand on the Grn. W4 . . . . .3H 5
Strand School App. W4 . . . . .3H 5
Stratford Cl. KT3: N Mald 1A 24
Stratford Gro. SW15 . . . . .1G 13
Stratford Rd. W8 . . . . .1K 7
Stratford Studios W8 . . . . .1K 7
Strathan Cl. SW18 . . . . .3H 13
Strathearn Av. TW2: Whitt 5G 9
Strathearn Rd. SM1: Sutt 2K 31
SW19 . . . . .2K 19
Strathmore Rd. SW19 . . . . .7K 13
TW11: Tedd 1K 15
Strathville Rd. SW18 . . . . .6K 13
(not continuous)
Stratton Cl. KT12: Walt T 5B 20
SW19 . . . . .6K 19
Stratton Rd. SW19 . . . . .6K 19
STRAWBERRY HILL 7A 10
Strawberry Hill 7A 10
Strawberry Hill KT9: Chess 3E 28
TW1: Twick 7A 10
Strawberry Hill Cl. TW1: Twick . . .7A 10
Strawberry Hill Golf Course 7K 9

Strawberry Hill Rd.
TW1: Twick 7A 10
Strawberry Hill Station (Rail) . . .7A 10
Strawberry Va. TW1: Twick 7B 10
(not continuous)
Street, The KT21: Asht 7F 33
Stretton Rd. TW10: Ham 6D 10
Strode Rd. SW6 . . . . .4H 7
Stroud Cres. SW15 . . . . .7D 12
Stroudes Cl. KT4: Wor Pk 4B 24
Stroud Rd. SW19 . . . . .7K 13
Stuart Av. KT12: Walt T 5A 20
Stuart Gro. TW11: Tedd 2K 15
Stuart Ho. W14 . . . . .1H 7
(off Windsor Way)
Stuart Lodge KT18: Eps 2A 34
(off Ashley Rd.)
Stuart Rd. SW19 . . . . .7K 13
TW10: Ham 6C 10
Stubbs Ct. W4 . . . . .2J 5
(off Chaseley Dr.)
Studdridge St. SW6 . . . . .6K 7
Studland Rd. KT2: King T 3F 17
Studland St. W6 . . . . .1E 6
Sudbrook Gdns. TW10: Ham 7E 10
Sudbrook La. TW10: Ham 5F 11
Sudbury Ho. SW18 . . . . .2K 13
Sudlow Rd. SW18 . . . . .3K 13
Suffolk Rd. KT4: Wor Pk 6C 24
SW13 . . . . .4C 6
Sugden Rd. KT7: T Ditt 5C 22
Sulivan Cl. SW6 . . . . .6K 7
Sulivan Ent. Cen. SW6 . . . . .7K 7
Sulivan Rd. SW6 . . . . .7K 7
Sullivan Cl. KT8: W Mole 7G 15
Sullivan Ct. SW5 . . . . .1K 7
(off Earls Ct. Rd.)
Summer Av. KT8: E Mos 2K 21
Summer Crossing KT7: T Ditt . . .2K 21
Summerfield KT21: Asht 7E 32
Summerfield La. KT6: Surb 6E 22
Summer Gdns. KT8: E Mos 2K 21
Summer Rd. KT7: T Ditt 2K 21
KT8: E Mos 2J 21
(not continuous)
Summers Cl. SM2: Sutt 4K 31
Summer Trees TW16: Sun 5A 14
Summerville Gdns. SM1: Sutt . . .3J 31
Summerwood Rd. TW7: Isle 2K 9
Summit Bus. Pk. TW16: Sun 4A 14
Sun All. TW9: Rich 1F 11
SUNBURY 7B 14
Sunbury Av. SW14 . . . . .1A 12
Sunbury Av. Pas. SW14 . . . . . . .1B 12
Sunbury Cl. KT12: Walt T 3A 20
Sunbury Ct. Island TW16: Sun . . .7C 14
Sunbury Ct. M. TW16: Sun 6C 14
Sunbury Ct. Rd. TW16: Sun 6B 14
Sunbury Embroidery Gallery, The
. . . . .7A 14
Sunbury La. KT12: Walt T 3A 20
Sunburylock Ait KT12: Walt T . . .1A 20
Sunbury Pk. Walled Garden 7A 14
Sunbury Way TW13: Hanw 2B 14
Sun Ga. Ho. KT3: N Mald 1C 24
Sun Life Trad. Est. TW14: Felt . . .1A 8
Sunna Gdns. TW16: Sun 6A 14
Sunningdale Av. TW13: Hanw . . .6D 8
Sunningdale Cl. KT6: Surb 6F 23
Sunningdale Ct. TW7: Isle 3J 9
(off Whitton Dene)
Sunningdale Gdns. W8 . . . . .1K 7
(off Stratford Rd.)
Sunningdale Rd. SM1: Sutt 1J 31
KT6: Surb 5K 33
Sunnybank W5 . . . . .5K 33
Sunnyhurst Cl. SM1: Sutt 7K 25
Sunnymead Rd. SW15 . . . . .2E 12
Sunnymede Av. KT19: Ewe 5B 30
Sunnyside KT12: Walt T 2B 20
SW19 . . . . .3H 19
Sunnyside Pas. SW19 . . . . .3H 19
Sunnyside Pl. SW19 . . . . .3H 19
Sunnyside Rd. TW11: Tedd 1J 15
Sunray Av. KT5: Surb 6J 23
Sunrise Cl. TW13: Hanw 7E 8
Sunset Rd. SW19 . . . . .2E 18
SURBITON 3E 22
Surbiton Ct. KT6: Surb 3D 22
Surbiton Cres.
KT1: King T 7C 36 (1F 23)
Surbiton Golf Course 1C 28
Surbiton Hall Cl. KT1: King T 1F 23
Surbiton Hill Pk. KT5: Surb 2G 23
Surbiton Hill Rd. KT6: Surb 1F 23

Surbiton Pde. KT6: Surb 3F 23
Surbiton Plaza KT6: Surb 3E 22
(off St Mary's Rd.)
Surbiton Raceway 7A 24
Surbiton Rd.
KT1: King T 7B 36 (1E 22)
Surbiton Station (Rail) 3F 23
Surrey Cres. W4 . . . . .2H 5
Surrey Lodge KT12: Hers 2A 26
(off Queens Rd.)
Sury Basin KT2: King T . . .1B 36 (5F 17)
Sussex Av. TW7: Isle 1K 9
Sussex Cl. KT3: N Mald 1B 24
TW1: Twick 3C 10
Sussex Ct. KT18: Eps 3B 34
(off Downside)
Sussex Gdns. KT9: Chess 3E 28
Sussex Pl. KT3: N Mald 1B 24
W6 .2F 7
Sussex Rd. KT3: N Mald 1B 24
Sutherland Gdns.
KT4: Wor Pk 5E 24
SW14 . . . . .7B 6
Sutherland Gro. SW18 . . . . .3H 13
TW11: Tedd 2K 15
Sutherland Rd. W4 . . . . .3B 6
SUTTON 2K 31
Sutton Cl. W4 . . . . .3K 5
(off Sutton La. Sth.)
Sutton Comn. Rd. SM1: Sutt 4J 25
SM3: Sutt 4J 25
Sutton Common Station
(Rail) 6K 25
Sutton Ct. KT8: W Mole 2E 20
W4 .3K 5
Sutton Ct. Rd. W4 . . . . .4K 5
SM1: Sutt 3K 31
Sutton La. Nth. W4 . . . . .2K 5
Sutton La. Sth. W4 . . . . .3K 5
Sutton Tennis Academy 6K 25
Sutton United FC 1K 31
Swail Ho. KT18: Eps 2A 34
Swallow Pk. KT6: Surb 7G 23
Swallow Pk. Cl.
KT6: Surb 7G 23
Swallows Cl. SM1: Sutt 7K 25
Swan Cl. TW13: Hanw 1D 14
Swan Ct. SW6 . . . . .4K 7
(off Fulham Rd.)
TW7: Isle 7C 4
(off Swan St.)
Swan Island TW1: Twick 7B 10
Swan M. SW6 . . . . .5J 7
Swann Ct. TW7: Isle 7B 4
(off South St.)
Swan Path
KT1: King T 6D 36 (7G 17)
Swan Pl. SW13 . . . . .6C 6
Swan Rd. TW13: Hanw 2D 14
Swanscombe Rd. W4 . . . . .2B 6
Swansmere Cl. KT12: Walt T 5B 20
Swan St. TW7: Isle 7C 4
Swanton Gdns. SW19 . . . . .5G 13
Swanwick Cl. SW15 . . . . .4C 12
Swathling Ho. SW15 . . . . .3C 12
(off Tunworth Cres.)
Sweet Briar La. KT18: Eps 3A 34
Swift Rd. TW13: Hanw 7D 8
Swift St. SW6 . . . . .5J 7
Swinburne Rd. SW15 . . . . .1D 12
Swinfield Cl. TW13: Hanw 7D 8
Swyncombe Av. W5 . . . . .1C 4
Sybil Thorndike Casson Ho.
SW5 . . . . .2K 7
(off Kramer M.)
Sycamore Cl. KT19: Ewe 2J 29
TW13: Felt 7A 8
Sycamore Ct. KT3: N Mald 7B 18
TW4: Houn 1D 8
Sycamore Gro.
KT3: N Mald 7A 18
Sycamore Ri. SM7: Bans 3G 35
Sycamore Rd. SW19 . . . . .3F 19
Sycamore Way TW11: Tedd 3D 16
Sydney Rd. SM1: Sutt 1K 31
SW20 . . . . .6G 19
TW9: Rich 1F 11
TW11: Tedd 2A 16
Sydney Simmons
KT21: Asht 7G 33
Sydney Ter. KT10: Clay 3A 28
(off The Green)
Sylvan Gdns. KT6: Surb 4E 22
Sylvestrus Cl. KT1: King T 5H 17
Syon Ga. Way TW8: Bford 4B 4
Syon House 5D 4
Syon La. TW7: Isle 3A 4

Syon Lane Station (Rail)—Tudor Cl.

Syon Lane Station (Rail) 4B 4
Syon Pk. 5C 4
Syon Pk. Gdns. TW7: Isle 4A 4

T

Tabard Theatre 1B 6
Tabarin Way KT17: Eps D 5F 35
Tabor Ct. SM3: Cheam 3H 31
Tabor Gdns. SM3: Cheam 3J 31
Tabor Gro. SW19 . . . . .4J 19
Tabor Rd. W6 . . . . .1E 6
Tadlow *KT1: King T* *7H 17*
(off Washington Rd.)
Tadworth Av. KT3: N Mald 1C 24
Taff Ho. *KT2: King T* *1B 36*
(off Henry Macaulay Av.)
Taggs Ho. KT1: King T 4B 36
Taggs Island TW12: Hamp 6J 15
Talbot Lodge KT10: Esh 2F 27
Talbot Rd. TW2: Twick 5K 9
TW7: Isle 1B 10
Talgarth Mans. *W14* *2H 7*
(off Talgarth Rd.)
Talgarth Rd. W6 . . . . .2G 7
W14 . . . . .2G 7
Talisman Way KT17: Eps D 5F 35
Tallow Rd. TW8: Bford 3D 4
Tall Pines KT17: Eps 7C 30
Talma Gdns. TW2: Twick 3K 9
Tamarind Ct. *W8* *1K 7*
(off Stone Hall Gdns.)
Tamesis Gdns. KT4: Wor Pk 6B 24
Tamian Ind. Est. TW4: Houn 1B 8
Tamian Way TW4: Houn 1B 8
Tamworth St. SW6 . . . . .3K 7
Tangier Rd. TW10: Rich 1H 11
Tangier Way KT20: Tad 6H 35
Tangier Wood KT20: Tad 7H 35
Tanglewood Way TW13: Felt 7A 8
Tangley Gro. SW15 . . . . .3C 12
Tangley Pk. Rd. TW12: Hamp 3E 14
Tangmere Gro. KT2: King T 2E 16
Tankerton Rd. KT6: Surb 6G 23
Tanners Cl. KT12: Walt T 3A 20
Tanyard Ho. *TW8: Bford* *4D 4*
(off High St.)
Tapping Cl. KT2: King T 4H 17
Tasso Rd. W6 . . . . .3H 7
Tasso Yd. *W6* *3H 7*
(off Tasso Rd.)
Tatchbury Ho. *SW15* *3C 12*
(off Tunworth Cres.)
Tate Rd. SM1: Sutt 2K 31
TATTENHAM CORNER 7E 34
Tattenham Cnr. Rd.
KT18: Eps D, Tatt C 6C 34
Tattenham Corner Station (Rail) 7E 34
Tattenham Cres. KT18: Tatt C 7D 34
Tattenham Gro. KT18: Tatt C 7E 34
Tattenham Way KT20: Tad 7G 35
Taunton Av. SW20 . . . . .6E 18
Taunton Cl. SM3: Sutt 5K 25
Tawny Cl. TW13: Felt 7A 8
Tayben Av. TW2: Twick 3K 9
Tayles Hill Dr. KT17: Ewe 6C 30
Taylor Av. TW9: Kew 6J 5
Taylor Cl. KT19: Eps 7H 29
TW12: Hamp H 2H 15
Taylor Rd. KT21: Asht 6E 32
Tealing Dr. KT19: Ewe 1A 30
Teal Pl. SM1: Sutt 2J 31
Teazlewood Pk. KT22: Lea 6B 32
Teck Cl. TW7: Isle 6B 4
Tedder Cl. KT9: Chess 2D 28
TEDDINGTON 2B 16
Teddington Bus. Pk.
TW11: Tedd *3A 16*
(off Station Rd.)
Teddington Cl. KT19: Eps 6A 30
Teddington Lock 1C 16
TEDDINGTON MEMORIAL HOSPITAL .3K 15
Teddington Pk. TW11: Tedd 2A 16
Teddington Pk. Rd.
TW11: Tedd 1A 16
Teddington Pool & Fitness Cen. 2B 16
Teddington Sports Cen. 3E 16
Teddington Station (Rail) 3B 16
Teesdale Av. TW7: Isle 5B 4
Teesdale Gdns. TW7: Isle 5B 4
Tegan Cl. SM2: Sutt 4K 31
Telegraph La. KT10: Clay 1A 28
Telegraph Rd. SW15 . . . . .4E 12
Telephone Pl. SW6 . . . . .3J 7
Telford Dr. KT12: Walt T 4B 20
Telford Rd. TW2: Whitt 4F 9
Tellisford KT10: Esh 1G 27
Temeraire Pl. TW8: Bford 2G 5
Templar Pl. TW12: Hamp 4F 15
Temple Cl. KT19: Eps 1A 34
Templecombe Way
SM4: Mord 2H 25
Temple Ct. KT19: Eps 1A 34
Temple Rd. KT19: Eps 1A 34
TW3: Houn 1G 9
TW9: Rich 6G 5
W4 . . . . .1K 5
W5 . . . . .1E 4
Temple Sheen SW14 . . . . .1K 11
Temple Sheen Rd. SW14 . . . . . . .1J 11
Templeton Pl. SW5 . . . . .1K 7
Tennis Ct. La. KT8: E Mos 7A 16
Tennyson Av. KT3: N Mald 2E 24
TW1: Twick 5A 10
Tennyson Mans. *W14* *3J 7*
(off Queen's Club Gdns.)
Tenpin
Feltham 6A 8
Kingston upon Thames *3D 36*
(within The Rotunda Cen.)
Terrace, The SW13 . . . . .6B 6
Terrace Gdns. SW13 . . . . .6C 6
Terrace La. TW10: Rich 3F 11
Terrace Rd. KT12: Walt T 4A 20
Terrano Ho. TW9: Kew 4J 5
Tersha St. TW9: Rich 1G 11
Thackeray Cl. SW19 . . . . .4G 19
TW7: Isle 6B 4
Thackeray Ct. *W14* *1H 7*
(off Blythe Rd.)
Thames Av. KT4: Wor Pk 5F 25
Thames Bank SW14 . . . . .6K 5
Thames Cl. TW12: Hamp 6G 15
Thames Cotts. KT7: T Ditt 3C 22
Thames Ct. KT8: W Mole 6G 15
Thames Cres. W4 . . . . .4B 6
THAMES DITTON 3B 22
Thames Ditton & Esher Golf Course 6J 21
Thames Ditton Station (Rail) . . .4A 22
Thames Eyot TW1: Twick 5B 10
Thamesgate Cl. TW10: Ham 1C 16
Thames Haven KT6: Surb 2E 22
Thames Ho. KT1: King T 7B 36
Thameside KT8: W Mole 7G 15
TW11: Tedd 4E 16
Thameside Cen. TW8: Bford 3G 5
Thameside Pl.
KT1: Hamp W 1A 36 (5E 16)
Thames Lock KT12: Walt T 7B 14
Thamesmead KT12: Walt T 4A 20
Thames Mdw. KT8: W Mole 6F 15
Thames Pl. SW15 . . . . .7G 7
Thamespoint TW11: Tedd 4E 16
Thames Reach KT1: Hamp W 5E 16
W6 . . . .*3F 7*
(off Rainville Rd.)
Thames Rd. W4 . . . . .3H 5
Thames Side
KT1: King T 2B 36 (5E 16)
KT7: T Ditt 3C 22
Thames St.
KT1: King T 3B 36 (6E 16)
TW12: Hamp 5G 15
TW16: Sun 1A 20
Thames Village W4 . . . . .5K 5
Thames Wharf Studios *W6* *3F 7*
(off Rainville Rd.)
Thatchers Way TW7: Isle 2J 9
Thaxted Pl. SW20 . . . . .4G 19
Thaxton Rd. W14 . . . . .3J 7
The . . . .
Names prefixed with 'The' for example 'The Alders' are indexed under the main name such as 'Alders, The'
Theatre Ct. KT18: Eps 2A 34
Thelma Gro. TW11: Tedd 3B 16
Theresa Rd. W6 . . . . .1D 6
Thetford Rd. KT3: N Mald 3A 24
Thetis Ter. TW9: Kew 3H 5
Third Cl. KT8: W Mole 1H 21
Third Cross Rd. TW2: Twick 6J 9
Thirlmere Ho. TW7: Isle 2A 10
Thistlecroft Rd. KT12: Hers 1B 26
Thistledene KT7: T Ditt 3K 21
Thistleworth Marina *TW7: Isle* . . .*1C 10*
(off Railshead Rd.)
Thomas More Gdns. KT10: Esh . . .7F 21
Thomas Wall Cl. SM1: Sutt 2K 31
Thompson Av. TW9: Rich 7H 5
Thompson Cl. SM3: Sutt 5K 25
Thompson Rd. TW3: Houn 1G 9
Thorkhill Gdns. KT7: T Ditt 5B 22
Thorkhill Rd. KT7: T Ditt 5B 22
Thorncroft Rd. SM1: Sutt 2K 31
Thorndon Gdns. KT19: Ewe 2B 30
Thorne Cl. KT10: Clay 4B 28
Thorne Pas. SW13 . . . . .6B 6
Thorne St. SW13 . . . . .7B 6
Thorneycroft Cl. KT12: Walt T 3B 20
Thorney Hedge Rd. W4 . . . . .1J 5
Thornfield Rd. SM7: Bans 6K 35
Thornhill Av. KT6: Surb 6F 23
Thornhill Ho. *W4* *2B 6*
(off Wood St.)
Thornhill M. SW15 . . . . .1J 13
Thornhill Rd. KT6: Surb 6F 23
Thornton Av. W4 . . . . .1B 6
Thornton Hill SW19 . . . . .4H 19
Thornton Rd. SW14 . . . . .1A 12
SW19 . . . . .3G 19
Thornton Rd. E. SW19 . . . . .3G 19
Thornycroft Ho. *W4* *2B 6*
(off Fraser St.)
Thorpe Rd. KT2: King T 4F 17
Three Bridges Path
KT1: King T *6D 36*
(off Bellvue Rd.)
Thrigby Rd. KT9: Chess 3G 29
Thrupp's Av. KT12: Hers 2C 26
Thrupp's La. KT12: Hers 2C 26
Thurleston Av. SM4: Mord 2H 25
Thurnby Ct. TW2: Twick 7K 9
Thursley Gdns. SW19 . . . . .6G 13
Thurstan Rd. SW20 . . . . .4E 18
Tibbet's Cl. SW19 . . . . .5G 13
TIBBET'S CORNER 4G 13
Tibbet's Ride SW15 . . . . .4G 13
Tichmarsh KT19: Eps 6K 29
Tideswell Rd. SW15 . . . . .1F 13
Tideway Cl. TW10: Ham 1C 16
Tiffany Hgts. SW18 . . . . .4K 13
Tiffin Girls Community Sports Cen. 3F 17
Tiffin Sports Cen. 6G 17
Tildesley Rd. SW15 . . . . .3F 13
Tilehurst Rd. SM3: Cheam 2H 31
Tilford Gdns. SW19 . . . . .5G 13
Tilia Cl. SM1: Sutt 2J 31
Tilley Rd. TW13: Felt 5A 8
Tilton St. SW6 . . . . .3H 7
Timbercroft KT19: Ewe 1B 30
Timberhill KT21: Asht 7F 33
Timbers, The SM3: Cheam 3H 31
Timothy Pl. KT8: W Mole 2E 20
Timperley Ct. SW19 . . . . .5H 13
Timsbury Wlk. SW15 . . . . .5D 12
Tinderbox All. SW14 . . . . .7A 6
Tinefields KT20: Tad 7H 35
Tintagel Cl. KT17: Eps 3C 34
Tintern Cl. SW15 . . . . .2H 13
Titan Ct. TW8: Bford 2G 5
Tithe Barn Cl.
KT2: King T 2E 36 (5G 17)
Tithe Cl. KT12: Walt T 3A 20
Tiverton Way KT9: Chess 2E 28
Tivoli Rd. TW4: Houn 1D 8
Toad La. TW4: Houn 1E 8
Tobin Cl. KT19: Eps 7J 29
Toby Way KT5: Surb 6J 23
Token Yd. SW15 . . . . .1H 13
Toland Sq. SW15 . . . . .2D 12
Tollard Ho. *W14* *1J 7*
(off Kensington High St.)
Tolson Rd. TW7: Isle 7B 4
Tolverne Rd. SW20 . . . . .5F 19
TOLWORTH 6J 23
Tolworth B'way. KT6: Surb 5J 23
Tolworth Cl. KT6: Surb 5J 23
TOLWORTH HOSPITAL 6H 23
TOLWORTH JUNC. (TOBY JUG) 6J 23
Tolworth Pk. Rd. KT6: Surb 6G 23
Tolworth Recreation Cen. 7G 23
Tolworth Ri. Nth. KT5: Surb 5J 23
Tolworth Ri. Sth. KT5: Surb 6J 23
Tolworth Rd. KT6: Surb 6F 23
Tolworth Station (Rail) 6J 23
Tolworth Twr. KT6: Surb 6J 23
Tomlin Cl. KT19: Eps 7A 30
Tomlin Ct. KT19: Eps 7A 30
Tomlins All. TW1: Twick 5B 10
Tomlinson Cl. W4 . . . . .2J 5
Tom Williams Ho. *SW6* *3J 7*
(off Clem Attlee Ct.)
Tonbridge Rd. KT8: W Mole 1E 20
Tonfield Rd. SM3: Sutt 5J 25
Tonstall Rd. KT19: Eps 6A 30
Topiary Sq. TW9: Rich 7G 5
Tormead Cl. SM1: Sutt 3K 31
Torrington Cl. KT10: Clay 3K 27
Torrington Rd. KT10: Clay 3K 27
Torrington Way SM4: Mord 3K 25
Torwood Rd. SW15 . . . . .2D 12
Tourist Info. Cen.
Kingston upon Thames 4B 36 (6E 16)
Tournay Rd. SW6 . . . . .4J 7
Tower, The *TW8: Bford* *2E 4*
(off Ealing Rd.)
Tower Gdns. KT10: Clay 4B 28
Tower Ri. TW9: Rich 7F 5
Tower Rd. TW1: Twick 7A 10
Towers Pl. TW9: Rich 2F 11
Tower Yd. TW10: Rich 2G 11
Towfield Ct. TW13: Hanw 6E 8
Towfield Rd. TW13: Hanw 6E 8
Town End Pde. KT1: King T 5B 36
Town Fld. Way TW7: Isle 6B 4
Town Hall Av. W4 . . . . .2A 6
Town Mdw. TW8: Bford 3E 4
Town Mdw. Rd. TW8: Bford 4E 4
Townmead Rd. TW9: Kew 6J 5
Townshend Rd. TW9: Rich 1G 11
Townshend Ter. TW9: Rich 1G 11
Town Sq. *TW7: Isle* *7C 4*
(off Swan St.)
Town Wharf TW7: Isle 7C 4
Towpath KT12: Walt T 2A 20
Toynbee Rd. SW20 . . . . .5H 19
Trafalgar Av. KT4: Wor Pk 5G 25
Trafalgar Bldg. KT2: King T 2B 36
Trafalgar Dr. KT12: Walt T 7A 20
Trafalgar Rd. TW2: Twick 6J 9
Traherne Lodge TW11: Tedd 2A 16
Tranmere Rd. TW2: Whitt 4G 9
Transport Av. TW8: Bford 2B 4
Traps La. KT3: N Mald 5B 18
Treadwell Rd. KT18: Eps 5B 34
Treaty Cen. TW3: Houn 1G 9
Trebovir Rd. SW5 . . . . .2K 7
Tree Cl. TW10: Ham 5E 10
Treemount Ct. KT17: Eps 2B 34
Treen Av. SW13 . . . . .7C 6
Tregaron Gdns. KT3: N Mald 1B 24
Trehern Rd. SW14 . . . . .7A 6
Trematon Pl. TW11: Tedd 4D 16
Trenchard Cl. KT12: Hers 2B 26
Trenchard Ct. SM4: Mord 3K 25
Trentham St. SW18 . . . . .5K 13
Trent Ho. KT2: King T 1B 36 (5E 16)
Trent Way KT4: Wor Pk 7F 25
Trevanion Rd. W14 . . . . .1H 7
Trevelyan Ct. KT3: N Mald 4B 24
Treville St. SW15 . . . . .4E 12
Trevor Cl. TW7: Isle 2A 10
Trevor Rd. SW19 . . . . .4H 19
Trewenna Dr. KT9: Chess 2E 28
Trewince Rd. SW20 . . . . .5F 19
Triangle, The KT1: King T 6J 17
Trico Ho. *TW8: Bford* *2E 4*
(off Ealing Rd.)
Trigo Ct. KT19: Eps 7A 30
Tri Ho. KT12: Hers 1A 26
Trimmer Wlk. TW8: Bford 3F 5
Trinder M. TW11: Tedd 2B 16
Tring Ct. TW1: Twick 1B 16
Trinity Chu. Pas. SW13 . . . . .3E 6
Trinity Chu. Rd. SW13 . . . . .3E 6
Trinity Cl. TW4: Houn 1D 8
Trinity Cotts. TW9: Rich 7G 5
Trinity Ho. W14 . . . . .1J 7
Trinity Rd. SW19 . . . . .3K 19
TW9: Rich 7G 5
Trojan M. SW19 . . . . .4K 19
Trotter Way KT19: Eps 1H 33
Trowlock Av. TW11: Tedd 3D 16
Trowlock Island TW11: Tedd 3E 16
Trowlock Way TW11: Tedd 3E 16
Trussley Rd. W6 . . . . .1F 7
Trystings Cl. KT10: Clay 3B 28
Tucklow Wlk. SW15 . . . . .4C 12
Tudor Av. KT4: Wor Pk 7E 24
TW12: Hamp 4F 15
Tudor Cl. KT9: Chess 2F 29
KT17: Ewe 6C 30
SM3: Cheam 2G 31
SM7: Bans 4H 35
TW12: Hamp H 2H 15

Tudor Ct. TW11: Tedd 3A 16
TW13: Hanw 1B 14
Tudor Dr. KT2: King T 2E 16
KT12: Walt T 5C 20
SM4: Mord 3G 25
Tudor Gdns. SW13 . . . . .7B 6
TW1: Twick 5A 10
Tudor Ho. W14 . . . . .1G 7
(off Windsor Way)
Tudor Rd. KT2: King T 4H 17
TW3: Houn 1J 9
TW12: Hamp 4F 15
Tufton Gdns. KT8: W Mole 6G 15
Tulip Cl. TW12: Hamp 3E 14
Tulip Tree Ct. SM2: Sutt 7K 31
Tumblewood Rd. SM7: Bans 5H 35
Tunstall Wlk. TW8: Bford 3F 5
Tunworth Cres. SW15 . . . . .3C 12
Turks Boatyard
KT1: King T 2B 36 (5E 16)
Turner Av. TW2: Twick 7H 9
Turner Ho. TW1: Twick 3E 10
(off Clevedon Rd.)
Turner M. SM2: Sutt 4K 31
Turner Rd. KT3: N Mald 4A 24
Turners La. KT12: Hers 3A 26
Turneville Rd. W14 . . . . .3J 7
TURNHAM GREEN 1B 6
Turnham Green Station
(Underground) 1B 6
Turnham Grn. Ter. W4 . . . . .1B 6
Turnham Grn. Ter. M. W4 . . . . . . .1B 6
Turnpike Way TW7: Isle 5B 4
TWICKENHAM 5B 10
Twickenham Bri. TW1: Twick . .2D 10
Twickenham Mus. 5B 10
(off The Embankment)
Twickenham Pl. KT7: T Ditt 6A 22
(off Woodfield Rd.)
Twickenham Rd. TW7: Isle 2B 10
TW9: Rich 1D 10
TW11: Tedd 1B 16
(not continuous)
TW13: Hanw 7E 8
Twickenham Stadium 3K 9
Twickenham Station (Rail) 4B 10
Twickenham Stoop 4K 9
Twickenham Trad. Est.
TW1: Twick 3A 10
Twining Av. TW2: Twick 7H 9
Twynholm Mans. SW6 . . . . .4H 7
(off Lillie Rd.)
Tybenham Rd. SW19 . . . . .7K 19
Tygan Ho. SM3: Cheam 3H 31
(off The Broadway)
Tynamara KT1: King T 7B 36
Tyne Ho. KT2: King T . . .1B 36 (5E 16)
Tyrawley Rd. SW6 . . . . .5K 7

U

Udney Pk. Rd. TW11: Tedd 3B 16
Ullswater Cl. SW15 . . . . .1A 18
Ullswater Cres. SW15 . . . . .1A 18
Ullswater Rd. SW13 . . . . .4D 6
Ulva Rd. SW15 . . . . .2G 13
Umbria St. SW15 . . . . .3D 12
Underwood Ho. KT8: W Mole 2F 21
(off Approach Rd.)
Union Ct. TW9: Rich 2F 11
Union La. TW7: Isle 6B 4
Union St. KT1: King T . . .3B 36 (6E 16)
University for the Creative Arts
Epsom Campus 3B 34
University of the Arts London
Wimbledon College of Art
. . . . .5H 19
University of West London
Brentford Campus 2D 4
Unwin Mans. W14 . . . . .3J 7
(off Queen's Club Gdns.)
Unwin Rd. TW7: Isle 7A 4
Upham Pk. Rd. W4 . . . . .1B 6
Upland Ct. KT18: Tatt C 7F 35
Uplands Cl. SW14 . . . . .2J 11
Upland Way KT18: Tatt C 7F 35
Up. Brighton Rd. KT6: Surb 3E 22
Upper Butts TW8: Bford 3D 4
Upper Ct. Rd. KT19: Eps 7K 29
Upper Dunnymans
SM7: Bans 3J 35
Up. Farm Rd. KT8: W Mole 1E 20
Up. Grotto Rd. TW1: Twick 6A 10
Up. Ham Rd. KT2: King T 1E 16
TW10: Ham 1E 16

Up. High St. KT17: Eps 2B 34
Up. Lodge M. TW12: Hamp H . . .3J 15
Upper Mall W6 . . . . .2D 6
(not continuous)
Up. Mulgrave Rd.
SM2: Cheam 4H 31
Up. Park Rd. KT2: King T 3H 17
Up. Richmond Rd. SW15 . . . . . .1C 12
Up. Richmond Rd. W.
SW14 . . . . .1H 11
TW10: Rich 1H 11
Upper Sawleywood
SM7: Bans 3J 35
Up. Sunbury Rd. TW12: Hamp . . .5D 14
Up. Teddington Rd.
KT1: Hamp W 4D 16
Upton Rd. TW3: Houn 1F 9
URGENT CARE CENTRE
FULHAM 2G 7
WEST MIDDLESEX
UNIVERSITY HOSPITAL 6B 4
Urmston Dr. SW19 . . . . .5H 13
Uxbridge Ct. KT1: King T 2E 22
(off Uxbridge Rd.)
Uxbridge Rd. KT1: King T 1E 22
TW12: Hamp, Hamp H 1F 15
TW13: Felt 6B 8

V

Vale, The TW14: Felt 3A 8
TW16: Sun 3A 14
Vale Cl. TW1: Twick 7B 10
Vale Cotts. SW13 . . . . .7B 12
Vale Cres. SW15 . . . . .1B 18
Vale Cft. KT10: Clay 6A 26
Vale Pde. SW15 . . . . .7B 12
Vale Rd. KT4: Wor Pk 7C 24
KT10: Clay 5K 27
KT19: Ewe 1C 30
SM1: Sutt 1K 31
Vale Rd. Nth. KT6: Surb 6F 23
Vale Rd. Sth. KT6: Surb 6F 23
Valery Pl. TW12: Hamp 4F 15
Valley M. TW1: Twick 6A 10
Vallings Pl. KT6: Surb 4C 22
Vallis Way KT9: Chess 1E 28
Valonia Gdns. SW18 . . . . .3J 13
Vanbrugh Dr. KT12: Walt T 4B 20
Vanbrugh M. KT12: Walt T 4B 20
Vancouver Cl. KT19: Eps 7K 29
Vancouver Rd. TW10: Ham 1D 16
Van Dyck Av. KT3: N Mald 4A 24
Vandyke Cl. SW15 . . . . .4G 13
Van Gogh Cl. TW7: Isle 7B 4
Vanneck Sq. SW15 . . . . .2D 12
Vanquish Cl. TW2: Whitt 4F 9
Vanston Pl. SW6 . . . . .4K 7
Vantage Pl. TW14: Felt 3A 8
W8 . . . . .1K 7
Vantage W. TW8: Bford 1G 5
Varley Dr. TW1: Isle 1C 10
Varna Rd. SW6 . . . . .4H 7
TW12: Hamp 5G 15
Varsity Dr. TW1: Twick 2K 9
Varsity Row SW14 . . . . .6K 5
Vaughan Av. W6 . . . . .1C 6
Vaughan Cl. TW12: Hamp 3D 14
Vaughan Rd. KT7: T Ditt 4C 22
Vaux Cres. KT12: Hers 3A 26
Vencourt Pl. W6 . . . . .1D 6
Vera Rd. SW6 . . . . .5H 7
Verbena Gdns. W6 . . . . .2D 6
Verdun Rd. SW13 . . . . .3D 6
Vereker Dr. TW16: Sun 7A 14
Vereker Rd. W14 . . . . .2H 7
Vermont Rd. SM1: Sutt 7K 25
SW18 . . . . .6G 19
Vernon Av. SW20 . . . . .3F 25
Vernon Cl. KT19: Ewe 3K 29
Vernon Mans. W14 . . . . .2H 7
(off Queen's Club Gdns.)
Vernon M. W14 . . . . .1H 7
Vernon Rd. SW14 . . . . .7A 6
Vernon St. W14 . . . . .1H 7
Verona Ct. W4 . . . . .2B 6
Veronica Rd. KT6: Surb 6F 23
Vicarage Cl. KT4: Wor Pk 5B 24
Vicarage Dr. SW14 . . . . .2A 12
Vicarage Flds. KT12: Walt T 3B 20
Vicarage Gdns. SW14 . . . . .2K 11
Vicarage Ho. KT1: King T 6G 17
(off Cambridge Rd.)
Vicarage La. KT17: Ewe 5D 30
(not continuous)

Vicarage Rd. KT1: Hamp W 5D 16
KT1: King T 3B 36 (6E 16)
SM1: Sutt 7K 25
SW14 . . . . .2K 11
TW2: Twick 6K 9
TW2: Whitt 3H 9
TW11: Tedd 2B 16
Vickers Way TW4: Houn 2D 8
Victoria Av. KT6: Surb 3E 22
KT8: W Mole 7G 15
TW3: Houn 2F 9
Victoria Cl. KT8: W Mole 7F 15
Victoria Cotts. TW9: Kew 5G 5
Victoria Cres. SW19 . . . . .4J 19
Victoria Dr. SW19 . . . . .4G 13
Victoria Mans. W14 . . . . .3J 7
(off Queen's Club Gdns.)
Victoria Pde. TW9: Kew 5H 5
(off Sandycombe Rd.)
Victoria Pl. KT10: Esh 1G 27
(off Esher Pk. Av.)
KT17: Eps 1B 34
TW9: Rich 2E 10
Victoria Rd.
KT1: King T 4E 36 (6G 17)
KT6: Surb 3E 22
SW14 . . . . .7A 6
TW1: Twick 4C 10
TW11: Tedd 3B 16
TW13: Felt 5A 8
Victoria Vs. TW9: Rich 7G 5
Victor Rd. TW11: Tedd 1K 15
Victors Dr. TW12: Hamp 3D 14
Victory Bus. Cen. TW7: Isle 1A 10
Victory Ho. KT18: Eps 2K 33
(off West St.)
Vidler Cl. KT9: Chess 3D 28
Viewfield Rd. SW18 . . . . .3J 13
Viking Cl. SW6 . . . . .3K 7
Village Gdns. KT17: Ewe 6C 30
Village M. SW18 . . . . .5J 13
(off Elsenham St.)
Village Row SM2: Sutt 4K 31
Villiers Av. KT5: Surb 7E 36 (2G 23)
TW2: Whitt 5E 8
Villiers Cl. KT5: Surb 1G 23
Villiers Gro. SM2: Cheam 5G 31
Villiers Path KT6: Surb 2F 23
Villiers Rd.
KT1: King T 7E 36 (1G 23)
Vimy Cl. TW4: Houn 2E 8
Vincam Cl. TW2: Whitt 4F 9
Vincent Av. KT5: Surb 6K 23
Vincent Cl. KT10: Esh 7G 21
Vincent Rd. KT1: King T 7H 17
Vincent Row TW12: Hamp H 3H 15
Vine Cl. KT5: Surb 3G 23
Vine Pl. TW3: Houn 1G 9
Viner Cl. KT12: Walt T 3B 20
Vine Rd. KT8: E Mos 1H 21
SW13 . . . . .7C 6
Vine Sq. W14 . . . . .2J 7
(off Star Rd.)
Vineyard, The TW10: Rich 2F 11
Vineyard Cl.
KT1: King T 5E 36 (7G 17)
Vineyard Hill Rd. SW19 . . . . .1J 19
Vineyard M. TW10: Rich 2F 11
Vineyard Pas. TW10: Rich 2F 11
Vineyard Path SW14 . . . . .7A 6
Vineyard Row KT1: Hamp W 5D 16
Vineyards, The TW6: Sun 7A 14
Viola Av. TW14: Felt 3B 8
Violet Cl. SM3: Sutt 5H 25
Virgin Active
Chiswick 5B 6
Chiswick Pk. 1J 5
Epsom 2A 34
(within Ebbisham Cen.)
Fulham 3H 7
(within Fulham Pools)
Hammersmith 1G 7
Kingston upon Thames -
Richmond Rd. 1C 36 (5F 17)
The Bentall Cen. 3C 36
Putney 1H 13
Sunbury 5A 14
The Twickenham Club 3K 9
Wandsworth,
Southside Shop. Cen. . .2K 13
Wimbledon, Worple Rd. 3J 19
Virginia Cl. KT3: N Mald 1K 23
KT21: Asht 7E 32
Virginia Ho. TW11: Tedd 2C 16

Vitae Apartments W6 . . . . .1C 6
Vitali Cl. SW15 . . . . .3D 12
Vivien Cl. KT9: Chess 4F 29
Vivienne Cl. TW1: Twick 3E 10
Voewood Cl. KT3: N Mald 3C 24
Vue Cinema
Fulham Broadway 4K 7

W

Wadbrook St.
KT1: King T 4B 36 (6E 16)
Wades La. TW11: Tedd 2B 16
Wadham M. SW14 . . . . .6K 5
Wadham Rd. SW15 . . . . .1H 13
Wagner M. KT6: Surb 2F 23
(off Avenue Elmers)
Wagtail Cl. SW15 . . . . .3F 13
Waight's Ct.
KT2: King T 1D 36 (5F 17)
Wainford Cl. SW19 . . . . .5G 13
Wainwright Gro. TW7: Isle 1J 9
Wakefield Rd. TW10: Rich 2E 10
Waldeck Rd. SW14 . . . . .7K 5
W4 . . . . .3H 5
Waldeck Ter. SW14 . . . . .7K 5
(off Waldeck Rd.)
Waldegrave Gdns. TW1: Twick . . .6A 10
Waldegrave Pk. TW1: Twick 1A 16
Waldegrave Rd. TW1: Twick 1A 16
TW11: Tedd 1A 16
Waldemar Av. SW6 . . . . .5H 7
Waldemar Rd. SW19 . . . . .2K 19
WALHAM GREEN 5K 7
Walham Grn. Ct. SW6 . . . . .4K 7
(off Waterford Rd.)
Walham Gro. SW6 . . . . .4K 7
Walham Ri. SW19 . . . . .4H 19
Walham Yd. SW6 . . . . .4K 7
Walker Cl. TW12: Hamp 3E 14
Walkers Pl. SW15 . . . . .1H 13
Walkfield Dr. KT18: Tatt C 6E 34
Wallace Flds. KT17: Eps 1C 34
Wallbrook Bus. Cen.
TW4: Houn 1A 8
Wallis Ho. TW8: Bford 2F 5
Wallorton Gdns. SW14 . . . . .1A 12
Walmer Ct. KT5: Surb 2F 23
(off Cranes Pk.)
Walnut Cl. KT18: Eps 4C 34
Walnut Flds. KT17: Ewe 5C 30
Walnut Gro. SM7: Bans 3G 35
Walnut Tree Cl. SM7: Bans 1H 35
SW13 . . . . .5C 6
Walnut Tree Cotts. SW19 . . . . . .2H 19
Walnut Tree Rd. TW8: Bford 3F 5
Walpole Av. TW9: Kew 6G 5
Walpole Ct. TW2: Twick 6K 9
W14 . . . . .1G 7
(off Blythe Rd.)
Walpole Cres. TW11: Tedd 2A 16
Walpole Gdns. TW2: Twick 6K 9
W4 . . . . .2K 5
Walpole Ho. KT8: W Mole 2F 21
(off Approach Rd.)
SW15 . . . . .2H 13
(off Plaza Gdns.)
Walpole Pl. TW11: Tedd 2A 16
Walpole Rd. KT6: Surb 4F 23
TW2: Twick 6K 9
TW11: Tedd 2A 16
Walsham Rd. TW14: Felt 4A 8
Walsingham Gdns. KT19: Ewe . . .1B 30
Walsingham Lodge SW13 . . . . . .5D 6
Walters Mead KT21: Asht 6F 33
Walter St. KT2: King T . . .2C 36 (5F 17)
Walton Av. KT3: N Mald 1C 24
SM3: Cheam 7J 25
WALTON COMMUNITY HOSPITAL
. . . . .6A 20
WALTON-ON-THAMES 5A 20
Walton on Thames
Camping & Cvn. Site
KT12: Walt T 4F 21
Walton-on-Thames Station
(Rail) 1A 26
Walton Pk. KT12: Walt T 6C 20
Walton Pk. La. KT12: Walt T 6C 20
Walton Rd.
KT8: W Mole, E Mos 1E 20
KT12: Walt T 2B 20
KT18: Eps D 6C 34
Wanborough Dr. SW15 . . . . .5E 12
Wandle Ct. KT19: Ewe 1K 29
Wandle Recreation Cen. 3K 13

WANDSWORTH 2K 13
Wandsworth Bri. Rd. SW6 . . . . .5K 7
WANDSWORTH GYRATORY . . .2K 13
Wandsworth High St. SW18 . . . .2K 13
Wandsworth Mus. 2K 13
Wandsworth Plain SW18 . . . . . .2K 13
Wandsworth Riverside
   Quarter Pier (River Bus)
   . . . . .1K 13
Warbank La. KT2: King T 4C 18
Warboys App. KT2: King T 3J 17
Warboys Rd. KT2: King T 3J 17
Warburton Rd. TW2: Whitt 5G 9
Wardo Av. SW6 . . . . .5H 7
Wardrobe, The TW9: Rich 2E 10
   (off Old Palace Yd.)
Ware Ct. SM1: Sutt 1J 31
Wareham Cl. TW3: Houn 1G 9
Warfield Rd. TW12: Hamp 5G 15
Warkworth Gdns. TW7: Isle 4B 4
Warner Av. SM3: Cheam 6H 25
Warner Cl. TW12: Hamp 2E 14
Warners La. KT2: King T 1E 16
Warnford Ho. SW15 . . . . .3B 12
   (off Tunworth Cres.)
Warren, The KT4: Wor Pk 1A 30
Warren Av. SM2: Cheam 6J 31
   TW10: Rich 1J 11
Warren Cl. KT10: Surb 1G 27
Warren Cutting KT2: King T 4A 18
Warren Dr. Nth. KT5: Surb 5J 23
Warren Dr. Sth. KT5: Surb 5K 23
Warren Farm Cl. KT17: Bans 4F 35
Warren Footpath TW1: Twick . . .5D 10
Warren Hill KT18: Eps 5A 34
Warren Ho. W14 . . . . .1J 7
Warren La. KT22: Oxs 7H 27
Warren Mead SM7: Bans 4F 35
Warren Pk. KT2: King T 3K 17
Warren Ri. KT3: N Mald 5A 18
Warren Rd. KT2: King T 3K 17
   SM7: Bans 3F 35
   TW2: Whitt 3H 9
Warrington Rd. TW10: Rich 2E 10
Warwark Ct. KT6: Surb 6F 23
Warwick W14 . . . . .1J 7
   (off Kensington Village)
Warwick Cl. TW12: Hamp 4H 15
   W8 .1J 7
   (off Kensington High St.)
Warwick Dr. SW15 . . . . .7E 6
Warwick Gdns. KT7: T Ditt 2A 22
   KT21: Asht 6D 32
   W14 . . . . .1J 7
Warwick Gro. KT5: Surb 4G 23
Warwick Ho. KT2: King T 1D 36
Warwick Lodge TW2: Twick 7G 9
Warwick Mans. SW5 . . . . .1K 7
   (off Cromwell Cres.)
Warwick Pl. KT7: T Ditt 3B 22
Warwick Rd. KT1: Hamp W 5D 16
   KT3: N Mald 7K 17
   KT7: T Ditt 2A 22
   SW5 . . . . .1J 7
   TW2: Twick 5K 9
   W14 . . . . .1J 7
Washington Rd. KT1: King T 6H 17
   KT4: Wor Pk 6E 24
   SW13 . . . . .4D 6
Watchfield Ct. W4 . . . . .2K 5
Watcombe Cotts. TW9: Kew 1K 5
Waterbank Ho. SW18 . . . . .5K 13
   (off Knaresborough Dr.)
Waterer Gdns. KT20: Tad 7G 35
Waterford Cl. KT11: Cobh 7D 26
Waterford Rd. SW6 . . . . .4K 7
Waterfront W6 . . . . .3F 7
Watergardens, The
   KT2: King T 3K 17
Waterhouse Cl. W6 . . . . .1G 7
Water La. KT1: King T 2B 36 (5E 16)
   TW1: Twick 5B 10
   TW9: Rich 2E 10
Waterloo Pl. TW9: Rich 1F 11
Waterloo Rd. KT19: Eps 1A 34
   . . . . .3F 5
Watermans Art Cen., Cinema & Theatre
   . . . . .3E 4
Watermans Cl. KT2: King T 4F 17
Watermans Ct. TW8: Bford 3E 4
   (off High St.)
Waterman St. SW15 . . . . .7G 7
Watermill Cl. TW10: Ham 7D 10
Water Mill Ho. TW13: Hanw 6F 9
Watermill Way TW13: Hanw 6E 8
Water's Edge SW6 . . . . .5F 7
   (off Palemead Cl.)

Watersedge KT19: Ewe 1K 29
Waterside Bus. Cen.
   TW7: Isle 1C 10
Waterside Cl. KT6: Surb 6F 23
Waterside Dr. KT12: Walt T 2A 20
Waters Pl. SW15 . . . . .6F 7
Watersplash Cl.
   KT1: King T 5C 36 (7F 17)
Waters Rd. KT1: King T 6J 17
Waters Sq. KT1: King T 7J 17
Watery La. SW19 . . . . .5J 19
   SW20 . . . . .6J 19
Watney Cotts. SW14 . . . . .7K 5
Watney Rd. SW14 . . . . .7K 5
Watson Av. SM3: Cheam 6H 25
Watts La. TW11: Tedd 2B 16
Watts Rd. KT7: T Ditt 4B 22
Wavendon Av. W4 . . . . .2A 6
Waverley Av. KT5: Surb 3J 23
   TW2: Whitt 5E 8
Waverley Cl. KT8: W Mole 2F 21
Waverley Rd. KT17: Ewe 2E 30
Wayneflete Ho. SW15 . . . . .7G 21
Wayneflete Twr. Av. KT10: Esh . .7F 21
Waynflete Ho. KT10: Esh 1G 27
   (off High St.)
Wayside SW14 . . . . .2K 11
Wayside Ct. TW1: Twick 3D 10
Wealdstone Rd. SM3: Sutt 6J 25
Weavers Cl. TW7: Isle 1K 9
Weavers Ter. SW6 . . . . .3K 7
   (off Micklethwaite Rd.)
Webb Ho. TW13: Hanw 7D 8
Weimar St. SW15 . . . . .7H 7
Weir Rd. KT12: Walt T 3A 20
Weir Rd. SW15 . . . . .7G 7
Welbeck Cl. KT3: N Mald 2C 24
   KT17: Ewe 4D 30
Welbeck Dr. W14 . . . . .1J 7
   (off Addison Bri. Pl.)
Weldin M. SW18 . . . . .2K 13
   (off Lebanon Rd.)
Weldon Dr. KT8: W Mole 1E 20
Welford Pl. SW19 . . . . .1H 19
Wellesford Cl. SM7: Bans 6J 35
Wellesley Av. W6 . . . . .1E 6
Wellesley Cl. SM3: Sutt 5H 25
Wellesley Cres. TW2: Twick 6K 9
Wellesley Mans. W14 . . . . .1J 7
   (off Edith Vs.)
Wellesley Pde. TW2: Twick 7K 9
Wellesley Rd. TW2: Twick 7J 9
   W4 . . . . .2H 5
Wellington Av. KT4: Wor Pk 7F 25
   TW3: Houn 2F 9
Wellington Ct. KT19: Eps 1A 34
   TW12: Hamp H 2J 15
Wellington Cres. KT3: N Mald . . .7K 17
Wellington Gdns. TW2: Twick . . .1J 15
Wellington Mans. W14 . . . . .1J 7
   (off Queen's Club Gdns.)
Wellington Rd. SW19 . . . . .6K 13
   TW2: Twick 2J 15
   TW12: Hamp H 2J 15
   W5 .1D 4
Wellington Rd. Nth. TW4: Houn . .1E 8
Wellington Rd. Sth. TW4: Houn . .1E 8
Well La. SW14 . . . . .2K 11
Wellmeadow Rd. W7 . . . . .1B 4
WELLS, THE 3H 33
Wells Ho. KT18: Eps 3H 33
Wellside Gdns. SW14 . . . . .1K 11
Wells Rd. KT18: Eps 3H 33
Well Way KT18: Eps 4H 33
Welstead Way W4 . . . . .1C 6
Weltje Rd. W6 . . . . .1D 6
Wembley Rd. TW12: Hamp 5F 15
Wendover Dr. KT3: N Mald 3C 24
Wensleydale Gdns.
   TW12: Hamp 4G 15
Wensleydale Pas.
   TW12: Hamp 5F 15
Wensleydale Rd. TW12: Hamp . . .3F 15
Wentworth Cl. KT6: Surb 6E 22
   SM4: Mord 4K 25
Wentworth Ct. SW18 . . . . .3K 13
   (off Garratt La.)
   TW2: Twick 7K 9
   W6 .2J 7
   (off Paynes Wlk.)
Werter Rd. SW15 . . . . .1H 13
Wesley Cl. KT19: Ewe 2K 29
Wesley Pl. KT18: Tatt C 7G 35
Wessex Av. SW19 . . . . .7K 19
Wessex Cl. KT1: King T 5J 17
   KT7: T Ditt 6A 22

West Acres KT10: Esh 4E 26
Westbank Rd.
   TW12: Hamp H 3H 15
WEST BARNES 2E 24
W. Barnes La. KT3: N Mald 7E 18
   SW20 . . . . .7E 18
Westbourne Av.
   SM3: Cheam 6H 25
WEST BROMPTON 3K 7
West Brompton Station
   (Underground & Overground)
   . . . . .3K 7
Westbrook Av. TW12: Hamp 4E 14
Westbury Av. KT10: Clay 3A 28
Westbury Pl. TW8: Bford 3E 4
Westbury Rd. KT3: N Mald 1A 24
   TW13: Felt 5C 8
Westcar La. KT12: Hers 3A 26
West Cl. TW12: Hamp 3D 14
Westcoombe Av. SW20 . . . . . . .5C 18
Westcote Rd. KT19: Eps 7J 29
Westcott Way SM2: Cheam 6F 31
Westcroft Gdns.
   SM4: Mord 7J 19
Westcroft Sq. W6 . . . . .1D 6
   W14 .1E 8
W. Cromwell Rd. SW5 . . . . .2J 7
   W14 .1E 8
W. Cross Cen. TW8: Bford 3B 4
W. Cross Way TW8: Bford 3C 4
West Dene SM3: Cheam 3H 31
Westdene KT12: Hers 1A 26
West Dr. KT20: Tad 7G 35
   SM2: Cheam 5G 31
WEST END 3E 26
West End Common
   (Local Nature Reserve) 4D 26
W. End Gdns. KT10: Esh 2E 26
W. End La. KT10: Esh 4E 26
Westergate Ho. KT1: King T 7B 36
Westerham Cl. SM2: Sutt 6K 31
Westerley Ware TW9: Kew 3H 5
   (off Kew Grn.)
Western Rd. SM1: Sutt 2K 31
Western Ter. W6 . . . . .2D 6
WEST EWELL 5A 30
W. Farm Av. KT21: Asht 7D 32
W. Farm Cl. KT21: Asht 7D 32
Westfield KT21: Asht 7G 33
Westfield Cl. SM1: Sutt 1J 31
Westfield Ct. KT6: Surb 2E 22
   (off Portsmouth Rd)
Westfield Rd. KT6: Surb 3E 22
   KT12: Walt T 4D 20
   SM1: Sutt 1J 31
Westfields SW13 . . . . .7C 6
Westfields Av. SW13 . . . . .7B 6
West Gdns. KT17: Ewe 6B 30
Westgate Cl. KT18: Eps 4A 34
Westgate Ho. KT18: Eps 4A 34
   (off Chalk La.)
   TW8: Bford 2E 4
   (off Ealing Rd.)
West Gro. KT12: Hers 2A 26
W. Hall Rd. TW9: Kew 5J 5
Westhay Gdns. SW14 . . . . .3J 11
   W8 .2J 33
WEST HILL 2J 33
West Hill KT19: Eps 2J 33
   SW15 . . . . .4G 13
   SW18 . . . . .2J 33
W. Hill Av. KT19: Ewe 2J 33
W. Hill Ct. KT19: Eps 2K 33
   (off Court La.)
W. Hill Rd. SW18 . . . . .3J 13
Westhorpe Rd. SW15 . . . . .7F 7
West Ho. Cl. SW19 . . . . .5H 13
WEST KENSINGTON 1H 7
W. Kensington Ct. W14 . . . . .2J 7
   (off Edith Vs.)
W. Kensington Mans. W14 . . . . . .2J 7
   (off Beaumont Cres.)
West Kensington Station
   (Underground) 2J 7
Westlands Ct. KT8: E Mos 1J 21
   KT18: Eps 4K 33
Westleigh Av. SW15 . . . . .2E 12
Westmark Point SW15 . . . . .5E 12
   (off Norley Va.)
West Mead KT19: Ewe 3B 30
Westmead SW15 . . . . .3E 12
WEST MIDDLESEX UNIVERSITY
   HOSPITAL 6B 4
Westminster Cl. TW11: Tedd 2B 16
WEST MOLESEY 1F 21
Westmont Rd. KT10: Hin W 6K 21
Westmore Cl. SW15 . . . . .2H 13
Westmoreland Rd. SW13 . . . . . .5C 6

Westmorland Cl. KT19: Ewe 6B 30
   TW1: Twick 3C 10
Westmorland Ct. KT6: Surb 4E 22
Westmount Cl. KT4: Wor Pk 5F 25
Weston Av. KT7: T Ditt 4K 21
   KT8: W Mole 7D 14
Weston Ct. KT1: King T 6C 36
WESTON GREEN 5K 21
Weston Grn. KT7: T Ditt 5K 21
   (Weston Grn. Rd.)
   KT7: T Ditt 6K 21
   (Weston Pk.)
Weston Grn. Rd. KT7: T Ditt 5K 21
   KT10: Esh 5J 21
Weston Pk.
   KT1: King T 3C 36 (6F 17)
   KT7: T Ditt 5K 21
Weston Pk. Cl. KT7: T Ditt 5K 21
Weston Rd. KT7: T Ditt 5K 21
   KT17: Eps 7B 30
   W4 . . . . .1K 5
West Pk. Av. TW9: Kew 5H 5
West Pk. Rd. KT19: Eps 7G 29
   TW9: Kew 5H 5
West Pl. SW19 . . . . .2F 19
West Point KT19: Ewe 5B 30
W. Point Cl. TW4: Houn 1E 8
   (off Grosvenor Rd.)
West Rd. KT2: King T 5K 17
   KT9: Chess 1D 32
Westrow SW15 . . . . .3F 13
W. Sheen Va. TW9: Rich 1G 11
W. Side Comn. SW19 . . . . .2F 19
West St. KT17: Ewe 6B 30
   KT18: Eps 2K 33
West Sutton Station (Rail) 1K 31
W. Temple Sheen SW14 . . . . . . .2J 11
West Vw. KT21: Asht 7D 32
Westville Rd. KT7: T Ditt 5B 22
Westway SW20 . . . . .7E 18
Westway Cl. SW20 . . . . .7E 18
Westways KT19: Ewe 1C 30
Westwick KT1: King T 6H 17
   (off Chesterton Ter.)
Westwood Cl. KT10: Esh 7J 21
Westwood Gdns. SW13 . . . . .7C 6
Westwood Rd. SW13 . . . . .7C 6
Wetherby Mans. SW5 . . . . .2K 7
   (off Earls Ct. Sq.)
Wetherby Way KT9: Chess 4F 29
Wey Ct. KT19: Ewe 1K 29
Weydown Cl. SW19 . . . . .5H 13
Weylands Cl. KT12: Walt T 5E 20
Weymouth Av. W5 . . . . .1D 4
Weymouth Ct. SM2: Sutt 4K 31
Wharf La. TW1: Twick 5B 10
Whatley Av. SW20 . . . . .7G 19
Wheatfield Way
   KT1: King T 5C 36 (6F 17)
Wheatley Ho. SW15 . . . . .4D 12
   (off Ellisfield Dr)
Wheatley M. KT8: E Mos 1J 21
Wheatley Rd. TW7: Isle 7A 4
Wheatsheaf La. SW6 . . . . .4F 7
Wheatsheaf Ter. SW6 . . . . .4J 7
Wheelers La. KT18: Eps 3J 33
Whitcombe M. TW9: Kew 5J 5
Whitcome M. TW9: Kew 5J 5
Whitebeam Cl. KT17: Eps D 4E 34
Whitefield Cl. SW15 . . . . .3H 13
White Gates KT7: T Ditt 4B 22
Whitehall 3H 31
Whitehall Cres. KT9: Chess 2E 28
Whitehall Gdns. W4 . . . . .3J 5
Whitehall Pk. Rd. W4 . . . . .3J 5
White Hart La. SW13 . . . . .6B 6
White Heron M. TW11: Tedd 3A 16
White Horse Dr. KT18: Eps 3K 33
Whitelands Cres. SW18 . . . . . . .4H 13
Whiteley's Way TW13: Hanw 7F 9
White Lion Ct. TW7: Isle 7C 4
White Lodge Cl. TW7: Isle 6B 4
White Lodge TW16: Sun 5B 14
White Lodge Mus. 5A 12
Whitestile Rd. TW8: Bford 2D 4
White Swan M. W4 . . . . .2B 6
Whitlock Dr. SW19 . . . . .4H 13
Whitmores Cl. KT18: Eps 4K 33
Whitnell Way SW15 . . . . .2F 13
   (not continuous)
Whittaker Av. TW9: Rich 2E 10
Whittaker Ct. KT21: Asht 6E 32
Whittaker Pl. TW9: Rich 2E 10
   (off Whittaker Av.)
Whittaker Rd. SM3: Sutt 7J 25
Whittingham Ct. W4 . . . . .4B 6

Whittingstall Rd.—Wootton Pl.

Whittingstall Rd. SW6 . . . . .5J 7
WHITTON .4H 9
Whitton Dene TW3: Houn, Isle . . .2H 9
TW7: Isle 3J 9
Whitton Mnr. Rd. TW7: Isle 3H 9
Whitton Rd. TW1: Twick 3A 10
TW2: Twick 3K 9
TW3: Houn 1G 9
WHITTON ROAD RDBT. 3A 10
Whitton Sports & Fitness Cen.
. . . . .6G 9
Whitton Station (Rail) 4H 9
Whitton Waye TW3: Houn 3F 9
Whyte M. SM3: Cheam 4H 31
Wickham Av. SM3: Cheam 2F 31
Wickham Cl. KT3: N Mald 3C 24
Wickham Ct. *KT5: Surb* *2G 23*
(off Cranes Pk.)
Wick Ho. KT1: Hamp W 1A 36
Wick Rd. TW11: Tedd 4C 16
Wicksteed Ho. TW8: Bford 2G 5
Widewing Cl. TW11: Tedd 4C 16
Wiggins La. TW10: Ham 6D 10
Wight Ho. KT1: King T 6B 36
Wighton M. TW7: Isle 6A 4
Wigley Rd. TW13: Felt 6C 8
Wilberforce Ct. *KT18: Eps* *3A 34*
(off Heathcote Rd.)
Wilberforce Way SW19 . . . . .3G 19
Wilbury Av. SM2: Cheam 6J 31
Wilcox Rd. SM1: Sutt 1K 31
TW11: Tedd 1J 15
Wildberry Cl. W7 . . . . .1B 4
Wildcroft Mnr. SW15 . . . . .4F 13
Wildcroft Rd. SW15 . . . . .4F 13
Wilderness, The
KT8: W Mole, E Mos 2H 21
TW12: Hamp H 1G 15
Wilfred Wood Ct. *W6* *1F 7*
(off Samuel's Cl.)
Wilkes Rd. TW8: Bford 3F 5
Willcocks Cl. KT9: Chess 7F 23
William Banfield Ho. *SW6* *6J 7*
(off Munster Rd.)
William Evans Rd.
KT19: Eps 7H 29
William Farm La. SW15 . . . . .7E 6
William Gdns. SW15 . . . . .2E 12
William Harvey Ho. *SW19* *5H 13*
(off Whitlock Dr.)
William Hunt Mans. SW13 . . . . . . .3F 7
William Morris Ho. W6 . . . . .3G 7
William Rd. SW19 . . . . .4H 19
Williams Cl. SW6 . . . . .4H 7
Williams Dr. TW3: Houn 1F 9
Williams Gro. KT6: Surb 3D 22
William's La. SW14 . . . . .7K 5
Willingham Way KT1: King T 7H 17
Willis Cl. KT18: Eps 3J 33
Willoughby Rd. KT2: King T 5G 17
TW1: Twick 2D 10
(not continuous)
Willoughbys, The SW14 . . . . .7B 6
Willow Av. SW13 . . . . .6C 6
Willow Bank SW6 . . . . .7H 7
TW10: Ham 7C 10
Willowbank KT7: T Ditt 5B 22
Willowbrook TW12: Hamp H 2G 15
Willow Cl. SM7: Bans 3H 35
TW8: Bford 3D 4
Willow Cotts. TW9: Kew 3H 5
TW13: Hanw 7D 8
Willow Ct. *W4* *4B 6*
(off Corney Reach Way)
Willowdene Cl. TW2: Whitt 4H 9
Willow End KT6: Surb 5F 23
Willowhayne Ct. *KT12: Walt T* . . .*4A 20*
(off Willowhayne Dr.)
Willowhayne Dr.
KT12: Walt T 4A 20
Willowhayne Gdns.
KT4: Wor Pk 7F 25
Willow Lodge SW6 . . . . .5G 7
Willowmere KT10: Esh 1H 27
Willow Rd. KT3: N Mald 1K 23
Willows, The KT10: Clay 3K 27
Willows Path KT18: Eps 3J 33
Willow Wlk. SM3: Sutt 7J 25
Willow Way KT19: Ewe 3A 30
TW2: Twick 6G 9
Wills Cres. TW3: Houn 3G 9
Wilmer Cl. KT2: King T 2G 17
Wilmer Cres. KT2: King T 2G 17
Wilmerhatch La. KT18: Eps 7J 33
Wilmington Av. W4 . . . . .4A 6
Wilmot Way SM7: Bans 3K 35
Wilson Rd. KT9: Chess 3G 29
Wilson's Rd. W6 . . . . .2G 7
Wilson Wlk. *W4* *1C 6*
(off Prebend Gdns.)
Wilton Av. W4 . . . . .2B 6
Wilton Cres. SW19 . . . . .5J 19
Wilton Gdns.
KT8: W Mole 7F 15
KT12: Walt T 5C 20
Wilton Gro. KT3: N Mald 3C 24
SW19 . . . . .5J 19
Wilton Pde. TW13: Felt 6A 8
Wiltshire Gdns.
TW2: Twick 5H 9
Wilverley Cres. KT3: N Mald 3B 24
WIMBLEDON 3H 19
Wimbledon All England Lawn
Tennis & Croquet Club 7H 13
Wimbledon Bri. SW19 . . . . .3J 19
Wimbledon Chase Station
(Rail) 6H 19
Wimbledon Cl. SW20 . . . . .4G 19
Wimbledon Common 1D 18
Wimbledon Common Golf Course
. . . . .2E 18
Wimbledon Hill Rd. SW19 . . . . . .3H 19
Wimbledon Lawn Tennis Mus.
. . . . .7H 13
WIMBLEDON PARK 7K 13
Wimbledon Pk. Athletics Track
. . . . .6J 13
Wimbledon Pk. Ct. SW19 . . . . . . .5J 13
Wimbledon Pk. Golf Course
. . . . .7J 13
Wimbledon Pk. Rd. SW18 . . . . . .6H 13
SW19 . . . . .6H 13
Wimbledon Pk. Side SW19 . . . . .7G 13
Wimbledon Park Station
(Underground) 7K 13
Wimbledon Pk. Watersports Cen.
. . . . .6J 13
Wimbledon Pk. Women's Fitness Suite
. . . . .7J 13
Wimbledon Station
(Rail, Underground &
London Tramlink) 3J 19
Wimbledon Theatre 4K 19
Wimbledon Windmill Mus. 6E 12
Wimborne Cl. KT4: Wor Pk 5F 25
KT17: Eps 2B 34
Wimpole Cl. KT1: King T 6G 17
Wincanton Rd. SW18 . . . . .4J 13
Winchelsea Cl. SW15 . . . . .2G 13
Winchendon Rd. SW6 . . . . .5J 7
TW11: Tedd 1J 15
Winchester Cl. KT2: King T 4J 17
KT10: Esh 1F 27
Winchester Ho. *KT19: Eps* *1H 33*
(off Phoenix Cl.)
Winchester M. KT4: Wor Pk 6G 25
Winchester Rd.
KT12: Walt T 5A 20
TW1: Twick 3C 10
TW13: Hanw 7E 8
Winchester Wlk. *SW15* *2J 13*
(off Up. Richmond Rd.)
Winchfield Ho. SW15 . . . . .3C 12
Winchilsea Cres.
KT8: W Mole 6H 15
Windermere Av. SW19 . . . . .7K 19
Windermere Ct. SW13 . . . . .3C 6
Windermere Ho. TW7: Isle 2A 10
Windermere Rd. SW15 . . . . .1B 18
Windham Rd. TW9: Rich 7G 5
Windlesham Gro. SW19 . . . . .5G 13
Windlesham M.
TW12: Hamp H 3H 15
Windmill Av. KT17: Ewe 7C 30
Windmill Cl. KT6: Surb 5D 22
KT17: Eps 1C 34
Windmill Ct. *W5* *1D 4*
(off Windmill Rd.)
Windmill End KT17: Eps 1C 34
Windmill La. KT6: Surb 3C 22
KT17: Eps 1C 34
TW7: Isle 2A 4
Windmill M. W4 . . . . .1B 6
Windmill Pas. W4 . . . . .1B 6
Windmill Ri. KT2: King T 4J 17
Windmill Rd. SW19 . . . . .6E 12
TW8: Bford 1D 4
TW12: Hamp H 2G 15
W4 . . . . .1B 6
W5 . . . . .1D 4
Windrush KT3: N Mald 1J 23
Windrush Cl. W4 . . . . .5K 5
Windsor Av. KT3: N Mald 2K 23
KT8: W Mole 7F 15
SM3: Cheam 7H 25
Windsor Cl. TW8: Bford 3C 4
Windsor Ct. *KT1: King T* *1E 22*
(off Palace Rd.)
KT18: Eps *2A 34*
(off Ashley Rd.)
Windsor Rd. KT2: King T 4F 17
KT4: Wor Pk 6D 24
TW9: Kew 6G 5
TW11: Tedd 2J 15
Windsor Wlk. KT12: Walt T 5C 20
Windsor Way W14 . . . . .1G 7
Windy Ridge Cl. SW19 . . . . .2G 19
Winery La.
KT1: King T 5E 36 (7G 17)
Winey Cl. KT9: Chess 4D 28
Wingfield Ct. SM7: Bans 4K 35
Wingfield Rd. KT2: King T 3G 17
Wingrave Rd. W6 . . . . .3F 7
Wings Cl. SM1: Sutt 1K 31
Winifred Rd. SW19 . . . . .5K 19
TW12: Hamp H 1F 15
Winkworth Pl. SM7: Bans 3J 35
Winkworth Rd. SM7: Bans 3K 35
Winslow Rd. W6 . . . . .3F 7
Winslow Way KT12: Walt T 7B 20
TW13: Hanw 7C 8
Winston Wlk. W4 . . . . .1A 6
Winter Box Wlk. TW10: Rich 2G 11
Winter Cl. KT17: Eps 1B 34
Winterdown Gdns. KT10: Esh 3E 26
Winterdown Rd. KT10: Esh 3E 26
Winterfold Cl. SW19 . . . . .6H 13
Winter Gdns. TW11: Tedd 1B 16
Winters Rd. KT7: T Ditt 4C 22
Winterton Ct. KT1: Hamp W 1A 36
Winthorpe Rd. SW15 . . . . .1H 13
Wisdom Ct. *TW7: Isle* *7B 4*
(off South St.)
Wishford Ct. KT21: Asht 7G 33
Withers Cl. KT9: Chess 3D 28
Withycombe Rd. SW19 . . . . .4G 13
Witley Point *SW15* *5E 12*
(off Wanborough Dr.)
Wittering Cl. KT2: King T 2E 16
Witts Ho. KT1: King T 5E 36
Wivenhoe Ct. TW3: Houn 1E 8
Woffington Cl. KT1: Hamp W 5D 16
Woking Cl. SW15 . . . . .1C 12
Wolfe Ho. W14 . . . . .1J 7
Wolseley Av. SW19 . . . . .6K 13
Wolseley Gdns. W4 . . . . .3J 5
Wolseley Rd. W4 . . . . .1K 5
Wolsey Av. KT7: T Ditt 2A 22
Wolsey Cl. KT2: King T 5J 17
KT4: Wor Pk 1D 30
SW20 . . . . .4E 18
TW3: Houn 1H 9
Wolsey Cres. SM4: Mord 4H 25
Wolsey Dr. KT2: King T 2F 17
KT12: Walt T 5C 20
Wolsey Gro. KT10: Esh 1G 27
Wolsey Rd. KT8: E Mos 1J 21
KT10: Esh 1G 27
TW12: Hamp H 3G 15
Wolsey Way KT9: Chess 2H 29
Wolverton Av. KT2: King T 5H 17
Wolverton Gdns. W6 . . . . .1G 7
Wonersh Way SM2: Cheam 5G 31
Wonford Cl. KT2: King T 5B 18
Woodall Cl. KT9: Chess 4D 28
Woodbine Cl. TW2: Twick 6J 9
Woodbine La. KT4: Wor Pk 7E 24
Woodbines Av.
KT1: King T 6B 36 (7E 16)
Woodborough Rd. SW15 . . . . .1E 12
Woodbourne Dr. KT10: Clay 3A 28
Woodbridge Av. KT22: Lea 7B 32
Woodbridge Cnr. KT22: Lea 7B 32
Woodbridge Gro. KT22: Lea 7B 32
WOODCOTE 4K 33
Woodcote Cl. KT2: King T 2G 17
KT18: Eps 3A 34
Woodcote Ct. *KT18: Eps* *3A 34*
(off Dorking Rd.)
Woodcote End KT18: Eps 4A 34
Woodcote Grn. Rd. KT18: Eps 4K 33
Woodcote Hall KT18: Eps 3A 34
Woodcote Ho. KT18: Eps 4K 33
Woodcote Ho. Ct. KT18: Eps 4A 34
Woodcote Hurst KT18: Eps 5K 33
Woodcote Lodge KT18: Eps 4K 33
WOODCOTE PARK 6K 33
Woodcote Pk. Rd. KT18: Eps 5K 33
Woodcote Rd. KT18: Eps 3A 34
Woodcote Side KT18: Eps 4J 33
Woodend KT10: Esh 6H 21
Woodfield KT21: Asht 6E 32
Woodfield Cl. KT21: Asht 6E 32
Woodfield Gdns.
KT3: N Mald 2C 24
Woodfield Ho. *KT7: T Ditt* *6A 22*
(off Woodfield Rd.)
Woodfield La. KT21: Asht 6F 33
Woodfield Rd. KT7: T Ditt 6A 22
KT21: Asht 6E 32
Woodgate Av. KT9: Chess 2E 28
Woodgavil SM7: Bans 5J 35
Woodhayes Rd. SW19 . . . . .4F 19
Woodies La. KT3: N Mald 3A 24
Woodland Cl. KT19: Ewe 3B 30
Woodland Ct. KT17: Eps 1C 34
Woodland Dr. KT11: Cobh 7E 26
Woodland Gdns. TW7: Isle 7A 4
Woodlands KT21: Asht 7F 33
SW20 . . . . .1F 25
Woodlands, The KT10: Esh 6H 21
TW7: Isle 6A 4
Woodlands Av. KT3: N Mald 5K 17
KT4: Wor Pk 6C 24
Woodlands Cl. KT10: Clay 4A 28
Woodlands Copse KT21: Asht 5E 32
Woodlands Ct. KT12: Walt T 5A 20
Woodlands Dr. TW16: Sun 6B 14
Woodlands Gdns.
KT18: Tatt C 6F 35
Woodlands Ga. *SW15* *2J 13*
(off Woodlands Way)
Woodlands Gro. TW7: Isle 6A 4
Woodlands Rd. KT6: Surb 4E 22
KT18: Eps 4H 33
SW13 .7C 6
TW7: Isle 6A 4
Woodlands Way KT21: Asht 5H 33
SW15 . . . . .2J 13
Woodland Wlk. KT19: Ewe 3H 29
Woodland Way KT5: Surb 6J 23
SM4: Mord 1J 25
Wood La. KT20: Tad 6J 35
TW7: Isle 3A 4
Woodlark Ct. KT10: Clay 3A 28
Woodlawn Cl. SW15 . . . . .2J 13
Woodlawn Cres.
TW2: Whitt 6G 9
Woodlawn Dr. TW13: Felt 6C 8
Woodlawn Rd. SW6 . . . . .4G 7
Woodlawns KT19: Ewe 4A 30
Woodlodge KT21: Asht 6F 33
Woodman M. TW9: Kew 5J 5
Woodmill Cl. SW15 . . . . .3D 12
Woods Cl. *TW3: Houn* *1G 9*
(off High St.)
Woodside SW19 . . . . .3J 19
Woodside Av. KT10: Esh 4K 21
KT12: Hers 1A 26
Woodside Cl. KT5: Surb 4K 23
Woodside Ho. SW19 . . . . .3J 19
Woodside Rd. KT2: King T 4F 17
KT3: N Mald 6A 18
Woodspring Rd. SW19 . . . . .6H 13
WOODSTOCK, THE 4J 25
Woodstock Av. SM3: Sutt 4J 25
TW7: Isle 2B 10
Woodstock Ct. KT19: Eps 2A 34
Woodstock La. KT9: Chess 1C 28
Woodstock La. Nth.
KT6: Surb 6D 22
Woodstock La. Sth.
KT9: Chess 2C 28
KT10: Clay 2C 28
Woodstock Ri. SM3: Sutt 4J 25
Woodstock Rd. W4 . . . . .1B 6
Woodstone Av. KT17: Ewe 2D 30
Wood St. KT1: King T 3B 36 (6E 16)
W4 . . . . .2B 6
Woodthorpe Rd. SW15 . . . . .1E 12
Woodview KT9: Chess 7D 28
Woodview Cl. KT21: Asht 5H 33
SW15 . . . . .1A 18
Woodville Cl. TW11: Tedd 1B 16
Woodville Gdns. KT6: Surb 4E 22
Woodville Rd. SM4: Mord 1K 25
TW10: Ham 7C 10
Woodward Cl. KT10: Clay 3A 28
Woodward's Footpath
TW2: Whitt 3H 9
Woolneigh St. SW6 . . . . .7K 7
Wool Rd. SW20 . . . . .3E 18
Wootton Cl. KT18: Eps 5C 34
Wootton Pl. KT10: Esh 1H 27

A-Z Kingston & Richmond 71

Worcester Ct. KT4: Wor Pk 7B 24
  KT12: Walt T 6B 20
Worcester Gdns. KT4: Wor Pk . .7B 24
WORCESTER PARK 5D 24
Worcester Pk. Rd.
  KT4: Wor Pk 7A 24
Worcester Park Station (Rail) . .5D 24
Worcester Rd. SM2: Sutt 4K 31
  SW19 . . . . .2J 19
Wordsworth Dr.
  SM3: Cheam 1F 31
Wordsworth Mans. W14 . . . . .3J 7
  (off Queens Club Gdns.)
Wordsworth Rd.
  TW12: Hamp 1E 14
World of Golf Cen.
  New Malden 7D 18
World Rugby Mus. 3K 9
Worlds End KT18: Eps 5A 34
Worlidge St. W6 . . . . .2F 7
Worple Av. SW19 . . . . .4G 19
  TW7: Isle 2B 10
Worple Rd. KT18: Eps 4A 34
  SW19 . . . . .6F 19
  SW20 . . . . .6F 19
  TW7: Isle 1B 10
Worple Rd. M. SW19 . . . . .3J 19
Worple St. SW14 . . . . .7A 6
Worple Way TW10: Rich 2F 11
Worthfield Cl. KT19: Ewe 4A 30
Worthington Rd. KT6: Surb 5G 23
Worton Ct. TW7: Isle 1K 9

Worton Hall Ind. Est.
  TW7: Isle 1K 9
Worton Rd. TW7: Isle 1J 9
Wotton Way SM2: Cheam 6F 31
Wrayfield Rd. SM3: Cheam 7G 25
Wray Rd. SM2: Cheam 5J 31
Wren Ho. KT1: Hamp W 3A 36
  (off High St.)
Wrenn Ho. SW13 . . . . .3F 7
Wrights All. SW19 . . . . .3F 19
Wrights Wlk. SW14 . . . . .7A 6
Wyatt Cl. TW13: Felt 5C 8
Wyatt Dr. SW13 . . . . .3E 6
Wyatt Ho. TW1: Twick 3E 10
Wych Elm Cl.
  KT2: King T 1E 36 (4G 17)
Wych Elm Pas.
  KT2: King T 1E 36 (4G 17)
Wydell Cl. SM4: Mord 3G 25
Wyeths M. KT17: Eps 2C 34
Wyeths Rd. KT17: Eps 2C 34
Wyfold Rd. SW6 . . . . .4H 7
Wyke Cl. TW7: Isle 3A 4
Wyke Gdns. W7 . . . . .1B 4
Wyke Green Golf Course 3A 4
Wyke Rd. SW20 . . . . .6F 19
Wymond St. SW15 . . . . .7F 7
Wyndham Cl. SM2: Sutt 4K 31
Wyndham Ct. W7 . . . . .1B 4
Wyndham Cres.
  TW4: Houn 3F 9

Wyndham Rd. KT2: King T 4G 17
Wynton Gro. KT12: Walt T 7A 20
Wyvern Est. KT3: N Mald 1D 24

Xylon Ho. KT4: Wor Pk 6E 24

Yale Cl. TW4: Houn 2E 8
Yardley Ct. SM3: Cheam 1F 31
Yarrell Mans. W14 . . . . .3J 7
  (off Queen's Club Gdns.)
Yeend Cl. KT8: W Mole 1F 21
Yeldham Ho. W6 . . . . .2G 7
  (off Yeldham Rd.)
Yeldham Rd. W6 . . . . .2G 7
Yeldham Vs. W6 . . . . .2G 7
  (off Yeldham Rd.)
Yelverton Lodge TW1: Twick 4D 10
  (off Richmond Rd.)
Yenston Cl. SM4: Mord 3K 25
Yeoman Ct. KT20: Tad 7H 35
Yeomanry Cl. KT17: Eps 1C 34
Yeomans M. TW7: Isle 3J 9
Yeovilton Pl. KT2: King T 2D 16
Yew Tree Bottom Rd.
  KT17: Eps D 5E 34
  KT18: Tatt C 5E 34

Yew Tree Cl. KT4: Wor Pk 5B 24
  KT17: Eps D 5E 34
Yew Tree Gdns.
  KT18: Eps 4K 33
Yew Tree Wlk. TW4: Houn 2E 8
YMCA Hawker Cen. 2E 16
Yoga Way KT4: Wor Pk 6D 24
York Av. SW14 . . . . .2K 11
York Cl. SM4: Mord 1K 25
York Ct. KT19: Eps 1H 33
York Gdns.
  KT12: Walt T 6C 20
York Ho. KT2: King T 4G 17
  (off Elm Rd.)
York Rd. KT2: King T 4G 17
  SM1: Sutt 3K 31
  SM2: Sutt 3K 31
  TW8: Bford 2E 4
  TW10: Rich 2G 11
  TW11: Tedd 1K 15
  W5 .1D 4
York St. TW1: Twick 5B 10
York Way KT9: Chess 4F 29
  TW13: Hanw 7E 8
  (not continuous)

Zenobia Mans. W14 . . . . .3J 7
  (off Queen's Club Gdns.)

SAFETY CAMERA INFORMATION

PocketGPSWorld.com's CamerAlert is a self-contained speed and red light camera warning system for SatNavs and Android or Apple iOS smartphones/tablets. Visit www.cameralert.com to download.

Safety camera locations are publicised by the Safer Roads Partnership which operates them in order to encourage drivers to comply with speed limits at these sites. It is the driver's absolute responsibility to be aware of and to adhere to speed limits at all times.

By showing this safety camera information it is the intention of Geographers' A-Z Map Company Ltd. to encourage safe driving and greater awareness of speed limits and vehicle speed. Data accurate at time of printing.